FULFILLED
JOURNEY

FULFILLED JOURNEY

THE WILDER-SMITH MEMOIRS

The Word For Today Publishers
Costa Mesa, California 92628

Fulfilled Journey

by Arthur Ernest and Beate Wilder-Smith

© 1998 Beate Wilder-Smith

Published by TWFT Publishers,
P.O. Box 8000, Costa Mesa, California 92628
(800) 272–WORD (9673)
Web site: http://www.thewordfortoday.org

ISBN 0–936728–75-2

Unless otherwise indicated, Scripture quotations in this book are taken from the King James Version of the Bible.

To our Children, Oliver, Petra,
Clive and Einar who shared all
joys and trials of life with us.
They also helped in the
realization of this biography by
means of their advice, editing
and encouragement.

CONTENTS

PART III
MEMOIRS

PART IV
THE LATER YEARS

FOREWORD
1

Paul the apostle declared at the end of his journey, I have fought a good fight, I have finished the course, I have kept the faith. This may also be said of Dr. A. E. Wilder-Smith. Not only did he keep the faith, he brought the faith, and continues to bring faith to multiplied thousands. His life was marked by a strong faith in God and an uncompromising belief that the Bible is the inspired, infallible Word of God. Add to this his keen scientific background, and you realize why he was able to give to every man a reason for the hope that we have of eternal life through our Lord, Jesus Christ. When teaching the Word of God he would have an engaging grin, and his eyes would twinkle in such a way that you could tell that he delighted in unlocking the great mysteries of God and His creation in such a way that even the young students could begin to grasp complicated truths. His ability to combine scientific truths with the Scriptures was unsurpassed.

The apostle John was commanded to write, "Blessed are the dead who die in the Lord, for they have ceased from their labors, but their works do follow them." This can certainly be said concerning Dr. Wilder-Smith, he has, having died in the Lord, ceased from his labors, but his works do follow him. The many books that he has written strengthen our Christian faith and challenge the fallacy of the so-called science of the evolutionary theory, he leaves a legacy to every believer in Jesus. The Bible tells us of Abel the son of Adam, who, "By faith offered unto God a more excellent sacrifice than Cain, by which he obtained witness that he was righteous, God testifying of his gifts; and by it he being dead yet speaketh." In this fascinating biography, Dr. Wilder-Smith, though he is now with His Lord, still speaks to us today as he shares the events and circumstances by which the Lord molded his life and made him a man of God and a man of science, in that order. He did not just finish his journey, but he fulfilled his journey. Through this book we have the joy to journey with him, and I can see the twinkle in his eyes as he, in his unique way, shares with us his story.

Pastor Chuck Smith,
Calvary Chapel of Costa Mesa, California

FOREWORD
2

Professor Dr. Dr. Dr. Arthur Wilder-Smith gave many Christians and non-Christians decisive impulses in their intellectual and their spiritual development through his lectures and literature. As a true pioneer he fearlessly confronted the seemingly all-powerful theory of evolution in universities and churches. His criticisms also included the theory of theistic evolution, which was especially widespread amongst Christians.

Among his over 80 publications on questions of faith and science, his standard work *Man's Origin, Man's Destiny*, published in 1966, in particular helped to abolish intellectual hindrances to faith. He was thus often able to open skeptical eyes for the uniqueness of God's Word.

His specialist research in the pharmaceutical industry was very successful as demonstrated by the great number of his publications and patents.

His special concern was for the young generation. During World War II, he helped and encouraged many German prisoners of war in England showing them the way out of their despair to the living Christ.

In a special assignment in the NATO Allied Forces against drug abuse, he helped thousands of soldiers to free themselves from drug abuse and to avoid drug dependency. He often personally assisted young people in their struggle against drugs.

But it was not only in the military context that Wilder-Smith won the confidence and respect of the young generation. His love towards young people showed in a special way in his teaching activity at the university. For example, his pharmacology students at the University of Illinois stated at the awarding of an academic distinction, "He not only made us better scientists, but also better men."

It was an unforgettable experience to listen to his lectures on fundamental problems on the evolutionary doctrine and biblical creation. His outstanding personality, his far-reaching knowledge and his unique talent to fascinate during lectures attracted many listeners.

As an example, his lectures at the University of Cologne in the "auditorium maximum" of the high-rise building were so crowded that even the empty floor right to the platform and the rostrum was densely filled with listeners packed head to head. Even the window sills were occupied by students who had climbed there with acrobatic agility. His extraordinary capability in relating with young students became especially obvious when answering questions from the audience. Even late at night after a strenuous lecture, Wilder-Smith did not lose patience when high-spirited firebrands threatened to leave objectivity behind in their arrogance. His answers had the imprint of genuine sensitivity and encouraging superiority, a fact that even irritable fanatics recognized without losing face, thus interdicting the destruction of the good climate of his lectures.

In the Pro Universitate seminars, founded by him, Wilder-Smith equipped academics and students for their studies and profession. He drew from his wealth of knowledge and experience gathered through his research at the universities of Geneva, Chicago, Bergen and Ankara.

In remembering Wilder-Smith, innumerable Christians are grateful to their Lord for this fearless witness who helped many to jettison pseudo-scientific ballast and to find access to the living Word of God.

May our Lord grant that the mighty witness of Wilder-Smith may continue to reach many people through this present work even after his home-going, and that it may glorify the Creator of heaven and earth.

Professor Dr. Dr. Theodor Ellinger, Cologne, Germany

INTRODUCTION

My husband and I began writing our Memoirs in 1990 some time before my husband's first brain operation. In March 1991, he had the operation. He picked up his pen again a few months later in 1991, while recovering from the surgery, when he was not yet able to travel and lecture again. Because of problems following the second brain operation, resulting finally in his death, I have completed the book.

In order to achieve a homogenous structure and continuity most parts of the Memoirs are written in the "I"-form, from the perspective of my husband, even though sometimes told by me. I hope the respected readers will excuse this liberty. Of course, the end of the book is told from my point of view.

Many times we both traveled and worked together, especially when our four children were grown up. So I had the privilege to take a close part in my husband's thinking and activities. When after all the years together, I leaf through his diaries, I am amazed at the diversity and amount of work he quietly accomplished. His great concern in life was not to waste time unnecessarily, to be a good steward of his time.

To give a quick overview of his activities I would like to mention only a few facts. Besides all his extensive literary work and, of course, his profession as a university professor, my husband traveled and lectured all over the world: eight U.S. tours, three New Zealand tours, one Australian tour, in addition to his innumerable European tours. In the course of these he lectured—merely counting the last twenty years—in over 1000 public halls and churches, and held 370 lectures and debates in universities. Furthermore, he regularly addressed businessmen in various continents and spoke on TV and radio programs.

Several times lecture tours took him to Scandinavia, Asia and most of Europe. As our home was in Switzerland until 1981, our first twenty years of professional and Christian work centered in Switzerland, Germany and the neighboring countries.

In the early 1970s, my husband became consultant on drug abuse for NATO, in which capacity he traveled widely, lecturing and consulting to thousands of servicemen all over NATO.

The motivation for writing our life story was

1) To show in which way God trained and shaped us for life and its special tasks;

2) To show how well and faithfully God looked after us in good and in difficult times.

We experienced the satisfying fact that God's presence and peace in any situation is more important than the situation itself.

May many people be blessed and encouraged by this book to commit their lives fully to God. We want them to make the same discovery as we did; namely, that He does not always spare you suffering and difficulties, but lovingly stays close by you in the middle of it. This assurance gives peace, joy and confidence.

Einigen, September 1996
Beate Wilder-Smith

PART I

ARTHUR ERNEST WILDER-SMITH

FIRST MEMORIES

EARLY YEARS

In our later years, memories of the earliest childhood seem to us like dreams. Dreams usually are soon forgotten. Yet, the first impressions of life have the tendency to live on. This is at least what I have experienced. I had the great privilege of growing up with three older sisters. It was especially my oldest sister who frequently looked after me. She took me for walks in the pram and—as I was firmly convinced—also patronized me enormously.

One day, when she took me for a walk, a number of elderly ladies had the desire to inspect me. They lifted the fringes of the pram hood—it had a kind of fringed sunshade as roof, intended to protect the baby from the gazes of inquisitive people (not only from the sun). These ladies pulled all kinds of faces to make me laugh. But obviously these grimaces were so frightening that I started to cry pitifully. Shocked, my sister pulled the fringes of the sunshade down to protect me from this intimidating view. This event became my first conscious memory.

One or two years later, my oldest sister again had to take me out for a walk. It was summer and hot weather. My mother, who had dressed me in a beautiful white suit, had given the strictest orders to my sister to keep me clean, as we were expecting visitors. In those times, there were no washing machines. Instead, my parents kept two maids to boil the washing and then scrub it by hand. My sister was helpful and kind but she treated us boys—my brother was sixteen months younger than I—like babies; at least that is what we thought. Thus, we often were resentful towards this patronizing. Now, here we obviously had the opportunity of the year to take our revenge. After a little walk of some hundred yards or so, we reached a spot on the road covered with fresh steaming horse apples. In those days, you did not have to deal with the stench of car exhausts, but rather with the sweet smell of horse apples! Here, now, was the great opportunity to take revenge for the hegemony of my poor sister. Resolutely—I was about two and a half years old—I lay down in the brown mass and rolled around in it. The walk was immediately interrupted. Desperately, my sister tried to brush off the worst of the manure. But in vain; for afterwards I looked worse than before. On our walk home all the passers-by admired my newly speckled brown suit—before it had been a beautiful white sailor's suit and now it had changed its political color. Mother was enraged when she saw it.

As expected, she severely scolded my poor sister, which was exactly what we had intended, although Mother, of course, was not aware of it. You can imagine that our three older sisters firmly stuck together against their two younger brothers; a state of war which I am sorry to say continued for a long time.

Parents often do not have the slightest idea how small children manipulate the rest of the family from earliest childhood onwards. Even as the smallest infants, humans are schemers and politicians! The task of parents—*the very difficult task of parents*—is to check at a very early age the drift in most children towards manipulating everybody. My parents firmly tried to do that—although my sisters maintain until this day that they never succeeded in achieving that goal in the two boys.

ON THE FARM

I was born on December 22, 1915, in Reading, Berkshire, England. My father came from an old family background of land-owners. Since the Danish invasions of East England, his forefathers had cultivated the good fertile soil of the southeastern plains, and spread from there towards the West where the Celts, the original inhabitants of the country lived. Today's population of East England still shows the Danish phenotype although mingled with other races. Biologically, these people were usually long-lived (as long as they kept out of wars), blue-eyed and of a tall stature. They often had fair auburn hair. My father sported a reddish mustache. My patient mother remarked that the reddish color had originated from the heated words which had often slipped over his lips. In spite of this, Father had a good and compassionate heart.

Father secretly took care of the poor in the whole area, especially of widows and orphans. In his taciturn manner, he went on his visits round the neighborhood and took fresh products from the farm—a chicken, some good vegetables, eggs, butter or milk—to old lonely men and women. Especially during the war, his discreet charity was highly appreciated.

Father was a strong adversary of the Anglican State Church. This attitude he held not without reason. As we will see later on, he opposed the unjust activity of the church in collecting the tithe (chapter V.1). Yet in the depth of his heart he was a religious man, for he was a freemason and rose up to the 32nd grade, the "Royal Arch." His memory was so phenomenal, that he had the task of examining kings and high members of the royal family on the word perfectness of the lodge rites. He was convinced that the Christian faith was for women and children and that his lodge possessed the real religion for men. Father was highly disappointed that I did not follow in his Masonic footsteps.

As a young man I thoroughly examined the doctrines of the freemasons and rejected them later as unchristian. In order to come to a just conclusion, I studied the rites and practices of the lodge in great detail, which often produced tensions at home.

My mother, a licensed teacher, came from an old generation of engineers. Her father had founded an iron-foundry, which is still in the family. My grandfather designed and developed machines of all kinds, especially agricultural machines which were sold to the farmers in our area. Both families—on my father's and on my mother's side—were large. Mother had seven brothers and sisters, and father four. A brother of my father's died in early childhood of a strangulated hernia, which threw a shadow on the family for a long time. My father was the oldest son of the family.

THE FARMERS AND THE ENGINEERS

On account of the farming activity in my father's family and the activity of my mother's family in the foundry, both families had always been in close contact. Father knew my mother as a child at school. We were told that, even as a young boy, my father had presented to my mother the best apples in their garden.

Mother was interested in sciences and became a teacher. She married late as often is the case amongst English academics. She was twenty-seven when they married, and Father was three months older. Mother's family was small in stature and dark-haired, but also blue-eyed like my father's family. Mother's forefathers were of Celtic, Father's of Anglo-Saxon descent. In the counties of Berkshire, Oxfordshire, Gloucestershire and Hampshire both types are to be found, now often intermingled.

My father bought his machines, tractors, big steam plows, etc. from the firm Walter Wilder & Co., the family firm of my mother. The firm Walter Wilder bought land to test their newly developed machines on from my father's family. Thus, a close contact existed between the two families.

Due to the shared interests of the two families as landowners and engineers, the young members of the two families also met regularly. Mother's brother Percy, an engineer and also a good musician, married Father's younger sister, Millie. They lived not far from us and had two children who went to the same school and later to the same public school as my brother and myself. When Father needed a new kind of threshing machine for the clover (Father had a contract with Sutton's Seeds in Reading to cultivate a new kind of pedigree clover for export to New Zealand and Australia) he bought this machine at Wilder's. Sutton's was a Christian company which was highly esteemed in those years. They came every year to our estate to inspect the seed. The firm, Walter Wilder's, saw to it that for each activity the right type of machine was available.

THE ANIMALS ON THE FARM

Before the invention of petrol and kerosene tractors the plowing was, of course, always done by means of a horse-drawn plow. We possessed big horse stables for our faithful horses, which carried out the plowing, the harrowing, the sowing and the rolling. In one of our stables stood a big intelligent pedigree stallion with the name of Framlingen Curfew, a noble animal, which obviously was fond of us children, for he never became cross with us despite all the jokes we played on him. He let us lead him during the harvesting. Even with our dog, Folly, our stallion got on well.

Once, Folly had given birth to six or seven puppies. Walter and I wanted to inspect the little ones—which one should not do, as animals in that state are often unpredictable. Folly lived in a pretty dog house not far from the back entrance of the farmyard. Walter and I inspected the newly born puppies through the door of the hut, but it was too dark to see much. So we both crept inside the dog house to the corner where Folly and her new family lay. I can still today see how her eyes stared at us nervously while the little ones were in the middle of having their meal. We talked to her and she tapped with her tail against the floor which meant that we were welcome guests. Then we picked up one little puppy with our hand— which one should never do, as it is a direct infringement against canine etiquette. Folly suffered the greatest agony, her eyes glanced even more nervously out of her dark corner trying to tell us; this is not allowed! She arose from the floor and implored us to return the puppy which we did immediately with many signs of good intentions. I can still hear her fearful whining while we held her little baby. As soon as she had her little one back again she lay down and continued tapping with her tail against the floor—the sign that everything was all right now.

Folly was our faithful companion throughout childhood. During the war, I was away from home for several years. After a long time, I returned home; my father had suffered a heart attack. As the oldest son, I had to return and look after the farm. Folly met me at the main entrance when I arrived from the station. Without hesitating, I opened the great wooden gate. She thought I was intruding on her rights and started to bark angrily at me. Somewhat reproachingly I called her name: "Folly, what are you thinking about!" She suddenly recognized my voice and stood still, looking at me and sniffing me. She realized her great mistake, wagged her tail vehemently to ask for forgiveness and licked my shoes with her tongue. As ultimate sign of repentance, she lay on her back and rubbed up against me. That is the expression of unconditional capitulation in dog sign language. She then jumped up and ran to the house, to announce my arrival. How good if people would recognize their wrong-doings and ask for forgiveness in a similar fashion! Yet, by nature, dogs do not possess such good manners. They learn these only from a good master. Is it not likewise with us humans?

But we must not forget the cat. Her name was Limpy. There was great rivalry between Limpy and Folly. If you showed any kind of favor to Limpy—took her on your lap and stroked her—then Folly expressed great uneasiness. Folly could not stand it. She would try to push our hand away from the cat with her nose! Folly disliked bread. She would only sniff a little at bread, before contemptuously leaving it alone. Yet if at that moment you called the name "Limpy," Folly would rapidly turn around and devour with one snap the whole piece of bread before the cat could come near! Did Folly also learn this attitude from us humans?

You cannot keep animals like Folly and Limpy in a small modern apartment because, like human beings, they need adequate space and useful tasks. If they lack space and regular tasks they can become unbearable.

Our chickens lived in good chicken houses and had their individual nesting sites, but they often preferred laying their eggs into small hollows underneath the hayracks. Thus we often had to search for the eggs, otherwise one day a hen would turn up under the hayracks surrounded by thirteen chicks. Folly, with her unerring nose, was best at sniffing out the eggs. She knew better than any other dog which methods and tactics to employ in looking for and fetching the eggs.

Her first rule, which she strictly observed, was to treat the hens very carefully, otherwise they would suddenly fly off their hidden nests and break the eggs. Therefore Folly approached the hens sideways or even from the back and pushed her snout cautiously and softly underneath the hen which sometimes had up to thirteen eggs under her wings— especially if one had not discovered her nest for some time— and took one egg between her two canine teeth. If we held our hands down to Folly she would carefully place the egg into our hands before trotting back to the hen and fetching the next egg.

I never saw Folly eat or break a single egg during this job—although she used to enjoy eating the breakfast leftovers which contained eggs. If nobody was at home, she would deposit the eggs in front of the door. They were always intact.

When Folly had grown very old and we five children had left home, she developed a special relationship towards my aging parents. She usually slept in the kennel or in the dog house where she had borne her puppies. One very cold night in winter, Mother and Father had retired to bed early. Folly noticed that she was not feeling well. She opened the door of the kennel—she was able to do this—and crept to the back gate of the yard which she was able to open by jumping up. But this time the strength to open the gate failed her. Next morning my parents found her dead in front of the gate. In her need she had tried to find my father who had always helped her. We buried her in our garden. This was the end of an era for our family. She died at the age of eighteen years.

It is such a pity that children growing up in towns no longer become acquainted with the ways of nature. They no longer see first-hand the kind of relationships between men, animals and plants which are needed for their full development. This certainly is one of the reasons why people easily fall victim to the false ideologies which usually thrive in towns. In a country population living so much closer to and in an interdependent relationship with nature, neither the Nazis, nor the communists, could have achieved much. The communists considered it necessary to liquidate the muschiks in the country by putting them into kolkhozes, because they could not have won over these country people in any other way. About one million of these peasants died by starvation (starvation in the country!) before the wrong communistic ideology was abolished. Like in Egypt in the days of old, starvation usually is a consequence of communism. Because of communism the entire rural tradition of Russia perished and the stabilizing effect of the country population disappeared for good.

CHAPTER II

THE EVOLUTION
OF AGRICULTURE

THE MODERNIZATION OF FARM EQUIPMENT

The conditions on the farm, which existed during my early years, could not last. The then ruling socialistic politicians required that the farm-laborers who had not earned much cash—but were given many supplies and amenities—would be paid higher wages. They wanted to introduce a "supply side" economy (an economy based on the concept that people should own more money in order to spend more). If the population spends more, then industry will flourish. But the English farmers at that time simply could not pay higher wages, because due to the high taxes and the high tithes, they just did not have that much cash.

For this reason, the farm laborers, with their nice little cottages and the large gardens in which they grew their vegetables, became unemployed. The farmers had to mechanize to survive. In my childhood, a farm laborer earned approximately eighteen shillings per week. He paid five shillings a week for a nice cottage with a large garden so that he could grow his own potatoes and vegetables, as well as keep some chickens and hares. So he paid about twenty-five percent of his wages for his house and garden! Is that possible today? The English socialists then prohibited "bound cottages" for farm laborers; the farmer was no longer permitted to build cottages which were specifically reserved for and rented at low cost to his own laborers. The farm laborer had to search on the open market for an apartment or house which was, of course, much more expensive. On account of this fact, his cash wages had to be raised. But the motto was socialization, and the farm laborer had to become equal to all other laborers: a uniform tax source! It is true that the farm laborer was now entitled to earn more cash—if he could find a farmer who was in the position to pay the raised wages. The ridiculous situation resulted, that in English farming areas there was simultaneously unemployment and a shortage of farm laborers! Inexpensive houses with gardens, chickens, goats or hares disappeared from the market!

My father now no longer had enough farm-hands on the farm because of this situation. He needed at least three farm-hands for the horses; the horses had to be fed and brushed every afternoon. Often horse-shoes had to be replaced, the foals had to be looked after and broken in, which was very costly. A single tractor driver could achieve the work of three grooms with his horses. The groom returned from the field at approximately 2:00 p.m. to feed and brush his horses. The tractor driver could plow until 6:00 p.m., leave the plow in the field and drive home on his tractor. To survive in spite of the raised wages, the farmer was compelled to mechanize.

After a few years, the horse stables were empty. The groom had learned to drive tractors, to operate the grain mill. A new era had begun. Soon, the farm was no more dependent on one's own farm-hands, own hay and own grain, but on expensive oil from the Middle-East. Now, the farmer was dependent on the oil economy rather than his own laborers and land.

THE STEAM-PLOW AND OTHER MACHINES

On our farm, mechanization began with the steam-plows. Our soil consisted of heavy clay which was well suited for growing wheat.

Heavy steam-engines were built, which had big steel-cable windlasses and reels under their boilers. In order to plow the field, a steam-engine was placed on one side of the field and another one on the other side. A distance of about half a mile or more lay between the two steam-engines. A six-furrows-plow was fastened to the cable. One of the steam-engines drew the cable and hauled the big plow towards itself on one side of the field. Then the second steam-engine drew the plow back to the other side. Both machines then advanced a few steps, after which the plow was again drawn forth and back. The steam-engines burnt coal, at that time a very inexpensive fuel—about fifteen shillings per ton. In this manner whole fields could be plowed very thoroughly and inexpensively.

As time went on, coal became more expensive, for the miners also justly began to earn more money. For a steam-plow-team at least two steam-engine engineers were needed, who, by standards of those times, were expensive. A third man was needed to provide water and coal. After a few years working with the steam-engines, my father risked the big step into the modern age. He bought two "Titan" kerosene tractors.

These big American machines had four steel wheels, which were so heavy that the ground trembled when they moved around in our farmyard. The motor was a two-cylinder boxer. There were heavy open fly-wheels on both sides of the machine. To start the machine, a big iron crank handle had to be applied and then turned with all your strength—and a little more, if possible. If the motor back-fired—which easily happened with that beast of a machine—one was hit over the head. This could be fatal. If the machine did spring into action—a fifty to fifty chance—the handle tended to remain attached to the fly-wheel, spinning around loosely, so that all bystanders rapidly had to seek cover. Detaching itself at high speed, the handle would fly in a wide curve into the air—or implant itself with a loud bang into the ground. If the spark-plug was dirty, which often happened, the unburned gases of the exhaust exploded with a roar which could be heard for miles. We owned two of those monsters for driving the corn-mill, later for making pig food, for driving the threshing machine and also the clover-threshing machine. For the plowing, harrowing and rolling, special steel wheels had to be attached. These machines were so heavy that they were not of much use on our clay soil. Only when the soil was totally dry was it possible to drive them on the unpaved ground, otherwise the tractor sank immediately into the mud right up to its axles. Within a few minutes, such machines had the habit of disappearing literally into the soil in front of Father's eyes. And then a steam engine fitted with a steel winch was needed to drag it out again. Of course, the old horse laborer watched smilingly; with his horse this difficulty had never arisen.

THE NEW HUMBER SNIPE

Uncle Frank was my mother's brother and also a good friend of us boys. He regularly came to visit us in Cholsey, for he was a freemason and Friday evenings he and my father used to sit together to memorize the rites of the lodge. Father and Uncle recited the entire rites after all the others had gone to bed, because nobody was supposed to know the contents of the little book which outwardly looked like a prayer book. Later on, I learned more about it—but that is another story.

One day, Uncle Frank bought himself a new Humber Snipe. There was a little rivalry between Uncle Frank and my father despite their close friendship. They were of the same age. He and Mother were both musical. Now, Father had just recently bought a three-liter Bentley and the car was the pride of the whole family.

One Sunday, quite unexpectedly, Uncle Frank with his wife, Auntie Emmie, and some of our cousins turned up for tea. Afterwards they wanted to take a little tour in their new car. We always enjoyed Uncle's visits. We children were very fond of him because he often played with us. Yet this fact did not protect him from our playing tricks on him. While the whole family was drinking tea my brother and myself sneaked out of the house and saw the sparkling new car properly parked in the drive in front of the house. It was beautiful—but, of course, by far not as beautiful as our Bentley—and probably it did not run quite as well, we were convinced of that. If anybody would have doubted it we could easily prove it! Yes, we surely could!

Quickly, we lifted the bonnet, and in a flash the ignition system lay open to our eyes. Deep in the distributor we found the tiny little screw. With our special pocket knife, boasting an inbuilt millimeter scale we screwed the contact breaker from a gap of one to two millimeters down to a much smaller interval. Nothing else, that sufficed! Distributor closed, bonnet locked again! We only needed to wait! We chatted with our Auntie Emmie, with the cousins and Uncle—perfectly acting our part. After tea with cake, strawberries and Devonshire cream, Uncle and his family intended to continue his trip in the new car. They got up, thanked us for the good hospitality, and walked proudly towards their new car. We two boys were in suspense! This was the long waited for moment! Would the new motor start?

It did, the first time, and quite well, and Uncle Frank with his family drove with great verve and in style through the big farm gate. When he reached the main street he put his foot down on the accelerator to demonstrate how well the motor accelerated—Humber Snipes were known for this, the motor was big and the body light and racy. But what was that? The motor started to spit noisily and hesitated. Uncle Frank now really put down his foot to show us Bentley owners what performance his car could produce. Suddenly the motor failed entirely. Uncle applied the self-starter, the motor started again a little hesitantly—it was embarrassing! But, as soon as the motor picked up full speed, it again started to spit and to cough noisily. The car jerked along like a skittish horse. Uncle obviously thought he could succeed by applying power—with the throttle full open. The answer of the tortured motor was a huge bang, accompanied by black smoke. Very embarrassing— but from our point of view totally expected! We quietly watched in amusement. Now, Uncle Frank, the engineer, tried trickery, he only touching the accelerator very lightly. But, soon as the motor picked up full speed again, it started spitting, coughing, spluttering and banging; the noise would have done honor to the best racing car.

In this manner, Uncle Frank and his family drove through our sleepy village on a Sunday afternoon, sounding like the best fireworks party; the banging, exploding, smoking, and spluttering would not stop. On the contrary, it became worse and worse. The noisy spectacle gradually became fainter, leaving the village. But we could still hear the slowly diminishing noise for a long time. Walter and I looked at one another merrily.

"Will he make it home?" wondered my father. We two boys did not utter a word. But what was the matter? The loud noise seemed to be increasing again. Had they turned back? Eventually, Uncle Frank with his shocked and pale-looking family re-appeared humbly in front of our gate. His smoking and fuming motor was still running albeit irregularly. He drove through the gate, got out of the car, opened the hood and began inspecting his prized new possession. The ignition and its regulator seemed to be in order. No flies and no water in the carburetor! He cleaned everything expertly. Meanwhile the ladies went back into the house to enjoy a second portion of strawberries and Devonshire cream. Uncle Frank, the engineer, could find absolutely no cause in the new car for his Sunday humiliation.

We boys were suddenly struck by an excellent idea. "Uncle," we said, "we know you love your tea, especially with lots of milk. Go back into the house and help yourself to a second portion. May we in the meantime investigate what might be wrong with your motor and possibly put it right?"

Uncle Frank was a very kind gentleman, always ready to help. He was somewhat pear-shaped and loved his tea, strawberries and cream. So he consented and disappeared to join the ladies.

Quickly my brother and I lifted the hood of the new Snipe. Down with the ignition distributor, out with the pocket knife to screw the gap of the contact breaker back to normal! Down with the bonnet!

Slowly and composedly we strolled into the house, ate a few strawberries and chatted loftily with our cousins who had the greatest respect towards us boys. "Well," said Uncle Frank, "did you find anything?" "Possibly," we answered, "but we have not yet driven the car."

Uncle rose from the table and climbed into the car for a trial run. He literally shot out of the entrance onto the main road, raced through the village and returned enthusiastically after five minutes. "My new car has never driven as well as this," he exclaimed. "I can clearly see that your mother is an engineer's daughter. It's hereditary!" My father did not say a word. He remembered certain past experiences with the sons of an engineer's daughter and obviously would not risk any comments. But our good uncle was not suspicious. He came to us, reached deep into his coat pocket and produced half-a-crown (two and a half shillings, we had not seen so much money for a long time) before our amazed eyes. "This is a small reward for following so capably in your mother's footsteps," he said, placing the large coin into my brother's hand. "Oh no, Uncle," we stuttered, "we really have not earned this, it was only a very small matter." "Don't mention it," he replied generously, "What's important is the know-how. Half a crown for the know-how," he added cheerfully!

Deeply ashamed, but not yet ready to own up to our misdeed, we pondered about the meaning of "know-how." Maybe know-how to trick an unsuspecting kindhearted uncle?

We never found out what he really thought about this affair. He was a good man, who was always open for a joke. He was also the only uncle who came to our wedding. All the others were very old or had passed away. Uncle Frank was well over seventy years old when he came to congratulate us on our marriage. Although he was a freemason, God blessed him, for he practiced the commandment, "Honor your father and your mother that you may live long in the country which the Lord your God has given you." He lived till he was nearly one hundred years old.

CHAPTER III

VISUAL EDUCATION

THE BENTLEY STORY

When I was ten or eleven years old my father drove to London for some business. At the dealership of the famous Bentley, he espied a three-liter Bentley. The price for this used, but very beautiful car was 275 British pounds, a horrendous price for those times.

The car was a four-cylinder saloon model, blue, with plenty of space for the whole family. It greatly delighted Mother and my sisters. The car was an excellent model, but expensive. The motor possessed a cylinder head which could not be disassembled. Bentley considered such added luxury unnecessary. In their opinion, a reassembled cylinder-head would never again be watertight. To polish the valves, one had to disassemble the whole cylinder block and polish the valves through the actual cylinders. There were four valves and two spark plugs per cylinder. Two magnetos provided the high tension for the spark plugs. Two silver buttons on the dashboard served as ignition keys. Apart from these ignition buttons, there was an extra hand-operated petrol-pump, to inject petrol directly into the cylinders. This was useful in cold weather, when the motor did not start immediately.

The sixteen valves were controlled by the camshaft, which was directly driven by the crankshaft with the help of a vertical shaft. The heavy dynamo acted as a "fly-wheel" for the camshaft to avoid unnecessary vibrations without adding unnecessary weight. The dynamo had to be so big because it was made of chromium steel and turned at half the revolutions of the engine. It was so long and so big that it was situated in front of the passengers' knees.

We two boys rapidly found out all about these technical details. The car had three forward gears and one reverse gear. The gears were not synchronized, so one had to double-clutch to change gear—my father was not always successful in this skill. The gears would then grate threateningly. We often drove around with my father in this new toy and observed everything closely. Would the motor run with only one spark plug inserted, were the magnetos really necessary? Maybe we could shift gears better than Father! My sisters were definitely not successful at operating the gears, the clutch was too heavy.

A) NOCTURNAL INSPECTIONS

In the evening, when the rest of the family was chatting, my brother Walter and I often inspected the new garage which my father had specially had built for the Bentley. After a short time, we had collected enough theoretical knowledge, we only lacked a little practice! The English—as everybody knows— are pragmatists! But the exact "How and When"—that was the big problem we had to solve!

One evening we all sat together having high tea and talking to one another. Without being much noticed, my brother slipped round the table and whispered into my ear, "It is open." I knew exactly what was meant by this cryptic remark. Several times in the morning in the garage when intending to drive the Bentley, Father had discovered a flat battery uttering only a weak groan and then dying completely when he pressed the big starter button. Although the battery was powerful— eighty to ninety ampere hours—it could not stand the many demands of two enthusiastic boys who operated the starter too long and too often. The consequence was that Father fastened a big lock on the garage door—and he alone possessed the key to it. That stopped our unofficial visits to the garage earlier than hoped for. But we regularly inspected the lock—who knows, Father was sometimes forgetful!

After some time my brother again whispered into my ear, "It is open," and added softly, "let's not go together, they might get suspicious. Follow in five minutes time and meet me at the garage!" After five minutes I too left the table, helped a little to clear the table and slipped out through the back door. My brother was already sitting in the car. But there was one difficulty. We could only look through the steering wheel instead of over it. We were too small! Quickly, we tiptoed back into the house and fetched two thick cushions to sit on. Now, we were able to look over the steering wheel although our legs were too short to press down the clutch.

B) THE EXPERIMENT

We started the three-liter motor. The sound of the exhaust was satisfying for our by now well-trained ears. The ignition on the left side was fine, so was the right side. The manual petrol pump was no longer needed. The big quadruple carburetor was heated by a water mantle, so that everything was quickly ready to start. We now practiced an often observed procedure; press down your left foot with all your strength, engage the reverse gear, a little more gas, slowly up with the clutch, and we drove backwards—supported by two big cushions—out of the garage. We circled a few times round the yard, to examine our theory regarding the necessity of double-clutching. Everything went smoothly. And then we slowly drove through the big farm gate out on the main road towards the station.

The space in front of the station was big. It was big enough to test a Bentley. We drove round the big place and changed gears. There was not a person to watch us—at least that was what we thought! We drove faster and faster, our technique of double-clutching became better and better. We changed drivers. My brother was younger than I, which meant that his legs were even shorter than mine. But he was strong—and very clever. Round and round the station place we drove. Fortunately, the tires and the springs were new, because the body sometimes nearly tipped over, especially in the bends, which several times we took too closely.

Many times we passed by the office window of Mr. James. Mr. James, the station master, was a kind man, who was well acquainted with my father. He possessed a telephone! His telephone number was Cholsey 1 and our number was Cholsey 2—not easily to be confused. After many rounds in our car it occurred to us that Mr. James might have been watching us. We did not see him, but he knew us well—and also Father's Bentley. Mr. James had a telephone, and Father too! Maybe Mr. James had already telephoned Father and he knew everything! Full speed back to the farm!

Through the main gate we speeded, the cushions started to slip and we nearly lost them. Quickly into the garage; we just negotiated the garage entrance for the car was big. Close the garage door, but leave the lock where it was so that Father would not be suspicious. Silently, we crept into the house and through the back door upstairs into our room. Ten minutes later my mother called for supper. "No, Mother, would you please excuse us, we are not hungry. And we have so much homework to finish for tomorrow."

The truth was that we did not want to meet Father. Maybe he knew already and was keeping silent? Father could keep silent for a long, long time. But his anger was different from other fathers, it did not decrease with time, rather it definitely increased. Maybe he knew the whole story and was not saying anything. But when he spoke out the punishment would be worse the more time had elapsed! Better to avoid Father, that was our strategy!

C) THE POWER OF THE CONSCIENCE

Father and Mother were very surprised that we did not want any supper. Boys, and not hungry? That was remarkable and unheard of! What is the matter with them?

In the morning before going to school, we had breakfast together. We could not avoid it! Mother served the porridge and afterwards bacon and eggs. The aroma of bacon and eggs for breakfast is delicious! And what an enjoyable taste, especially when it is cold and rainy outside. Father watched us suspiciously as we huddled in our corner. We choked the porridge down our throats. Father said not a word, which did not mean that he was not thinking. As soon as we had the troublesome breakfast—that is, Father's presence—behind us we rushed to the station to board the train to Wallingford for Grammar school. School usually did not mean the greatest pleasure to us, but today it was.

At noon, we always returned home by train—Wallingford being only three miles away from our house. At home at about 12:30, Father sat at the head of the table and dished up the meat—and Mother, as usual, doled out the vegetables. Did Father know or did he not? This was our vital question. He did not say anything about the car, at least the battery was not ruined! We had driven fast enough to make the dynamo turn quickly to recharge the battery. Father said nothing. Neither did Mr. James whom we met every day on our way to school.

Every meal was now a torture for us boys. We kept away from Father, but he did not say a word although we felt in our bones that he suspected something. Maybe he was waiting for us to confess our guilt of our own free will—we were always expected to "own up." It was now unbearable for us to be alone with him. In the evenings, we often used to play checkers with Father—he played checkers very well and built many "chicken traps" for the feet of the unwary, as he called them.

But now, under such tension, in this torturous situation, it was out of question! We preferred to retire to our boys' room and read. Maybe our sisters knew already and were also keeping silent, they were very close to Father.

Our paradise on the farm had changed overnight into a hell—a hell of uncertainty and loneliness. After three weeks of torture, my brother and myself conferred with one another what to do, for this tension and torture were unbearable. After much consideration, we agreed we should go to Father to confess to him the whole truth. But when? Obviously, not when Mother or the sisters were at home. We had to talk with Father alone, when all the others had gone shopping or were in bed. The difficulty was that the others went to bed later than we. All right, on Friday, when Mother and the sisters had gone shopping! It was a deal!

D) THE THOROUGH CONFESSION

Usually Father sat in his leather armchair after lunch, put up his legs and read the newspaper—The Daily Telegraph— for some fifteen minutes. While reading, he quickly fell asleep, but at least we had him alone in this situation. So he rested, dozing off, and the house was very silent. My brother and I softly sneaked into the room, but he woke up. He looked at us asking; "What do you want?" "Dad, we wanted to have a private talk with you." Now he really was awake. "Hm," he said, "it must be something of great importance, because it seems that you have been eagerly avoiding me for a long time. What is the matter?" "Well," we stuttered, "didn't you tell us that your garage was out of bounds for us?" "Surely, I did," he replied. "Did you enter it alone in spite of my prohibition? For tactical reasons I had fastened a lock to the door. Have you damaged the lock or produced a new key to it?" "No, Father. One day you forgot to lock the garage." "That's possible, is anything else the matter?"

"Dad, not only did we enter your garage, we climbed into your Bentley and started the motor." Now Father's anger rose. It was not for nothing that he sported a sandy mustache! "How often have I forbidden you exactly that!" He was furious and rose. "What else did you do?" The tears rose in our eyes—although, of course, boys do not cry!—as we watched Father rush to the door. On the sill above the door in a niche lay his riding-whip which he rarely used, but which he knew very well how to use! A few times we had already experienced it, when having committed bad transgressions. "What else did you do? Is the battery flat again?" "No, Father, we drove fast enough for the dynamo to pick up full speed and charge the battery at twenty ampere!" "I see," he said, "gradually everything is coming to light. You not only started the engine, you even drove the car. You drove it so fast that the dynamo picked up full speed!" He was in the process of taken down his riding-whip from the niche. "Now, my little rascals, I slowly begin to understand your behavior during the last days!"

The tears rolled down our cheeks—although boys never cry!

"Is there anything more to confess?" Father apparently wanted to know the whole story before administering the punishment. "Remember, if you do not confess everything, the punishment will be worse!" Maybe there was still some hope if we were honest and told him all we had done. But there was so much to confess, that was the great problem.

Obviously, Father had not known anything. Mr. James had not betrayed us, for which we must be grateful to him all our life and not to be so impudent when he insists on tidiness and cleanliness in the railway. The poor man had to deal daily with many young passengers riding to school by train. My father always remarked that those many schoolboys in the train were craftier than a wagon-load of monkeys. Only later in life did we recognize that Father was not so wrong in his judgment of boys and their manner of life.

"Father, we started the Bentley, let the motor warm up with garage doors open and recharged the battery. Than we fetched two big cushions—without them we could not see well. We backed out of the garage, drove a few times round the yard, and then straight on to the main road, round the corner to the station place where the other cars are parked all day. How often we circled the place we cannot really tell you—we did not count it.

"Maybe it was twenty times, maybe even forty times. We never drove more than fifty miles per hour, mostly less. We wanted to drive fast enough to recharge the battery (at that time the automatic mechanism to regulate the recharging speed did not yet exist)." This list of our shortcomings was too long for us, and it was profoundly depressing. We thought we were fine boys in confessing exactly all we had done and we felt great sympathy with ourselves. We started to weep. Guilt and angelic honesty combined (as we saw it) were too much for us!

Father was visibly moved but very concerned; "Did you hurt anybody or do any other harm?" he asked hesitantly. He was obviously afraid that a confrontation with the police might have occurred. "No, Dad, the car is in perfect order. We tested it all nearly three weeks ago. And you have driven the Bentley yourself since. Everything is in best order."

Father played pensively with his riding-whip. The danger was not over yet. "What should be your punishment?" he asked after a while as we were still sobbing. "Administer to us the due punishment, Dad, so that everything is all right again." We had not taken the precaution of stuffing our pants with newspaper to dampen the effect of the whip on our rearward portion. These tricks were known to every boy, but we did not risk it with our father. It could have cost us another fit of rage with unpleasant consequences.

E) THE JUST, YET LOVING FATHER

We were prepared to receive our punishment. We fetched a chair to bend over while the six lashes of the riding-whip were administered. Usually, one was ordered: "Bend over!" But remarkably nothing of this sort happened. Father, whip in hand, still hesitated. We wanted the whole affair to be over quickly, but apparently not so with our father. "No," he finally said, "I will not do it. It would be wrong. You were honest of your own free will. I had not the slightest idea of this affair. I noticed that something must be wrong on account of your altered behavior, but I guessed nothing. I will not punish you because you have made a clean breast of it. It would be very wrong of me to punish you as a consequence of your honesty. Have you really told me the whole truth? Is there nothing more on your conscience?" "No, nothing more." "Then get up!" And he gave each of us a kiss on the cheek (which he seldom did, being a reserved English farmer), and said, "the matter is over, let's never mention it again."

Can you imagine how ashamed and at the same time grateful we were? We respected and loved our father in a new way because he had been so just. Although there remained some bashfulness towards him the bane of the bad atmosphere in the room was broken. We could face Father again and look into his eyes. Our appetite at table had returned as befitting to boys. When Father went hunting with his twelve bore shotgun we could accompany him with our "0410" gun. And the evenings were again harmonious and normal. He played checkers with us after the English manner and again built his "chicken traps." So, we learned early that guilt and sin separate spiritually, and destroy any kind of fellowship. Only forgiveness heals and restores this separation. Later, my brother and I learned that the same principle applies to the relationship between God and us. Guilt and transgression of the good laws of God separate us and exclude us from fellowship with Him—just as guilt and transgression of the laws, which my father rightly had established, excluded us from fellowship with him. But forgiveness, after a thorough confession, removes this estrangement. In this way, we learned the principles behind the Christian message early—although only later did we get to know this message personally—namely that examining yourself honestly, owning up with the intention to give up the cause of the separation signifies the first step to a reconciliation with a just, yet loving God.

I believe if we had talked to Father about the above event in later years he might even have forgotten it. For him, to forgive meant to forget. With regard to other matters, Father had a fabulous memory.

THE ERA OF OIL-LAMPS IS OVER

One of my earliest memories is the cleaning of smoke blackened oil-lamps. Until 1921, many villages in England possessed no electricity and therefore people used kerosene lamps.

For bigger rooms one used oil-lamps with a ceriumoxide mantle which looked like a small white stocking. These incandescent mantles, when new, were quite robust, yet once used they became very fragile and easily fell apart with the slightest shock. Those lamps developed a fine white light in which one could easily read. The other oil-lamps possessed a long wick of fabric dipped in kerosene, which was lighted at the upper end. A screw regulated the size of the flame. Such lamps developed a yellow light, and because they generated smoke their "glass chimney" became dirty and black. Every Saturday all lamps and their glass chimneys were cleaned, which meant a lot of work. Both kinds of lamps had the disadvantage that they always smelt of kerosene.

In 1921, my father decided that electricity on the farm and in the house would save much work. It would not be much more expensive than the old oil lighting, with the continual danger of fire in the old farm-house. However, there were hardly any public power plants in the country—only cities had electricity at their disposal. Father was acquainted with the chief-electrician of the big hospital in Moulsford which owned its own generator. In the same hospital worked a carpenter who had helped to install the generator in the hospital. The carpenter's name was Cox, and the name of the electrician was Philips. Mr. Cox was thin as a lathe and witty, while Mr. Philips was stout, wore a big mustache and was an introvert. Father bought fifty-four big 108-ampere per hour lead oxide cells with large glass containers for the sulfuric acid and installed it all in a converted stable. Then he procured a big generator capable of delivering up to fifty amperes at 130 volts. From his second farm, which he managed in Littlestoke, he fetched a big Crossley kerosene engine.

I had just turned six years and was very interested in the electrical installations. I watched Mr. Philips and Mr. Cox set up the big accumulators on wooden benches. Then they wired our house and the farm with leaden cables. It was fascinating for us small boys to watch the bulbs in the generator building glow immediately after the batteries were filled with sulfuric acid. The meter on the big instrument board in a separate building at once indicated the 110 volts.

The great moment arrived when a concrete bed was cast for the big Crossley oil motor (hot balloon kerosene motor). The flywheels for this monster each weighed a ton—there was a flywheel on each side of the engine. The piston of this motor had a diameter of about twenty centimeters (twelve inches). The crankshaft carried two mighty counter-weights. The one-cylinder motor then was coupled to the generator (Ransome, Symes and Jeffries) by means of a leather belt. A soldering lamp was ignited to render the hot balloon glowing hot. These motors did not have an electrical ignition, the compressed mixture of hot air and kerosene was pressed into the hot balloon where it ignited with explosive strength and delivered the expanding gases into the cylinder. The intake-valve operated itself by vacuum. The outlet-valve was driven by a massive crankshaft, which at the same time regulated the speed of the motor.

At last the great moment arrived: The hot balloon glowed in the flame of the soldering lamp. Spindly, small Mr. Cox tried with all his strength to put the big flywheels into motion. Mr. Philips dripped some kerosene into the motor through the intake-valve. But, unfortunately, the motor kicked back, and Mr. Cox very nearly was thrown against the roof. The motor preferred to run backwards instead of forwards. Clouds of kerosene vapor streamed into the engine room so that everybody had to flee the room. It was a miracle that the soldering lamp did not cause the cloud of kerosene to explode!

All windows were opened. A new strategy had to be found. Mr. Philips had an idea. He had one useful characteristic: Although he was not as strong as Mr. Cox he was corpulent. In other words, he possessed a large amount of weight. He placed himself resolutely on one spoke of the big flywheel so that the motor could not run backwards; against his weight not even the Crossley was able to argue. Just at the vital moment, Mr. Cox put a lot of kerosene into the motor. There was a mighty jolt and a dull explosion as the compressed kerosene vapor exploded, the piston shot out and this time the motor turned in the correct direction. The motor slowly and majestically started to pulsate. It needed some time until the motor reached full speed, but full speed it certainly reached. It ran faster and faster so that we became afraid of the flywheels and flying counter-weights weighing tons. Mr. Cox desperately worked at the regulator of which he really did not know enough. But Mr. Philips quickly loosened the spring regulating the outlet-valve so that the speed slowly diminished.

When the motor was running at a reasonable speed Mr. Philips switched on the generator, which rapidly restrained the motor. Everything went according to calculations, the motor delivered about twenty-five amperes at 120 volts which sufficed for our requirements. Now, the soldering lamp was turned off, and an asbestos cover was put over the hot ignition-balloon. In this fashion, the hot balloon stayed hot enough without a lamp and the ignition automatically continued to run—at least theoretically! When after five or six hours the accumulators were charged the motor ran more easily. The hot balloon cooled down with the result that the ignition of the kerosene intermittently did not take place, and the motor partially failed. Under these circumstances the unburned kerosene gases collected in the big muffler. As soon as the motor restarted the new hot gases ignited the old gases in the muffler. The result was, of course, a huge explosion in the muffler, an explosion to be clearly heard at two to three miles distance! Mother was much afraid of such explosions although they actually were quite harmless.

When I was eight or nine years old, my father entrusted me with the maintenance and supervision of the whole plant. Every week the batteries had to be recharged. I learned to operate the big Crossley although I was only a child. To start it, I applied Mr. Philips method: I stood on one flywheel (my weight unfortunately was not the same as Mr. Philips) and so prevented the motor from turning backwards. Then I reached with my left arm to the intake-valve to put in the kerosene at the right moment. In a fraction of a second I had to jump down from the flywheel otherwise I would have taken a journey to the moon through the roof of the engine room! In later years, my brother and I built an electric ignition system (with magneto and spark-plug screwed into the hot balloon). We then used petrol to start the motor. After a few minutes the motor was warm enough to be changed to kerosene. In this manner we could avoid the explosion in the muffler caused by the cooling of the balloon.

I practiced this job as chief of the electric plant on the farm until my brother and I went to boarding school. Later, when I was a student in Oxford and Reading, I resumed the job. It taught me many practical things. My brother and I had an inclination to engineering, and besides looking after the electric power plant, we tinkered at lot with cars. Probably, this love for engineering came from my mother's family.

CHAPTER IV

BOARDING SCHOOL

THE PUBLIC (BOARDING) SCHOOL

Between 1922 and 1930, my brother and I went to Grammar School in Wallingford. Every day we traveled there by narrow gauge train. Other boys from nearby villages joined us in the same train, and we usually had lots of fun.

My mother, who was a teacher, was not very satisfied with the teaching staff in Wallingford. For example, I was judged too stupid to learn Latin and therefore was forced to study bookkeeping instead. Mother tried to teach me Latin. Obviously, she did not believe the school report and the grading. The same applied to Mathematics and Chemistry. My brother and I passed for beyond hope, although with Mother, we learned quite well.

Father and Mother discussed the situation and asked themselves if a boarding school would be the solution. Mother was of the opinion that the principle of the Wallingford School, Mr. Haywards, was not a man who should be entrusted with children's education. He was easily enraged and called his pupils "ineffable apes" and other "endearing" names, instead of teaching them something useful. Mother questioned his teaching ability. He was the Latin teacher. There was another gaunt, chronically bad-tempered chemistry teacher with the name of Hyslop. He wore a pince-nez and looked ascetic and fear-inspiring. Apart from chemistry, he also taught physics. After one year of his teaching, I had learned absolutely nothing. My grades in his subjects were "rock bottom;" i.e., the lowest possible. My brother was even worse. We just did not get the meaning of what he was waffling on about in a low voice.

A) MOTHER'S INTERVIEW WITH THE TEACHER

One evening, my mother went to see Pinney Hislop and asked him about her son's IQ. The teacher gave a positive report of me; he is always polite, attentive, obliging, etc., etc. "Why then does my son always fail his exams?" my good mother questioned the teacher. "That's a mystery," he answered. My mother could not stand for this any more, so she gave notice to the school—a private school, for fortunately the state did not have a monopoly on schools. She told him flatly so many pupils had already left the school that she also was taking her sons away because they were not learning anything.

My father agreed with my mother's decision, especially as he had to pay for the Grammar School. Father was of the opinion, if a school did not teach well, one should take the children out of this school as soon as possible. For what one misses in early youth can never be made up later on. One learns best and most thoroughly before and during puberty. John and Charles Wesley were able to enter the university in Oxford at the age of twelve, because they already knew Latin, Greek, some Hebrew and some French. They had been taught it by their mother.

Today's youth generally know very little of Mathematics, languages and grammar. The reason for this lies not with the children's incapability, but probably more with the fact that they suffer from stimulus flooding (too many impulses from the mass media into the brain, so that the information storage and retrieval system cannot cope any more). Over and above that the teachers also suffer from the same disease—too much information flooding through the TV, the mass media, and through cheap, inferior quality literature.

So my good parents decided to send Walter and me to a boys Public School. My sisters had also been sent to Boarding Schools with good results. "We will have to send the boys to a Boarding School. Otherwise they will not learn anything and suffer from it."

In Public School, the boys have to go to bed at 9:00 p.m., they have to rise at 7:00 a.m., wash in cold water and sleep with windows open in summer as well as in winter. They were taught manners. The teachers were addressed with "Sir" and the lady teachers with "Ma'am" (Madam). Boys did not enter a door before a teacher or a girl. And the weaker sex was to be treated respectfully. Most English boys and girls from educated families attended such a Public School from twelve to thirteen years onwards—which by the way is very private and not "public" at all.

B) TAUNTON SCHOOL

It was decided that we boys should go to Taunton School in Somerset, West England. Taunton School, in the village of Taunton, is a boarding school which, at that time, accommodated about 700 boys, ranging in age from three to eighteen years. The very small children were "cared for" in a special "house" by the name of Thone. Why were children so young sent to boarding school? The reason was that England, at that time, had a large colonial empire, that had to be supplied with administrators. The circumstances in certain parts of this colonial empire were wholly unsuitable for children, so that they could not be educated properly. Often in the colonial territories there was no school which prepared students for English colleges and universities. The children of these officials in the English colonial empire were, consequently, sent to boarding schools like Taunton School and, in particular, to places such as Thone. They were left there, on their own, at three to nine years of age.

It was often moving to observe how these children, as young as three years old, Sunday after Sunday, would be marched to church behind the older boys. Most often, groups of five to ten boys were led by the hand of an elderly woman, who was their teacher. Even more moving was the scene that was repeated so often when their parents had to leave for three to five years. At that time, one could not fly to India in a couple of hours.

In the trimester-break (half term)—in the middle of each trimester there was a weekend off—children, whose parents lived close by, could have their parents come to visit. However, the very small children naturally did not know their parents at all any more when they came to visit after three to five years. Mothers stood in front of their own children, who had no idea who or what parents are. There, my brothers and I learned what it meant to have a family and a father and mother behind you. You could always recognize the "Thone-children" when they were in middle or high school later on. It was somehow written on their faces; "I am an underprivileged child, I have no concept of family."

When our own children became teenagers, they faced the problem that in Switzerland, they being foreigners, could not acquire the same medical degree as the Swiss student, but rather only a "Fakultätsdiplom" which would not entitle them to have a medical practice of any kind, neither in Switzerland, nor in any other country. So, we decided to send all of them, including our daughter, to boarding school in England at thirteen or fourteen years of age.

Most European children of sixteen to seventeen years of age could hardly wait until they could leave home and get their own place. Our children were much more attached. They liked to come home to us and be a "child" again—even though they have all long since become doctors.

As our children experienced today's boarding schools, we came to see that the situation was similar to fifty years ago, when I was in boarding school, but for completely different reasons. In every boarding school, one finds children today who are underprivileged because they also do not know what it means to have a family and a father and mother. This is not, however, because England is a colonial empire, but rather because England, like most Western countries, today has so many broken homes.

The result is the same whether divorce or the colonial empire is the cause. It is literally written on the faces of these underprivileged children: "I do not know the warmth of a family. I have neither a father, nor a mother that wants me."

LIFE IN BOARDING SCHOOL

Taunton School was originally a "Dissenter School," that means a school that did not belong to the Church of England. (It was, in other words, a "free-church" school). We, as a family, had had some trouble with the Anglican Church, so mother was of the opinion that her sons should experience all aspects of religious life.

Some teachers in Taunton had made a conscious decision for Christ, many, however, unfortunately had not. Most of the boys did not come out of Christian homes. They were, at that time, most likely, sons of higher officials of the British Commonwealth: patriotic, proud, but unfortunately often lazy. A boarding school boy from that era was often very conscious of his social status. So public schools often instilled snobbishness. Today that danger is not as great, but it still exists.

ORDER IN THE OLD PUBLIC SCHOOL

Our boarding school was highly regimented. We were brought up in a Spartan manner. For example, there were no carpets on the floor in the bedroom, only concrete floors. In the large bedrooms, there were often twelve or thirteen beds, all on the bare concrete floor. The windows were open day and night, even in the coldest weather. Washing was done with cold water every morning. The bathroom was unheated. Once a week there was a hot bath under the supervision of a house master—six bathtubs in one bathroom with a concrete floor. Today, one can still recognize which English children went to boarding school, because the boy or girl who did not experience public school cannot stand a cold draft in the house. No true Englishman ever complains about a draft in a room. In English public schools, one becomes tough! A fresh breeze in the bedroom is healthy—it doesn't hurt anyone! One must have air, otherwise one cannot breathe!

When my brother and I first went to boarding school, our father and mother brought us in the Bentley to the train station in Reading. There, we were put on the 10:45 a.m express train and shipped to Taunton and that was that. We had never been to Taunton and knew absolutely nothing about the school or what awaited us. We found some boys on the train that had the same destination. They were also being sent to boarding school. We were met at the train station in Taunton by the vice-principal himself, Mr. Record. He gathered us together in military-like groups of about thirty to fifty boys and marched us to the school. The distance was perhaps two miles. Our baggage was brought up afterwards. Once we arrived, we were personally "debriefed" by the vice-principal: Have you had relatives attending here? How old are you? Do you have brothers and sisters? Have you ever been in a boarding school before? What kinds of diseases have you had? Then we were given over to a "Matron," an elderly lady, who saw to it that we received a bed for the night, that we had a space for our things, and were assigned a place at the table for "supper"—a piece of bread and butter without anything on it and a bowl of an indescribable mixture that the boys called "Stingo."

An important matter that I must not forget at this point: Every boy had a lockable wooden chest, in which he put his "goodies" or "tuck": edibles locked up and safely stored away. This chest or "tuckbox" was guarded with a padlock and bolt. During the school recess in the morning and in the afternoon, one could go to one's tuckbox to get something good to eat. Tuckboxes are to boarding school boys as water is to a fish. My own children still have their tuckboxes hidden away. They are the one thing a boarding school boy cannot do without. If a boy robbed another boy's tuckbox, which rarely happened, this was a very serious offense.

THE FIRST IMPRESSIONS OF BOARDING SCHOOL

My brother and I scouted out the big complex of buildings the next day and were not very impressed. Outside, nearly everywhere were sports fields, for rugby, hockey, cricket and on and on; and inside the buildings, looked like barracks. Absolutely nothing was private, but there were all sorts of places that were off limits. The terraces at the public school were only for "masters" (teachers) and "prefects" (senior boys with special disciplinary function). Everything was very elitist—and we were only "new boys" and "juniors." We had many duties and few rights. One felt constantly watched to see if one happened to break a rule.

While we were scouting out the place, a group of older boys approached us "new boys" and said with very serious expressions that the duty of all new boys was to loudly greet all prefects by their "proper" names. We said that we could not do that because we did not even know the names of the prefects. "We want to help you," they said earnestly, "that tall one over there with the bright red hair and the stylish off-white trousers is the Head Prefect. He comes and goes on the terrace as he pleases since that is his privilege. If you do the right thing you won't be punished. You just go over to him and address him as "Lighthouse" since that is the proper greeting. Then you will have called him by name and he will not punish you. But do not step onto his terrace!"

Now we knew enough to know that one should not call a teacher or a prefect by a nickname. And this name "Lighthouse" seemed odd for a redhead! So we thanked them very politely for their friendly information and said that tomorrow we would, according to regulations, carry out the official greeting when we were completely sure that he was really called "Lighthouse." My brother and I were not that stupid! A rude name like "Lighthouse" would have cost us six lashes with the whip. The redhead was well known to be arrogant and humorless. So the boarding school boys came to know whether the "new boys" had any sense or not. Woe to the boys that were naive. They would be teased until it was knocked out of them.

DISCIPLINE AND UPBRINGING IN THE OLD STYLE

We were awakened in the mornings at 7:00 a.m. sharp by a big hand bell rung outside on the meadow. The old gardener would go between the houses and swing the big bell back and forth so that (theoretically) every boy woke up. One can become accustomed to anything, however, and I often did not hear the bell. But the other boys would wake up anyone who slept through the bell. At 7:20 a.m., the House Master stood at the top of the big staircase of our house (I was in the "East House") and called out a loud, "Tallyho" (this is the call of the hunter, when the hounds have just gotten the scent of a fox). With this call, all the hunters (that is, boys) dashed after him. Whoever had not finished dressing when the House Master closed the door to the Assembly Hall was considered late. Whoever was still struggling with his tie or collar in the Assembly Hall or whoever had a dirty shirt on was also regarded as late. The names of all the boys would be called out alphabetically and each boy had to answer with "adsum" which means "I am present" in Latin. Being late cost "two" with the cane. If one was cowardly, one could exchange the "two" for 200 "lines." "Lines" meant that one had to write 200 times, "I must not be late for Roll Call." Or, "I must dress properly before appearing for Roll Call" 200 times. Most preferred to endure the whip. It was more honorable!

Today, this all seems totally impossible and brutal. But I have never seen the whip to cause harm. Of course, the whip was not used with girls. They were girls! And we were boys!

Schools that had stopped using the whip when I was in school had done so because they had girls instead of boys. At least that was the word among the boys! Discipline of this kind never hurt anyone as long as there was a just school master to administer the system. As soon as weak, unjust teachers appear in the boarding schools, the system failed. It became brutal and this threatened the dissolution of the disciplinary tradition.

The Bible teaches: "He who spares the rod hates his son, but he who loves him is careful to discipline him" (Proverbs 13:24). I do not believe that the rod achieves much after childhood—even though many brutal murderers fear the whip more than twenty years of imprisonment. Perhaps the rod would help such people. But in the upbringing of children— taking into consideration the disposition of the child, and whether the child is a boy or a girl—the rod plays a quite definite and healthy role. In my book, *Terrorism—The Criminal Mind,* I sketched out the position of psychology in this field. The threshold of a new era of criminality can be very favorably altered through a wise application of corporal discipline early in life. Why is criminality in most countries of the world increasing so terribly? Man stays the same—genetically at least. The factor that has changed is surely the factor of upbringing. Does the increasingly lax upbringing of children have something to do with the climbing crime rate and with the growth of terrorism? Pedagogues and educators should thoroughly examine these possible causes. This is exactly the question that is scientifically scrutinized in my book, *Terrorism.*

A FEW MISERIES IN THE DAILY LIFE
OF BOARDING SCHOOLS

Under the supervision of Mr. Record, the vice-principal of the boarding school, I never again had trouble with Latin and French. An iron disciplinarian, Mr. Record, whom we called "Chew," because he always worked his mouth, was, in reality, a devout, fair and just man whom we all respected. Every Sunday morning, he personally inspected all seven hundred students as they marched together into the town to the various churches. The parents decided which church was to be visited. Mr. Record saw immediately whether a young churchgoer had on a clean, white or a no-longer-so-white shirt. Or whether his black tie had a spot on it. Or whether his handkerchief was white or not. Often, at random, as we were marching along, he would demand that a handkerchief be produced. Woe to the boy who had forgotten his handkerchief, or whose handkerchief did not look like an ad for laundry soap. He would have to step out of line and go get a fresh handkerchief while the whole school waited impatiently for him. Such boys were not popular. So Mr. Record's discipline worked. In the end, the boys themselves saw to it that there was order.

For a boy who has gone through such schooling, it is often difficult to come to terms with today's "relaxed" fashions. Not a single boy or girl from that time would ever have dared to appear in church or in other society as is common today with dirty and sloppy jeans. Cleanliness and orderliness in one's clothing certainly relate to inner purity.

Although our Director, Mr. Record, had the nickname "Chew," the pupil who was caught with chewing gum or any other similar hideousness in his mouth would regret it. Whoever in the class chewed tobacco was gambling with his academic fate. Luckily, bubble gum had not been invented yet. Mr. Record would have had an apoplectic fit.

Other sources of trouble at our boarding school soon became apparent to us new boys. If a boy spoke to a teacher or some other adult with his hands in his pockets, he was in trouble. Such an ill-mannered boy, received, at first, a series of caustic veiled remarks; e.g., would he please be so kind as to pay attention to his social unacceptability. When one was too dull to understand these oblique comments—there were such boys even then—one could expect a direct, sharp rebuke: "Boy, take your hands out of your pockets when you are conversing with your elders and betters."

Three times a year all the parents received a report card on their children. It was sent directly to the home. Not only was the academic performance of the pupil assessed, but also his overall conduct, his progress in the area of personal development, his refinement and his manners were all written out with a corresponding record of evidence. How often the pupil had to be punished, what kind of punishment and the reasons for it were also recorded. "Cheek," that is insolence, was a serious offense, especially towards one's elders.

A sermon was given by the school director or a minister in the school chapel the summer mornings and evenings. Our behavior was strictly observed and one had to be decently dressed. There was a school uniform, which helped prevent class envy between the boys who came from very wealthy families that could afford fine clothes and those who were of more modest means. Boys, however, left to their own devices, are less vain about their clothes than are girls. Woe to the boy who stood before God and prayed disrespectfully. Today, I have, myself, very often observed even Pastors in their pulpits who pray to God as if he were their buddy: with their hands deep in their pockets while they lead their congregations in prayer to God. Such a sight takes away from the reverence of worship for me. Does today's lack of self control and discipline have something to do with the disintegration of our western society? I think it does! Today no one has respect, neither for man, nor his elders, nor for God.

I do not want to say that this Spartan upbringing is without fault. There are people who are incorrigible. There were such people in the boarding school. There was much immorality at Taunton. The older prefects often had their "bum-boys"; they had a sexual role to perform. The older pupils often brought loose girls into the boarding school—they said they were their cousins or some other relative. Sex was the usual topic of conversation in the bedrooms. Dirty jokes were often the rule, even though there were pupils that did not join in. These pupils who did not participate were often considered "prudes."

I know of Christian boarding schools apparently free of such problems. But, in the purely secular schools, immorality is very often the rule. We sent our children to Christian boarding schools where the atmosphere was certainly better. However, the danger in such Christian boarding schools is that of legalism and hypocrisy. There may well be a Christian headmaster, but often there are many non-Christian teachers. The children can see for themselves the difference between Christians and non-Christians, which may help them in choosing their own faith. There the Christian teachers are often truly lights in a world, that is to a large degree non-Christian. In this way, they are prepared for the real world where Christians must shine in a non-Christian world.

SOME ADVANTAGES OF BOARDING SCHOOL

Nonetheless, boarding schools also had great advantages. Even though boarding school was very expensive for my dear parents—and that in the time of the Great Depression (1930–1934)—there were far fewer distractions from schoolwork. One started at 7:00 a.m. in the morning with rising and washing. Chapel was from 7:30 to 8:00 a.m.; breakfast was 8:00 to 8:30 a.m.; classes from 9:00 a.m. to 1:00 p.m. Lunch was from 1:15 to 1:45; then classes lasted from 2:00 p.m. again to 4:30 p.m. Then sports—soccer, rugby, hockey (in the winter), cricket (in the summer). These were all mandatory. Excelling in sports meant, perhaps, even more than academic achievement. Dinner was at 6:30 p.m.: bread and butter with very little cheese, marmalade or even less Marmite (a yeast extract) and a "mug" of cocoa—an indescribable concoction of water, milk powder, more water, sugar and cocoa. Homework, in a large hall under supervision followed from 7:30 to 9:30 p.m. ("prep time"). Bedtime was 10:00 p.m. (for the older boys; half an hour earlier for the younger boys in the Junior House). "Lights-out"was 10:30 p.m., on the dot. All lights in all bedrooms must be turned off, all must be quiet, and woe to the boy who tried to listen to his radio quietly under the covers. One senior boy in every bedroom ("dorm leader") was responsible for enforcing this rule, and he was highly respected.

CHAPTER V

THE ATHEISTIC SEED

THE CHURCH CONFLICT IN ENGLAND

While my brother and I were at boarding school, a conflict was raging over the Church of England. The Church of England had its roots in the time of the Reformation under Henry VIII, when the Anglican Church broke with Catholicism. The English King, Henry the VIII, did not want to be subject to the Pope in Rome, because the Pope gave him grief over his many wives (with good cause).

Now, Henry was not an especially devout man, quite the contrary. He did not necessarily want to change the doctrine of the Church in England, just its political structure and hierarchy. The political power of the Pope was troublesome for the proud English King. So he, in effect, made himself Pope in that he himself appointed the Archbishop of Canterbury. Doctrinally, he held to almost everything else. So the Church of England today still teaches, as far as the Book of Common Prayer is concerned, several Roman Catholic doctrines such as that of child baptism.

Now, the conflict in the Church, while we were in boarding school, had nothing to do with these problems. These problems had been taken up at the time of the real Reformation of England, through the Reformers, Charles and John Wesley, George Whitefield and later, Spurgeon. The conflict in the Church from 1925 to 1935 was solely over money, a problem that even the contemporary church—especially on the European continent—is plagued with. The

Church of England, whose head is the King (or the Queen as the case may be), did not have a church tax. The country required a "tithe." Every landowner, with the purchase of his land, had to pay the church a cash sum every year. Earlier this "tithe" was paid "in kind," that is with the produce of the land. Every Pastor or priest had his own "tithe-barn" where he stored his wheat, potatoes, straw, etc. In later years, the ministers no longer wanted to accept the tithe in the form of goods and demanded the equivalent of the tithe in cash. In this way, the ministers' work was made easier. There are still "tithe-barns" to be found all over England that are now used for other purposes.

At the same time, whether the landowner belonged to the Anglican Church or not, the fact remained that because he owned a certain piece of property, he was obliged to pay the "tithe" to the Anglican Church.

Often Methodists, members of non-denominational churches, and even atheists owned land and therefore were obliged to pay this "tithe" to the Anglican Church. Many members of free churches (non-Anglican) and atheists objected to supporting the Anglican Church financially. The Church of England was enormously wealthy and owns—or owned— much property throughout Britain.

In times of plenty, people do not bother to object to paying such taxes, even though they are unjust. But when the Great Depression started in 1929, and farmers and landowners became poorer, people started to object to paying this church tax. Farmers were having to lay off their farm workers because they did not have the money at their disposal to pay their wages, much less the money to pay the "tithe." When it came down to whether "John" and "Harry" would be laid off or whether the church "tithe" would be paid, many farmers refused to pay the church. The Anglican Church was almost empty anyway—worship services often consisted of the Pastor, the organist and the custodian. Sermons lasted ten minutes at the most and the minister was usually totally liberal. The theology professors at the universities, principally Oxford and Cambridge, had seen to that. The churches with liberal ministers were and still are the most empty.

THE GREAT DEPRESSION 1929–1932

Every day jobless men roamed by our farm. They were young men who had been discharged from the army. Often as many as 100 to 200 "down at heel" young men would come through our little village and stop and beg from us. They would go from one "workhouse" to another, to find a bed for the night. A "workhouse" was an institute for jobless men who were also homeless. They would be required to perform certain tasks, such as digging the garden or weeding, then they received a meal and a bed for the night. Everything was very primitive, but it was better than sleeping in a ditch. Father had no money to give away. When one gave these people money, they often wasted it on alcohol, which was understandable because they wanted to forget their misery for a time. These jobless were mostly young men who had put their lives on the line for England in World War I. Such discharged soldiers were often very bitter against the state and against society altogether, because they felt unfairly treated. So my father, when he could, would give them short-term work, a meal and a bed for the night for which most of them were very thankful.

My father was of the view that the Anglican Church was a dead organization which swallowed up too much money compared to what it produced. He was most certainly not wrong. So when the time came to pay the church "tithe," my father said that he would rather help these poor unemployed men than the church. My dear mother, a devout lady who was a practicing Christian, wavered between the two loyalties. She was, however, very just and saw that the Church represented a direct impediment to the faith of the people in its care. So she supported father. We children were naturally of the same opinion; why should a minister, who very often did not believe or live what he was paid to preach, take food out of the mouths of the poor?

So, father and many other neighboring farmers simply did not pay the "tithe." The consequence was foreseeable. The church had to bear the cost of the ministers' salaries, otherwise they and their families would starve. The church therefore also urgently wanted money and promptly sent the local auctioneer with the power of law into each house to get the "tithe." They received however, no money; nothing was available. As a result, everything the family owned, furniture, beds, tables, and cutlery was publicly auctioned. It was publicly announced what was to be auctioned.

THE AUCTION

On the predetermined day, the farmers and a crowd came into the house to see what the now hated Church would do next in the name of Christ. The auctioneer extolled the kitchen table and said that it was perhaps worth ten pounds and asked for firm bids. Dead silence followed. No one made any kind of bid, because the farmers that were present were our friends and good neighbors. And, because they also had refused to pay their "tithe," later the same day their farms would be auctioned also. As a result, the auctioneer pressed the crowd for a bid. One farmer then said, mockingly, that the table had scratches in the middle of it and that the price was too high! "What do you bid me for it?" asked the annoyed auctioneer. "One farthing (one quarter penny) at the most," answered the farmer with a very serious expression. "But the table is still good," answered the official, "please, may I have serious bids?" Dead silence again, even though some faces were showing light grins. "Yes," said another farmer after a while, "the scratches are very serious and I bid a half-penny. I am doubling the first bid, Mr. Auctioneer," he pointed out very seriously. (A half-penny is two farthings). In the end the poor auctioneer received three farthings, that is, three quarters of a penny for the kitchen table. The farmer solemnly paid the amount on the spot and received an official receipt that the table now belonged to him to use as he pleased. Then he went seriously to my mother and presented the kitchen table to her to use as she pleased.

But worse was to follow. As the whole crowd and the auctioneer came out of the house and went over to father's car to auction it off, suddenly there was an enormous commotion. The young men suddenly vaulted over the fence. The ladies screamed loudly. And the auctioneer fled with a leap into the barn loft—four to five rungs of the ladder at a time—a very undignified climb. Why the commotion, the sudden clambering? One seldom sees such agility in state officials. It did not take long at all to determine the cause for the rapid movement of the official and his retinue. Our bull was standing there, scanning the group with his head down and his tail standing up like a flagpole! A farmer, a good friend of ours, who had a robust sense of humor, had crept into the stable. There he had untied our very mean, wild bull. The bull had never ever been allowed to wander around free! One led him around on a chain and with a rod through the nose-ring. As he enjoyed his newly found freedom, he glared at the auctioneer and his following. In a fraction of a second, everyone disappeared and the farmer responsible for this fun showed himself, grinning, from behind the other side of the courtyard door, from absolute safety himself.

There was no way the auctioneer could come out of his hiding place to the floor of the barn to auction father's car off. He had to wait pathetically until we could find the Swiss man whom the bull knew and would obey. The Swiss man could not be found for quite a time. Strange! Later he very slowly ambled out of the other barn and calmly went to the bull, placed the rod into the nose-ring, while reassuringly talking to the dangerous animal. He then led him back into the stable and tied him up. Only then did the auctioneer dare to come back down to the floor. Somehow his authority seemed to have evaporated. All the farmers were now in the very best of moods and congratulated my father.

But the afternoon's work was not yet done. The auctioneer had decided that it was already too late to continue with the auctioning of the car. Therefore he walked to the barn where the beautiful car was parked. But Oh no! Oh dear! He could not recognize the car at all anymore. Someone had obviously gone into the hen house and gathered a whole lot of feathers and droppings. And someone else had, at the same time, poured warm, runny tar, which was being used to asphalt the street in front of the property, all over the car. The feathers had been strewn onto the wet tar. This car was "truly" tarred and feathered.

Strangely enough, the police looked on from afar, but did not see much. Poor men, they had to work in a village which consisted mostly of farmers. It would certainly not have been very good for the policemen's health if they had interfered. Similar incidents occurred throughout the country and were considered fair sport. The whole county laughed about this passive resistance against the unrighteousness of the Church. The police could count on the farmers and vice versa. No one wanted anyone to get hurt. This humorous and innovative happening was a form of self-defense. English humor often happens that way.

THE CONSEQUENCES OF THE AUCTION

Now, what was the consequence of this obstruction? The Church was a state institution. The State appointed the Bishops and collected the "tithe" for the Church and was one with the Church. If the State Church were to go bankrupt, the State would have to bear the costs. The money that the Church could not collect as its "tithe" had to be paid by Father State. So, Father State was directly affected. What to do? Very simple! The Church must be financially secure, but less obtrusive. So a new law was quickly drawn up and, with dizzying speed, passed through Parliament in order to resolve the question of the "tithe" for all time. The "tithe" was converted into a state tax for the state church, and this tax would be collected by the policing power of the State just as income tax is collected. The landowners that wanted to, could pay off their entire tithe in a lump sum. It was declared that whoever did not want to accept this regulation and resisted the power of the state would be guilty of tax evasion.

So the State won this argument, in as much as the Church identified itself with the power of the State. The Church of England lost forever the right to assert that "My kingdom is not of this world" (John 18:36). This debate in a financially depressed country was naturally not without consequences for us boys. Already before we went to boarding school, we had decided that this Church for the most part was a "humbug" and that no man who thought in this way could be "religious." We confused being a Christian with religiosity—or picusness— and the power of the State with moral authority. So we imagined ourselves to be atheists. It is due to an especially gracious God that my brother and I later became Christians, despite all these negative experiences.

While in boarding school, I decided to study at Oxford or Cambridge. At that time, Oxford was directly under the influence of the Church. Most scholarships came from sources controlled by the Church. It was therefore advantageous for me to go through confirmation. I had been baptized as an infant in the Anglican Church, so I could become confirmed later. So I let myself be confirmed while I was in boarding school. The poor minister who confirmed us boys was somewhat hard of hearing, but was a gentleman in every respect. During the lessons, we told him unsuitable jokes that he did not understand. But I learned nothing about being a Christian. When I was confirmed by the Bishop of Taunton, I could not even recite the Ten Commandments. So, I committed for the first time, the sin of taking Holy Communion as an atheist and even did it for the sake of academic advantages. I was wholly and completely an unbeliever and was confirmed without serious investigation. What kind of rationalization can a Church have that has a Bible and does not use it?

THE HONORABLE MINISTER RECEIVES A HIGHER CALLING

To conclude this segment about the Church and the "tithe," we must describe still one more small occurrence, that has to do with the Church. We had in the parish in Cholsey a very kind, gentle minister. He was in poor health and as far as I remember, he had two daughters. Rather early, he suffered from a type of colon cancer and had a colostomy.

He preached a sermon once a week which lasted about ten minutes (seldom longer) and belonged to the "Middle Church" (between the Evangelicals and the Anglo-Catholics). His church-going people, or regulars, were few—ten to fifteen people each Sunday—because his sermons were very boring and also irrelevant. He made almost no house visits. Because most of the inhabitants of his parish worked on farms and the Church was very unpopular due to its politics and the compulsory collection of the "tithe," the situation of the pitiful minister in the village was very difficult.

One day the minister surprisingly contacted us and said that he would like to come to visit. The reason for this visit was not spiritual—this probably never happened and would have certainly not been desired by us. No, he wanted to say good-bye to us. So he was invited to Tea with us at 5:00 p.m. The poor, sick man appeared punctually and was welcomed by my dear mother. The situation was naturally very delicate because my good father also turned up to bid good-bye to the minister.

After a while, my father asked the minister where he would be going. The good minister naturally answered very piously, he had received a higher calling. My father wanted to know where this calling was. But the minister did not want to come out with it. My father would not back off until the minister named the new village where he would be working. The village lay not very far from us. Father, who was a member of the District Council, was very well oriented and knew that the new parish which the minister named was twice as well endowed as the parish in our village. When the minister named the rich village where he would be going, an awkward silence fell on the whole family, because the place was well known to be a rich parish. Then my father said very loudly and clearly that he expected that the Lord had surely called the minister to that place. And that He, the Lord, would surely bless this calling richly. But then my father said that he suspected that the Lord would have had to call very long and very loud if the remuneration there had not been twice as high as in Cholsey.

At that, the minister stood up and politely said good-bye. I felt very sorry for him because he was a kind, but also an ailing man, who found himself in an extremely awkward situation.

As a confirmed member of the Anglican Church with good academic grades, Oxford University was open to me. Today, the circumstances are completely different. Only very few parents nowadays are required to finance their children's education at Oxford or Cambridge on their own. At that time, the parents had to completely finance their children's education, which encouraged a strong sense of family unity. One knew that the family was sacrificing much financially in order to secure a good education for their children. For that reason many students were very thankful for their parents who supported them. In light of that, they used every second of the trimester in order to gain the most benefit for their parent's money. Today, in a state that has become financially irresponsible, taxpayers' money is being flung at young people in the form of university grants. Unfortunately, when the students have the government money in hand, they are often not motivated to study at all or to get the most out of the money. Many students maintain that they will be unemployed anyway, why should they educate themselves for that? This is unfortunately only too true.

CHAPTER VI

THE REALITY OF LIFE BEGINS

MY FIRST EXAMINATIONS IN PUBLIC SCHOOL

Because the financial situation in the country was so drastic and because the boarding school was so dreadfully expensive, I decided that I would finish boarding school more quickly than normal. (Today, this first examination is called the GCSE-Levels.)

I began at the boarding school in 1930, and should have written my "Middle Exam" in the summer of 1933. At the end of 1931, I decided to have a try at my Middle Exam in December of 1932. But the Director of my school thought that if I did not pass in December of 1932, that I would then have only two Trimester's time left to prepare for the Middle Exam of the Summer of 1933. Therefore, he insisted on my preparing during the day for the Exam in the Summer of 1933 with the normal class and in the evenings, during the "Prep," the homework period, I would be allowed to study privately with the older boys, who were preparing for the Exam to take place in December of 1932. So I had to plow through two curricula at the same time.

As December of 1932 came nearer, I was really very poorly prepared because the teachers were not supportive of my plan. In the end, when I was successful, the teachers could be regarded as superfluous, because I had prepared myself without their help. This, in a time of the most difficult financial need, was unthinkable both for the teachers and for the administrators. To what extent were the teachers indispensable? The last months, I had worked literally night and day on both curricula (they were different every year, one year Milton, one year Shakespeare, one year Coleridge, one year Molière, one year Goethe and the German philosophers). Shortly before the exam, I became sick and went into the School Clinic. There, I finally had some peace and quiet to work only for the December exam, as I desired. I dropped the curriculum for 1933 completely and concentrated on the exam in December of 1932. I got up directly from bed and went straight to the Examination Hall (although I was very shaky). In England, one was tested both in writing and orally in a foreign language, so when the time came for me to be tested in German, I was so weak and hoarse that I could only whisper for the oral part of the Exam.

THE BIG SURPRISE

When the results for December became known, I could hardly believe my eyes. I had passed with honors—six "credits," plus a "Distinction" in chemistry. I was promoted on the spot. From one day to the next, I no longer belonged to the Junior School, but rather, came into the sixth form, where one prepared for the Higher Certificate (what is now called "A"-Levels).

THE COMPETITION BETWEEN BOARDING SCHOOLS

The standard of academic achievement varied from one boarding school to another. There was also competition between the different boarding schools. Parents chose a boarding school according to its area of renown—academics or sports. Some schools were known for their achievements in the area of sports, others for their achievements in academic fields. There were even specializations in sports and in the academic subjects. Taunton was known for the humanities and for rugby. This fact had unforeseen consequences for me. When I was suddenly promoted to then Sixth Form, I chose the natural sciences for further study. Then came the big surprise: the school did not have a single capable science teacher on staff because there were so few boys who chose to be taught in natural science. Humanities scholars were in abundance, but not scientists! The biology teacher was a very old, politically active communist who was not at all interested in his teaching profession, and completely outdated. There was also no teaching for chemistry and physics. One cannot teach oneself in these subjects, because there is so much practical course work to be absolved.

As I had passed through self-study to receive the School Certificate, perhaps, I could also succeed in the Higher Certificate. So for almost two years, I simply memorized the textbooks. But the microscopy work and the chemical syntheses were a whole different story. When the big day of the Exam in Bristol arrived, I read the first question and realized I had no chance at all of passing. Even the language of the questions was completely foreign to me. I had never gone through any old Exam questions! The result was foreseeable: I failed completely.

CHAPTER VII

CHANGES IN MY EDUCATION

THE ACADEMIC CAREER BEGINS

The Boarding School fees were high, but my dear parents recognized that my O-Levels would be sufficient for Oxford Entrance Exams, because I had received an "Honors Certificate with Distinction." Oxford was somewhat more expensive than the boarding school in Taunton, where I had wasted much of my time. So, my father spoke with his friend, Professor Chattaway, the Professor of Chemistry in Queen's College Oxford, who was a freemason "lodge-brother" of my father's. He arranged for me to take the entrance exam and then to study directly at Oxford University. The last two years in the boarding school had been wasted. I was so pleased when the actual lectures began at Oxford. The quality of teaching was incomparably better than that which I had experienced at boarding school. It also became possible for me to commute by car to Oxford in my first year, to avoid expenses until I had my "First Public Examination" in Natural Sciences.

I became affiliated with St. Edmund Hall and studied under Professor Gavin de Beer, Professor E. B. Ford, Professor Robert Robinson, Professor Chattaway and others. De Beer gave outstanding lectures in evolution and zoology. He was French, spoke perfect English and was a prominent atheist, evolutionist and Darwinist. In later years, he moved to

London to the "Royal Institute." But he was not very tolerant and had the inclination to despise people who did not think and reason exactly as he did. Ford was an inspiring genetic scientist and his favorite animal was Drosophila melanogaster—the fruit fly. His whole life, he worked on "maps" of the chromosomes of fruit flies. Chattaway was the dear tutor who watched over me. Robert Robinson, the organic chemist, who was a top expert in his field, had a laboratory in South Parkes Road, with a superb team of chemists there.

After one year, I had made up for all the time I had lost in boarding school and passed my First Public Examination of Oxford University with "good." Then I had the right to be a student in residence at Oxford.

My examiner in General Knowledge in the area of Mediaeval English History was C.S. Lewis. He was a very strict examiner and insisted that students should be able to express themselves clearly and accurately in their mother tongue. A number of students feared him for this reason. When a student started to stutter and stammer while trying to answer C.S. Lewis' questions, he used to interrupt him: "Sir, would you please step outside to reorganize your thoughts and come back when you can give me a well-structured and clear answer?"

On the other hand, C.S. Lewis was famous and respected by students and academics for his excellent lectures. On Sundays when C.S. Lewis preached the church was always crowded in contrast to other times when churches were very badly attended.

THE GREAT DEPRESSION REVISITED

The year was 1933. The whole of Europe was once more in a deep crisis. England was not much better. Hitler was elected in Germany and re-armament began, even though all the nations were bankrupt. Then Neville Chamberlain came to power in England, a man who was totally manipulated by

Hitler, who returned to London from Munich with a piece of paper in his pocket and proclaimed to the world that he had peace in hand. In such times, I started my studies at Oxford. My father had become very quiet. But mother reported to us that father could not find the finances for our further education. We had to buy new machines to replace the farm workers because they had become too expensive. Father had sold whole flocks of sheep without a word, in order to pay for the education of his children. The bank began to refuse to grant credit for the property, because the deficit was already very high.

Our workers were paid every Friday. Each one came to my father's office window, to receive his wages and any overtime. We had good, loyal people, who nonetheless were dependent on their wages, because they had their own responsibilities. Most of them had their own children. One Friday evening, shortly before 5:00 p.m., my poor father came to me with a moving plea. Could I please be his banker for today? The bank had given him no money for the wages due this evening. In half an hour, the workers would stand in front of his window to receive their wages. Both he, as well as my dear, good mother had not even a shilling left with which they could pay. Now, my brother and I had always received six pence a week as pocket money. We had always saved this money. Mother brought us up to be thrifty. My brother Walter and I counted our collected savings out of the savings book and presented them to our dear, good father. He was able to pay the wages due to the workers completely. We were so happy that the problem was solved for at least one week.

But what then? Next week, with its wages would come quickly. Although the harvest was already sold, the wheat buyer had no money with which to pay father. Until the wheat dealer paid, father could not pay any more wages, could not buy kerosene for the tractors, and also could not buy groceries for the household. At the end of the week, my father asked if I could help him financially once more, but I had no more money. Walter, my brother, also had nothing left. Daily, hundreds of young, unemployed men went by the farm and begged for some work and for something to eat. The situation was hopeless and desperate. What was father's plan now? Would I, please, try the following for him: I should travel for him to the bank in Reading with a bank check, explain the situation to the bank manager and ask him for help until the wheat dealer paid. The manager would not listen to father. Perhaps he would listen to a half-grown child. The plan was extremely awkward, but desperation had driven him to it.

Everyone begged for credit and the bank, in order to survive, had to be hard. Maybe one would help a youth out of pity! So I took on this extremely embarrassing task. We were proud farmers who were used to owing no one anything. The bank clerk sat behind the counter as I came hesitatingly to her. I showed her the check, explained that it was almost payday (Friday) and that we had sold a lot of wheat, but the payment for it had not yet come through. She listened very carefully and then disappeared. After what seemed an eternity to me, she returned. Miracle of miracles—this time, she smiled and said that everything was now in order. She had just spoken by telephone to the grain merchant, whose name was Soundy. He had sent the check to pay for the grain today! So I, a mere youth, went home triumphantly with a full wallet! My family was so happy over this success! I was beginning to be recognized as a budding financial genius!

But the family's financial situation seemed unbearable to me. My father just could not carry on like this anymore. I could not burden him with further expenses for my education. I had to find an alternative solution for my education. Oxford was too expensive. I had to find a less expensive university, or do without any study at all and immediately set about earning money myself.

IMPORTANT DECISIONS

We lived between Oxford, the county seat of Oxfordshire, and Reading, the county seat of Berkshire. Reading had a young university that offered most of the disciplines except medicine and theology. So I went there to inquire. There, it turned out that this university would admit me with pleasure—indeed, I came from Oxford University and had passed my First Public Examination in Natural Sciences with success. They offered me a degree course in the natural sciences and the course would cost about a third as much money as it would at Oxford. Without saying a word to my parents, I matriculated there in Reading and started right away in September 1934. The lectures and the professors were pleasant—mostly younger people who wanted to make careers for themselves. Some already had their FRS (Fellowship of the Royal Society, the highest honor of the academic world in England). I got on well with them and, in 1937, received my Bachelor of Science (Honors in Chemistry) with a "good." This diploma is roughly the same as passing the state exams with a "good" on the European Continent.

But what now? If I wanted to go into the teaching profession, I would have to earn a diploma in education, which would take another year. Only then would I be certified to be a secondary school teacher. The prospect of being a teacher did not excite me at all even though my mother was a teacher and had even graduated from Reading. My parents and I talked for a long time about my future. I wanted to become a natural scientist and researcher, especially if I could be associated with biology and structural organic chemistry. I then went and spoke with the professor of organic chemistry, Dr. A. K. Mills, who had received his doctorate in Heidelberg, Germany. Mills knew me well and was my tutor. (Every student in English universities has a professor from his discipline set over him who watches over the progress of his protégé.)

A tutor, however, does not watch only over the academic progress, but also over the development of his charge's character. As my tutor said, he was there to advise me in all areas from marriage to mathematics. Therein lies a great difference between the British and the continental universities. The continental universities educate a student purely on the academic side and do not pay attention to the condition of the man—as to whether he is of a moral character. On the continent, if a criminal or a drug-dealer wants to become a pharmacist, that is his business—as long as he is certified. The continental university only needs to find out if the candidate knows his subject. If he knows his subject, then he passes his exams. The English system was based on a holistic concept that an academic should be a moral character. Only a person of good morality, for example, should become a judge, and only a person of integrity, a doctor. No psychopath may, for example, become a pharmacist. That is why a tutor watches over the development of character in his student.

Now, this is in theory an excellent system—if one has good professors. When, however, materialists or egoists hold the university chair, then the tutorial system fails. I had the good fortune, both in Oxford and in Reading, to have excellent tutors.

So, I asked my tutor which path he thought I should follow for the future. He thought I had a gift for doing theoretical work and that being a secondary school teacher would not satisfy me intellectually. He knew me very well. His wife was German. She had come to know him during the time that he had studied in Heidelberg, Germany, under Professor Karl Freudenberg. Sometimes we would speak German with each other. I had begun to study German, which, incidentally, the other professors did not care for. Hitler had come to power in 1933, and the English people were polarized with regard to the Germans.

As my tutor and I came to this conclusion about my future, he said suddenly, that he had, just at that time an open position for a Ph.D. student. Would I be interested? He had two research problems for doctoral work. They were theoretical questions with far-reaching academic consequences. He could also offer me, along with that, a stipend of fifty pounds a year! I had never been so rich! At that time, fifty pounds was worth as much as 5000 pounds today! I accepted right away and drove to my parents at home with the good news. My father and mother were so pleased! But that was not all! Right afterwards, I was to take part in a BAAS Conference in Aberdeen (BAAS = British Association for the Advancement of Science). To cover the hotel and travel expenses, my tutor offered me, in those hard times, five pounds!

So, I became a Ph.D. student in physical and organic chemistry. The year was 1938, and Hitler held the whole of Europe under his spell. Neville Chamberlain was too much of a gentleman and too naive to understand Hitler. He believed what Hitler said! This naiveté soon led to World War II, with all its devastating consequences.

MY WORK ON SYNTHETIC COMPOUNDS BEGINS IN TURBULENT TIMES

In the meantime, I started with the first research topic regarding chemical synthesis and worked six months without success. As these dealt with the synthesis of two compounds with asymmetrical carbon atoms, half racemates resulted, whose behavior was problematic with regard to characterization. Through my endeavors, I had gained some experience in dealing with intricate problems, so my activities had not been a waste of time. My tutor proposed that I tackle the second research topic, because it was considerably more promising. So, I began with the asymmetrical synthesis of different alpha-amino acids as the basis for developing the formation of optically active ketones. This work with the smallest amount of optically active substances went very well and advanced quickly after I had worked out the exact methodology. In a very short time, I synthesized a whole series of pure, optically active ketones, which should help with the measurement of electronic forces in a conjugate molecule. The work thrived until the outbreak of the war in September 1939. I had worked a year on the problem and my supervisor was enthusiastic about the work.

OUTBREAK OF WAR—1939

In the fall of 1939, Hitler invaded Poland, and England and France declared war on Hitler. The university was reorganized because of the war. Many professors joined the military forces. Those of us who stayed had to safeguard the whole area around Reading against a feared offensive as well as we could. We produced models of the various poisonous gases—often a very tricky matter. In the meantime, I worked on my dissertation day and night. And so the first year of the war passed, with synthetic work, work on poisonous gas protection, and fire brigade service.

During the summer of 1940, Hitler occupied France, Holland, Belgium, Denmark and Norway. The international situation became very, very serious. England had lost the European harbors for supplies. Hitler occupied the whole of Europe right up to the borders of Russia, which cost him much in energy and soldiers. In September 1940, he had a try at conquering England by air, but lost so many airplanes that the attempt had to be abandoned (by September 15, 1940, he had lost about 180 airplanes), which in turn brought on disastrous consequences for the whole German war effort.

As England finally came to understand Hitler's real purposes and aims—that he wanted to conquer Great Britain—the country prepared in earnest for war. Until 1940, it had been the "mock war." Now it was deadly serious.

Churchill was elected Prime Minister and the Nazis' goal of ruling the world was explained to the people. Hitler had prophetically described all his goals, in clear and precise details, in his book, "Mein Kampf." But most Germans and also most Europeans simply did not take Hitler's described plan seriously. Unfortunately, today's world seems to have learned very little from that time, because the communists' goals of world domination are also clearly put forth and described in communist literature. But who takes them seriously nowadays? Even now, after the collapse of the Berlin Wall, much of the world lies under communist terror. The Germans thought, at that time, that Hitler's dictatorship would bring a solution to the world's problems. Many think today, especially the left-leaning Western mass-media, that democratic freedom brings only chaos, while communistic rule would bring justice. In this way, the West has let communist subversion go on until, as in the summer of 1940, the tyranny was right at their own door! Only then did the Englishmen wake up. But just a hair too late! If the United States had not helped, England and Europe would have been lost.

THE EVACUATION OF THE UNIVERSITIES—1940

The result of all these terrible events was the evacuation of the universities. I was offered a position as a research scientist in industry in the northeast of England. Because of the catastrophic situation, I willingly agreed to give up my flourishing laboratory in the university. But, before I left the university, I reached an agreement with the University Senate that I could finish my dissertation while working in industry. I had already carried out most of the syntheses with success and concluded the optical measurements with the polarimeter. Only the many micro-analyses remained, which I completed at my new home in Stockton-on-Tees.

In September 1940, I took the train to Stockton-on-Tees. One could not travel through London, because the city was being bombed daily from the air. Later, I often traveled through at night. The situation was serious in London. Thousands upon thousands of people rented places on the platforms of the Tube (the subway, or "Underground") where they would sleep for months out in public. The trains kept running the whole night through, but did not disturb the sleepers. They had become used to it.

After a train ride of over ten hours, I landed in Stockton-on-Tees, where I would work in the chemical industry as a professional researcher for the next four years.

CHAPTER VIII

OVERCOMING MY MATERIALISTIC EDUCATION IN SCHOOL AND THE UNIVERSITY

"THE GERMAN CONNECTION"

Some personal developments, which took place between my time at boarding school and my university career, need to be described in order to portray the development of my character.

The materialistic education at boarding school—especially the teaching of evolution as if it were a fact of natural science—led me to become an atheist. This step happened when I was at boarding school and had just acquired my School Certificate. My dear, good, believing mother was shattered over the knowledge that my expensive education had degenerated me in this way. Father was a Freemason and did not comment much on this change. He despised the Church and mistook the Anglican Church for Christianity. But he believed in God.

Personally, I was very unhappy. The numerous struggles at boarding school and the economic situation had depressed me very much. At this time, a young German came to the boarding school in Taunton as a pupil. He had red hair, was very self-disciplined, and spoke excellent English. We soon became friends. He invited me to his house in the Westerwald in Germany. So I spent a few weeks vacation during the summer of 1933 in Germany and learned some German. There I also got to know some other German families. The son of one of these families was in financial need at that time. The family owned a men's and women's ready-to-wear clothing business. The National Socialist Party invited the son to become a member of the SS. Then they would assign to his family's business the sole contract for the party uniforms for that region. This step would help him to relieve his financial difficulties. For that reason, he became an SS-man and his business began to flourish.

In the year 1936, this son invited me once more to the Westerwald for my holiday and I accepted the friendly invitation. The situation in the National Socialistic Party had, by that time, become very tense. One night, my friend was ordered to report to headquarters immediately in order to carry out a secret mission. Even the SS men did not know what that secret mission would be, but they were used to obeying without asking questions. A large group of SS-men had to carry out a mission which required the use of an automobile. For this purpose, the Party had supplied a DKW (a German car). The difficulty was that no one in this select group was able to drive. Then my friend asked me if I would be willing to take charge of driving the DKW for the group. I asked about the purpose of the nocturnal drive, which seemed very suspicious to me, but he did not know himself.

A few hours later, my friend, the SS-man, returned to the house very depressed and beaten down mentally. He had told the SS Section Chief that he had a foreign visitor who was able to drive a car. But, of course, he wanted to know the purpose of the nocturnal mission. Should he ask him? Whereupon the Chief immediately became enraged, and called him a "dummkopf." Did he not know that I was an Englishman? And that no foreigners should be included in an important SS mission?

Of course, I did not take part in the nocturnal drive. Only the SS leaders knew about the secret mission to be carried out—they expected blind obedience from their subordinates. It is always wrong to pledge unconditional obedience to man, a sinner, who can easily misuse his power.

This night was what later turned out to be the "Kristallnacht" (The Night of Broken Glass), when so many Jewish synagogues were destroyed—and the local SS-group had itself participated in the destruction. My friend had joined in, even though he had been warned. This event broke him. Later in the war, he was sent to the Baltic States and was killed. We do not know where his grave lies.

GENERAL FROST

At this time, a young English general moved into our area of Berkshire and bought a large pleasant bungalow on the Thames. He was the youngest general in the British-Indian army and had been stationed for some years on the north west frontier between India and Afghanistan. When this youngest general in the British-Indian armed forces became about forty-five years old, he was won by Christ through the witness of other Christians and through reading the Bible. He had seen much hardship and strife in life, was not emotional, but rather was a genuine soldier: straight, fearless, intelligent and utterly honest.

On his conversion he decided without delay, that he would use the rest of his life in a better way than being a soldier. He wanted, as he said, no longer to live his life for the King in London, but rather for Christ, the Eternal King, who had given His life for him! So, he took an early retirement and bought a house on the Thames, which was right in our neighborhood. There, he built a small chapel on the lawn. Because there was no active congregation nearby, he gave evangelistic sermons every Sunday. Everywhere he went, he held devotions—in churches, free-churches and community halls. He quickly became very popular, as there was no evangelical competition in our neighborhood.

My dear mother was invited to the lectures. She went and was very impressed and blessed. Mother invited her sister (Aunt Addie) to go and she became a believer. Then a cousin of mine, who had experienced many difficulties in life, went. She also became a believer. Then my mother invited me to accompany her to the general's house. However, I said that a student of Oxford University does not go to an evangelical gathering—not even if a general is speaking! Mother poured out her distress to the General personally, who said cryptically, when Mohammed will not come to the mountain, then the mountain must go to Mohammed! He invited me to high tea at his home. Now in England, when a General invites a person to high tea, he must go. Otherwise, in better English society, he would no longer be socially acceptable. So, whether I liked it or not, I had to go.

On a lovely afternoon, I drove to "Watersmeet" (this was the name of his house on the Thames), and received a friendly welcome. We played tennis, rowed a rowboat on the Thames and had a proper tea with the family. After tea, the General took me into his study to talk with me privately. He asked me if I was a Christian. I answered that I was a committed atheist, even though I was baptized and confirmed. He said that he was a committed Christian. He knew that Christ had died for his sins and was resurrected. Then I laughed at him and his naiveté and asked him how he could, as an educated man, believe in the fairy tales of the Bible? Christ identified himself, for example, with Genesis, and the account of creation in the Bible. No educated person could today believe in such a thing. Adam and Eve were not real persons, they were not historical people. But Christ believed in the myths of the Bible and confused history with myths. Now, if Christ were really the Son of God, he would not have mixed up truth with nonsense and myths.

During the course of the conversation, I said to him that Darwin's theories were hard facts of history and natural science. The world came about through chance and natural selection. Natural selection and mutations had caused the development of the amoeba right on through to people. The idea of an intelligent creator was the ultimate in unscientific thought, the theologians today did not believe that anymore. There was no proof of the existence of God: Feuerbach and others had long since proven that. His (the General's) religion was uneducated fantasy and his belief, concentrated imagination.

The good, honorable General, who actually was not at all uneducated, looked at me with more of a sad than an angry look in his eyes, and admitted that he knew next to nothing about natural science and that he had not made much progress with me (the conceited young student). Around 11:00 p.m. I said good night. I was sure that I had beaten him in discussion. His dear wife, Mrs. Frost, was a true lady. Later she said to me that she had found me to be unbearable and conceited and that she had advised her husband to give up on me. I was not ripe for such things, I was absolutely hopeless, "unconvertible."

But the faithful, courageous General had a weapon of which I knew nothing. He understood the power of intensive prayer. So, for three weeks, he prayed for me. Not until he was fully certain that God had "sent" me to him did he invite me once more to Tea. He was, in some respects, like Samuel Hebich, the German missionary who worked among the British soldiers in India many years ago. Hebich did not visit any home nor did he invite anyone to visit him until he had first received certainty of victory from God. Only then did the General invite me to visit again.

This time I had no reservations against the visit. The house on the Thames was beautiful, I enjoyed rowing on the river and the tennis court was pleasant. I could easily dispense with the

General and his arguments. He understood practically nothing about science. I could silence him with ease at any time. I am ashamed of myself to this day when I think of my insolence toward a proven and distinguished General. My academic education had instilled in me an attitude of arrogance. I was not able to appreciate how unwise, rude and even naive my actions and thoughts were.

When we were finished with playing tennis, rowing and Tea, we went to his study to speak man to man. He was a very gracious man—even though as a General he was intrepid. His experience as a general had made him a man with an obvious strength of character and authority—a man with a gift for command. This time he used a completely different strategy with me, as befitting a good General. This time, he began not with natural science, where he was inferior to me, but rather with life style, formation of character and with self-discipline. In this area, he was naturally at a great advantage. Inside, I was often very frustrated. I lacked motivation, was often despairing, and also was bad-tempered. He had learned as a general to deny himself, (as the Lord Jesus Christ himself says, "Whoever cannot say 'no' to himself, cannot be my disciple," Matthew 16:24, Mark 8:34, Luke 9:23). Now, the General, who sat with me in his study and willingly gave his time for me, was a living example of the discipleship of Christ. He said "no" to himself and "yes" to Him and His Will. And this disciplined choice actually came from the heart. His whole life was reflected in his manner. It shone in his eyes, was revealed by his love, but was also proclaimed in the severe aspect of the creases and wrinkles in his countenance.

The whole person of the General—not only his words and his manner of arguing—had an effect on me as he spoke. His words made quite an impression, but his whole being underlined every word. He lived what he proclaimed. I, as a natural scientist, could speak lofty words, but had precious little to back them up. I was hollow, he was solid. So, he made it clear to me that my sins—my violation of the eternal law of

God—had ruined me. The power of God, through the forgiveness of his sins, streamed into the General's life so that he was made strong in Christ. I needed more than a little of this "river," or I would stand as firm as a wet washcloth! I felt like a wet washcloth in front of this man. Obviously, he liked me or he would not have spoken so truthfully. To do exactly that took a lot of love, patience and perseverance. And this love, perseverance and patience he had in abundance.

After a long conversation, he asked me directly if I needed this forgiveness and this power in my life? The answer was crystal clear: "A thousand times, yes." Then he asked me if I would like to have the forgiveness of God in Christ in my life. What should I answer? The answer of every honest man is "yes." "In that case," he said, "let us both kneel down to ask His forgiveness through Christ's death and resurrection." He always spoke so directly of his relationship to Christ, who was his constant companion, that he was irresistible!

So, we knelt down in his study and he prayed aloud for me. When it was my turn, not a word would come to my lips. I was speechless! How should I speak with Him and want to pray to Him in whom I did not believe? Then the General asked whether I believed that Jesus Christ lived in his (the General's) heart? I had to be honest and said that the Spirit of Christ obviously lived in him. The next question was whether I wanted to have the same Spirit in my heart? To that, I resolutely answered yes. Then he said that I should only ask for the Spirit if I was completely honest. Because Christ always gives to those who ask.

The General did not try to manipulate me like so many evangelists do today, only to achieve results and statistics for their mission societies. He spoke man to man. So I felt a sense of ease when I was with him, which ensured that in the end I would pray for the forgiveness of my failures and my sins. I was ready, very soon, to whole-heartedly accept this forgiveness in faith, because I knew that Christ had heard me and that I had made a contract with the Lord Jesus. So, I stood up again and the General shook my hand and he spontaneously thanked God for hearing my prayer.

But the faithful man was not yet finished. He read me the Bible verse where it is written that whoever believes in his heart is justified and whoever confesses with his mouth is saved (Romans 10:9–10). He asked me then whether I believed in my heart, which now I could answer in the affirmative. But the second question was different: whether I was ready to confess Christ with my mouth? I was astonished because I thought I had just done that and, in fact, had done it in prayer. "No," he said, "I mean confess Him before men." That was no problem, I thought, if I can confess before God, then I can also confess God before other people. The General, however, was skeptical. He was a pragmatist, he said, and he wanted to see it in practice before he ventured an opinion. "How would it be, if you go into the kitchen now and tell my wife and children what you have just confessed here"?

I hesitated because his children were either older than me or were my own age and Mrs. Frost, although she was a perfect lady, held me at somewhat of a distance. That, I had noticed. As a woman, she recognized the nature of people quicker than most men! She had so much intuition and knowledge of human nature that I did not know how to approach her or her two daughters. The son was a young officer and had neither time nor appreciation for academics. "Is it really necessary to give an account of my private experiences to the family in the kitchen?" I asked. "No," he answered, "but if not, you will never be a soldier of Christ. You are actually far too cowardly! We learned in the military to obey the word. You have probably never done that! And therefore you also would not experience the promise of Romans 10:9–10—the salvation—without the uncomplicated confession with the mouth of what you believe in your heart!"

Now, I did not want to be a coward in front of such a General—especially not in front of his family! So, I quickly made a decision, knocked on the door of the kitchen and confessed with my mouth what I believed in my heart after the Word of God. In the blink of an eye, this act of obedience over my own will fulfilled the Word of God in my spirit. The confession with the mouth, the overcoming of my own inhibition, pride, and fear brought the knowledge of the promised salvation. My righteousness was dependent on my faith in my heart, while frank confession with the mouth was linked with the knowledge of salvation of the heart.

Mrs. Frost was overjoyed when she heard my confession. She exclaimed: "The days of miracles are not yet passed!" and cordially shook my hands.

From that day on, I began to be a confessing Christian even though I had very much to learn! The intellectual difficulties concerning Adam and Eve, the teachings of evolution, and the reliability of the Bible were in no way totally cast off, naturally! If the Bible is full of scientific errors, how is it that Christ, the Son of God, held fast to these errors? That was a real problem for me. Was he a hypocrite? Because as the Son of God, who created the universe, heaven and earth and all that lived, he must have known, even as a man, that that which Moses had written in Genesis 1–3, did not correspond with the facts—the scientific historical facts. I discussed these problems very often with the good General. But he could not help me. He thought that I must "just believe," and then everything would be all right. Nevertheless, he actually gave me, indirectly, the solution to all problems of this type. He remarked that when I trust Christ and his Word, even when I, rationally, simply do not understand, God would send people in my path who are in a position to give me the necessary conclusive scientific solutions.

And so it has been in my life. I had to study long and hard until the answers were clear to me. Problems do not evaporate by themselves! But I have asked God daily to send me people that know the solutions to my difficulties. I met Professor Rendle-Short, Professor of Surgery at the University of Bristol. We were immediately on the same wavelength. As a confessing Christian, he occupied himself in detail with the Bible and also with the newest scientific theories. He was a theistic evolutionist because he was not familiar with the chemical knowledge rendering Darwinistic evolution impossible. Through him, I learned the "Gap-Theory," where an interval is supposed to exist between the first and second verse of Genesis. God had, according to this theory, created a world before our present world that was destroyed through the fall of Lucifer. After this ancient destruction God allegedly created our current world from the beginning and in fact, in six days.

PROFESSOR RENDLE-SHORT

Now, this theory seemed to solve some problems regarding geological ages. But the theological evidence for the Gap-Theory and the paleontological facts do not support this theory. We possess no evidence for this assumed second, late creation. Professor Rendle-Short was himself rather inclined to think that God had secretly guided Darwin's evolution— therefore he had a tendency toward theistic evolution—or progressive creationism. It was to no avail to try to make the fine old professor see that the foundation of the evolutionary theory of creation lay in chance and not in intelligence. If God created everything through chance, he no longer worked through intelligence. But the Bible teaches explicitly that everything came about through plan and intelligence. I could not agree with him on the teachings of evolution because intelligence always eliminates chance and does not use it as a tool. Intelligence effectively destroys chance. If God replaced intelligence with chance, it would not take long at all until man negated and even despised the personality and intelligence of God. We later learned, through Professor Rendle-Short's son, who later became a good friend of ours, that at the end of his life, he changed his mind and adopted creationism.

General Frost took the view that the eternal God, in a miraculous way, transcends the dimension of time, and was thereby able to carry out in eternity His whole creation in six literal days. Naturally, the natural scientist did not take the General very seriously on this point. And the General did not know the language of the natural scientist. But his point of view was that the Word of God is stronger than the whole universe—heaven and earth will pass away, but my Word will not pass away (Matthew 24:35, Mark 13:31, Luke 21:33). The Bible, as God's plan and Word, will always exist long after heaven and earth have passed away.

WISDOM AND PRACTICAL OBEDIENCE GO TOGETHER

Now these and other problems I have kept in thought for over sixty years. Constantly, I have worked on them and have also written a number of books about them. Knowledge comes once in a while like a flash of lightning, but also grows slowly. If one endeavors, to truly live in accordance with the newly-won knowledge, it has been my life-long experience that God always entrusts further and more complete knowledge. When one denies the already available, God-given knowledge or is unfaithful, then the growth of insight and understanding stops. He no longer entrusts his mysteries to us. One no longer grows in the grace and the knowledge of the Lord. I have discovered and experienced this for over sixty years. "Whoever can be trusted with very little can also be trusted with much," (Luke 16:10), says the Holy Scripture. This is also a valid fact for growth in Christian knowledge. Whoever can be trusted with a little knowledge will receive more. Therefore theological study alone will not bring great spiritual insight.

When we attempt to live out the basic teachings of the Bible, our spiritual knowledge will grow further. God progressively entrusts more wisdom—exactly as he did with Daniel the prophet. Daniel was faithful to the Law of Moses and the dietary laws, which were the aspects of the Law and diet he knew. Therefore, God entrusted to him so much more insight, that according to King Nebuchadnezzar's measure he was ten times wiser than all the other scribes in the land. The same principle is true today, as it was in the Old Testament, so it is also the case in the New Testament.

General Frost loved the prophetic word of the Bible and often spoke about it. As a young Christian, I did not understand this prophetic aspect of the Christian life. The same was true for many theological questions, such as the question of free will and the eternal election. I read Paul Humberg (can a free will and eternal election coexist) and profited from it. But how can man possess a really free will if God has chosen him from eternity for salvation? Humberg thought the parallel teachings were consistent in the eternal dimension.

I read a great deal and came to know many good authors through the General. But I still did not have clear answers to many questions. However, I learned one fundamental principle from the General: If you have clarity in one thing, act and live accordingly, otherwise you will lose this clarity. What was not clear to me was overcome with sincere prayer to God for clarity. Read and hold in your heart the Word, even when you do not understand various things. Ponder the other things in your heart until God gives you enlightenment. So I have been, for sixty years, a practical student of the Word of God. The more one learns and does, the greater are the resulting insights.

MY BROTHER WALTER DIES

Shortly after this time, my good brother also came to the Lord Jesus Christ—and also through the General. Although he had some difficulties, he accepted God's Word and was faithful for a long time in his Bible reading. But when the

General moved, he could not find good Christian fellowship any longer and his faith became cold.

To recount the whole story about my brother, who was so close to me, I have to skip many years in this chapter.

I had long since left home and lived with my family on the European Continent. Later, when we lived in Norway, my brother came to visit us with his whole family and always took part in the Bible readings. He visited us in Geneva, and later in Wheaton, Illinois, USA. In "The Bible Church" in Wheaton, he asked if he could take part in communion and really made a new beginning. But he did not have a local fellowship of Christians in Wantage, Berkshire, where he had his farm.

More than thirty years later he died very tragically at the age of fifty-eight. He was a very loyal brother and person. He developed gallstones and the large university clinic, the "Radcliffe Infirmary" in Oxford, suggested a gall bladder operation. He was operated on without incident, but very soon afterwards had a strong pain in his calf—a sure sign of a beginning thrombosis. After the operation he was not examined or visited by any doctor, and not even by a registered nurse. He lay in his pain in hospital; and when he attempted to go to the bathroom, with all his infusions and tubes, unassisted, he collapsed and died, probably secondary to a neglected pulmonary embolism.

His death was announced to us by the Swiss police in Einigen at 4:00 a.m. in the morning. The next day, we flew to London and went to the clinic in Oxford. I asked for an interview with the surgeon, who had just arrived in his Rolls Royce. He sent his most junior doctor to deal with me. It turned out that since the operation my brother had never been seen by any doctor or even by a nurse. When I began my investigations, I ran into the profound inefficiency of the English State Medicine. No one accepted responsibility, just like everything else, the State takes over! I had to start my inquiries at some ministry or other in Oxford (not in the hospital), where they had absolutely no idea what happened in the Oxford hospital! Even the patient's clinical assessments and notes were not complete. In the end, I confronted the responsible, well-known surgeon who informed me that the incident was "an Act of God." I made him quite aware of what a very serious matter it is to make God responsible for our own irresponsible, disorganized and incompetent work.

We could not bring my good brother back, however. His dear wife and his five daughters were, like all of us, absolutely shattered. But my dear brother had gone from us forever and we felt very lonely, because he had been my only brother and schoolmate. God's ways are often completely unfathomable. We can only worshipfully say that we "shall understand hereafter" (John 13:7), even if we do not comprehend here and now.

FREEMASONRY AND CHRISTIANITY

MY FATHER'S BELIEFS

After I became a Christian, I tried to understand my father and his Freemasonry better. Father's attitude, as I had already ascertained, was that he had found the true religion for men. We, on the other hand, had adopted the religion for women and children. But he never said anything specific about his faith. This was forbidden to Freemasons. They are sworn to absolute silence. The British Freemasons were especially closed. They were not permitted to advertise or promote their lodge at all and are not allowed to directly invite anyone to become a Freemason. They know the Bible well—especially the Old Testament. If one asks them directly what they believe, they never give an informative answer. But they are not interested in the Gospel of Christ. God's Son is, for them, only a good man, not our Creator or the One who died for us on the cross. My father was, in this respect, no exception. He went to church with my mother—off and on—and when the minister was a lodge-brother.

One must consider the fact that many Anglican ministers are Freemasons. At the time of Oliver Cromwell in England, there was a saying that the "Priests of Baal" will be stamped out. As school children, we never understood these words. Oliver Cromwell was made out to be, for us, a politician who was a religious fanatic and fundamentalist. Later through my studies of Freemasonry, I came to understand what Oliver Cromwell meant with this saying about the "Priests of Baal." He was talking about Anglican and other ministers who were Freemasons, because the name of Baal is part of the name of the Freemasons' deity. The Freemasons align themselves with the old Babylonian mysteries. The ritual of the lodge belongs to the ancient pagan cults of Babylonian origin, even though it is filled with Old Testament quotations.

But we could never determine for certain what Father believed in. For forty years, Mother read to him in bed from the Bible. In the first years of their marriage, he turned away from her when she began to read, but in later years, he asked Mother to read to him from the Bible every evening. When he was old, he could not sleep without Mother reading to him from the Bible. He was especially interested in passages in the Old Testament and seemed to know them well (for example, Ecclesiastes 12). But Mother never found out what Father actually believed. She only knew that he did not believe in the Lord Jesus Christ, as the Son of God, who died on the cross for our sins and was resurrected. He smiled pityingly at the General and his influence on Mother and her sons.

Now, in order to successfully carry on a conversation with another person, one must really find common interests. We could not find anything in common with Father in the area of spiritual matters. So, there was just no rational conversation to be had with him over inner things. But he was not anti-religious. Anti-Anglican, for sure, but not anti-religious. We found out that he secretly did much good for the poor, the widows and the orphans in the village.

I had an aunt in the United States, who was a believer and who sometimes visited us. She was an intelligent, devout lady who was very knowledgeable. I spoke with her about this mystery of Father's beliefs and freemasonry, on the occasion of one of her visits with us. She revealed to me that she had books on this subject at home in the United States. But one could not send these books through the public post. They had a habit of disappearing without a trace while in transit. The books had been published long ago. The publishing house that printed these books was mysteriously destroyed several times by arson.

My aunt said, however, that she would send me the books in a sealed and registered letter—not as printed matter—if I would promise to safeguard them carefully and discreetly. I promised her this and after a few months, received a thick registered letter that contained the promised books. One of these little books is still in existence today.

This book contained the complete key to the "prayer book" of the Freemasons. Perhaps some of my readers know nothing of these things. Therefore, I must provide some background details. Uncle Frank and Father usually got together on Friday evenings to read out of a small black book that looked like an Anglican Book of Common Prayer (the "prayer book" I mentioned before). Sometimes, Father inadvertently left this book lying around and we inquisitive children looked inside. But we did not understand anything—or very little. The book was written in English but crucial passages in most sentences contained only initials—usually consonants—and not complete words. So one could only make sense out of it if one knew the meaning of the letters. For example, the initials "J.B.O." that stand for Jehovah, Baal and Osiris. The book was, in short, strictly encoded, so that the uninitiated could not get anything out of the text. Father became very angry when he caught us leafing through the pages of his little book.

On June 13, 1985, at 8:00 a.m. in the morning on Radio BBC 4, I heard from the BBC London a report about the nature of Freemasonry by the Methodist Church in Great Britain. A Methodist minister gave a presentation on the official Methodist report about Freemasonry and insisted that Freemasonry is a danger for Christians. As a reason for this danger, he cited that informed Freemasons believed in a god whose name is known. This name is derived from three religions. Two are purely pagan and not Christian. One name of this deity is Jewish. The interviewer asked him to name the triple-name of the Freemason's god. The minister hesitated, but the radio interviewer was not satisfied until the Methodist minister explicitly named the name of this Freemason god: "Jaobulon," a composition of Jehovah (Yahweh), Bul or Baal, and On or Osiris. In the Freemason's books, this name is only named in encoded form, always J.B.O. Freemasonry is therefore an acute form of syncretism: a fusion of many religions, among them, pagan religions.

This was the first time in my life I had heard the Freemason's god mentioned by name—and publicly over the radio—rightly named and pronounced. Freemasons themselves may not pronounce the secret name of their god alone. Each individual may only pronounce a syllable of the "inexpressible" name. So, they must be in a group of three Freemasons standing in a circle holding hands with each other worshiping together, softly saying the name syllable by syllable in sequence, each Freemason pronouncing only one syllable. The first Freemason says "Jao." Then comes the second, who is holding the hand of the first and the third Freemasons and he says "Bul." Then comes the third, who worships as he holds the hands of the others. He says "On." No one may pronounce the whole name of their god in its entirety. Whoever does that is considered worthy of death.

My father and Uncle Frank were both high up in the Freemasons' hierarchy. Father was in the 32nd grade, "the Royal Arch." So both of them were fully initiated. But most Freemasons do not know all that. Only in the very highest degrees—if one advances so far—do they learn the name of their god. If they get that far, they are already older experienced Freemasons who have taken oaths their whole lives long never to disclose the inexpressible name, even though, for years, they did not know what kind of a name or a secret they were keeping! For genuine Freemasons, there was a connection between "Yahweh" of the Old Testament and the two great pagan deities "Baal" (bul) and "Osiris" (on). The whole Old Testament and the whole New Testament strictly forbid exactly this kind of syncretism. According to the Bible, it is outright idolatry.

The oaths that the Freemasons must take from the level of "entered apprentice" on are really hair-raising, and absolutely unchristian. If a man wants to be initiated into the lodge, he must inquire discreetly whether one would admit him. He would then be discreetly examined. Uneducated people off the street are not admitted, rather only people who have a status in life. Once a man is admitted to the lodge, nothing very bad will happen in his life, because Freemasons promise to always favor other lodge-brothers whether it concerns business or professional affairs. If, for example, a Freemason is a judge, and the accused before him is also a Freemason, the latter can give the sign of the Freemasons. He thereby identifies himself as a Freemason. The judge must then help the accused brother out of his difficulty. The judge cannot abandon him. He need only to say, hidden in the middle of the conversation so that an outsider does not notice it, "Is there then no help for the son of a widow?" (Hiram, the King of Tyre, was the son of a widow and played an important role in the ritual of the lodge). When a Freemason hears this call for help, he may not rest until he has helped his brother in need.

I was born the eldest son of my father and my mother, in the year that my father was "Master of Chairs" in the lodge. For this reason I was, in the freemason's terminology, a "Louis." I would have had, as a Freemason, special rights and responsibilities. If my father had died, or had not been in the position to bear the costs of my education, the Freemasons would have funded my education. Even though I was often, in a round about way, invited to join the lodge when I was active in Middlesex Hospital as a Countess of Lisburne Memorial Fellow in cancer research, I always firmly rejected this step because I was a Christian.

Are we completely sure that all this information about freemasonry is factual or is it only a fairy tale that the enemies of the Freemasons have invented? One should not adopt evidence from only one source. One must have confirmation from as many sides as possible, otherwise one can be very deceived in such questions. It was really very important to me to understand my good father, because he was a good man and did much good for the poor. Freemasons are often exemplary in their life-style and morally of very high standards. My father was a good example of this, even though he never confessed the name of Christ.

To be completely sure that my sources were genuine, I took the following action: I took my books from the United States about freemasonry and very carefully memorized the code. Then I memorized the ritual of the "entered apprentice," that is, the questions and answers that are posed to the "entered" when he stands before the closed doors of the lodge and knocks. He knocks three times. Before he knocks, a blindfold has been put over his eyes, so that he cannot see anything at all, and his clothes have been taken off. He has put on a special pair of trousers that have only one leg and then, he knocks. Someone stands behind him with a drawn sword. The point of the sword is always pushed in his back so that he knows that he may not turn back. After the triple-knock signal, he is answered, through the lodge door, with "Who goes there?" Then the candidate must answer "A poor candidate in search of light."

The door opens then and the candidate, who naturally cannot see where he is, is forced forward with the sword in his back. He notices that many people are around him. Then he is forced to kneel down and the holy book of laws is pushed between his folded hands. This action is a freemasonry signal—when he takes the Bible (that is, the Old Testament) between folded hands, every informed Freemason knows what that means! The first oath he must swear is then read aloud, sentence by sentence. The candidate must repeat every sentence and every phrase even though the syllables that he must repeat in sequence are not yet meaningful. Without knowing what the complete oath will mean, he must repeat everything syllable by syllable until he is finished with the statement.

In short said, the candidate swears that he will let his tongue be torn out by the root and will let his corpse be buried on the sands of the sea, where ebb and flow twice daily flow. The absurd thing about the whole experience is that he, after this terrible oath, has not learned anything worth keeping secret. Therefore many young Freemasons maintain that everything in the lodge is compatible with Christianity. In the lodge, they learn much out of the Old Testament—about the building of the temple, etc.—which all seems to be harmless. Only much later, at the 33rd degree of the royal ark (from Noah's Ark), and in other higher degrees, do they come to know the actual nature of Freemasonry, including the "inexpressible" name, J.B.O., of their deity. And only much later do they learn that the lodge believes in the existence of a secret chamber in the temple in Jerusalem where the priests of God secretly served Baal and turned their backs on God! That is why Oliver Cromwell in England called for "the slaughter of the priests of Baal": Oliver Cromwell knew various things that we today have long since forgotten.

I soon found further confirmation of the correctness of my increasing knowledge of freemasonry.

It happened this way: Uncle Frank and his family came to visit us for supper one evening. Afterwards, he intended to practice the Freemason's ritual with Father. Our family went to bed and the others went home. I, however, stayed up and read a book in the living room. Father and Uncle held their little books (their "prayer-books" of the Freemason kind). They read in their books and said not a word. They were waiting for me to leave.

But I did not go. So, they continued to read to themselves out of their small black books further. All was as quiet as a mouse. The clock ticked. Upstairs in the house all had become still. Then I began very quietly to recite the ritual of the "entered apprentice": Knock, knock, knock, "Who goes there?" "A poor candidate in search of light! . ." I said everything verbatim, exactly as it was encoded in the books. But naturally I said it without the key. My father and uncle looked on in obvious consternation, but did not say a word. Then I concluded the ritual, which had lasted about twenty minutes, with the dreadful final oaths: that I would let my tongue be torn out by the root and my corpse be buried in the sands of the sea, where ebb and flow twice daily flow, if I should ever tell what I had now learned. Then I stopped and sat still over my scientific book. I made absolutely no comment. I had only, very quietly, but verbatim recited the ritual, the pure ritual, nothing else.

Father and Uncle both looked mutually frightened. Then my good father exploded. (One must forgive him this outburst under the provocative circumstances.) And he cried out: "You want to be a Christian and are a devil. You have stolen my little book, my black, secret, private little book." "No," I said, "You know, Father, that I would not do that. I know that everything that is in your little book is encoded. Without the key to the code, I cannot read it. But one thing I now know for all time, that all that which I have recited must be in your little black book. Otherwise you two would not have reacted so. Is that true or not?"

The two old men still looked shattered. My father regained his composure first, and said that all of that was rubbish. That he did not know where I had obtained this foolish nonsense which I had recited. However, I was prepared with an answer for this, because I knew that the Freemasons were sworn to use just such a special reaction in cases where the truth of their secrets comes out. When a secret of the ritual or of the Freemason's beliefs comes out, and someone finds out what the Freemasons really believe, without being a Freemason themselves, then the Freemason is obliged by oath to mock and to maintain that the truth that came out about Freemasonry is not the truth. So, I said to the two men that I also knew of this oath to lie when the truth comes out. This was confirmation for me in my conviction that the two were under oath to react in this manner if the ritual should be revealed. The two men rigidly maintained that my quotations (the whole ritual) were unknown to them until I stood up to go to bed. Both had committed themselves to lie if someone learned what they believed. Whereupon I naturally asked why my father had, as his first reaction, maintained that I had stolen his little book after I had recited the whole ritual? If I had been on the wrong track, he would never have made such an accusation!

After this event Father and Uncle Frank were especially kind and obliging to me—which I certainly did not deserve. And, as I expected (because I knew the oath that they had taken), they tried indirectly to win me for the lodge. But every time they discreetly presented the advantages of the lodge to me, I drew their attention to the fact that no genuine Freemason will recruit for the lodge, either covertly or publicly. That is, after their own rules and oaths, tabu. Then they would always, immediately, stop their discreet recruitment!

I am still ashamed of myself today for my radical methods to "help" my dear father and my good uncle. I should have exercised more tact and deeper respect for my elders.

Later, in London, out of fun and for a practical joke, I fooled my Director. He was like most leading people in England, a Freemason. When I was saying good-bye to him, I just casually gave him the Freemason's handshake. (I am able to "identify myself as a Freemason.") He looked at me, genuinely amazed, and sincerely said that he was really very happy to hear that I was "one of us."

GLASSBLOWING AND FREEMASONRY

One day, during the war, I sat in the laboratory in London at the glassblower's table. Because we no longer had a glassblower in the laboratory, I had learned to do glassblowing from a Master glass blower. At the start of the war, the glassblowers were recruited into the army. Thus, I was very thankful that I could blow the delicate micro-apparatus that I often needed for research.

One time, in London, I was working at the glassblower's table and had just finished making a micro-distillation apparatus. This device used three "double internal seals" that were tricky anyway. During the war, we had no Pyrex at our disposal, so we had to fabricate everything in soda glass, which breaks easily while it is cooling. The whole laboratory watched because the apparatus was a work of art and very beautiful to look at. I held my artwork in a smoky flame in order to cool everything down slowly and carefully. This was a very thrilling moment.

The Vice-Director of the laboratory was also a Freemason. He was never on the same wavelength with me! He suspected that I knew more in various areas than was pleasant for him, but I never spoke with him about these things. He was also somewhat intolerant, but had lived through many difficult times. His house was bombed by the German airplanes, and he and his wife were buried for a whole day until the rescue team got the pair out. He was a German-hater, which one could understand under the circumstances. So I handled him with kid gloves.

Now, this Vice-Director looked on at my glass-blowing mockingly. He thought that I would never be successful with the work. And I was successful with it! But what was that "crack" in the middle of the flame? Through the double seals a crack appeared and then the whole work of art exploded. On the table lay nothing but black fragments. So, then I turned, grabbed a shovel and broom, and began to brush everything away and tidy up. The mocking gaze of the Vice-Director annoyed me. "Mr. L.," I said, "this reminds me of the prophet Zerubbabel in the temple, when he swept away the broken pieces of the old temple in order to make room for the new building." I had naturally referred to the Freemason's ritual where Zerubbabel is mentioned in the lodge. He wants to rebuild the ruined temple and first clears away the old rubble—as I did on the glass-blower's table! The Vice-Director turned around lightning fast and disappeared like a rocket out of the laboratory! He ran up the stairs to the Director, and burst into his office, where by chance, a colleague of mine was standing and conversing with the Director. The Vice-Director burst into the room without seeing who was there and shouted out loud that we must immediately dismiss this Wilder-Smith, he knows too much, far too much! He took his Freemasonry very seriously—in contrast to the Director, who dealt with religious matters superficially. Nothing happened!

FREEMASONRY AND SYNCRETISM

Freemasonry is an absolutely anti-Christian syncretism. It is an enemy of Christianity and also of Judaism. Worship of Baal and On (Osiris) as deities is not compatible with the Old Testament! But, in the beginning stages, the young Freemason or the Freemason who is not very ambitious, knows practically nothing important about the Freemason's doctrine. Charles Finney, the father of the American awakening, was Freemason before his conversion to Christ. He tried to witness for Christ in the lodge after his conversion. Finney learned very quickly that in the lodge, one may name and admire any religious leader, as long as one does not name the name of Christ as the Son of God, who died for the sins of the world.

CHAPTER X

THE SECOND WORLD WAR: THE RELATIONSHIP OF THE CHRISTIAN TO THE STATE

RESEARCH PROBLEMS AND THEIR CONSEQUENCES

Throughout the whole war, I worked as a researcher at the Imperial Chemical Industries (ICI) in Billingham. Stockton on Tees on the northeast coast of England. The climate was hard and cold up there. The east wind was so bitter that in the afternoon the temperature could easily fall about twenty degrees. With my first paycheck, I bought a very thick winter coat which I still have. But on the bicycle, the wind would even whistle through this thick coat. The sleeve of this coat had a built-in windbreak so that the wind would not penetrate up to the shoulders—theoretically anyway! After the mild climate of the Thames Valley, I had difficulty with the harsh climate and suffered from influenza very often.

Throughout the whole war, I lived in a small room that lay between the fork of two train lines. This was a good target for the regular visits of the night bombers! During the bombings that were aimed at Billingham, we had to put out fires in the city and in the factory. One night, I saw a fleeing cat that had been in the area of an exploding bomb. She was dragging something behind her. With horror, I realized that it was her own fur, which the force of the explosion had ripped away. She had been skinned alive.

On another night, we were doing fire-service in the factory and some of us stood before the entrance to an air raid shelter to be on the look out after the bombing. When we saw the flashes get too close, we dived into the bunker for shelter. A few seconds later a bomb fell exactly on the spot where a colleague of mine had been standing.

When the bombs became too numerous, the factory would shut down. It was a high-pressure factory that produced gasoline, ammonia, and fertilizer. Because it was a high pressure factory, it was too risky to maintain the pressure during an attack. Therefore, the safety valve would be opened to reduce the pressure during an attack. The howl of the safety valve was a frightening thing. It sounded like wailing from beyond the grave. One could hear it for miles in the night. Afterwards, it would take many hours until the factory was back at the right pressure and ready for operation.

At that time the German U-Boats (submarines) were sinking many ships carrying food to England. The consequence was that food became scarce. For a while, we received one egg a month, two ounces of meat and about one hundred cubic centimeters of skimmed milk ("blue wonder") a day. Since we ate in the cafeteria, we never went hungry, but the situation was serious and caused many health problems. I noticed one day that I had an infection in my gums and my teeth were loose. I visited a dentist who wanted to pull all my teeth on the spot. I thought it would be better to handle this myself, rather than to let all my teeth be pulled! I dealt with it in a simple and effective manner: I went to my landlady, who was a dear lady, but not excessively scrupulous, and said that I, in the future, wanted to have my milk ration, not as cocoa-drink, but rather as raw milk. She had acquired the habit of taking my milk ration for her own purposes and giving me cocoa and water. In a few months, my teeth were strong again and the gum infection had healed on its own. I still have all of my teeth.

Occasionally, my dear mother would send me eggs from the farm, but that was illegal! Mother knew that my health was poor and said that she would accept responsibility for these small contributions. She was very courageous and a strong character.

I worked with nitrogen tetroxide, which is a light brown liquid that boils at 22°C. The gases are very poisonous and the liquid is extremely volatile. For this reason it was very difficult to keep the air in the laboratory clean. We always worked behind Plexiglas hoods that were constantly ventilated by strong fans (fume cupboard). Our laboratory was situated on the large lawn of a country house, not in the factory, because research of this type would have been too dangerous for the factory.

Our goal was to work out new methods and techniques to directly nitrate double and triple compounds in order to acquire new aliphatic nitro compounds. This goal had been attempted before I arrived in 1940. The responsible chemist at that time had caused so many violent explosions in the laboratory that the Director demanded an organic chemist who would be better able to understand and avoid potential fireworks of this kind. The previous chemist had had so many failures that, as was the custom at ICI, he was immediately promoted and became my supervisor. The poor man understood next to nothing of organic chemistry. He was a physical chemist and was now Director of Organic Research! In England this activity is expressed as: "Fitting square pegs into round holes."

Now, the previous research work was always carried out at 160°–200°C and the result was naturally foreseeable! These conditions were far too extreme. Every day there were powerful explosions and the product was always an indefinable oil. My boss then calculated, with the help of complex differential equations, how much of the desired products should have been available in this indefinable oil! The component parts were never characterized. Everything was done mathematically and never chemically. In reality, we discovered on nearly the first day that none of the desired products were available because the boiling point of the desired products would have been about 100°C at 760 millimeters of pressure. The products they had found showed a boiling point of 90°–100°C at 0,1 millimeter pressure—a small difference!

We soon discovered that the right conditions for the desired reactions were at 40°C in liquid N_2O_4, rather than in the gaseous phase. This early success opened the door to a whole array of new substances which were promising for organic synthesis: namely the aliphatic alpha-beta-dinitro compounds and aliphatic beta-nitro-ether compounds. We were then able to immediately apply these new compounds in the synthesis of even newer compounds for medical purposes. As a result of all this work—we worked four full years in this area—about forty patent applications were written and there was a series of publications in leading natural science journals.

We did not only encounter success in this new area of chemistry; there were also serious medical problems. My chief assistant slowly became sick. His illness was not immediately diagnosed, but it proved to be sub-acute bacterial endocarditis. His health was already endangered when he came to work for me. One must remember that at that time, penicillin was not yet discovered or was still in its infancy. After two or three years working in our area of the laboratory, he became seriously ill and died. Then others also became sick. In the end, I too became sick. My blood pressure fell steadily and I suffered from orthostatic hypotension. I could no longer climb any stairs. At the same time, I developed symptoms of angina pectoris, rashes appeared on my fingertips that would not heal, so that I was no longer able to work with my fingers.

I was sent to a skin specialist who healed my fingers with X-rays. But my heart was very weak. In the end, it turned out that for four years we had been breathing small concentrations (one to five parts per million) of nitrogen tetra-oxide in the laboratory air. The strong ventilators in our Plexiglas chambers had pumped the N_2O_4 out into the atmosphere very efficiently. But these same ventilators were so strong that they had drawn the same poisonous gases from the Plexiglas chambers back into the laboratory through the laboratory windows! So, for four years we had been breathing diluted poisonous gases until my assistant, who was already weak, died because of it and others became sick.

My good mother was very frightened when she saw me again at this time. I had lost a lot of weight, could not climb any stairs, and had aged rapidly and significantly. I was given three months leave at home during the summer of 1944, so that I could recuperate from this poisoning. But as a result of this poisoning, frequent symptoms of angina pectoris have persisted ever since. The nitrogen functioned pharmacologically somewhat like the more toxic amyl nitrite.

After three months, the doctors reported that I had to give up the work with these substances completely, if I wanted to regain my strength. I was now allergic to nitrite, nitrate, and nitro compounds of all kinds. I had to completely change my research so that I would no longer come in contact with these substances.

Consequently, I searched for a new field of work as the war was drawing to its close. But, before we go into this new chapter of my life, I must recount a completely different development. The military authority wanted to train me directly for military purposes. More soldiers were needed, but they did not want to use me exclusively as a soldier or an officer, because I was in an area of research that few people understood, and that was useful in their eyes. This development produced unexpected consequences.

THE RELATIONSHIP OF CHRISTIANS AND OF THE INDIVIDUAL TO THE STATE

One fine day officers of the "Home Guard" came in and wanted to recruit me.[1] I asked these colleagues, who were mostly academics from ICI what the conditions for the additional service were. In response, they showed me a long document, which I asked to study before signing any document. My father had taught me most emphatically that one must thoroughly understand what one is committing oneself to.

One requirement included in this document troubled me: I had to swear, unconditionally and without question, to immediately carry out all orders of the crown and its officers. I asked the responsible officer what this passage meant exactly. To which he answered, that it meant just what it said—unconditional obedience is a foundational principle of all armies throughout the world.

Now, in our company, some colleagues were working on a very secret project called "Tube Alloys." They were secretly developing the atomic bomb. I was not involved in it and heard only rumors about it. But we knew that it was going on. We suspected all sorts of things. No one was forced to work on this project, because the company was a civilian concern.

So I asked the officer whether these obligations were all-embracing (whether one, for example, could receive a command to detonate a potential atomic bomb). At that time, no one was sure whether or not the detonation of an atom bomb in the atmosphere or in the water would trigger a chain reaction so that the whole world would explode. Only later did we find out in practice that this feared chain reaction

---

1. The "Home Guard" was a branch of the army that consisted of soldiers and officers who stayed in their professions during the war, but practiced air defense, fire-service and other military duties in their free time in the evenings and on Sundays.

would not take place. At the time, one did not know, and so there was a great deal of anxiety. We also took into consideration the threat of biological warfare. New viruses could be created and unleashed on an enemy only to end up destroying all of humanity. Today, we have similar fears in the area of gene manipulation. One spoke of all these possibilities.

Yes, the officer said, we would possibly have to carry out these measures in order to win the war, and we must be prepared to limit our own free will so that we could achieve victory. He wanted to have a "carte blanche" over my life with my signature on that agreement. "I do not give such a carte blanche over my life to anyone except God, and you, my good sir, are not God." I was ready, as a civilian, to go and help wherever I needed. But I was not prepared to give unquestioned obedience to command. If I became a soldier, I would in principle, be required to switch off my personal conscience totally and I was not prepared to do that. At ICI research, I could always say "no," because I had a civilian contract. In the military, I would just be a cogwheel in a mechanism. I wanted to keep my freedom as a person with my own independent conscience.

The officer was very polite in his approach. He knew me in civilian life, but reported what I had said. As a result, in the course of the next week, I was summoned to appear before a court. England was engaged in war against a ruthless dictator who wanted to take all freedom from us. Therefore one must sacrifice one's own freedom in order to dispose of Hitler and his dictatorship.

Now, it was known that I spoke German, that I had many German friends and that I was a Christian. So one could easily come to the conclusion that I had acted out of political or personal grounds. The judge was a ruthless man and did not listen much. He started out with patriotic tirades and suggested that everyone thought I was an enemy of the nation. He rejected my petition without listening to my defense. If I did not sign up for the military as an officer, I would be put in jail.

What was I to do? It was war time and every petition of that nature was very suspicious. My Christian friends at Stockton advised that I just join the military forces; it was just a technicality, they argued. It was very difficult for me to find a proper solution to this question. One cannot trust feelings alone for decisions in such situations. One must try to think and act on principle. But how? That was the question.

I decided after much thought and consultation with other older Christians, that this Word of Scripture was the deciding factor: "do not become slaves of men" (1 Corinthians 7:23). I wanted to preserve my freedom of conscience and never, where I could avoid it, become "a slave of men." So I appealed the judge's ruling.

In the meantime, shortly after the so-called "Baedeker Attacks," the Appellate Tribunal in York, where one could file an objection to a judgment, was bombed by the German Luftwaffe. At that time, the Luftwaffe was attacking many old cities in England, which in peacetime were major tourist attractions. So the mood of the population there was very bitter against the Germans and also against the defendants at the Tribunal, because we did not want to join the military.

On the morning that I came to the Tribunal in York, the city had again been badly damaged by the Luftwaffe the previous night—and the mood in the city was accordingly explosive. Over a thousand people came to the large courtroom in order to hear my defense. They wanted to see if I was only an "odd bird" or a dangerous criminal and traitor. Before the hearing began, I saw that there were three judges, of whom the Chief Justice, who should be neutral, was the son of a devout Bishop. The two other judges represented the War Ministry and the Ministry of Labor. The Chief Justice was the chairman of the Court.

The Chief Justice interrogated me in detail on my convictions, how I lived, what I did, etc. He was a very pleasant person and also scrupulously fair. One could hardly maintain that of either of the other two. They could not understand how anyone could hesitate for an instant to bring to bear all conceivable means against Hitler. "All is fair in love and war": that was the English saying. But the Chief Justice was not like this, he was a man of principle. He inquired whether I was a Christian, and when I had become one. Whether I was active as a Christian and where? If I held that the military was unchristian? I gave him the relevant information, which was not at all easy in front of 1000 critical people. I said I was precisely as little against the military as against the police. Christ had put the sword in the hand of the State and a sword is a potentially deadly weapon. Sins and sinners would become even more active without the sword, as is now the case. But just as not everyone should take on the role of the policeman, so not everyone can take on the role of the soldier.

One cannot condemn the role of the police and the military. Cornelius was an officer (in the Acts of the Apostles) and his soldier's prayers were heard by God. But it is not the vocation of all to play the role of policeman or officer. There is one vocation for every man.

For me, there was only the one major difficulty. I was not in a position to, from the outset, commit myself to doing everything which my still unknown superior might demand of me, without knowing in advance what he might demand. If he required that I should make the earth uninhabitable—or annihilate humanity in a bacterial war—I would always and emphatically say "no." Therefore, I could only offer conditional obedience.

"But," said the Chief Justice, "we cannot run an army on this basis. We must require unconditional obedience. If an officer cannot rely on his people to obey, he will be endangered and powerless himself." I made clear to him that the reason for my being there lay precisely in this point. If an officer ordered me to do what I would not do, I would be court martialed for disobedience.

"Milord" (that is how one addresses an English judge), "If you, or the King, or his officers were to order me to do something which is forbidden by the Word of God, namely to sin, I am obliged to make a solemn announcement that I would refuse—with God's help."

The Justice then wanted to know, what I would do if my company, ICI, asked something of me which did not agree with my conscience? I said that under my contract, I would be compelled to resign; which is exactly what I could not do in the army. I said, that as long as I was genuinely allowed to resign, there would really be no misgivings.

The Judge understood me well. Where real freedom of conscience is, the conscience is allowed to function, and one may act with peace of mind. Where, however, compulsion of conscience exists, then one may not voluntarily take part.

Now, the Chief Justice was satisfied, but not the other two Judges on his right and left. The Judge who represented the army became very aggressive and said this position was subversive and intolerable. But the worst came from the Ministry of Labor Justice who began to swear. "It is known," he shouted, "that your company, ICI, manufactures gasoline for the Spitfire fighter planes. It is known that ICI is cooperating on other secret military work. I worked for this company, as so many did, which was obviously against my conscience and I had not resigned. I was a wretched hypocrite." His tirade went on and on. I was convinced that I had surely lost.

But just then something happened which no one could have foreseen. Suddenly a gentleman in the audience stood up in the middle of this tirade and appealed to the Chief Justice for order and quiet. The Chief Justice rose and asked his swearing colleague for quiet. The latter stopped immediately because even in times of war, the average Englishman does not appreciate cursing against the accused. Such talk is contrary to English notions of fair play. The Chief Justice asked for order, so that someone from the public could express his opinion. "We are here," said the Justice, "to ensure that justice is done, not to support propaganda."

The whole hall was as quiet as a mouse. Such a thing had never occurred in the history of an Appellate-Tribunal. The man that now arose, was totally unfamiliar to me. He was between forty-five and fifty-five years old, gave the impression of sound character, and spoke very quietly with the accent from Northeast England. "The accused does not know me," he said, "but I have observed him unseen for four years at work in the laboratory. What he testified to about his way of life is completely true. The work that the defendant does in the research department is purely organic chemistry and has absolutely nothing to do with warfare." The volunteer witness stressed once more that I did not know him and had no idea that he would make a statement for me.

The aggressive justice then asked me if my research could be used for war purposes. I answered that one could just as well use it for pharmacology as for the manufacture of explosives. The judge then rejoiced triumphantly once more as if I had condemned myself. Then I asked him whether I could pose an indirect question? Mockingly he permitted that. The question was the following: There was once a farmer, who grew barley. His harvest was good, because he was a first class farmer. He used his barley as feed for his cows in order to produce milk. But one day, the country in which he lived came into military difficulties. It needed acetone in order to manufacture explosives for the war. So, the government came to our farmer, took his barley away and used it to synthesize acetone that would be used for explosives. So, the farmer originally grew barley in order to produce milk. But now he grew barley that would be used for the production of acetone. The question is, therefore, is it wrong to grow barley? Obviously it is good to grow barley because with it, one can do all sorts of good—feed livestock and produce milk. The real questions must be formulated in another way, namely: Is it wrong to misuse barley in such a way that one synthesizes acetone in order to manufacture explosives for the maiming and slaughter of people? The attainment of technology is certainly good, but the misuse of technology for evil purposes is surely bad. I had developed new technology with my research. Out of the "know-how" one can, so-to-speak, produce "milk" or "explosives." The people that misuse technology must bear responsibility for it, not the one who provided the potentially beneficial technology. The responsibility is borne individual and also step-by-step—exactly like the farmer with his barley production. If others misuse my "know-how," they must bear the responsibility for their misuse, not I. Atomic energy can just as well be used for good purposes as to contaminate the whole of mankind. The guilt lies in the misuse of the potentially good, not in the neutral technology. For the misuse of his good barley, the good farmer cannot be held responsible. This situation applies to all areas of life.

The Chief Justice nodded, said that it is so and that he wished there were more young men with such moral insight. Insight was the foundation of true justice. Many in the hall who had obviously been hostile towards me, sat quietly. Some even nodded their heads. Then the Justice made his summary and verdict. There was no "jury" at this Tribunal, the Justice with his two colleagues had to pass judgment. The judgment was as the law of the Medes and the Persians: once it is decreed, it cannot be appealed.

The judgment was really amazing. I could not believe my ears as it was solemnly read aloud: The accused is not guilty, he poses absolutely no danger to the State, he will see to it that he is useful. He may carry out and perform any work that he is suitable for, or he can, if he is so inclined, continue with his research. The decision was applauded and I was free, even in wartime, to do what I wanted!

I thanked the Justices very much, first and foremost, the Chief Justice. The two other Justices did not say much, but they also seemed to be satisfied. Many of the spectators came to me afterwards and thanked me for so clearly explaining the problem of personal responsibility. Also, I thanked the honorable gentleman who had rescued me in the middle of the hearing. Without his help, I never would have pulled through. To this day, I have never learned his name. The Bible teaches us that we are the living lessons that God uses to demonstrate his divine wisdom to the angelic beings as he works in us. How God deals with us in this world demonstrates his character to the angels! (Ephesians 3:10). How often we fail in this commission!

Personally, I think that a State that looks after the freedom of conscience of its citizens, like the British State did for me and for many others, is worthy of respect and loyalty. In the midst of war of the worst kind, the State maintained justice and order so that every citizen could enjoy freedom of conscience. This attitude naturally carries with it heavy responsibility for the citizen. If I had gone ahead and joined the military despite my doubts and my conscience, I alone would have had to bear the guilt. But a State that shoots its citizens, because they cherish genuine conscience, does not deserve the loyalty of its citizens.

Through the strict separation of the executive from the judicial and legislative branches, the fathers of Anglo-Saxon law sought justice of this sort. Many States, especially certain European States, cannot grasp such fairness in practice. Especially not under the Napoleonic code, because in such States they unite the power of the police (as executive) with the power of the judiciary to create a dictatorial power.

CANCER RESEARCH 1944–1950 AT THE UNIVERSITY OF LONDON

After the doctors recommended that I change my field of research, I obviously had to look for other possibilities. One day I saw in a scientific journal an advertisement issued by the Middlesex Hospital of the University of London. Middlesex was and is still a university clinic of the University of London and carries out good research in many fields. In the Biochemical Institute (Courtauld Institute) the synthetic female hormone Stilbestrol, which was formerly used in the treatment of breast and prostate cancer, was discovered by Prof. E. Dodds and his colleagues. The substance is used much less today, because it may trigger certain side effects, including cancers of various kinds.

It turned out that breast and prostate cancer could be treated successfully in some cases with Stilbestrol. The effect, however, was of a palliative nature only, because, after a certain time interval, the hormone lost its efficacy and the patient, literally, became resistant to the cancer inhibiting effect of Stilbestrol. In the beginning of the treatment, the effect of the hormone was quite striking; however, after a while efficacy diminished and the cancer became rampant again.

Middlesex was looking for a biochemist who would be able to investigate the problem of tolerance development in Stilbestrol: why the initially favorable effect was not sustained and ceased entirely after some time. The biochemist sought was to investigate the reason for the efficacy of the hormone with patients who responded, and to investigate the reason for the lack of efficacy in patients having become tolerant ("relapsing") to it. If one could find out to what extent the metabolism of the hormone differed in reacting patients and those who had become tolerant to it, it might be possible to change the chemical structure of the hormone so that the metabolism of both types of patients would remain the same. Then it might be possible to treat patients who had become tolerant to the altered hormone successfully. In order to carry out this cancer research project, the university clinic therefore was looking for an organic chemist who could investigate the relationship of the metabolism with the chemical structure. I applied immediately and was invited for an interview. First, I had to describe my allergy and my illness in detail. Despite the fact that I now had been sick for more than three months, I was offered the position on the spot. After a few days of thinking it over, I accepted and signed the contract with the university as a "Fellow." From then on I was officially a "Countess of Lisburne Memorial Fellow" at the University of London, "tenable" at the Courtauld Institute of London University.

At that time, it was quite difficult to find an apartment in London. The city had suffered from bombing throughout the whole war, and the military required all the living quarters left. I thus had to rent a permanent room in a hotel on Manchester Square (across from the Wallace Collection). The room was on the top floor of the hotel. The owner was an emigrated German lady who quite often could be found in a drunken stupor under the table. I frequently had to come down-stairs at night because the servants were concerned for her life.

For cooking I had a gas ring. The gas was metered, and I had to put a shilling in the meter every time I wanted to cook water or heat the room. In the morning I had breakfast at the hotel, and in the evening I cooked for myself. I did not like to go to a restaurant, because during the war the quality of the food was bad and expensive. I lived for five years in that room—just as I had lived for almost five years in a room in Stockton-on-Tees.

Manchester Square lay in the western part of London, not far from the BBC building. Every morning I walked by the BBC on my way to the Institute. On the occasion of these walks of about twenty minutes I usually inspected the bomb damage from the previous night. It was during the time of the V-1 and

V-2 missile bombings. The V-1 were genuine flying bombs equipped with a pulsed ram jet. They did not fly very high and were pre-programmed to impact after so many miles.

Spitfires (fighter planes) would fly along side them and depress one of the V-1's wings with the tip of their own wing, so that the V-1 flying bombs turned around and flew back to France to crash there instead of in England. In this way, the RAF-pilots intercepted them half-way on their pre-programmed flights, so that they flew in the opposite direction and crashed at about the location they had started out from. The V-1 were so programmed that at the end of their flight they would fly at full throttle straight into the ground. When the pre-programmed distance was flown, the nose of the machines turned toward the ground and accelerated to maximum speed for the impact. The sudden dive of the machine temporarily deprived the motor of fuel. As a consequence, the motor sputtered, and then with full speed raced into the ground. When one heard this momentary sputter, one knew that one had still a few fractions of a second to find safety! One really had to make a quick decision and act accordingly. In general, however, the V-1 machines were not very effective, because they could not be guided well enough to hit specific targets. The psychological effect was much stronger: people who did not understand them panicked so easily—but not the others!

The V-2 weapon was quite different. It was shot up into the stratosphere as a rocket and then descended with supersonic speed down onto its "target." At that time, a missile following this fast ballistic trajectory was difficult to detect or track. As a result, these missiles arrived without any warning and exploded where they were not at all expected. You could see the V-1 coming, but you could not see an approaching V-2. Suddenly, somewhere there was an explosion and one did not know where it came from. The whistling and howling of the rocket could only be heard after the explosion had taken place: this was a consequence of the hypersonic speed with which the missile flew.

The explosions caused by the V-2 were not particularly large, even though a V-2 explosion completely destroyed Whitfield's Tabernacle (the large church that the reformer of England and North America built). After the first use of the V-2, the English government tried to calm the people by claiming the explosion had been caused by a natural gas leak under the street. But lies rarely have a calming effect, and this lie did not explain the subsequent whistle of the missile's flight heard after it exploded!

One Monday morning in 1944, I came late into my laboratory and found everything in a chaotic state. The windows of the laboratory were almost all broken, the doors blasted away, and a tangle of fire hoses lay in the middle of the building. During the night, a V-2 had hit and destroyed Whitfield's Tabernacle which was located just a few hundred yards away from the Middlesex Hospital. Our kennel cages looked the worst of all, because they were accommodated on the top floor of the building. The monkey cages were open, the mice and rats had escaped and the guinea pigs were squeaking around in the ruins. But the cats were happy—they had never seen so many mice and rats in all their lives! It took weeks until all was brought back to order.

As with the V-1, the psychological effect of the V-2 was its strength. There was never any kind of warning; at once, out of the blue, a building would be hit and the people in it killed or buried alive. But precise targets could not be had with the V-2 either. It was clear that one could never win a war in this way, because terror incited the terrorized to even fiercer resistance. And so it was at that time in England. When the V-1 and V-2 weapon systems were discovered, and even before they came into use, the Allies had decided to accelerate the invasion of Europe in order to ward off the danger of these weapons of terror. As a matter of fact, the V-1 and the V-2 were only in action during a relatively short time, because the launching pads in Northern France, Belgium and Holland were occupied by Allied troops after the invasion in the summer of 1944. However, these times were not well suited for serious research in the laboratory. There were too many distractions the whole day and also through the whole night.

Although there were no further V-1 attacks after 1944, new V-2 attacks continued taking place. Nevertheless cancer research made relatively good progress in London as one can still read today in the professional journals. But even though hormones for the treatment of certain types of cancer can be useful, they do not provide a definite therapeutic answer to the problem of cancer.

CHAPTER XI

ENGLAND AFTER THE INVASION OF EUROPE 1944

WORK AMONG GERMAN PRISONERS OF WAR

When the allied troops landed in Northern France, tens of thousands of the Axis Troops surrendered. So many prisoners were taken that they became a real burden to Eisenhower's troops. Everywhere in England make-shift camps were established in order to accommodate this flood of prisoners. All the country mansions that had lain empty for years due to high taxes were quickly renovated in order to handle this new "invasion" of England.

The old aristocracy of the country owned many large country manor houses with extensive parks surrounding them. However, when the war started, the taxes for such estates became so unbearably high that the owners simply could not pay any more. Consequently, the tax authorities of the State (Internal Revenue) came and tried to auction the estates. But no buyers could be found because nearly all had already been crushed by the tax burden. Furthermore, it was no longer possible for most of the owners to pay the costs of the labor needed on these large country estates. In addition, most young people were serving in the army during the war, so these large properties lay empty. They became state property by default. This sad situation reminds us of the politics of the state in the "tithing"-crisis that I previously described. The state received all these beautiful country mansions and estates as "profit," but then had to leave them empty. The state left it this way rather than to grant any tax relief.

Jurisprudence in England may be generous and reasonable— as in the case of conscientious objectors. However, when it is a matter of money and finances, any reasonable governing ceases to exist and the state shows itself as a genuine predator of the most unreasonable sort. In that situation, the state behaves similarly to a family which has learned to live beyond its means. Neither such a family, nor such a state, will ever again manage to live within the given means. Neither one can cut back. Both continue to go into debt until they are crushed by their own debts. Private families have maintained such a desolate and chronic state for quite some time. What should one write about politicians and states? States in this world still try by means of criminal rates of inflation of their currency to eliminate their debts without liquidating them. That is, they attempt to rob the private citizen in order to pay the state's debts (because inflation is nothing but common theft). (See also my book *Inflation, der Dieb im Haus—Inflation a Thief in the House*—A.E. Wilder-Smith, Altherr Verlag, St. Gallen, Switzerland).

Many prisoners of war were shipped to the USA and to Canada. The vicinity of London was host to nearly one million POWs. The English officers who were running these camps often were men who themselves had been in Hitler's camps and thus were experienced in such situations prior to their liberation by the Allied Troops. They understood the special problems of war imprisonment and often ran their camps relatively well. There are obviously always exceptions. Food was scarce, not only for the prisoners of war, but for the civilian population of England as well. This shortness of supplies during the first months caused some dissatisfaction among the prisoners of war. But most prisoners were glad to have more or less escaped the slaughter and murdering of the battle field.

The greatest problems of these prisoners of war, however, had little to do with food. Most of them knew absolutely nothing of the fate of their own families: whether they were alive or dead. And if their relatives were alive, they did not know where they were staying. The chronic uncertainty brought a lot of stress with it. Fathers did not know whether their children, wives or parents were still living. It is possible to keep up moral and esprit de corps in a victorious army with a few tricks. But, within a beaten army, fallen into imprisonment, hope very quickly evaporates.

British authorities also made sure in a drastic manner that the prisoners found out about the true character of Hitler and the Nazis. They were shown pictures of the mass murder camps, of the gas chambers and the experiments with people that were carried out in the extermination camps. The result naturally was, that some of these men, who had risked their lives for Hitler, came to see that they had been cheated. Others simply dismissed this news as enemy propaganda. Many were not able to handle this stress; they were totally demoralized and disillusioned. They began to accuse each other, to curse each other and to steal from each other. The esprit de corps sank to zero, particularly, in the SS-camps, of which there were a great many in the vicinity of London.

When May 1945 approached and victory in Europe was proclaimed by the Allies, the POWs naturally all wanted to return home immediately in order to search for their families. But Europe was a heap of rubble, and the authorities in England did not want to let the prisoners go. It was felt that the POWs should help now with the reconstruction work after the war. This resulted in even more frustration and also in bitterness.

Those among the prisoners who volunteered could leave the camps in groups and work in the civilian economy for the prevailing British wages. The unions in England took good care that the POWs received exactly the same wages as the British workers, with the one difference, however, that the entire amount was not paid out at once. The money withheld was deposited in a bank account and returned to the POW at the time of his repatriation. This way these men had something with which they could start a life in their home country again.

Obviously, among the SS-POWs there were almost no German speaking chaplains who would have been able to help these men with the problems of those days. Among the other prisoners of war there were a few conservative chaplains who were capable dedicated clergymen, but those were really rare. But, in my opinion, liberal theology does not produce good clergymen for such a plight. Many German imprisoned pastors were liberals. The theology departments at the German universities had radically taken care of that. But among these millions of prisoners of war there was much worry, stress and dire need and far too few clergymen genuinely able to help the desperate men and their needs.

Once the combat activities in Europe had ceased, the Allies had a new quite different fight on their hands: How to alleviate all the needs, the hate and stress of the POWs? There were simply not enough German speaking chaplains to manage this problem. The German chaplains confined in the camps often did not know how to solve their own problems—let alone anyone else's. Their own wives, children and relatives were often missing.

THE RECONCILIATION COMMISSION

At that time the British Department for Religious Affairs (headquartered in Buende, Germany) approached me and asked whether I would be willing to help to implement the reconciliation between the nations recently fighting each other? I was not to be involved on a full time basis, but to do it in addition to my research.

Well, as a Christian I was very able to take this responsibility. First, the authorities wanted to make me an officer—I was to become lieutenant-colonel and to go to Germany in uniform. I, however, rejected this with the reasoning that I would never be taken seriously if I showed up as a well-nourished and well-protected British officer among the hungry and unprotected people there. However, if I went as a civilian, without special rationing coupons and without uniform, I would be a German among Germans to them, and they would listen to me.

The authorities showed understanding for my reasoning, but new difficulties appeared. Europe was a military camp. One could only get in as a soldier. Civilians from the outside were not allowed. I thus asked that a civilian contract with a military rank be set up. I thus would then be able to identify myself in military fashion without having to be a soldier. The border guards would have to let me pass. The friendly British officer agreed because the situation in Germany was grim, and he provided me with the papers for the rank of lieutenant-colonel, but in exchange for the favor, no salary and no protecting uniform. Thus, I traveled across the Channel by military ferry in early 1946 and went by military train all the way to Krefeld.

I will never forget the way this city looked: simply disintegrated, demolished, bombed out. I was traveling with some high ranking officers of the British army. All of them were in "full regalia," so to speak: uniforms and medals everywhere. Subordinate officers were flitting about me as I sat in my corner of the train in a simple suit and rain coat. I was the only civilian among the hundreds of high level personalities who were traveling to their official assignments.

There was a peculiar difficulty, which I had never expected when I worked out my plan. The "top brass" started to wonder why such a simple civilian was traveling among them.

Everything was supposedly reserved for VIPs, what about this simple person in a rain coat?

A high-ranking officer sitting across from me, however, whispered that one should be doubly careful (I could partially understand what they were whispering), since they would never allow a simple civilian to travel with VIPs. The one in the corner (= myself) was probably more important than all of them combined, otherwise it would certainly be impossible to travel without insignia and without uniform in a military train. Care was to be taken, since I probably had a highly secret assignment. When we arrived at Krefeld in the early gray morning hours, my name was paged on the loud speakers: "Lt. Col. Wilder-Smith, please report immediately at the RTO-Officer, the private car (with chauffeur) is waiting for you." The "top brass" who sat in the first class compartment with me, looked at each other triumphantly and nodded understandingly when I quickly rose: It was not an error after all, we were right, he is a high ranking secret agent. Exactly as we suspected!

I thus was driven in the general's car to Cologne, where I reported to the City Commander. The misery and the dire needs I saw there in Cologne were almost beyond description. Starving people were standing in great masses around the bombed out train station. They stood there all day waiting for anything that they might be able to grasp. One simply could not leave anything standing around—not for a moment. This was the age of the "Kohlenklau," the theft of coals. The Ruhr Area had to deliver many tons of coal daily to France for reparations. It was cold (minus 25°C) thus the people were terribly cold and starving. The City Commander first offered me a good meal, because he was completely informed about my contractual conditions and he invited me, to come once a week for a meal personally with him, since my stomach would not yet have adjusted to the German diet of that time: pea soup in the morning, noon and evenings. One can freeze as long as one is not starving at the same time! One can also be starving, as long as one is not also freezing at the same time. But both together would have been too much. Once in a while the Commander put a military vehicle at my disposal, so I would not be completely immobilized. Once in a while, with this car, I picked up food for myself and my starving friends in the city from farmers I knew. The German driver liked to participate in these expeditions, for he thus received a few extras for his young and hungry family.

Former POWs whose acquaintance I had made in England invited me everywhere to speak, at their houses and their bombed churches and destroyed parish halls. I often spoke in churches that had not yet had a new roof. In one church both outside walls were missing since the bombing. But all churches, no matter how damaged, were always crowded. There was a great hunger for the Gospel at that time. My office of reconciliation was easily exercised there—an office of reconciliation, after all the murders, the slaughter of the war.

The fact that I also was personally hungry and freezing along with everybody else—and not even wearing the uniform of the victors—helped me a lot. The people quickly found trust in my assignment and often in Christ as well, who had called upon me to do this type of work. Since I did not posses any kind of food coupons, all the German friends had to share their food stuff with me—pea soup usually!—and then, for a change, pea soup again. The Germans had already become pot bellied from this diet some time ago. In order to just barely survive, they had to eat—or try to—very large amounts of this soup. My stomach was not as distended as theirs and I could not absorb sufficient amounts to keep myself sufficiently nourished. For that reason and due to all the cold and hunger, my old friend from ICI reappeared: angina pectoris. Furthermore, I just had a thin coat—an English macintosh— available. Thus during the winter of 1946, I learned how to go hungry and to freeze.

THE BAVARIAN JACKET AND THE RECTOR

The friends with whom I lodged had returned to their old bombed house. I lived in the living room, because space was very scarce. This was a Christian family and we already knew each other from visits before the war. They had even visited us on the farm in England. The father, my host, had been injured in World War I (he had lost one arm), and lived with his wife and three daughters in Cologne. Now, only two daughters were left because the oldest, who had visited us with her father before the war on the farm in England, had been transferred from Cologne to Dresden. She was living there when the Americans and the English annihilated the city from the air during a single night. She was missing without a trace in the flames. The gigantic firestorm caused a lack of oxygen and thousands thus suffocated due to the lack of oxygen. She died in the flames.

During my temporary furlough from the laboratory in London, the task of reconciliation on the continent started becoming reality. My professor, although a hater of Germans, gave me the time off to do this work, because he wanted to go along with the politicians and to help them.

One day, the British City Commander told me that he was very strongly in favor of the plan to redevelop and rebuild the University of Cologne again. As I was a Fellow at the University of London, he was certain that I could be of help to the German rector and provide the professors at the university there with much good advice. I therefore scheduled an appointment with the rector to meet him and the faculty one afternoon, in order to present the internal organization of the University of London.

At the date agreed, I was eating—that is, was drinking—my lunch (pea soup) with my hosts in Cologne, when I suddenly heard the street car that I needed to catch to get to the university. There were only two or three street cars daily, but they were naturally always overcrowded. The passengers formed what we used to call a "grape formation" in order to just get a ride somehow; they hung like grapes from the sides of the vehicles.

When I heard the street car, I hurriedly pulled the raincoat over my usual everyday clothes in order to get a ride quickly. I must add, however, that it was so extremely cold during that season (we did not have any wood or coal and the temperature was -25°C) that I had needed to borrow extra clothing. Obviously, nobody had much to lend, everything had been lost during the war. However, up in a closet in a roofless room (open to the heavens) an old moth-eaten jacket, a hunter's jacket had been found. The jacket looked like those worn by the Bavarians when they go hunting. Moths had carried out a few fashionably racy alterations to the cut of the jacket. But the jacket at least was made of wool, which was the most important factor in that cold. It was clearly two sizes too small for me and the corresponding green hunter's hat with feather was also missing, but it was warm. Thus, I had put on this Bavarian jacket and now I quickly pulled my raincoat over it for extra warmth as I heard the streetcar. Everybody in the house made fun of my looks, but I did not care, the jacket wasn't beautiful, but it was warm. The rest of the inhabitants of the house, by the way, did not look much better than I did; there was actually no real reason to laugh.

I charged out of the house and into the streetcar, where I was promptly pressed flat by the mass of passengers. As I was standing there I remembered that my Bavarian jacket was still underneath my raincoat. This attire was likely to attract attention at the university in the office of the rector! What was I to do? I could barely breathe in the street car, much less try to take off my raincoat in order to remove my borrowed Bavarian jacket. I therefore had no option but to go on as I was to the university—whether I wanted to or not.

When, after an almost endless trip, the streetcar finally stopped in front of the university, many of the almost crushed passengers streamed from that horrifying vehicle. I tried to shake myself back into shape, but really did not look particularly presentable after this trip for sardines. But the war had just ended, nobody will look better, I thought. And thus consoled myself. It also was bitterly cold, and it did not even occur to me to take off my rain coat and my Bavarian jacket. In the cold, this would unavoidably have resulted in pneumonia.

I marched up the great stairs in front of the main building and arrived at the main gate above. Wonders never cease, they opened by themselves, because a servant standing at a small window in the door recognized the visitors and opened the gates in time. I presented my business card and he read: Dr. Wilder-Smith, Countess of Lisburne Memorial Fellow at the University of London. The servant made a deep bow and led me, directly into the office of the director.

The rector sat behind a gigantic desk in his office. When the servant, standing at the door, announced my name—as well as he could pronounce it—the rector hesitated, then stood up, bid me welcome and asked me to come in. Apparently, my clothing surprised, if not disconcerted him. In England, an old dirty raincoat is considered noble, particularly if it looks really greasy—just as dirty, filthy and greasy Lederhosen are seen as the hallmark of a genuine Bavarian. Then the rector proceeded to say that the entire faculty was assembled in the hall next door, waiting for my esteemed visit. He opened the door leading to a large side room where thirty to forty elegantly dressed gentlemen sat in dark suits with their festively adorned ladies. They all sat around a large oval green table, conversing, when I entered. They rose when they saw me, and when the rector announced my name, I thought I could see a slight shadow flitting over the faces of this distinguished gathering. Could this destitute looking young man really be the important guest from London University?

In the room itself I was engulfed by a wave of very hot air. I started to sweat. The rector realized this right away and explained that the Military Government had allowed for a special allotment of coals to the university so that they could spend a nice afternoon with the English guest from London University. The rector approached me and wanted to help me to get out of the greasy raincoat. "In here," he said, "it is much too warm. You must take it off or you will catch pneumonia afterwards." I protested, I thought of my moth-eaten Bavarian jacket hidden under the raincoat! I would prefer not to take my things off, I said clumsily. However, the rector insisted on carrying out his plan.

Well, I had a bit of a cold and said so, to explain why I would prefer to keep my coat on. "No," the rector said. "You will catch pneumonia if you sweat in this hot lecture hall and then get back out into the severe cold." With these words he approached me from behind and helped me out of my coat. And thus the Bavarian jacket appeared—including all the moth-holes, the worn-out pockets and the faded green-yellow colors. Furthermore, as I said before, the jacket was at least two sizes too small for me. One could actually hear the stylishly dressed distinguished gentlemen and their festively adorned ladies holding their collective breaths. Thus, I stood there, helpless in front of this distinguished gathering, specially dressed up in my honor. "If only the earth would open up and swallow me," was my most sincere wish.

When the rector began introducing me for the lecture on the organization of English universities, he seemed at a complete loss for words: thunderstruck. I did not do much better either. How would you, dear reader, like to give a lecture in front of an audience who had searched for the most beautiful robes in order to honor the speaker who, however, was himself dressed worse than a beggar?

The lecture was certainly the worst I had ever held. I could feel the ladies counting the moth-holes in my pockets, and the gentlemen guessing how many sizes too small my Bavarian jacket actually was. Humor, élan, self-confidence, and eloquence of speech completely left me. The audience all remained polite, although they did not seem to have much humor with regard to my situation. With my friends in the city we were all about equally shabbily dressed and my clothing gave no cause for any particular attention. There no one could be better than the other. Here, however, the situation was quite different.

I have often thought about this event and drawn the conclusion from it: Here, among people we are all sinners, one a bit better, another a bit worse, but more or less alike. But how will it be when we all have to appear in front of God in all His Glory? "And it is appointed unto man once to die, but after this the judgment" (Hebrews 9:27). Facing this distinguished audience I had only one wish, namely to take off my jacket and to put on something more correct under the circumstances. Then I might have been able to speak for myself, but this way, the words got stuck in my throat. What an image of Christ and ourselves! Christ takes off our shabby clothes and gives us the gift of wedding suits and dresses for free. What splendid salvation when we have to appear before God. I am overjoyed to know that Christ did not only invite us to the wedding by His coming, but that he gives me the appropriate "clothes" as a gift. On earth among men we are good enough in our shabby clothing (our own deeds), and nobody among us attracts special attention. But there, facing Him, it will be completely different and we will be grateful for His festive clothing (His deeds adjudged to us). The most beautiful aspect remains that we may already claim this heavenly clothing of celebration as of today. The result is that the Christian is already allowed to enjoy this great gift now.

"DER KOHLENKLAU"—THE THEFT OF COAL

As previously mentioned, the days of the winter of 1946 were the days of the so-called "Kohlenklau" (coal-theft).

Winter 1946 was bitter, just terribly cold. Even in the Ruhr area, the Germans had difficulties obtaining any kind of heating material for their bombed houses. Coal was produced in the Ruhr area, but under the reparation laws the Germans had to deliver daily quotas of train loads of coal to France. These reparations just about consumed the entire production of the Ruhr area.

Every day, long freight trains fully loaded with coal crossed the Rhine bridge in Cologne on the way to France. The bridge near the Cologne train station (very close to the Cologne cathedral) was crowded with these freight trains. It had been temporarily reconstructed after its destruction. When the trains coming from the Rhine valley rolled towards France, they had to overcome quite a difference in elevation. During frost and icy conditions in winter the steam engines often could barely pull the long and heavily loaded freight cars. One could hear all day long how the locomotives started to slip and slide.

Consequently, men and women climbed onto the very slowly moving trains and threw coal from the moving wagons down the embankment. At the bottom of the embankments men stood with push carts, handcarts and even old baby buggies, loaded the coal up and took it home. At especially steep escarpments, the trains moved particularly slowly. Often the locomotives could not get sufficient traction on the rails, because the rails had been quietly smeared with oil and fat beforehand. The locomotives thus lost traction and often came to a complete halt. Therefore the freight cars were often almost empty before the train had made it over the mountain. It actually happened that coal trains arrived empty in France, a fact that obviously made the French very unhappy.

One afternoon a friend showed me the great "Kohlenklau" (coal-theft). I asked him what all the uniformed men standing on both sides of the rails—and bearing weapons—were all about. He laughed and said that this was the police that had been sent to stop the coal-theft. Peculiar, however, was the fact that these policemen looked directly away from the trains, with their backs all turned towards the rails and the trains. My friend laughed quite heartily once more, but then turned serious saying that it was a good thing that these policemen at least had a heart. They also were no longer capable of seeing the misery of the freezing and starving population. Furthermore, the fact that they (the police) and their wives and children were also freezing at home meant that they were actually grateful for the coal-theft, because all of them received a percentage provided they did not interfere with the operation.

Well, what was one to say considering the unspeakable need? The military authorities knew very well about the coal-theft, but did nothing about it in light of all the misery. It was better to have empty trains roll to France—all the misery had become too much to bear.

THE POW WORK—A GLANCE BACK

We now have to back up a few steps in order to better understand the relationships and roots of this reconciliation project. Before I was invited to participate for the first time in 1946, I had already worked a lot among German POWs. This gave the military authorities the reason to have me invited to the British zone in Germany.

When the war in Europe was won, England was full of POWs from almost all the nations of Europe. All those who were fighting on the side of the Nazis, i.e., all those who were captured in German uniforms, came into POW camps. In the occupied part of Russia, the Nazis forced Russians to work for the Wehrmacht. Partially as a result of deceit and partially by honest recruitment, Russians, Frenchmen, Italians, Finns and Norwegians surfaced who had been captured wearing German uniforms. All these people had to be sorted out, because from then on, even the Germans no longer wanted to remain German, but to be of some other nationality.

As we have established already, there were too few chaplains in the Wehrmacht to handle the concentrated despondency in these camps. In addition, POW chaplains were preferentially repatriated. The needs in the bombed homeland were so urgent that chaplains were sent home first. This was even more to the disadvantage of the remaining POWs, because then there were almost no chaplains left to help them.

POWs often came to the hospital where I worked, to clean windows and to scrub the floors. They volunteered for these jobs in order to earn some money and to escape the boredom of imprisonment. Every morning, when the group of Germans marched towards the hospital, there was a small group of Jews at a street corner spitting at them. They shouted curses in German at them. The situation of the POWs was difficult. SS-men came out less frequently. They were considered dangerous although often they were not highly dedicated Nazis at all. Their tattered SS-uniforms gave them away.

A few Christian friends in Cholsey, where father's farm was located, saw them and discussed their situation with me. We asked ourselves whether it would not be a good idea for us to visit these POWs in their camps as our Lord Jesus Christ has called upon us to do. At home in Cholsey, I visited a small church of the so-called Open Brethren. Thousands of POWs worked nearby in agriculture, and the misery of the POWs in the region was very great. Although nobody in the community—except myself—spoke German, we went to the commander of a camp in Didcot and asked for permission to hold German Bible studies and lectures.

The POWs sat around evening after evening, with nothing to do but to worry about their families and relatives. Diversion of any kind was certainly welcome. I personally had not spoken a word of German for almost five years, but I diligently read the Luther Bible every day and had learned many texts by heart; otherwise I am sure I would have completely forgotten the language. We thus started Bible studies and held lectures in this POW camp. The men at first came out of curiosity. In one camp, close to Oxford (Shottover House), the commander himself was a dedicated Christian, and very much welcomed the idea of lectures and Bible work. Often about a thousand men showed up for an evening lecture. Propaganda was not necessary, spontaneously the men streamed into the halls where I spoke. I have to emphasize that my German was not good, and that I spoke a biblical Luther-German, because this was the only German I knew at that time. But it was precisely this Luther-German which fascinated the men. It was pure German and no dialect, they admitted that much—however it was very old-fashioned (much like speaking Shakespearean English today!).

Once I talked about the dying thief on the cross—the dying man who cursed the Savior on the cross and still received the promise of paradise without being capable of doing any good deeds. These hardened men listened, fascinated, as I described the crucifixion and its purpose. They had never heard anything like it. It spoke to their hearts and for the first time many understood how deep a love towards us men God had, and how great a sacrifice He had invested to redeem His fallen creation from eternal ruin.

In the course of time, the military authorities invited us to serve everywhere in the camps. Many men started reading their Bibles. A number became believers and began working among their comrades. Together with our friends of the Open Brethren, we worked at St. Albans at Mr. O.C. Hartridge's place. There, a large number became believers who then asked for New Testament baptism. These public baptisms were a blessing for the camps. We then went to the camp in Harpenden with similar results. Afterwards, we went on to Didcot where a SS-camp was located, then on to Woking and then again to Oxford. Many men, in particular the SS-men, really did not know at all what kind of book the Bible is and what it represents. In those days, I had many in front of me who did not even know the name of Jesus Christ—for them the name was not much more than a derisive nickname, nothing more.

As time went on, we gained a lot of trust from the POWs and the military authorities as well. It grew to the extent that the latter permitted us to send busses into the camps to bring the POWs to our small congregation. I know that the well known evangelist from Altenkirchen (Westerwald), Anton Schulte, found Christ through similar evangelistic activities by the Open Brethren in Scotland. Now he heads the large missionary work "Neues Leben" (New Life) in Germany. The work done at that time did bear fruit a hundred fold.

Thus the spiritual situation was happy and fruitful, although the external misery in the land was great after the war. Food was rationed—severely rationed. What was one to do with all these young men without a country? We did not want to send them straight back to the camps after Bible studies and services but wanted to offer them a little bit of informal Christian fellowship. We thus decided to invite all POWs who had been at the service to our house. The invitation was announced after services and unanimously the POWs accepted. They were really looking forward to being among young and happy people for once.

But this arrangement brought a severe problem for the housewives. For they were to offer tea and cake as was the custom after the hours of fellowship.

But where would you get so much tea, cake, butter and bread for so many young men? The result was that every family sacrificed a part of their own rations. However, when large crowds of these inwardly and outwardly neglected POWs showed up at our place, we stood there like the disciples in front of five thousand hungry people at the time of Christ. Should we send them home empty? We did not have much food. We prayed about the situation.

It was Saturday evening and after the Bible study. Many POWs had come in order to read the Bible with us and they knew that we had no more bread, no butter and no other spreads in the house. Directly after the prayer was finished, the telephone rang. A grocery store in Wallingford was on the line. The owner knew us quite well since we did our shopping at his place. He was not a convinced Christian but a dear, nice man. The manager of the grocery in Wallingford said that it was Saturday evening and there was a lot of bread left over and he simply could not take the responsibility of having it turn old. He would sell us the bread without coupons—under these circumstances this was allowed and legal. He knew very well that we would not have wanted to do anything illegal.

Thus, we sent a small car to Wallingford to the grocery and the manager packed the car fully up to the roof with bread. "But what are you going to do with the bread, do you have butter or margarine to spread on it?" We stood there embarrassed because we had nothing of the sort. We just looked at each other, because nothing was there, and we knew it. He did not ask any more and came back with a large basket full of butter—it must have been several kilograms, we had not seen that much butter in years. "The expiry date of this butter," he said, "has passed. If you don't take it, it will turn rancid. You can get it a bit cheaper from me—and also without rationing coupons." Again, under the circumstances, this was allowed. With heartfelt thanks we accepted the butter and bread, both without rationing coupons, but for money. We were really happy to have received in this manner our "fish and loaves." We paid and thanked him again warmly. But he seemed absent-minded for a moment, then he said: "What are you using as a spread on your buttered bread?" We again looked at each other in embarrassment and did not say anything. We had nothing to report and it is always better to keep quiet. "Wait a moment," he said and disappeared into the pantry. After a few minutes he returned with a gigantic box filled with jars of marmalade. "These also have expired, but they are still good," he said. "I may also sell you these without coupons." We worked out the bill—he provided us with a hefty volume discount, because everyone knew what we were going to do with these large amounts—and triumphantly we returned home with the loot.

Some of our POWs who had accepted Christ were well informed about our critical food situation and observed, with great joy, how God was taking care of His children who wanted to work according to His will. These and other prayers answered reinforced their faith, because they recognized the reality of how God hears prayers. But some who had not yet progressed to this point simply could not believe what they saw with their own eyes. They wondered why the friends from the Open Brethren did these good works for their former enemies.

A young POW who had observed the entire scene—only later did he become a Christian himself—one evening came to see me with the specific question: "Why are you doing all these good works. You have experienced nothing but evil from the Germans and the Nazis. Why are you doing good deeds? Is it not true, as many openly assert in the camp, that you are an agent of the British government and that you are actually just spying on us?" These young people could not understand why good deeds are done—particularly to those who had done evil. I thus asked the young man, who was nominally a member of the church, what the Lord Jesus Christ had meant when he asked his disciples to love their enemies, to repay evil with good and to feed their hungry enemies? I showed him the passages in the Sermon on the Mount, where these commandments appear, and read them to him. I then asked him to read these parts out loud for me himself, which he did. I then asked him what these passages express: loving enemies, feeding the enemy when he is hungry, repaying evil with good? He looked at me, bewildered. A small light had finally lit up in his head.

The meaning of these passages had become clear to him. Then I asked him what he would do if God, his Creator, asked him to love his enemies, and to feed them when they were hungry, and to repay evil with good? What would this POW do, if God from the heavens called upon him to act in this manner? A shadow of a smile crossed his face when he answered with just one word: "Obey." "Do you, my dear friend, personally have anything against our doing as you yourself would do, that is 'obeying'?" "Well," he said, "now I understand that faith is not just some religious matter sitting in the heart without obligations. Obedience is really the point, otherwise one does not really believe." He thoroughly understood what the New Testament means when it says: "If a man loves me, he will keep my commandments" (John 14:23). Later on this young man came to believe in the Lord Jesus Christ as the Son of God.

We did this type of work from 1945—1950 until most of the POWs were repatriated. When the men returned to their homeland, they often found very sad conditions. Although some churches and congregations were alive, many were dead—they did not believe in the word of the Scripture, or the word of the Bible was not personally binding to them. Faith without works is dead, exactly as the apostle James wrote. Thus, many of the men who had become Christians wrote to me from their Germany and invited me to come and evangelize further in their home towns, just as I had done in the POW-camps. Therefore, I went as often as I could to the continent accepting such invitations from the men I knew. Often I preached in churches that were full but had no roofs. I remember a church near Cologne that had neither front nor back walls. The wind whistled through the nave during the entire service. At that time, such small things did not bother people. They hungered for the good news of the dying love of the Savior. Where this message was delivered in an uncomplicated but dignified way, the halls and churches were full—filled to bursting-point.

Meanwhile, England was no longer governed by Churchill, but by Mr. Attlee, the head of the Labor Party. As a direct consequence, England recovered less well from the war than Germany, although the latter had lost the war. Germany had Adenauer, who was very conservative, as Chancellor, with Erhardt as Minister of Finance, and together the two managed to achieve the so-called "Wirtschaftswunder" (economic miracle). During my visit in 1946 in Germany I was told the following joke: At a meeting between the occupation force and the German authorities, the English officer asked how long the Germans would need to get back to normality? The German responded that this question needed to be restated more precisely before he could offer an objective answer. "Because," he said, "if you (Englishmen) help us with the normalization of the state and the economy, we will not have made any progress in twenty years. If, however, you leave us alone to solve our problems, five to six years will suffice." This is how the defeated Germans correctly appraised Attlee's Labor government.

Why all this? The answer to this question is easy to explain. I made good money as a Fellow at the University of London, but was unable to do anything with the money I earned. It was, for example, not permitted to take money into foreign countries. If I remember correctly, we were allowed to take fifty pounds sterling a year along to a foreign country. Well, fifty pounds per year as money for expenses in a foreign country did not get you very far—the amount was written into your passport, and one could not easily get around the law. Before monetary reform, one could hardly expect the Germans to finance the lectures and evangelization carried out in Germany. Thus, I earned money in London that I wanted to spend on the continent. But it was precisely such financing of work on the continent which was not allowed under Mr. Attlee's directions.

Until 1949, I managed. We used the money earned to send Care-packages to the continent as well as to organize trips and to invite Christians from the continent to England. But every time something happened that would make necessary the export of finances, there was a barrage of regulations that had to be overcome. Finally, I was of the opinion that I would have to seek work on the continent, preferably in Switzerland, since the currency there was the most solid in the world and one could use it any way one wished to. But how to implement such a plan? The idea of the European Union had not matured yet and the borders between countries were very strict— especially with regard to finances. How this plan was realized will eventually require a chapter all by itself.

CHAPTER XII

IMMIGRATION FROM ENGLAND

HOW I MET MY WIFE—AND HOW SHE MET ME

In 1948, a Swiss evangelist by the name of G.R. Brinke visited the Christians in England. He had heard about the work among the German POWs and he wanted to see the poverty with his own eyes and be helpful. Thus, we invited Mr. Brinke to our home and enjoyed brotherly fellowship with him. He was, so to speak, on the same wavelength as we. Brinke was a native German, but a naturalized Swiss citizen and came from the circle of the Open Brethren. A few other Swiss came to see us at that time to help us, among them Karl Neuhaus, an engineer who was working at Brown-Boveri in Baden, Switzerland. He diligently helped us, and his lightheartedness and cheerful personality was, so to speak, "a breath of fresh air."

As a result of these connections with Switzerland, I was invited to Switzerland shortly thereafter. The first Swiss congregation I visited at that time was the Freie Evangelische Gemeinde in Thayngen near the Swiss-German border. A former Salvation Army officer, Voegelin, was minister at that church and had much understanding for evangelization.

In the course of this trip, I met an old Englishman by the name of Eoll who lived in Zürich with his son-in-law from the Scripture Union, Mr. Aebi. He also had a lot of interest in evangelization and was of the opinion that I should move to

Switzerland to take advantage of the many doors currently open on the continent. Switzerland was centrally located; its currency was stable and I would lose less time traveling. He said he knew a wealthy Christian industrialist in Switzerland who was looking for somebody to help with research in his pharmaceutical department. Mr. Eoll then contacted his friend, the industrialist, by telephone and introduced me to him there in Central Switzerland. As a result, I was immediately invited to get acquainted with these Christian friends.

They were touchingly hospitable and received me like their own son. The master of the house was a widower. A housekeeper had brought up his four daughters. She was not exactly the person he was really looking for, but she took care of the household until the death of his first wife who had been ill for many years. After that the industrialist married a second, younger woman who was as hospitable as one's own mother.

After all these travels in 1948, I went back to London and continued working on my research. Since we made good progress, my Professor, E.C. Dodds, was very satisfied and often granted me leaves of absence to continue my reconciliation projects. He knew that the British authorities considered this task to be important and he did not make any difficulties for me.

During the spring of 1949, I received an invitation from the German branch of "Youth for Christ" to Frankfurt/Main to give some lectures for young people and also to speak in a student seminar organized by the SMD (Students' Mission, Germany). Well, I was very familiar with the student work, because in 1946 I had helped with the founding of the SMD. Fritz Laubach was studying theology at that time in Marburg. He invited me to Marburg where I was allowed to preach the Gospel to the students from the desk of Professor Rudolf Bultmann. Günter Dulon, Fred Runki and Uli Weber from

Wuppertal were also most actively involved in the Christian students' work in Marburg at that time, together with the engaged couple Zittelmann and Schwöbel. As an SMD team, we evangelized in Ehringshausen where a revival was taking place among the farmers. The farmers, their wives and children sang the praises of the Lord in the fields during the hay harvest. The joyful hymns could be heard everywhere until dark.

I still remember how the SMD students at that time were upset with me, because I was of the opinion that one should not evangelize in a farm village during harvest time—it was not realistic to expect farmers to show up at the evangelization hall while the fields were being harvested and the farmers with their families had to work hard for long hours. The SMD students at that time were of the opinion that the Bible was calling upon them to preach at any time, at convenient and inconvenient times, the unfathomable riches of Christ. When I realized that I was dampening their spirit, I agreed and helped them. Many still remember it today—the spiritual awakening in Ehringshausen!

I am actually a founder member of the SMD. For many years, I served the SMD-Circle Marburg regularly together with other lecturers. In the course of this work I was quite frequently invited to Frankfurt/Main—the first time being in the winter of 1946. There I rode in an open American truck in icy cold (-20°C) from Fritzlar, where I had held lectures to Americans, to Frankfurt. I was dropped off at the train station, and the truck drove away without waiting to see whether any trains were running. There were no trains along the Rhine in the direction of Cologne until the morning hours. Everything was hopelessly overcrowded, there were no hotels and I had no pass from the Americans that would have allowed me to get allied military lodging. Thus, I stood with hundreds of other people the entire night at -20°C next to a steam locomotive to get a little bit of warmth. It was the longest and also the coldest night of my life. By morning, I had a severe attack of angina pectoris and no medication with me to alleviate the attack.

In 1949, I received the previously mentioned invitation from the German branch of "Youth for Christ" to speak in Frankfurt. In Frankfurt, the American and the German branch of "Youth for Christ" worked harmoniously together.

At the same time, I was asked by the SMD (students mission) to hold a three day series of lectures on "The Bible and Science" for students. The hall that was offered to us was the hall of the Nordost Gemeinde (Northeast Church) in Frankfurt. Its members were in the process of rebuilding the bombed church building. They personally took care of this work: hammering bricks, removing rubble, etc. They carried out everything on their own and without any paid workers, as often was the case at that time. The result naturally was a beautiful and lively congregation—although the church hall still left much to be desired.

Every evening the auditorium in the Nordost Gemeinde was full to bursting with young people from all walks of life. I spoke about scientific aspects of the Genesis account on the first pages of the Old Testament and showed that there were no contradictions with the natural sciences. Then, every evening, we had the evangelistic application of the truths we had previously discussed.

I realized during these lectures that every evening three pretty young ladies, sisters, sat in one of the front rows. They paid close attention to what I explained and showed no tendencies to fall asleep while listening. I often selected lesser known texts from books of the Bible which most superficial readers of the Bible would not find—books such as Nahum, Obadiah, Haggai and Ezra.

Well, if one stands in front at the pulpit, asking listeners to read such a text out loud, one finds out rather quickly who reads their Bible seriously. My observation in that regard quickly indicated to me that clearly these young ladies knew the Bible extraordinarily well! It turned out that they were not only pretty, educated and feminine young ladies, but apparently also devout Christians. In the course of the evening, I found out that they were the daughters of the pastor of the congregation.

I was already over thirty years old and still a bachelor. My mother was very worried about me, because she was of the opinion that I would become "peculiar," if I remained a bachelor much longer. I had attained the "critical age," in her opinion, a long time ago. She was convinced that it was no good for a man (or a woman) to remain alone. It is, she thought, important that one not only love, care and tend to the other, but that one also educate the other and to reprimand the other when necessary. My answer to my dear mother was always the same: it is better to not get married if one has not been able to find the woman without whom one cannot live. She was of the opinion that I should try harder.

A young man has to master a difficult task if he wants to make progress in this regard. First, he must find out the name of the young lady who is of interest to him—no easy task if one is somewhat clumsy and if one does not want to get embarrassed. In the higher circles of society, it was not the custom at that time to do as in the USA: "dating" a young lady was simply unthinkable. The young lady was only invited home to the family. When dating, a young man often invites a young lady to some restaurant or other entertainment. There they converse and see whether they are compatible.

Such a "forward" method was never to be chosen by me, it was too much like horse trading. Furthermore, a girl can much easier play-act than a man. The atmosphere of a restaurant or an entertainment hall is artificial and real life is not like that. In a restaurant you are being served, which is rare in life. In life you have to serve yourself. In the restaurant or on any other pleasure-outing one is well dressed, manners are fine-tuned and one makes every effort to make a good impression.

In life these conditions are usually not found. I wanted to see a possible future partner in life, not in a restaurant under artificial conditions! I wanted to see how she gets along with her mother, with her father and her sisters. In the family you can see whether he (or she) really lives and acts according to the example of what one professes to believe in one's heart. The family is the real foundation, not just for social life, but for the life of faith. Politicians who issue anti-family decrees are enemies of the Christian faith.

Well, I was invited into the home of the pastor of the said family in Frankfurt/Main. All three daughters were not only pretty young ladies, they were also Christians with an apparently genuine and heartfelt relationship with their father and mother—and the maid. What I saw there with regard to family life really impressed me. However, as a somewhat experienced scientist and Christian, I could not simply let myself be swept off my feet by a young pretty lady while on a trip to a foreign country. It seemed wiser to wait before deciding whether the matter should be further pursued. I prayed a lot at that time about this situation and came to the following conclusion: During this visit I would not say anything and not show my inclination at all. If, however, God would direct that I was to be invited once more to Frankfurt, then I would know that this meeting was a sign of God's providence.

This decision was not at all easy to make, because one of the daughters of the Gottwaldt family—this was the name of the pastor's family—was already engaged, and this was easily understood. The one already engaged was the youngest daughter. I thought the daughter who interested me the most was the youngest. In that regard, I erred, because the one who interested me was actually the middle daughter, and her name was Beate.

Thus, I went back to England to my laboratory and continued my work there in London. In the course of the summer I suddenly, out of the blue, received a letter from Youth for Christ in Frankfurt. I was asked whether I could come to Frankfurt again soon and lecture, because the youth of Frankfurt were very receptive to my type of message. I wrote back, telling them that I could come during my vacation time, and that the only condition would be that someone would provide lodging. The answer came back: lodging had been found for me, but they did not say where.

When I arrived in Frankfurt in late summer I was taken right away to my place of lodging. I had really been wondering where that would be. Wonder beyond all wonders, it was the study of dear Pastor Gottwaldt! I was told that there was unfortunately no other room to be had in all of Frankfurt. Hotels and homes had been destroyed by bombing and thus rooms were very scarce and rationed. The housing office permitted pastors an extra room for counseling and study, otherwise not even this pastor's family would have had the possibility of hosting a guest. Thus, I moved in exactly where I wanted to be: into the nest itself, so to speak.

After the evening services, we often talked in the family, sometimes until very late at night. We conversed about prophecy, about progress in cancer research, about freemasonry and the chances of avoiding a new war. At that time the political relationship with Russia was often very tense. The situation in Berlin and the events that led to the Berlin Airlift were all burning issues. We spoke about modern science and its relationship to the Old Testament and its teachings for us in today's world. In the course of the week, we got to know each other quite well in that family.

Everything I saw confirmed my deep conviction that I should ask Beate for her hand. The big difficulty consisted of the fact that this lady was so shy and unobtrusive that I had not the slightest idea whether she would accept my hand. It is quite acceptable to fall in love with a pretty girl, but it is quite a difficult situation if one does not know at all whether this feeling might be mutual. As far as I was concerned, everything was clear that I should ask her; but whether it was also as clear from her point of view and her family's remained a great question. She did not give me the slightest point of reference. During my days there I never progressed beyond "Good morning, Miss Gottwaldt" and "are you very busy today." She always had lectures to attend at the Institute for Church Music where she was studying Music, or she had just organized an organ somewhere to give her a chance to practice. Most instruments had been destroyed during the war, thus the study of the organ and practicing on this instrument was difficult. She simply was always gone. But in the evenings she always came to my lectures. She was also always there for the discussions. She always helped her dear mother diligently. She showed evidence of a fine sense of humor too, but to be alone with her, or even to talk to her alone proved impossible. Here I remained completely without success.

One evening as we sat together with the family discussing some topic, I was in the process of conversing with the Pastor who had posed some question. In the middle of our conversation I found myself deeply involved in providing some proof, when, for some reason I suddenly looked in her direction as she sat there between her sisters. And I caught her, as she was in the process of searchingly looking at me. For a fraction of a second our eyes met. I still remember the meeting of our eyes today as if it had been yesterday. In this look it seemed to me that I had discovered more than just simple interest. But I could not be sure, I never had talked to her personally after all. However, I relied on this one meeting of eyes alone, which had lasted for a fraction of a second, and which was completely spontaneous.

The last evening in Frankfurt was upon us. The next day I was to depart for Hof on the border of the Russian zone. But I still had not been able to achieve any communication with

Beate. I could not get in a private word with her. We sat together until 11:00 p.m. in the family. The location of the conversation was obviously in the pastor's study, that is, I could not go to bed until the study was cleared out. First, the daughters and their mother bid farewell. The last one to go to bed was the pastor himself, who always made sure that I had everything I needed. Thus, we were alone together for a few moments in the study. When he rose to say "good night," I told him that I would very much like to address a question to him. He seemed very surprised, came back to the room and looked at me in a genuinely questioning way. What kind of question could this well be? I was very embarrassed, one has to keep in mind that I was groping in the complete dark. I did not even know whether Beate was still available. Thus, I said that it concerned his daughter Beate. I was trying to be simply sober and objective, but it was still very embarrassing. In what regard, he said helplessly as fathers often are helpless. "Well," I said, even more embarrassed than before (and that was already maximum embarrassment), "would you be opposed if I were to ask Beate for her hand?"

Now, the good father protecting his beloved daughter appeared. "Well," he said, "do you have any understanding with Beate, have you talked with her about it?" "No," I said, "I could never find the opportunity to exchange two words with her privately and alone. She is so shy after all." Then I added with the urgency of desperation that I did not even know whether she was still available or whether she was already engaged. Since she was so shy, I wanted to ask him, the father, first, because I would not want to hurt her in any way. No, the father said, he knew nothing, he did not know of any kind of relationship as far as Beate was concerned. He really knew nothing, he added thoughtfully. Then he rose as if completely lost in his thoughts. After a few moments, he said: "I will ask her and tomorrow morning I will give you your answer." He said a very friendly good bye and disappeared.

You can imagine that I did not sleep very much that night. But others in the house could not sleep much either, because the father immediately discussed the situation with his wife and the next morning both parents went to their daughter and talked about it. Beate, the main one involved, said she would want to think about the situation very carefully. The youngest daughter, who was engaged already and who was always quite sharp and mischievous (loving jokes and pranks) said she had always thought that those two would make a couple. The parents then said that Beate would have to think carefully about this, as I was an Englishman. This would bring about a separation from her family. We would probably have to live far away from her loved ones, and she would have to speak another language and integrate into my family. On the plus side of the relationship was that I had an unbroken relationship with the Holy Scripture, something that would play a very important role for the father and the entire family as well. On the other hand, it had to be considered that the entire family was Lutheran whereas I was a devout Open Brother. We would have to discuss all these things by way of the Bible before we could come to any final conclusion.

The previous night, when she still did not know about the question I had posed, Beate had a dream. She rarely has dreams and does not normally pay much attention to them. However, this peculiar dream she was never able to forget. In the dream, she was confronted with many situations in war and peace. In every situation, she was asked in her dream whether she could imagine living together with this Englishman under these circumstances. "Peculiar," she thought when she awoke from the dream, "how can you have such a dream?"

After the loving description of the preliminary details of our engagement by my husband, I (Beate) would like to add just a few words from my side. At that time I was just twenty-one years old. According to the Holy Scripture, my education, and the example of my parents, it was clear to me that I would never marry a non-believer. Conscientiously, I thus far had not engaged in close friendships with young men, because my dear mother had provided us daughters with very good advice which I would like to pass on to every young girl, since, after over forty years of observations, it has proven to be true. This advice from my mother was: "Every little game of love takes away part of the large and genuine love. Therefore wait and save your heart for the one, the one man designated by God for you!" Day in and day out we saw with our own eyes how happily our parents lived together joyfully and unified, and how they loved each other with all their hearts until the very end. They both had followed the same advice in their youth, and they passed it on to us.

I am convinced that, among the many other factors for the innumerable family catastrophes today, an important one is, that, by going through numerous love relationships before marriage, a person is often no longer capable of one great love which will keep them together "for better or for worse" and thus for growth within.

At that time Beate, at twenty-one years, had said that she was so happy with Lady Music that she repeatedly declared to others: "I shall never marry! I shall marry my violoncello!"

And now this charming Englishmen, who was a devout Christian and a gentleman as well, appeared in our house. Should my love not belong exclusively to music after all? I drew back. And then came the dream and directly thereafter the completely unexpected question. Suddenly, it became clear to me that God in his Grace had spoken to me through this dream and wanted to prepare me.

The next morning we had to discuss many things. Beate gave me her answer, her yes. For many years, she has now been my wife and constant companion on all of my many wanderings across many different continents. Never did I do a better day's worth of work than on that evening when I dared to ask her father for her hand without knowing whether she even was available or whether she would take me. I did the best work of my life and it was the best chance I took since becoming a Christian. I learned for once and for all the truth that is the base for the famous English saying: "Faint heart never won fair lady!"

I was able to postpone the trip I had planned to Hof a little without causing complications. This I did, in order to have time to discuss many things and to allow us to get to know each other on a purely personal basis. Then I had to depart. From Kreiensen, as I was waiting for a train connection, I wrote the first letter to my fiancée. On my birthday, December 22, 1949, we publicly got engaged. Since my conversion to Christ as a student, I had never taken a more important and happier step in my life.

IMPORTANT DECISIONS

Now, it seemed to become quite clear that my calling would lead me to the European continent or at least that the first steps would take place on the continent. Thus, we decided to first visit my parents on the farm in England. My younger brother Walter was already married and had three children. My good mother and my dear father would want to get acquainted with my chosen one. My father and mother both were already elderly and wanted to see me settled somewhere.

When my fiancée and I stood in front of the familiar gates of the farm, my dear old mother met us with extended arms and bid us welcome. She immediately took my fiancée to her heart (who wouldn't) and right away was motherly and considerately caring for her. My father, who was always cool (in spite of his red-blonde mustache that now was gray) inspected the newcomer to the family from a distance. He was not unfriendly, rather neutral, until he was sure of having formed his own opinion. He decidedly did not love the Germans, but was always ready to make exceptions. He thus welcomed Beate politely. He always called her Beat-tie. Right away he found out that she was a devout Christian—he always surmised that the young lady who would become my wife would obviously have to be a Christian—he knew that.

He observed Beate very carefully, saw how she quietly gave mother a hand. No work was too much to her. She had good manners. She helped mother with darning, doing dishes, vacuuming, she conversed quietly and unobtrusively with him, spoke to him about his interests, had no problems with the language. She played the piano beautifully and knew British history. All this he noted. My father was a man in the best sense of the word, that is, he had a distinguished sense for ladies. He very well knew how a beautiful, pretty and educated woman should behave. He did not like "men-women" and "emancipated" women at all; he detested such "species." A feminine, pretty lady—those he eventually always appreciated with time. But even those had to win my old father over first. In the course of a few weeks, the slow "melting" of the ice started with father. Who could resist Beate's warmth for any length of time?

We knew that "thawing weather" had started because of what was actually a small event. Every morning shortly before 7:00 a.m. Father received his cup of black tea at his bed side. He drank a lot of black tea, but the most important cup was the one at 7:00 in the morning in bed. This tea had to be brewed exactly according to instructions, otherwise it did not taste right to my father. The teapot had to be thoroughly preheated with boiling hot water. Then the pot had to dry on the inside—the boiling hot water was emptied and the pot dried by itself. Then one put as many spoons of tea as one wanted to have cups of tea into the teapot, plus an extra tea spoon (one for the pot) for the pot itself. Then half a cup of boiling water was poured onto the tea. The mixture steeped for three minutes. Then water just coming to a boil again was added, depending on how many cups of tea were to be poured. Two more minutes of waiting, and only then the tea was served. It was a genuine ritual that had to be observed. However, the ritual only works where the water actually boils at 100°C. In the mountains, where water comes to a boil below 100°C (due to the altitude), everything fails!

Well, my dear mother showed my fiancée all these important secrets and she quickly became a tea expert. One morning she brought my good father his tea to the bedside at 7:00 a.m. He looked somewhat suspiciously into the new day, but out of politeness tasted the offered cup. A smile lit up his entire face, and then he proceeded to say with full conviction "That's a good cup, my dear." The ice had melted for good and my Beate had completely won over even the "crusty old man." From then on, she was always "my dear," when he talked to her. But who could resist her tender, but reasonable, ways!? When such a thawing occurred with father, then it had to happen with everybody, because father was, so to speak the tough nut (in the good sense of the word) to crack. When he no longer provided resistance, who could?

At this time, I received an invitation from a wealthy Swiss industrialist to move to Switzerland to help him with research in his company. He offered us a chalet with a nice apartment into which we were to move after our wedding. My fiancée and I visited the industrialist in Switzerland to clarify the plans. However, I wanted to continue my lecturing activities in addition to my research. Since the industrialist was a devout Christian, he fully understood. He even hoped that I would be helping his little congregation, because it was quite stodgy and in need of some fresh air.

We agreed with him that we would take the unfurnished apartment in the chalet for a nominal rent of 100 Swiss francs (Sfrs.) per month. I would be receiving about one third of the normal salary for two thirds of the normal working time—that is I would be working twenty days a month and ten days would then be at my free disposal for evangelistic work. Thus I would be receiving approximately 400 Sfrs. (minus rent of 100 Sfrs.). However, for any useful inventions and discoveries that could be exploited by his company, I would receive an appropriate licensing fee. We were of the opinion that we could do without some of the salary, since, at a later time, when the research was successful, we would have an independent income available. This thinking—to do without something in order to provide for future freedom—proved to be a success. Within a few years, I was independent enough to take a position as instructor at the University of Geneva. However, at the beginning, from a financial point of view, it was very difficult for my wife and me, because we had to buy everything a young couple needs. It was also our principle not to take on any debt. Thus, we only bought whatever we could pay for by cash. The industrialist often offered us a loan, but we rejected it. The first months of our marriage, we slept on a simple couch—not a double couch, but on a very narrow couch that we still have stored in our house in Einigen as a souvenir.

PREPARATIONS FOR THE WEDDING

Now, once again, we have to go a few steps back in order to get the correct overview. The international situation was such at that time that we both were of the opinion that it would be better if both of us were of the same nationality with the same type of passport. My wife could have remained a German citizen; however, the two different passports often caused problems while traveling. The currency restrictions were also quite strict, an often disagreeable fact.

Once the two of us, engaged at that time, traveled to Switzerland and had to go through customs in Basel. I had a British passport, my fiancée was still traveling with her German passport. There was great interest in making sure that the new D-Mark (this was immediately after the currency reform) did not get into Switzerland. Well, as an Englishman, I was subject to a different customs inspection and Beate, as a German, had to go through another. We intended to meet on the other side of the inspections again. But she did not appear.

I went to the customs officer and asked what was the matter. I was angered about this chicanery, because it really was nothing other than chicanery.

The reason was easily explained. Beate had given me her billfold after we got off the train, because I wanted to have all the money with me—the rules for us English were easier than the more restrictive ones in effect for Germans. On the top of the train station an observation post was established from where all passengers could be observed unknown to them. The officer had seen Beate give me her billfold—she did it very openly, which was within her rights—and thought that we wanted to smuggle something out of Germany. As I was an Englishman, he was not allowed to search me, which is why they checked her as she went through the inspection by herself. She was checked out to the skin and they repeatedly told her as the last pieces of clothing were taken away that she still could confess what she wanted to smuggle without punishment. They were very surprised since they, as a matter of fact, did not find a thing.

I proceeded to do a bit more with the responsible official than just tending to his soul and asked him whether he had ever heard of psychology. I told him that one should first clearly look at the victims of such chicanery. It was quite obvious that a person with such a face would never do anything that was not right or something criminal. He saw that I received the billfold, why did he not check me? The answer was that he was afraid to take a risk; he had seen my blue passport and had also seen that my fiancée had a green one— he could take out his frustrations on her without taking any personal risks. Unfortunately, one does quite often find this attitude with officials—taking advantage of those falsely considered meek. For this and other reasons, we decided in favor of a common nationality, a common right of citizenship.

CONSIDERATIONS REGARDING FAITH

When my friends from the Open Brethren heard that I was going to marry a Lutheran lady, most of them emphatically shook their heads. Not only that: When the Lutherans heard that the daughter of a Lutheran pastor wanted to marry an Open Brother, that is a member of a Free Church, they also had plenty to talk about for a while. We would never achieve the inner union which is a "conditio sine qua non" for a Christian marriage. As always in such cases, it is important to clarify things before one jumps to a conclusion. First, I was educated in the Anglican State Church, which according to its doctrine is almost Catholic. The Anglican Church practices child baptism and confirmation, similarly to the Lutherans and Catholics. I was thus very familiar with the practices of the State Churches. It was not at all that I was just a "stubborn" Free Church member; subsequent to my conversion, I had often served in State Churches.

Second, my fiancée and her family served in State Churches, as well as in Free Churches. For all of them, as for me, the genuine biblical conversion to Christ was the central issue and not membership in any kind of fellowship of believers. The entire family had always had fellowship with the Open Brethren. Hudson Taylor and George Müller (both Open Brethren) were their examples of the Christian life style. In fact, the later two men were actually the founders of the movement that is known as Open Brethren.

We had to begin with much in common with regard to most areas of our faith. But it was clear that differences due to our different Christian educations would surface sooner or later. Questions with regard to baptism, holy communion, confirmation, the relationship of works and grace certainly would appear. How could they be solved? The conjugal union is a deeply committed relationship. One should be able to attain common consent if one wants to master the stress of life together. One can never force such unanimity, that was clear to us. My wife could not simply say that she was supporting me in all my convictions when in reality she herself was not convinced.

Why do the Open Brethren, as based on the New Testament, not baptize any babies, but only people who evidently have experienced a conversion? Why do they receive at the Communion table exclusively those who are committed devout Christians, having led a corresponding life, or wanting to do so? Why, in general, do Lutherans baptize infants and assert thereby that they become members of the Kingdom of God by means of the baptism of babies? Is this affirmation biblically based? Do the Open Brethren believe in the so-called "Full Inspiration" of the Holy Scripture, something that is rejected by many theologians of the State Churches—and of the Free Churches today as well?

Well, the newly engaged couple had to find a solution in principle for these and many other problems before they dared to launch their ship of marriage. We were striving for a genuine spiritual relationship, which was very important for us. We wanted (and want) to solve everything in our marriage in the sense of the spirit of God, that is according to the word of God. We believed and believe, that the word of God is Spirit ["the words that I speak unto you, they are spirit" says the Son of God (John 6:63)]. If we thus wanted to live in the spirit of harmony in God, we consequently had to arrange everything in our marriage according to the biblical word. "But seek ye first the kingdom of God, and his righteousness; and all these things shall be added unto you" (Matthew 6:33) was the basic principle on which we wanted and still want to base everything for all practical purposes in our marriage. But, how do you do all that in practice?

Beate and I came to the conclusion that a couple like us should best proceed as follows: If questions of doctrine and practice appear, e.g., whether a child should be baptized as a baby or not, we wanted to make the decision for our actions together through the study of the practice and the teachings of the Bible, by means of a good concordance. We wanted to leave old fashioned traditions by the way and try to find out how the apostles acted and thought, and then unanimously act accordingly together. Thus, we often sat together with a *Young's Concordance* (or a *Strong's Concordance* later on) and first tried to find all relevant passages of the Bible. After we had read all the corresponding Bible passages which gave information about the problem in question, we tried to explain by means of the original texts what they have to say. We then prayed about the understanding thus gained, and tried seriously to conduct our marriage accordingly. The practice of the word of God was to characterize our married life.

As a believing pastor, my future father-in-law was very satisfied with this solution, my mother-in-law as well, because they all were a family of this same book and had taken on a lot in their church due to their Bible-oriented attitude. They thus were quite happy about the fact that we had decided to go the biblical way together. Even today, we cannot recommend a better way and council for newly engaged couples. Unanimity in marriage is attained by growth in practice and understanding of the word of God. The First Epistle of John teaches us, that if "we walk in the light (and the word of God is light), we have fellowship one with another." This fellowship is exactly what we have experienced during our entire married life.

Thus, we started to grow together spiritually during the months of engagement. The closer we grew spiritually, the more beautiful our relationship became. We enjoyed each other more and more in a child-like way. During family vacations, we went into the mountains with the parents and took hikes together in the Swiss Alps. A few times we chose the Ticino as a vacationing site and enjoyed the Italian culture of that time and the gondolas on the Lago Maggiore (they no longer exist today). All this can barely be seen anymore in the Ticino—the old Italian culture disappeared relatively quickly. The Italian part of Switzerland literally became a German and Swiss-German colony so that even the Italian language became threatened. Now, Switzerland is doing a lot to preserve the Italian language and culture. When we celebrated our wedding on Beate's 22nd birthday on September 17, 1950 we chose the Ticino (San Nazzaro), on Lago Maggiore, across from Locarno, as a vacation site for the honeymoon.

This brings us to our wedding itself. Beate told me that in the midst of the many wedding preparations with her mother and Martha—their good housekeeper—her mother gave her much good advice regarding our future life together. One of them we want to pass on as it might be helpful to others as well. She said: "Beate, to become really happy in marital life you have to marry twice. The first time you say "yes" to one another because you are so in love that you hardly see any faults in one another. But in your life together you notice that your partner also has faults—just as you have. Then for the second time you should say "yes" with all your heart to one another—accepting one another with all your faults and weaknesses in love before God just as you are."

PART II

BEATE WILDER-SMITH
(NÉE GOTTWALDT)

CHAPTER I

FAMILY AND EARLY LIFE

THE FAMILY

Breslau, the city of my birth, is situated in Silesia, which at that time was in Germany. My mother descended from a family of ministers, teachers and industrial businessmen, which has been traced far back on the family tree.

My father, also a pastor, came from a very musical home on his mother's side. My grandmother—with Viennese blood in her veins—played the piano well, liked to improvise on it and composed music occasionally. Unfortunately, she died very young and we know of her loving and gracious ways only from tales.

My paternal grandfather came from an industrious family of craftsmen. Finances were tight and they had to be very careful in managing their money to make ends meet for their five children. Since his father died very young, much of the responsibility for the family fell on my grandfather, a very responsible son. As a student, he tried to make money on the side whenever he could, in order to help his mother and support the family. With diligence, hard work, and talent he provided himself with a solid background of higher education. Later, he worked at an advanced level of the postal administration. A most characteristic trait of his personality, keenly remembered by my sisters and myself was that he loved to make others happy and he was very inventive in doing so. After his retirement, he lived in our house for many years. He even accompanied us on our vacations several times.

Those he always greatly enlivened with his original ideas and kind generosity.

From my very earliest years, my parents organized music performances and artist evenings, readings by poets and lectures at our large old parsonage. These events greatly enriched and enhanced our youth, which was a difficult era. My sisters Rosemarie and Christiane and I grew up during the Hitler regime and World War II with all its associated stresses and terrors, and our safe and happy family life was a paradise in the midst of hell, where we were able to find strength and encouragement for everyday life.

KRASCHNITZ AND THE HOME FOR
MENTALLY HANDICAPPED

My very first memories go back to the time (1933—1937) when my father was director of a training school for Christian social workers in Kraschnitz, Silesia. The social workers were trained according to the principles of the Bible for service in churches, in hospitals and with the chronically ill. Many of them later worked in a Christian institution in Kraschnitz. This home for 700 mentally ill and 700 mentally handicapped patients was founded by a devout nobleman, Count von der Recke. Here the mentally disabled were taken care of with exemplary Christian love.

The common present-day assertion that the life of such handicapped individuals is not worth living just is not true. Many handicapped people live a happy, fulfilled life in their limitations and we can learn a lot from it. Suffering and illness—whichever kind they might be—are sent from God and we should help alleviate them whenever we are in the position to do so. Sometimes suffering is sent to us for the developing of our character and spiritual growth.

My father and my mother sometimes visited the handicapped in their free time. We were often allowed to accompany them. I remember especially the visit to a young man, about thirty years old, who lay in a nicely prepared wicker bed. He had neither arms nor legs—or only very crippled ones—and he was only able to lie. But many visitors loved to visit him, because of his radiant personality and firm faith which made him joyful and content even in his difficult situation. The male nurses loved him and many a "healthy person" came to him for encouragement.

More details from this time of my life are described in my little booklet *The Day Nazi Germany Died*. There I also recount the sad happenings under the Hitler Regime.

STEALING AND ITS CONSEQUENCES

Our family lived in one part of the training school. My younger sister Christiane and I—we were at the time about six and seven years old—sat on the lawn in front of the stately building and discussed what we should play. Our older sister was still in the house doing her homework. It was fall, and the grapes on the house were ready to be harvested. Although the grapes were growing on our side of the house, they belonged to the training school and not to us. We owned our own large and beautiful garden with flowers, fruit trees and a swimming pool—but no grapes. "Actually the grapes on our side of the house should belong to us and not to the Lachmanns," one of us began the conversation. "I agree, I think we could taste a few of them in good conscience," the other responded, although our conscience bothered both of us mightily. We knew very well that it was a sin to take the fruit of others. Not far away from us stood a tin bucket, which we sometimes used when playing. We carefully looked around, as we did not want to get caught and quickly, with trembling hands, we picked two or three nice bunches of grapes. Suddenly, we heard the door to the verandah click open. With lightning speed the grapes disappeared underneath the bucket and we sat on top in order to be completely safe. Our older sister

Rosemarie had finished her homework. Happily she ran towards us to join us playing. With innocent faces, we greeted her from our perch. Suddenly she stopped, staring at our bucket she said: "Where did you get those grapes?" In our haste, we had not managed to completely hide the grapes under the bucket and a few were peeking out from one side of the bucket. Stunned silence. My older sister had a very tender and sensitive conscience. She guessed what had happened: "Come, let's go and see Mother." Greatly embarrassed, we followed. And there, with our mother, everything came to light. There were no valid excuses. It was clearly established what we already knew very well deep down inside. We had committed a sin, we had stolen.

Our mother did the only right thing in such a situation. She took us two penitent children by the hand and went to the housemother of the training school, Mrs. Lachmann, to whom we confessed our deed and whom we asked for forgiveness. How much better we felt! But then, something truly humiliating happened: The good housemother handed us a whole bowl full of the most beautiful grapes, gave us a friendly handshake and said: "If you ever have the desire for grapes again, just come see me." On that day I learned a lesson for life and I have never forgotten it! At bedtime we rectified the entire affair in our prayer to our Creator.

ICE SKATING ON THE VILLAGE POND

One of our favorite winter pleasures in Kraschnitz was skating on a large deep pond outside of town, not far away from the windmill and its industrious plump miller, Mr. Schnecke. What a joy it was to gracefully glide over the mirror-smooth surface with all our girl friends.

Only one part of the pond was strictly forbidden to us by our parents, the part where workers regularly cut ice and where for that reason a gigantic water hole gaped. The huge ice blocks that were cut there all winter long were stored in caves and later sold to businesses, hotels and individuals for the cooling of food and wine cellars as then refrigerators were scarcely used.

Although the ice surface was certainly large enough for extensive skating sports, we were attracted magnetically and irresistibly to the vicinity of the ice cutters and the dangerous open water area. Because of mutual admonitions and reminders of the parental ban, up to now we had been able to resist the temptations of this magnetic field.

As it happens, one winter afternoon, we three sisters and our girl friends and acquaintances went skating again, and we saw a particularly large ice floe swimming far out in the area hacked free of ice. An older neighbor boy we knew jumped with a big leap onto the floe and challenged everybody who might be courageous enough to come out onto the floe and to drift around on the water. One or two "courageous" souls heeded his challenge and jumped onto the ice floe. When he saw us, he also invited us to join the adventure.

We discussed this together and then we went on our skates to the edge of the water and Christiane, my younger sister, jumped with her skates on (in those days all skates were attached to high lacing boots and screwed on with a special key—today's type of skate permanently attached to the boot was practically unknown) onto the ice floe which was floating away from the edge of the hole. It became evident that there were now too many people on the floe as it quickly started to sink while the distance to the edge of the hole also increased. My little sister was probably the youngest on the sinking ice. The other two "courageous" souls just managed, with great effort, the leap back to the icy "terra firma." They were, however, not wearing skates.

A terrible fear seized Rosemarie and me: Will we be able to save Christiane? We had great pangs of conscience. If only we had listened to the admonitions of our parents. If something should happen to Christiane, we would never be able to look our parents in the eye again. We felt miserable and terrible. Rosemarie suddenly saw a long stick lying on the ice. She grabbed it and reached the other end to Christiane on the sinking ice floe and shouted: "Hang on to this and jump, we'll pull!" Christiane grasped the stick and after a lot of enticement and encouragement she finally dared to leap. With one skate she just reached the solid ice, with the other leg and much of her body she landed in the water, but we all pulled and supported and worked until we got her to safety. She was dripping wet.

However, the danger was not yet over. Dripping wet in an icy wind, she could quickly catch pneumonia. Fortunately, the miller's son, Paul Schnecke, was among the group of friends; he was kind enough to invite us home to the cozy warmth of their tiled stove. There Christiane was able to get warm and dry and the good miller's wife revived us with hot tea.

A few hours later when we got home there were quite a few things that had to be settled with our parents. In our evening prayer we begged our Heavenly Father for forgiveness for our sins and thanked Him for his gracious protection and help in the danger we had caused by our lack of obedience. Our parents had taught us from early childhood to reflect on the day every evening before God, to confess all evil deeds of the day and to ask for the forgiveness of man and God. How easy it was to fall asleep with a clear conscience!

THE PRE-WORLD WAR II YEARS

The years before World War II were hard years of depression and misery. Many people were without jobs and lived in utmost poverty. Rebellion and crime flourished. At that time my father was a Lutheran pastor in one of the poorest workers' quarters in Berlin. The misery of the people around us caused him and my mother many a sleepless night. So they initiated a warm shelter and a soup kitchen where people could find some warmth during the cold winter and food for their ever hungry stomachs. By caring for people's personal needs they soon won their confidence and were able to tell them also about the good news of the Gospel (for further details see my booklet *The Day Nazi Germany Died*).

You can well understand that in 1933, when Hitler promised to provide work and bread for everybody and to build again a strong and respected Germany, he was elected by a great majority of the German people. And he immediately began to fulfill his promises. But, at that time, very few asked about the terrible price that was to be paid that brought about World War II and the Holocaust (see *The Day Nazi German Died*). If people had only read Hitler's book *Mein Kampf,* which was given to every young couple at their wedding. Here Hitler clearly laid out his intentions to set up a world tyranny, to liquidate the Jews and non-Aryans and to achieve rule by the German "Herrenvolk" (master race) over the world.

But most people do not like to ask questions as long as they have enough to eat and are prosperous. Unfortunately, they often have to pay bitterly for this uncritical and egotistical attitude in later life.

I believe that every person once or twice in his life is confronted with a similar decision: Food, a job, a career, prosperity, honor or personal conviction, truth, absolute values, poverty, humiliation, etc., which can lead to great renunciation and sacrifices, even sometimes to the loss of life. There are always only very few who choose the second alternative, though most persons know in the innermost of their heart which is the right decision. And yet, if we chose the right decision—although often painful—our heart is at peace and our conscience untroubled, because we know God stands by us.

GOLLNOW

The greatest part of my early childhood I spent with my two sisters, Rosemarie and Christiane, and our parents in a small Hanseatic town in the eastern part of Germany. The town, Gollnow, lay in the midst of beautiful pine forests and the old historic houses were surrounded by a picturesque city wall with four towers and city gates. Our large old vicarage lay near the impressive Gothic brick church, where Father regularly preached, and the square, cobblestone market place. Our family lived happily together and our parents surrounded us with love. They lived a genuine Christian life and were an example to us. The standard in our family life was the Holy Scriptures, the Bible, according to which we tried to regulate our daily life—not legalistically, but in loving obedience towards our Heavenly Father.

World War II broke out in the midst of the harmonious years together. Most of the pastors were called up for military service. As Father suffered from a valvular heart disease, he was not drafted and could stay at home. But besides his own churches in Gollnow and in the surrounding villages, he had to look after a number of other churches of pastors who had to fight in the war.

As there were no cars—all private cars were requisitioned by the army—he had to travel to the various churches by horse and coach or by sleigh in winter, driven by his faithful "Herr Grund." Mother usually rode with him, as she was the organist in the various village churches, with their old mechanical pipe organs. In winter, they were dressed in heavy fur coats and caps and wrapped up in warm blankets. If the Pomeranian winter blew too cold over the country, foot warmer and hot chestnut bags (horse-chestnuts warmed in a little compartment of the tiled stove were put into linen bags and used for warming) were a great comfort. When we children were younger, we usually stayed at home with our nanny, especially in winter when the thermometer sank considerably below zero centigrade (32°F). When we were a little older, we enjoyed accompanying our parents and treading the old organ bellows—quite a good physical exercise. In winter, it was an enchanted fairy land around us as we glided with the jingling sleigh through the glittering snowy forests.

In the old cozy country churches, which in those times were never heated, we were always greeted by a friendly crowd eager to listen to God's Word. In spite of the Nazis, who were very antagonistic towards real biblical Christians, these faithful people were not to be intimidated and stuck to the Bible and their pastor. Church attendance in these villages was very high, which enraged the Nazi leaders.

MY SCHOOLING: ALL KINDS OF TEACHERS

From the very beginning my parents made a great effort to provide us three daughters—we were all very close in age—with a good, well-rounded education and good skills. Since for many years we had two young ladies to help with the household, my mother could spend quite a bit of time in the education of her daughters in addition to her work as a pastor's wife. She was an excellent counselor to ladies and a loving mother to many lonely people.

Both of our parents were musically gifted. Even before we went to school, they purchased for us a quarter sized violin. Mother taught us the basis of playing the violin and the reading of music using colored notes and colored violin strings. The first years of piano lessons were also provided by our patient mother until we reached that age when it is better that children learn and practice with teachers who are not family. When we came into the teen years, Rosemarie specialized in the piano, Christiane in the violin and I in the violoncello. We formed our own family choir and enjoyed singing classical choir works together, often to my father's masterful accompaniment on the piano or organ. Or we organized folk song evenings. At Christmas, or for birthdays, we often accompanied our father on his visits to the ill or aged and sang chorales and hymns.

At the age of six, I entered public school in Kraschnitz, and at ten the high school (Gymnasium) in Gollnow. Since Gollnow was only a small town of 13,000, it only had a high school for boys, the Barnim-Oberschule. At that time, during the Hitler era, there existed for a short time a law against girls taking the first two years of Latin at school. However, if they learned Latin privately at home and mastered the curriculum and passed the entrance examinations they were allowed to participate again in Latin classes in the later semesters and also to take the Abitur (final examination). Since we all wanted to go to the university, and the complete final examination including Latin was a prerequisite, our father taught us, and several girl friends, Latin at home. Since we were just a small group, we learned faster than the students at school. Later, the restrictive law was rescinded and we were allowed to join the Latin classes with the boys earlier than expected.

In the Sexta-class, our teacher was a remarkable man, whom we loved but also feared. He was very strict but fair, punished hard, but praised whenever it was deserved. He had a unique talent for teaching, although he was the only teacher who was not an academic, as he was trained at a teacher training college instead of the university. He taught German, mathematics, biology and religion. Grammar and oral math taught by him was unforgettable for the rest of one's life. I was often grateful to him later on in life. As a human being he was disciplined, selfless, always helpful to his students, although some of the pupils feared him for his severe punishments he meted out if his high standards of motivation were not met. He was a Christian, which he courageously professed even during the Hitler era, although it earned him many reproaches.

In summer, every student had to bring a complete plant including roots to botany class. We then proceeded to identify and classify it according to its flowers, leaves and roots. It almost never happened that Mr. Gehrke could not identify our plant although we all made efforts to present the rarest of species. Thus, we devised a plan to embarrass him. With a lot of effort and skill we assembled a plant whose flowers, leaves and roots each came from a different plant, but which still looked very genuine. Mr. Gehrke took this rare piece into his hand and inspected it from all sides; from the top, from the bottom, took off his glasses in order to see better and finally shook his head perplexed. "This plant is new to me, it furthermore does not seem to fit into any classification clearly. Before I can tell you its name, I will have to look it up in my book." We all grinned. He did not feel quite comfortable about the whole thing, but he did not say anything more and took the plant home. At the next class he arrived laughing: "You played a good trick on me with your unknown plant! The artistry was so perfect that I did not notice the hoax until I got it home."

In his religion classes he made us love the Bible and its truths. He repeatedly recommended warmly to us to faithfully attend children's Sunday School Services, since they would provide us with a foundation for life.

Once we had mastered the given curriculum for a semester, he revised and reviewed with us until even the last of us knew all the rules of grammar and punctuation, the large and small multiplication tables, the mathematical theorems and operations, by heart (even in our sleep), and then, as a reward during the last hours before vacations, Mr. Gehrke read us stories from a yellow book called *Spies*. These were the thrilling biographies of great spies from various countries which were enormously captivating to us ten- or eleven-year-olds. We looked forward to it for weeks ahead of time and worked hard to finish the curriculum in time. I was so enthralled by these spy stories that for years I cherished the desire to someday also become a great spy.

However, we also had other teachers at our school; a teacher of history and German, a dedicated and spineless Nazi who spied on his students' conversations and essays. He inquired about parents political opinions and denounced them; he betrayed Jews and half-Jews in our town—some of whom then disappeared. None of the students cared for him, as he was a moody and a bad teacher who mocked everything that was holy. He caused my sensitive older sister much distress.

Furthermore, we had a teacher, Fräulein Dr. F., at our Gymnasium, who moved there from Stettin and who was a unique character. She introduced herself to my parents with these words: "I am Fräulein Dr. F.—Doctor, please, because I have sacrificed a great deal of time and money in order to receive my doctorate. I teach German, English and French. I play the piano (which she did excellently), recite and dance solo! Well, and what else could you wish for?" She lived with her elderly father for whom the not exactly uncomplicated and very self-assured lady cared with love and devotion.

Our music education was provided by a very capable music director and conductor who introduced us early to the fundamentals and rules of harmony, music history and choral singing. Music was his life. When he discovered my sisters' and my own interest and talent for music, he took a lot of time and made great efforts to further our education. We continued our piano lessons with him. He provided for me a three-quarter cello (I don't know where he found it during these times of war where nothing was available) and taught me to play it. In addition, he put together a recorder quartet consisting of us three Gottwaldt-sisters and a musically gifted friend. In our little town, he thus organized many varied classical music evenings, either vocal or instrumental—often together with the school choir and sometimes accompanied by his orchestra.

Our musical education was later completed by two competent musicians from Stettin; the pianist, Suske-Fromm, and the cellist, O. Philipp. These two artists used to travel to our home by train from Stettin once a month to instruct us children. Stettin was often attacked at day and nighttime by British, American, and Russian bombers and the artists enjoyed traveling to Gollnow to be out of danger for at least a few hours during the month. After the music lessons in our home, the artists sometimes played together with my father. This was always the greatest musical delight for the family.

Later, I became a student of the Frankfurt concert cellist Ilse Bernatz.

One elderly German, French and English teacher in Gollnow changed personality during the last years of the Hitler era to the extent that she reproached her students in her German classes every time they used expressions such as "mercy," "charity" or "pity": "Our people must be hard, proud and victorious. Thus, these words have to be eradicated from the German vocabulary and may no longer be used."

CHAPTER II

THE WAR YEARS

POTATO HARVEST SERVICE DURING THE WAR

She was the same teacher who was sent along with us girls from two grades as a supervisor to a large country estate in Pomerania for the potato harvest service during the war. Since all male workers on the estate were drafted as soldiers for the war, schools were employed for the harvest. On that farm our teacher lived in a small room that she could only reach by passing through our room (three friends and I), because there was no direct entrance from the hallway. Since she often infuriated us during the day, standing stiffly on the field without lifting a finger herself, yet constantly shouting at us working girls: "Beate, there is still a potato left on the ground; Gerda, look back, there is still a small potato behind you, you haven't picked it up; Ute, hurry up; Ursula, quickly bend over again, you missed one again!" we were waiting for a chance of sweet revenge.

Over and over again, field mice charged fearfully out of their holes in order to escape the harvesting machine. We had not failed to note that the "Spider" (our nick name for this teacher) did not seem to be particularly fond of these four-legged animals, that they actually gave her the shivers. When one day one such mouse got caught by the potato harvester and killed, we secretly picked it up, put it into a bag and took it home in the evening.

As usual, "Spider" talked for one to two hours with the estate administrators before she retired to her room. We used that time to hide the dead mouse in her bed. The four of us then went to bed and turned the light out. When she tiptoed through our room, we were obviously all very much "asleep." We all waited for a scream as soon as she went to bed. Not a sound! After about 10 minutes the door opened, we heard some scratching with a wooden coat hanger and then in one swoop a mouse flew into our room and... the door snapped shut. Neither she, nor we, ever exchanged a word with regard to this mouse matter. We were very much disappointed that our joke did not have a stronger frightening effect.

The estate to which we were sent to help in the potato harvesting was very large. Eastern Germany—East and West Prussia and Pomerania—consisted of huge land estates often belonging to the old German aristocracy. A number of Russian and Polish prisoners of war were allotted to big estates, by the German authorities, for agricultural work to replace the German farm laborers sent to fight in the war. So, the prisoners of war from Eastern countries worked side-by-side with us girls in the fields.

The young Poles were quite temperamental and often fought one another. They kept to themselves and we had little contact with them.

Quite different were the Russians. They sometimes helped us to lift and empty the heavy baskets full of potatoes into the trucks. They started to communicate with us in broken German, which they had picked up as war prisoners and told us a little about their life. One, Nikita was his name, had been a mail man in Sibiria. Another, Gruglow, told us about the beauty of the Ukraine for which he was so homesick.

I also remember vividly the little slender witty fellow who was extremely good at imitating musical instruments with his mouth. He explained that in the village band in his little home village he had the job of replacing the instruments of absent musicians by imitating them with his mouth. We were impressed.

Of course, we German girls were not really allowed to speak to prisoners of war. A German girl had to be proud! And a German girl should not communicate with the war enemy! The war prisoners lived in barracks behind barbed wire when not working in the fields.

One day the Russians secretly invited us to visit them in their barracks in the evening after work. Of course, the estate inspector was not supposed to know of this invitation, because it was strictly illegal. But that made the whole affair more attractive to us.

After work and after supper, we five or six girls sneaked through the barbed wire entrance into the primitive prisoners of war barrack. The Russians gladly welcomed us and then sang Russian folk songs and played some lively music on their few instruments. What really intrigued us was their dancing, the cossack dances, in squatting position, kicking out their legs straight, growing faster and faster and more intense all the time. It was dark outside, nobody on the farm knew where we were. The Russians who had been away from home a long time behaved perfectly correct and we thoroughly enjoyed the evening. Maybe they saw us rather as allies—because we worked together at the same job—than enemies?

Later, our school class was again ordered to help at another big estate in Eastern Germany with the potato harvesting. Here not only male Russian prisoners of war were put to work but also women, some of them with children. They helped in the fields, in the farms and also in the moonshine distilleries (brandy). The "schnaps" was produced from potatoes. The Russian women used to secretly approach us and beg for food, as their rations were minimal. My sister, Christiane, and I once or twice—when we did not feel watched—gave them some of our sandwiches which we had brought from home.

One young Russian girl—Dunja—had a small baby wrapped in newspaper for want of clothing. She had been working in the fields with a German farmer's family. The farmer's son had misused her. On account of her being pregnant, she was sent away and put to work on this big estate where she gave birth to her baby. She begged me to give her the big apron which my mother had sewn for me from a thick old mattress cover for the potato harvest—when kneeling in the cold autumn soil. Dunja wanted my apron to wrap around her baby. "Dunja, you can have my apron next week when I come back from our weekend at home. But, first I must ask my mother's permission." We went home that weekend by train. But they told us we need not come back to the same estate next week because the harvesting was nearly over. So, I was not able to return and poor Dunja never got her much needed apron for the baby! How tragic! If only I had given her the apron right away! Of course, my mother would have agreed, even encouraged me to give her the apron. But I was too timid and hesitant to react spontaneously. This wrong decision plagued my conscience over years and even now I feel bad about it.

Another time we were assigned to various farms for the potato harvest. I remember the night trip from the train depot to the farming village by horse drawn wagon. There were probably five or six of us fourteen year old high schoolers and we were picked up by two affable young lads. I had to sit right next to one of them. It was a long road leading mainly through forests and the night was pitch black. Suddenly, the boy started to make advances and put his arm around me. I objected and to defend myself I took a swing with my elbow and with a fervent prayer in my heart gave him such a good hit between the ribs that he stumbled backward and cried: "Oh, now I can see the stars twinkle." From then on, he behaved. It must certainly have been all the prayers of our parents around us that protected us from many things.

In Hermelsdorf, I was assigned to a farmer who drove out to the field with me every day. He drove the potato harvester pulled by his old horse, and I, the city girl, gathered the potatoes into baskets and sacks from morning to evening. I really had to hurry in order to keep up with the farmer and his horse. For a while another school girl also helped, but she was taken home by her mother, because she didn't feel well. The two of us slept with the daughter of the house in a room that could not be locked. The boys of the village were very much interested in the young high school girls from the city and in the evenings knocked on our windows or even tried to invade our room; this scared and worried us, since we had been very much sheltered at home and had not the slightest interest in such affairs.

In order to protect ourselves and to lock the door, we tied a strong thick string from the door knob around the broad tiled stove on the corner and wrapped the string three times around the stove. Now we were able to sleep in our room safely. Our worried parents were very much amazed that the farmer people were not more concerned about our well being, but just laughed about our fears.

BILLETEES (COL. TORTORELLA)

During the war years, we had to accept all kinds of people in our large parish house by order of the housing office. Many mothers with children were evacuated from the large cities because of the endless bombing attacks in these areas and were temporarily housed in the East. For instance, a very nice, timid, pale woman lived with us with her two children. She had escaped the bombing nights in Stettin. Her husband was a soldier at the front and she was very anxious about him. The bombing nights had undermined her health, so that she was relieved to have found a sheltered place in our home. She was receptive to the Christian message in our house.

Mother's beautiful antique work-room with all its elegant furniture we surrendered to a lady FLAK (anti-aircraft battalion soldier) assistant. Furthermore, our guest room was occupied by an Italian colonel of the Carabinieri, a very noble, highly educated man, a genuine Roman. Hitler had some of the Italian officer corps and soldiers transported to Germany after 1944 to make sure they did not attack him from the rear and ally themselves with the English and the Americans. Colonel Tortorella was very attached to his family and suffered greatly from being separated from them. He was especially worried about his oldest son who had also been drafted and of whom he had no news. In the evenings, we daughters often stood guard on the street and at the house door while my parents with Colonel Tortorella and his Carabinieri friend, Major Vita, secretly listened to the strictly forbidden English radio station, where the list of Italians taken prisoner were regularly broadcast. How relieved our friend was when he found out that his oldest son was safe as an English prisoner of war. We all thanked God together.

On an almost daily basis, our Italian guest provided us three daughters with Italian instruction while we taught him German. Otherwise, daily communication between him and the family was in French. Since he was a good teacher and a perfect gentleman, we learned quickly, not only the Italian language, but also about customs and manners, and the art and culture of the country. From his spirited orderly, we learned many a good Italian joke. He was a good singer and particularly around Christmas he sang his Italian tunes. Colonel Tortorella and his friend were very devout Catholics with whom we could pray and have spiritual fellowship. After a while, they were like members of the family.

THE TOWER WATCHMAN

Our wealthy old Hanseatic town of Gollnow on the Ina—a tributary of the river Oder—was surrounded by gigantic forests. Since a fire could do irreparable damage, the city traditionally employed a tower guard. He had a small room on the very top of the large church steeple that had windows looking out in all four directions. From there he observed the entire surroundings day and night and if he spotted something of a suspicious nature he would ring a special bell reserved for that—later he had a telephone. We pastor's daughters loved to visit the old tower watchman in his private world. He was virtually separated from the rest of the world and looked at it quite differently, from high up. He knew every house, every tree, every kind of weather, every bird and he provided us with a lot of worldly wisdom. His heart was almost broken when the beautiful old bells were transported away during the war since the metal was needed for the war effort. A church steeple without a full set of bells was an anachronism to him.

CAMILLA MEYER COMES TO TOWN!

Once, however, the withdrawn, quiet watchman had his peace completely disturbed. Something happened that turned our little town upside down: A traveling circus group with the acrobat Camilla Meyer appeared in Gollnow. For days already the large open area outside the city where the itinerants always set up their horse drawn wagons, the circus tents, carrousels, shooting booths and roller coasters, was prepared for the great special presentation. Part of the preparation was also the visit to the tower watchman by a few circus men who entered his imperium by his permission and connected a thin but strong two to three kilometer long rope to one of his tower windows and over the tiled roofs of the innumerable houses all the way to the circus square.

Now the big day was here. Almost the entire town was watching: Most of them came to the crowded circus square; others were just leaning out of the windows. Since our parsonage was right next to the church, we children could observe everything very well. A small group of acrobats, in their midst Camilla Meyer, entered the church and started climbing up the many hundred stairs of the steeple. Suddenly a window way up in the watchman's room opened, two legs appeared and thereafter a tiny female figure to which a few leather straps were attached with a small wheel at the chin. This wheel was put on track on the rope. With élan and gracefully extended arms, Camilla Meyer now flew amidst the loud cheers and the astonishment of all the spectators from the church steeple window through the air across the entire town out to the circus square where she was received by a wildly applauding crowd. For a long time thereafter the "jump from the steeple window across the city" remained the small talk conversation topic of the day.

The circus and gymnastic square outside of town hosted all types of guests, among which many, unfortunately, became subjected to inhumane treatment during the Hitler era. They were gypsies, itinerant knife and scissor sharpeners, beggars and musicians. On that same square there were also the numerous trailers and wagons, tents and menageries of the, at that time, very famous Hoppe Circus. A special attraction of this circus was the advanced school of elegant riding horses.

One day the owner came to visit my father with her sixteen year old son. She very much wanted to send her son to my father's Bible classes and for him to be confirmed at a later time. Because of all the traveling around, the instruction had to be individualized. My father very much enjoyed this son who was quite open to spiritual things and who also studied diligently.

MISSIONARY FESTIVITIES AND MISSION PRINCIPLES

The annual missions meetings, for which we drove into the Silesian and later the Pomeranian villages, were always a special experience, for body, soul and spirit. Father usually was the principle speaker, followed by the testimonies and reports of the various missionaries. The Christians would come from far away with their families on foot, by bicycle, by carriage or horse-drawn wagons to hear about the missionary work in the various parts of the world, for which they regularly prayed and provided financial support. Often the large barns, which in summer were prepared and festively decorated, could hardly hold the enthusiastic crowds. At the same time, there were special events with missionary reports, games and singing for all the young people. How our hearts burned eagerly for the important and often hard work of the loyal missionaries and for the African, Japanese and Chinese Christians who gave testimony of their faith under great sacrifices and sometimes even by giving their lives. It is often claimed today that these people do not need the efforts of missionaries, since they would be much happier and more satisfied with their gods and religions than with the Christian Gospel which was forced upon them as a foreign religion by American and European missionaries. This is simply not true. Many of them are yearning for it, because:

a) Most pagan peoples live in fear and trembling of demons and evil powers, to which they are abandoned to all life long and which they try to appease with ritual sacrifices.

b) All religions, other than Christianity, do not offer a just and legally righteous solution to the problem of sin in man. The Muslim, for instance, hopes that he may pacify Allah and persuade him to overlook his sins. This finally results in a "bakshish-society" where bribery is accepted. If Allah may be manipulated in this manner, he is not just, neither true nor omniscient. He loses the characteristics of a holy, almighty god. In contrast, through the atoning death of Jesus Christ, the sinless son of God, Christianity offers a complete just and legally acceptable solution to the question of sin whereby

God is and remains the just, the holy, the almighty and omniscient loving God.

c) Many non-Christian people in other parts of the world do have an idea of the great invisible Creator God. Most of the people who have the original revelation of a Creator God longingly await the lost message of a saving, merciful God. They thus welcome the Gospel of Christ as the God-given message of salvation (See Korea, Burma, etc., see also Don Richardson, *Eternity in Their Hearts*).

These missionary meetings allowed us to hear of the actual liberation of human beings who were trembling in fear of demons, unable to find salvation for their sins and who yearned for true freedom and now were able to lead a happy redeemed life without fears. This spurred us on even more to fervent prayer and love for these people. In the afternoon, coffee and cake were served at long tables and benches in the garden. I still can see the laundry baskets filled with plum and apple streusel and poppyseed cakes, everything home-baked by the diligent and faithful farmers' wives. I will never forget the spiritual conversations, open questions and the happy fellowship.

We always had many visitors in our home. Villagers who came into town for their shopping often passed by and loved to have a little chat with my mother, seeking some encouragement or wanting some advice for their small and big family problems. Especially in the later years of the war, people full of fear and desperation, as well as some Nazis burdened with guilt, came to seek help, comfort and advice from my parents.

THE WAR MOVES CLOSER

When it was clear that Hitler was losing the war and the Russian army began to invade East Prussia, the first refugees turned up in our area. At that time, Hitler and his followers attempted everything to save the hopeless situation. Boys down to sixteen years and men up to sixty years were called up for military service. Even women had to join the army for certain tasks.

My sister Christiane and myself—then in the middle of high school—were transported eastwards together with other girls and women and ordered to dig infantry and tank trenches against the Russian invasion. Of course, we were not used to this kind of hard labor as schoolgirls of fourteen and fifteen years. (More about our war service in the East can be read in my book *The Day Nazi Germany Died*) At the same time my father lay seriously ill at home with cardiac failure and several times he was near death. It was a hard time for my mother.

We carried out our work with shovel, spade and pick, and were lucky to return home before the Russian invasion reached our home town.

The Russian front rapidly moved towards East Germany. For weeks we had observed the great misery of the refugees arriving from further east in the severe winter, trekking with their horse carts through our town continuously day and night for months.

FLIGHT BEFORE THE RUSSIANS

In the middle of the night of March 4, 1945, the sirens of our town suddenly started wailing. At the same time, we could hear cannon shooting and machine-gun firing. We jumped out of bed, put some clothes on and ran into the streets to learn the latest news. Frightened people with baggage and fully loaded hand wagons, men and women nervously running in circles, crying children and soldiers crowded the streets. "Did you not hear the sirens? It is the signal for everybody to flee. The Russians are at the city gates, hurry, hurry!" a soldier shouted. But we did not really want to flee. The roads were already blocked, only one single bridge across the Oder, the big river, was still usable for escape—all other bridges were either occupied or blown up by the Russians. The order was given that every single civilian had to leave town, because the town was to be defended. All the 13,000 inhabitants streamed out of the town and mixed with the flood of refugees from the surrounding area. Most of the SS soldiers fled in trucks while old regular soldiers and young boys sometimes down to the age of sixteen had to take up the battle positions for fighting the already hopelessly lost war. We realized we also had to leave the town. With my parents and us three daughters were Martha, our faithful housekeeper, and our grandfather. Everybody grabbed one or two suitcases, buckled on his rucksack and off we marched.

After we had struggled a few miles—we advanced only slowly because of the overcrowded roads and the attacks by low-flying aircraft—a retreating SS truck took us aboard on our request. When one of the SS soldiers, who was slightly drunk, learned that my father was a cleric, he tried to shoot him. He suddenly aimed his machine pistol at him, so we threw ourselves between my father and the half-drunk SS soldier while praying fervently for help and deliverance. At this very moment, the low-flying Russian airplanes came diving down and started to attack the crowded road with their machine guns. All trucks, in fact, all traffic—cars, refugees and infantrymen—stopped moving and kept as motionless as possible. We used this unexpected, yet prompt help to call some ordinary soldiers for help. They snatched the dangerous weapon out of the SS-soldier's hand and transported him into the truck driver's cabin. This sudden attack from the air had obviously been an act of God in answer to our prayers to save Father's life. How grateful we were!

During our flight, we experienced God's protection and divine guidance so often that it gave us confidence for each further step (for details see my booklet *The Day Nazi Germany*

Died). God had even provided for an apartment for our family in the midst of a West Germany overcrowded with refugees.

A young Christian—a soldier who was stationed in Gollnow—had visited my father's church services. We had invited him to our home when he had some leave, because he had no relatives in Eastern Germany and needed Christian fellowship as he often felt lonely in the army. His wife and parents lived in Western Germany in the Lüneburger Heide. When the Russians started to invade Germany, one day he told us: "If ever you should have to flee from your home, go to my parents-in-law who own a farm in the Lüneburger Heide. They will help you."

We had no relatives in the West. All our relatives lived in Eastern Germany. So, the only place we could aim for in the West was the home of our soldier friend, the farm of his parents-in-law. We only knew of one another through their son-in-law. During the whole flight my mother prayed that God might prepare these people for our arrival. How could we, strangers—a family of six—impose ourselves on this unknown farming family? Maybe their house was already crowded with refugees. After all every house and family in western Germany had to take in refugees from the east and the area was already flooded with homeless people.

When after many days on the road we reached the little village of Neuenkirchen in the Lüneburger Heide, we consulted amongst ourselves how to proceed. My father and my youngest sister took courage and started out to find our soldier friend's family. The rest of the family stayed at the bombed station. The appearing of six people all at once would have been too overwhelming for the farmer and his wife. When my father and Christiane had found the old straw-thatched, half-timbered farmhouse and approached it, the huge wooden door opened and an elderly kind farmer walked toward them, stretched out his hand to greet them, and inquired: "Are you Pastor Gottwaldt?" Astonished, Father answered in the affirmative. "But how could you know me? We never met before!" "That's right," he said, "but my daughter (our soldier friend's wife) had a strange dream last night. She dreamed that you and your family had to flee from the Russians and were asking us for shelter. So, Frieda prepared her small apartment for you. Everything is ready. Welcome here! My daughter and her baby son have moved to our farm." My father and Christiane could hardly believe their ears and eyes. God had answered my mother's continuous prayer in such a special way to prepare the farmer's family for our arrival.

We stayed in this nice little apartment until the invasion by the British army, which confiscated it and used it for their officers. We had to move into an old church hall, where we camped very primitively for a whole year. We partitioned off our various "rooms" with old school maps, which we found rolled up in a corner under some debris. We had thus divided up the big hall into smaller rooms. As there were no beds, we acquired some rusty bedsteads with straw sacks from an empty, dilapidated prisoner-of-war camp.

To our great delight, Mother found an old piano under the wreckage of the bombed part of this church building. We all set to work excavating this precious find and cleaning it thoroughly. It needed a lot of repair; many of the strings were broken and some of the keys were damaged. My mother was not only a good organist, but also an excellent mechanic. So, by talent and diligence, as well as know-how, she repaired this old war invalid into a functioning piano which we used for a long time—for social music evenings, which we organized for refugees and villagers to help them get through these difficult times.

THE BRITISH ARE COMING

Not long after our arrival in Neuenkirchen, the Western Allied Forces moved nearer and nearer every day.

One day a tired, depressed group of German soldiers, with a sinister looking officer, entered Neuenkirchen. The villagers willingly showed them the quickest and safest way to retreat. But the officer became very angry and shouted at them: "We have come here to defend the place and to fight to the last man. There is no question of retreat." Everybody in the village was depressed. They all had hoped for a peaceful occupation by the Allied Forces. The soldiers had to dig manholes and prepare everything for the battle. Shortly afterwards, the shooting started. The inhabitants of our village fled into their cellars. The superb English "Desert Rats," who had fought so efficiently against General Rommel in the North African desert, conquered the village in half an hour.

A huge English soldier in his khaki uniform tore the door of our cellar open and aimed a menacing-looking machine gun at us while mustering us. My eldest sister addressed him: "We are only civilians." Several soldiers with machine guns searched the house. When they found no resistance, they talked to us kindly and let us come out of the cellar. "You are not allowed to leave the house for several days or to go nearer the window than two yards. People who disobey will be shot."

One soldier and a civilian were killed during the fighting. An English officer asked Father to put on his clerical garb—he was allowed to leave the house if dressed and recognized as a Lutheran clergyman—and bury the two corpses.

During one of the first occupation days, Father was visited by a British colonel, the commander of the area, followed by a sentry. All three of them had left the house and driven away in a military car. At first we were shocked. What were these men going to do to Father? After an hour they brought Father back. The colonel had asked him to help find a new mayor for the village. "The old frightened Nazi mayor had barricaded himself in his house. They took him into custody preliminary to his trial. The colonel made investigations and thought that I was the person to help him find a good reliable new mayor. So, we visited the gentleman I suggested for a first contact."

GETTING A JOB

Until the local Lutheran pastor returned home from the war to Neuenkirchen, my father acted as pastor in his place. But after that, of course, Father was without a job and our family practically without an income. Each day this delicate situation was the object of our family prayers.

One day Father started to thank God for the church He had ready for him and us. Only a few days later, we received a letter from a good church in Frankfurt to say that they were inviting Father to be their pastor. We stayed at that church for seventeen years.

During the whole time of our flight from the east to the west, our parents had been examples to us three daughters in the way they faced difficulties and loss. It had been their personal trust in God that had carried them through and also enabled them to help others in need. It was our decision to follow along the same way.

CHAPTER III

GRANDMOTHER ELSE URBAN

HER EXAMPLE IN THE FAMILY

In the southeastern part of Germany, in the midst of the idyllic mountain range called "Eulengebirge," which now belongs to Poland, my grandmother, Else Urban, owned a beautiful sixteen room country house with a large garden around it. We had spent very happy holidays there together with our relatives. My grandmother was a remarkable personality. She had become a widow at the age of thirty-six, shortly before her fifth child was born. She was active in Christian work among women and helped many people with their problems, because she herself had experienced God's help from day to day in very difficult times. She told us God had given her a wonderful task in life; the task of consolation.

She and her husband, my grandfather, were wealthy. After my grandfather finished his theology studies at the university, both—following their spiritual calling—emigrated to Hungary. They wanted to preach the Gospel to the German speakers, of whom there were quite many, particularly among the nobility. They experienced a true awakening, where many people became devout Christians.

My grandfather was an educated, independent character who set his priorities strictly, since he saw time itself as the highest good given to him by God. Thus, it frequently happened at society events of the nobility, that after dinner, when increased drinking and empty gossip began, he quietly rose and with a bow excused himself from his hosts; "Ladies, gentlemen, I beg you to forgive me, I have important work to do: Widow X. is sick and my help is required." He never missed a single opportunity in this society to give testimony of his faith. Since he had excellent manners and was a radiant and joyful personality, he was popular everywhere and among his friends he was nicknamed "Brother Sunshine."

My grandmother stood loyally by his side and took care of women and children. The very first thing she did was to tell them about the message of love of Jesus Christ and she instructed them in the Bible; she furthermore taught simple people useful things, such as the managing of the household, child rearing and etiquette.

Once my grandparents were traveling in Hungary by train to some meetings. Right across from them sat a young lady who stared at my grandmother during the entire trip which lasted several hours. When they eventually started a conversation with the lady, she declared: "My lady, you may wonder why I keep staring at you. The reason is, I am expecting a baby. I wish that my child will have the beauty of your face and expression. Thus, I want to engrave in my memory your face and that is why I keep steadily looking at you." My grandmother looked at the person across from her with her radiant blue eyes and explained to her how a life of love, forgiveness and following of Christ makes a person radiant and beautiful.

My grandfather later suddenly died from a severe intestinal disease. He was a young man on a missionary trip in Hungary far away from home. Grandmother was expecting her fifth child. She had to go through very, very hard times with her five small children. Because of inflation and perfidious lawyer "friends" who cheated her, she lost her entire fortune. The way she was able to get her family through these difficult years in faith and to make a good education possible for all is a great example of a series of prayers wondrously answered.

Her son Johannes was already accepted as a young boy into the Dresden Kreuzchoir because of his magnificent voice. He went to high school there—the Dresden Kreuzchoir like many of the famous boys choirs was integrated into a boarding school. On account of the many music programs in which they had to perform Johannes traveled all across Europe with the famed boys choir. How miraculously God can protect from danger is shown in the following experience from his school days in Dresden:

Johannes was a sturdy boy with blond hair and blue eyes and of lovable character. He had learned from his mother early on the value of love and obedience towards the word of God and his parents. Johannes was about twelve years old, when one free afternoon when there were no classes, he went into town with a friend to shop. As they walked along the main street, a friendly gentlemen with a bouquet in his hand approached them and said: "Young gentlemen, could you be of service to me? I have to leave by train right away and my train is leaving in a few minutes. But this bouquet should be delivered to a young lady. Would you be so kind as to take the flowers in my name to the address written here. It is very urgent, please go right away." He handed my uncle the address while emphasizing once more the urgency of the matter and disappeared in direction of the train station.

The two boys started off with the flowers. Suddenly Johannes stopped and said to his friend: "We first have to go back to school and ask for permission. School rules forbid to visit people without permission." "We just have to drop something off." "Well, anyway, let's just let the school know." So, the two of them ran quickly back to the boarding school and there they just happened to meet the headmaster of the school whom they told their plan. The headmaster asked the boys for the address for the flowers. When he read it he became pale: "How good of you to come back and not to have secretly tried to go there. You just escaped grave danger. Just very recently I received a warning that children have disappeared due to boy slave traders here in Dresden. This is one of the suspected addresses given to me." He assembled the entire school and told them what had happened and severely impressed on the students never to go to unknown places.

When my grandmother heard of this event, she was deeply shocked, but grateful in her heart that God had protected her son due to his sense of obedience. After that, my grandmother sent her oldest daughter, my mother, who until that time had been enrolled in a good boarding school in Hermannswerder, to Dresden for her further education and to keep an eye on my brother. There are actually quite a few more similar stories from these years, showing God's help and protection but that would be too great a digression.

Grandmother dedicated her entire life to work among women and became a blessing to many in all parts of Germany. She also was a friend of Mother Eva von Thiele-Winkler, the well-known founder of many children's homes for orphans and foundlings in the East of Germany.

HAUSDORF

In Hausdorf, in the Eulen Mountains (Eulengebirge) where grandmother had her house, there were two children's homes for which grandmother cared greatly. A children's home consisted of a "family" of about fifteen children of various ages, and their "Mom"—a co-worker of Mother Eva's—and an assistant. They lived together as a family and shared joy and sorrow. The children were brought up with a lot of love and received education according to their talents and inclinations. The funds for maintenance and education came from gifts.

What personally impressed me and what really showed spiritual conviction was the fact that Mother Eva and her children's homes never begged for money, but brought all the needs of their "families" to God in their prayers, expecting His direct help and His answers to prayers. Thus, the children learned very early to trust in God alone because there was no begging from people, as unfortunately so many missionary societies are doing today. All requests were brought directly to God and no mention was made to other people. What joy each answered prayer brought, what affirmation of the work of God! Only through direct dependency on the Lord can we know whether we are acting according to God's plan or whether God has other plans. With this attitude one remains very sensitive to God and consistent in sanctification; each sin blocks complete dependency, leaving prayers unanswered. This spiritual safety-valve is often disregarded in today's missionary works. The mass mailing of donation requests has little to do with spiritual principles.

Grandmother prayed very faithfully. When she was already advanced in age she visited us for a few weeks in Switzerland. She started her day very early in the morning with Bible reading and prayer in her little room. She then brought out her list of intercessions and prayed for hours, individually, for each person who was listed on her "hundreds-of-people-list" and thanked God for all the answered prayers. Thereafter she happily got up. She always washed herself extensively and meticulously, because she believed physical cleanliness was a symbolic expression of inner cleanliness. While washing herself she always sang her favorite hymns.

THE RUSSIANS OCCUPY GRANDMOTHER'S HOME DISTRICT

On May 8, 1945, the day of armistice, the victorious Russians stormed over the mountains to occupy the whole of eastern German territory. They drove into Hausdorf, my grandmother's home village, late in the evening. The house was crowded with forty people—refugees and other homeless people, as well as her two daughters and one daughter-in-law with their children. Their husbands were in the war, so most of the people in the house were young women, girls and children.

Grandmother used to tell us the following story:

The Russians encircled the house which had been pointed out to them by some Poles, because of the many young women and girls in it, and hammered at the front door, smashing the glass panes in it.

Grandmother unlocked the door and about seventeen strong men dashed up the stairs. When they perceived all the young women around her they let out a long wolf whistle. "Ah!" My grandmother declared in all simplicity: "Gentlemen, we ladies and the children are without protection, we put ourselves in your care." Some of the Russian officers understood German.

Grandmother sent the young people into their rooms and asked the Russians if she could prepare them a meal. They refused and searched the whole house with the help of a huge dog and turned everything upside down into a complete chaos. Then they plundered whatever was valuable in their eyes, but miraculously they did not touch a single woman, as the Russians usually did everywhere. Grandmother gathered the women and children around herself constantly praying for God's protection. When the tension grew unbearable the women started to sing the beautiful German hymns and songs of faith. This was apparently something new to the brutal Russians, many of them officers. They restlessly came and went all the time and stared at the singing women, but nobody touched them.

Then suddenly the men signaled to my grandmother to follow them out into the kitchen. They wanted to separate her from the young people, somehow feeling that she possessed some spiritual strength which hindered them from doing what they wanted to do in this house. They ordered grandmother to prepare a meal; she had to fry all the eggs she had. They brought other food for her to fix and finally they handed her a very long smoked sausage and ordered her to cut it ever so thinly and bring it to their colonel downstairs. She noticed their wide-set, deceitful eyes and felt they wanted her isolated as long as possible from the young people. So, she looked the two Russians straight in the eyes and prayed loudly: "Lord Jesus Christ, please prevent that which these wicked men are planning!" At that moment the Russians looked terrified, turned around and fled out of the room.

Grandmother carried the meal down to the colonel and afterward went back to the young women and children. Not one of them was molested—it was a miracle! Her daughters told her that after they had fetched her away to the kitchen, many Russians, one after the other, had come and tried to enter the room, but every time had left the room after a few steps, as if blocked by an invisible power. God had sent his angels to protect them, they were full of thanks and praise.

A little later in the night two more Russians knocked at the door (can you imagine Russian soldiers knocking at the door of prisoners?) and asked for cigarettes. At 3:30 a.m. another officer appeared; he was tall, broad and strong, and his chest was full of decorations and ribbons. His glances were devilishly unpleasant. He stared at the scene protractedly and penetratingly. "Let us sing some more Gospel songs," grandmother suggested when the tension and fear increased. They sang—and he sat himself down on a chair in front of them. Finally, after one or two hours, he stood up from his chair, bowed to the ladies and said politely: "Now you can go to sleep safely—good night."

What a miracle! Unprotected women preserved in the middle of peril! God answered the prayers of His children, of those who trusted in Him. None of the forty people in the house were molested. During the same night in the village many young women and girls went through a night of terror. (More of grandmother's experiences during these hard times can be read in my booklet *The Day Nazi Germany Died*.)

CHAPTER IV

Rebuilding the Bombed Nordost Church

THE NEW BEGINNING

In Frankfurt/Main my father then started to rebuild the bombed and scattered Nordost Church. He conducted the first church services in the auditorium of a nearby school that had not been destroyed, the Komenius school. Since he very much cared for the members of his community, he preached the word of God with all his might, and also made many visits at the homes of parents of confirmation candidates, the sick, lonely and old. Attendance at the services grew very quickly. The space in the auditorium became too small.

After a building permit had been granted, the members of our church started to rebuild the bombed-out church building themselves, as finances and building materials were not available in those times. First, everybody among the young and old who was able came to help, cleaning the stones and knocking the old mortar and plaster off the bricks from the ruins of the bombed old church so that they could be used for construction again. Now the entire building was rebuilt by the members of the congregation as much as possible, and craftsmen were used only for specialized work. How proud everyone in the church felt when after a lot of work and toil with great sacrifices the church building, including side rooms, was completed.

Now the spiritual work could be expanded. Through the regular preaching of the Gospel by my father and special crusades of men of God, such as Pastor Hans Brandeburg, Oswald Smith and others in our church, a number of people put their trust in the Lord Jesus Christ and became active members of our congregation. The leaders of the church greatly emphasized their work with children and youth. Frankfurt was always thought to be a liberal city where spiritual work was hard. Yet in the difficult post-war era we had overcrowded services with up to 700 worshipers, whereas most other churches around us remained empty Sunday after Sunday.

My father educated male and female Sunday School teachers. My sisters and I also participated in teaching the Bible to children on Sundays during our high school years. We had up to 300 children in the children's Sunday School. A great number of the children came from entirely non-Christian homes. They were invited by us from the neighborhood and picked up Sunday after Sunday. We regularly visited the parents of these children and explained what we taught the children and tried to also help them personally. Many of them had endured much suffering during the war and had lost husbands, brothers or property, so many were going through their life embittered. But they were receptive to help and love. Even today, after thirty-five years, we still meet some people who at that time found their faith in the children's services and who have remained with it.

Child evangelization began in the post-war years, first coming from the USA under the leadership of Mr. and Mrs. Kiefer. My older sister Rosemarie was studying theology at that time. She had a special gift and love for children. When, during her studies she had to teach candidates for confirmation, she was assigned to a congregation of Frankfurt-Sachsenhausen, where the candidates for confirmation were infamous for their bad behavior. The sexton, a strong man, had to sit in during the pastor's lessons to keep order. When my tender, good sister got there—smiling to herself—she sent the sexton home and managed the notorious rowdies quite well. Her very fine, saintly personality was somehow fascinatingly attractive and admirable to young people.

After her studies Rosemarie worked in a leadership position in the child evangelization movement in Frankfurt where she became engaged to a theologian who also was a believer. Later, they headed their own church. Sometimes, when I was in high school, I helped in child evangelization. During the summertime, we visited play areas and parks and told Bible stories using flannel boards. It was not just a mass of children who flocked around us, but often also adults—mothers and grand-parents—who listened and asked questions.

We also worked with the gypsy children and visited the gypsy caravans which were permanently settled in Frankfurt. The gypsy women never let their children out of their sight and listened attentively.

My younger sister and I went to the Bettina-Oberschule for Girls in Frankfurt, near the university. The high school was partially destroyed by bombs during the war, but was still usable for classes. The directress of our school was also our classroom teacher in the lower and upper grades of high school and we girls are very much indebted to her for her philosophy of life. During those first years of the post-war era, the years of the fight for survival, many teachers meant a lot more to us for their advice, deeds and example than is usually the case. They, like all of us, had to come to grips with economic difficulties, hunger, cold and lack of homes, and they were confronted with new political and philosophical ideas and school systems. We had great role models, for example, in our excellent, self-disciplined mathematics teacher, a dedicated and devout Catholic, and our extremely capable history teacher, who vividly opened up past history so that we felt a part of those bygone times. I was in close contact with her until her death a few years ago. Looking at the teachers of my children and now at most of today's teachers, it is remarkable to me how the number of genuine personalities and role models has incredibly shrunk. This perception is confirmed by many people. What could be the reason for this?

THE DETERIORATION OF THE EDUCATIONAL SYSTEM

When reading the history of public education in the USA (John Dewey) one can quickly find out which teachings have stolen the richness of personalities from us and what has caused the decline and disintegration of our education system.

Just one example: The teaching of evolution has robbed our society of absolute values. Because the Lord Jesus and even more so Moses (with the Ten Commandments) lived thousands of years ago, they must have been less developed than we, according to the teachings of evolution. Their teachings and ethical laws accordingly must be more primitive than ours. Each era needs its own suitable ethical standards and laws, they say. There are no absolute values, only relative ones, depending on the current situation (situation ethics). Thus Hoimar von Dithfurth writes that the Sermon on the Mount is "based on feet of clay" since, as a higher developed species, we have now grown beyond it.

The destructive work of Dewey's and his followers has been continued and expanded by the Frankfurt school in Germany and its followers. Thus, school is too often no more than a means for the manipulation of opinions and the leveling of society for ideological reasons. It is no longer for training in independent thought and the formation of one's own opinions based on facts and data. In such a school system the development of an independent personality is neither possible, nor desired.

This sad process in the development of our educational system seems to be irreversible. It is therefore urgently important for the salvation of our society that deliberately Christian schools be founded to teach by example strong absolute values and ideals again, so that genuine personalities may again be formed.

Until these schools become established, we Christian parents must carefully monitor and oversee the teachers of our children in the state schools. Corrupt teaching and philosophies must be objected to, the curriculum must be discussed with our children and we must provide them with Bible-based Christian answers and guidelines. If we fail to do so, our children will suffer damage that can probably never be remedied and which already has ruined many a child of devout parents.

MUSIC EDUCATION

The last years before my Baccalaureate (school-leaving examinations from high school) I decided to study music. Both my parents were musically gifted and our family life was at all times full of music. Whenever possible, our parents took us to good concerts, had us meet with artists and also invited many of them into our home. My father introduced us to many musical scores, playing from them, explaining them. He also regularly gave us musicians' biographies as gifts. Thus, my love belonged to "Lady Music." With great enthusiasm I pursued my violoncello education with the concert cellist, Ilse Bernatz, and also developed my piano skills during my last years of school.

I am grateful to my parents with all my heart that they sacrificed so much for our education during those difficult years. Both lived a very modest lifestyle and gave up many personal desires and much comfort in order to enable us to receive good schooling and university studies, which were expensive at that time and not free, as in many countries today. However, during that time my father donated a good part of his salary for the rebuilding of the church.

In 1948, I passed my Baccalaureate. School was very demanding and during the last two years our class became much smaller. During the winter, school classes were often canceled due to cold and lack of coal in the post-war years; every three days we came together for abbreviated lessons with huge amounts of homework until we either received a new coal allocation or the weather turned warmer.

In those days, students had to know the syllabus material of all subjects at the time of the exam: German, mathematics, Latin, English, French, biology, physics, chemistry, history, social sciences, geography, religion, music and art. In all subjects there was the possibility of an oral exam and in each of the four major subjects—German, mathematics, English and Latin—we had a one-day written exam. The subjects to be examined orally were decided upon by a committee based upon the grades of the previous and the current year. However, one was not told until the day of the exam which one of the subjects one would be tested in, so one had to be fully prepared.

I would also like to mention that for the written exam in German, we were given a selection of three topics. I chose the theme: "Discuss three books that personally influenced you in your life. One of the books should be discussed in detail." I decided on the following three books: *Torquato Tasso* by Goethe, *The Paintings* by Rudolf Schäfer and the Bible.

Torquato Tasso was one of my favorite dramas by Goethe because it taught so much wisdom regarding conduct in life.

Rudolf Schäfer was one of the very great German painters who is especially known for his brilliant Bible illustrations. We visited him later personally and were touched by the deep understanding and love of Scriptures shown in his works and the magnificent intensity of his colors.

The Bible is the word of God and guiding principle of my life. I selected it for its special and explicit meaning to me and

I discussed it in detail from a historical, literary and theological point of view, as well as from its practical significance in my personal life.

When we had passed the exams, and the entire faculty shook every student's hand and congratulated us. The Curate, who taught the Catholic religion classes, approached me and shook my hand saying: "I particularly enjoyed your German composition and your attitude towards the Bible. Thank you so much for your courageous testimony. We do need more young people like you!" These words made me very happy, particularly as I only knew the clergyman by sight.

Our Protestant pastor also shook my hand like all the others, but did not say a single word about my written work, which obviously he also had seen. I had regularly and actively participated in his religion classes, but he sadly undermined our trust in the word of God, rather than reinforce it.

GRATITUDE AND THE AMERICANS: THE CARE PACKAGES

A great amount of gratitude, and this we should never forget, is owed to the American people. Particularly the American Christians sent us, the starving and poorly dressed Germany—their original enemy in the war—millions of CARE packages after the end of the war in exemplary and sacrificing fashion. The English and the Swiss also participated in this effort. Many refugees or big city dwellers probably would have starved or frozen to death without these charitable deeds from a country that treated its enemies in accordance with the Biblical commandment of practicing love. I know of very simple people in the USA, Switzerland and England who took extra jobs to earn extra money in order to be able to send food and clothing packages to needy Germans. This aid often came from genuine financial sacrifices and not simply from abundance.

Even today, we see the generous helping deeds of the USA with regard to suffering nations—certainly food for thought. Not the slightest gesture in that regard came from Russia and other countries with atheistic ideologies. Is this surprising?

MY FURTHER EDUCATION

It was very difficult to get a study place at the university in the post-war times even with good grades. Thousands and thousands of young and not-so-young men who had been fighting in the battle fields west and east had come home and needed an education. They had irreparably lost a good number of their formative years and it was very difficult for them— war-hardened men as they were—to return to the strict discipline of starting a university or other mental training.

It was only just that these men received priority regarding study places at the university and youngsters fresh from high school had difficulty to get in.

So, I started my music studies at the College of Church Music in Frankfurt/Main where I learned to appreciate even more the old hymns of faith, proclaiming the firm truth of faith.

Here I studied music history, music theory, composition, organ-building, solfeggio, reading and playing of full scores, singing and choir conducting. I continued my violoncello and organ lessons.

Later, at the University of Geneva, when already married, I continued my piano training with a French lady professor. In Geneva, I also continued my language studies followed by final examinations.

Mother Elfrida Smith
with baby Arthur

Father Arthur Smith Sr.
in full Freemason regalia

The Wilder factory in Crowmarsh, Wallingford,
England

Arthur Smith Sr. with sons
Arthur and Walter

The old Bentley

Arthur as a student

Brother Walter

General F.D. Frost preaching from his van

Dr. Wilder-Smith with prisoners of war

Dr. Wilder-Smith and German prisoners of war
studying the Bible

Beate's parents Reverend Wilhelm and Erna Gottwaldt

Rosemarie, Beate, and Christiane Gottwaldt

Beate with her 1/4 violin

Beate at her confirmation
(14 years)

The three Gottwaldt daughters with their fiancés

PART III

MEMOIRS

CHAPTER I

OUR WEDDING

Beate's and my wedding was in no way a normal wedding! The circumstances made it a big exception! My fiancée still possessed German nationality. We wanted to have the same passport in order to avoid bureaucratic harassment, and also so as not to be separated in case of war. So, we decided to celebrate our civil marriage in England. It took place on September 17, 1950, in Wallingford, England. Beate did not receive the British nationality automatically, she had to officially apply for it. At the same time, she had to give up her German nationality, she had to renounce her German passport. Today, the State does not demand this step anymore. If the person concerned desires, he or she can keep the original passport, as well as the new one. But at that time—five years after the end of the war—it was different.

We wanted our civil wedding to take place in England, because my parents were too old to travel to our church wedding in Germany—traveling right after the war involved many inconveniences. So, first of all we had a little wedding feast with our relatives in England on the date of the civil marriage. As we wanted to spend a few days with my parents in England, we lived for a time as it were in a marital limbo. After the state rules, we were now married. But for us, only the church wedding before God was to be valid. We could not celebrate our church wedding until October 21, 1950. Until this date, we lived separately just as we had done as a betrothed couple. We both wanted it this way.

But this state of marital limbo caused some unexpected difficulties. When we traveled back to the continent via Hoek van Holland to prepare our church wedding, we had to spend the night on the ferry-boat on the North Sea. We booked separate cabins with the purser although we were married! I do not know what kind of thoughts the purser on the boat had. Maybe: "How sad it is that quarrels or separation take place so early in married life"?

The religious marriage ceremony took place at my father-in-law's church in Frankfurt am Main, Germany, with my father-in-law officiating, some five weeks later. It was a glorious service characterized by Christian joy and radiancy such as is befitting for such an occasion where the horrors of the last five years of terror, war and bloodshed were overcome in the consummation in matrimony of two members of the erstwhile warring nations.

The Church, the well-known Nordost Gemeinde in Frankfurt, is a church which confesses the Lutheran faith and is therefore a part of the state church, but its particular statutes require that all its members personally confess a saving faith in Christ before they can become members of the Nordost Gemeinde. In the run of the mill state church, infant baptism followed by confirmation suffices for membership. For membership of the Nordost Gemeinde, mere infant baptism does not suffice, only a confession of a personal saving faith in Christ does.

The church building of the Nordost Gemeinde had been personally rebuilt by church members who scraped and cleaned the old bricks of the destroyed building by hands. The church had been totally destroyed by bombs during World War II. It was now packed to the last seat.

Little girls from Beate's Sunday school class sprinkled rose petals under our feet as we left the church after the ceremony. It was a symbol of the love and good wishes of the whole church towards the daughter of their well beloved Pastor who had now shown in her choice of an ex-enemy national as her husband that Christ overcomes the difficulties of nationality and culture. This surely was a very beautiful and practical way of showing the Christian's love of all nations. Rose petals under our feet now after so many years of bloodshed and terror! (For details of my wife's and my parents-in-law's war experiences see my wife's own account in her book *The Day Nazi Germany Died*, TWFT, P.O. Box 8000, Costa Mesa, California 92628, U.S.A.)

My wife, it must be said, was a general favorite with the whole congregation; her gentle, loving and considerate ways together with her feminine style all combined to make her a favorite with young and old.

After the service, all present were invited to a reception which had been arranged for by my parents-in-law at the Lydia Haus which was run by the Christian Endeavor (E.C.) friends of the Nord Ost Gemeinde. The occasion was a joyous success in every way and a worthy beginning to our married life.

Beate was radiant throughout the whole proceedings and found time and occasion for a kind, caring word to most of the numerous guests who were present at the reception at the Lydia Haus.

Our American missionary friends, Velma and Pastor Jim Kiefer of the Child Evangelization Organization, were present too. In fact, they made a movie film of the wedding and presented us with a copy of the film as a wedding present afterwards—it is one of our treasured possessions to this day. I recently had the whole film transferred to 8-millimeter film as the original film was becoming old and brittle. So, we now possess the original 16-millimeter film, as well as the 8 millimeter film copy.

Meanwhile, some friends of ours who were active in the student evangelization work had secured us the offer of a small house on the far side of Lago Maggiore, opposite Locarno in the Italian part of Switzerland for our honeymoon. The small house was hidden in the hillside overlooking Locarno. A small ferry boat crossed over Lago Maggiore from San Nazzaro, the name of the small village in which the honeymoon house was situated, two or three times a day to Locarno on the other side of Lago Maggiore. As Beate spoke some Italian, we were able to communicate with the locals.

We paid the princely sum of fifty Sfrs. (Swiss Francs) (about forty-five American dollars today) for the whole month of our honeymoon in this idyllic situation in the chestnut woods opposite Locarno. As winter was approaching, most of the holiday makers had already departed. The holiday houses around us were empty and we enjoyed being together in this quiet solitude. We had so much to say to one another!

Because our financial means were slender, we often walked—or took the local train—the several kilometers from San Nazzaro to Luino on the Italian side of the Swiss-Italian frontier. There in Italy we bought butter and meat at the considerably cheaper Italian prices compared with those asked in Switzerland.

My wife having been through the Second World War was given to economy, but told me later that she really did wonder whether she had married an Ebenezer Scrooge when I suggested one day that we manage on two meals a day to save house-keeping money. One fine day I saw in the greengrocer's store some dried corn grains—what one calls maize in the U.K. I suggested that we try some of that for lunch, because maize fresh on the cob is edible and as dried grains one feeds it to the chicken. It was tolerably cheap.

So, we bought several handfuls of these dried grains and boiled them for some hours. But it was all to no avail for at the end of our treatment with boiling water the corn grains were just as hard as at the beginning of the experiment, namely as hard as bullets! So we gave up that experiment in economy.

But life in Italy—or at least on the Italian-Swiss frontier near Luino—has its interesting aspects, especially if one is spending one's honeymoon in that part of the world. The young men of Luino soon noticed that we came over from the Swiss village of San Nazzaro and returned in the evening with the allowed amount of butter and meat.

Especially the young people, in the Tessin seem to be very observant where young couples are concerned, for they soon deduced that we obviously had not been married for very long! These youngsters loved to embarrass my wife by wolf-whistling after her—the beautiful young lady hanging on the arm of a man of whom she appeared to be rather fond! So, we could rely on a chorus of whistling youngsters every time we walked arm in arm through the streets of Luino. They had noticed, of course, that my wife blushed very easily. And this was just what they apparently wanted for the whistling and merriment were redoubled as soon as she colored up.

I instructed our three boys in later years never to think of marrying any young lady who could not or did not blush, for something might possibly be seriously amiss with her morals if she could not or did not!

Every time we went over the frontier to buy the meat and butter we enjoyed this free serenade. I think we must have enjoyed receiving it as much as they all appeared to enjoy giving it. The whole operation had the additional advantage that it provided us with cut-price butter and meat at the same time. So, everybody in the garden was happy.

One day when walking down to the post-office and the little pier in San Nazzaro, we met a lady who wanted to pay us a visit. How she got hold of our address, I do not know. But here she was standing in front of us. She was a daughter of a very wealthy gentleman whom we knew. She only worked occasionally in her father's firm and was divorced. But she regularly spent time in expensive luxury hotels and stayed there as long as she had credit and the hotel owner did not send her away. Here she was in Ascona, in a hotel so expensive that we would not have dared to even stand in front of the luxury portal.

We kindly asked her into our house and offered a cup of tea. But she had a big request which we easily guessed. The hotel manager had demanded his money from her before she left. Now, she was without a single penny, she was not even able to pay her fare home (first class, of course). Would we lend her some money? She knew we were Christians and cited that we should not turn away from those who are needy and have to borrow money. I told her we did not possess much ourselves. Could she not telephone home and ask her wealthy father to help. No, her father would be furious if he knew that she had again stayed in such a luxury hotel. She implored us and begged us with tears in her eyes to give her the money for her ticket home. Maybe today my reaction would have been different.

I had no Swiss francs to give her. We lived on twenty francs per week in addition to the rent of fifty Swiss francs for the house. I told her I had only ten U.S. dollars to *spare*, a present from an American friend. She took it and told us that this amount would just cover her fare home. Then she left with the promise to repay the money when home. Of course, we never received the money. Even the wealthy father did not mention a word when we met one or two weeks later although he knew of the episode.

Every week I receive by mail hundreds of begging letters mainly from Christian organizations. I examine them thoroughly and find that some of these organizations receive literally millions from church taxes which they use for office costs, the most modern computers, electronic data processing, telephone calls (long distance) and all kind of expensive equipment.

The spiritual work in the Kingdom of God is not as much dependent on money and finances as we are often told. We have mobilized whole universities in Germany, America, Canada, Austria and in Switzerland and had full audiences. The cost of this work often amounted to only a few thousand Swiss francs. Through these outreaches people regularly became believers. Sensible people often are repelled from Christianity when seeing the high expenses of Christian organization. They are convinced that Christians and Christianity have become a matter of big business—and they are often right and therefore they reject it.

We spent our honeymoon very simply, but were extremely happy in our little paradise. A gentleman later remarked about my wife that she lived by "air and love alone"—she might have learned this in those first weeks of our married life. I had given up my Fellowship at London University and my job in Switzerland had not yet started. I could not bring money with me from England as there were severe restrictions in these post-war times on taking money out of England. Therefore, we had to minimize our expenses until I started earning in my new job in Switzerland. But to be able to spend our honeymoon in Southern Switzerland was so wonderful.

We often went for long walks in the chestnut woods on the mountain sides surrounding Lago Maggiore. There we encountered with reptiles, lizards and snakes of kinds which one seldom sees in the colder parts of Switzerland. One type of lizard sported a kind of crown on the top of its head and did not seem to be particularly timid as it noisily waded its way through the deep layers of dried autumn leaves in the chestnut woods.

In San Nazzaro, we found the ideal setting for a study of "The Song of Solomon." Just take your honeymoon there in the autumn and read the book together with your bride to find out for yourself! When there are fewer restraints on one's time and the ordinary duties of routine life are less pressing, it is much easier.

During our honeymoon, we started the practice which we followed through all our life: To read the Bible—continuously—and pray together before getting up early in the morning. We did the same at night in bed before going to sleep. Because once out of bed, there were so many "important" things to distract us.

Those weeks of our honeymoon in San Nazzaro will remain with Beate and myself as long as we draw breath, for we used them to deepen our understanding of both the Old and the New Testament.

CHAPTER II

THE PRANK GONE AWRY

One evening I had to run down to the village to post a few letters at the post office. My wife preferred to stay at home to prepare the evening meal. So I went alone. The walk to the post office took about fifteen minutes and the way back uphill a little longer. "My dear," I said, "in about half an hour's time I will be back with you." The woods around us were lonely and void of people and it was already dark. But my wife declared that she was not afraid—she was always courageous and never wanted to give in to any tendency towards timidity.

I wondered if she really was so courageous! I rushed down the hill as fast as I could, delivered my letters and hurried uphill. I made it in fifteen minutes. I walked on tiptoes so that she would not hear me. She could not expect me home yet. Next to the main entrance to the house, a door led directly from the kitchen to the outside. The upper part of this door into the kitchen consisted of frosted glass so that one could see shadows moving inside the lighted kitchen. I saw the shadow of my beloved one as she was busy in front of the stove. Cautiously, I crept nearer as I heard her softly singing for herself. Beate has a charming, clear soprano voice and she sang the beautiful old hymns of which we both were so fond.

I wondered: Is she really not timid or does she just pretend not to be? Or is she perhaps singing because she is secretly afraid to be alone in this house in the middle of the woods? Let's see!

I found a long stick, stuck my hat on top of it and moved the hat slowly in front of the frosted glass so as to make it look like a stooped man creeping around the door. Obviously, while still singing her eyes had wandered to the door. She saw the hat slip by the lower part of the frosted glass—as if somebody was trying to look through the key-hole. Immediately the singing stopped; there was dead silence in the house. I presumed that she was watching the glass door. After a few moments, I let the hat on the stick glide back to the other side so that the shadow could again be seen through the door. My good little wife thereupon called authoritatively: "Who's there?" No answer. I rattled the window shutters a little. Again she called: "Who's there?" Again no answer.

Usually the door-handle creaked when being opened. I turned the door-handle a little until it creaked and let the hat move again from one side of the glass door to the other. Now, came the great revelation, which I had never anticipated. She called again: "Who's there?" courageously approached the door and resolutely unlocked and opened it wide to see who was busying himself around the house. She knew that her husband could not yet be back from the village. All the holiday houses around were empty. It must be some vagabond prowling through the lonely woods in the dark as sometimes was the case.

Just at that moment, I disappeared round the corner of the house; my good, gentle, shy darling chased after me. Just as I disappeared round the next corner, she caught the tip of my overcoat and held me firmly so that I could not escape. Then she recognized me.

The whole time I had thought that she had played the game with me. But no, she really was afraid.

When Beate confronted danger, she left her fear behind and became brave like a lion. Ashamed, I apologized deeply, because she felt hurt. Through this experience, I learned that the so-called weaker gender is often misjudged. I seriously had to revise my conception of a lady's psychology!

This prank gone awry taught me to cherish and appreciate Beate in a new way—although my love and respect had been maximal before. I learned to value the courage and determination of a gentle lady who had gone unharmed through the Nazi-rule and borne all the troubles more faithfully than many men. Yet, I should not have played the trick, I should never have played frivolously with her timidity. I often regretted my inexperience and thoughtlessness and apologized for it.

Over thirty years later, my wife and I went back to San Nazarro after having been absent abroad for some years from Switzerland and having lived for some time in Norway and the United States. Much of the Italian culture of those honeymoon years has now disappeared, but the old house with the frosted glass door in which we then lived is still standing, although it has an extra story built on upstairs.

We found the name of the store owner, too, who used to serve us with our groceries at the local village store; but this time his name was on a tombstone in the churchyard and not on the village store; he had gone to other worlds some four years ago. Worlds about which we had often talked while on our honeymoon. He was a pious Catholic. His widow still remembered the young couple of yesteryear who lived in Casa Hortensia, San Nazzaro, on their honeymoon.

We walked the same old paths and remembered past times. We were full of thanks for the many bygone years and for our four children with whom God had entrusted us and who had grown up to be our joy.

The days of joyful reflection and what we had to communicate with one another in San Nazzaro after all the years of happy marriage remain our secret for ever.

CHAPTER III

PLANS FOR THE FUTURE

During these idyllic honeymoon days, we started to think about our plans for our life together later on, after the honeymoon was over.

Beate and her parents were concerned at the apparently largely ineffectual Christian testimony in the European academic world and universities. It was pretty clear to us all that much Christian witness in Europe was rendered less effective than it could have otherwise been by becoming what the European considers to be "professional."

If it could be said that one earned one's living as a professional evangelist or theologian, one's testimony, at least in Europe, was often weakened thereby. Thus, under no circumstances did I wish to be financially dependent on a salary from my Christian activities. I did not wish to earn my living as a paid evangelist, because it was my experience that in the special mentality of European academics, financial dependence on Christian work definitely weakens one's Christian effectiveness. "You repeat the Christian testimony only for your bread and butter," is a regular commentary heard in European universities during and after Christian lectures.

Years ago a kind and very wealthy American Christian friend of mine offered "to set me up in Christian work" by founding and financing a European student mission for me personally. As he put it, he would found the broad basis of a financial "pyramid" for me, pay me a salary and charge dues from the members to keep the organization out of the red. I would be at the top of the pyramid and be "set up for life" as he expressed it.

I turned the plan down, although it was pure kindness on his part that had prompted it. I did not think that God necessarily works optimally that way. Since that time there have been numerous Christian evangelistic academic organizations founded on this basis to work among European continental students. In my humble opinion, personal private faith, especially on the financial side of the operation, is much more vital than assured finances for maximal success in any "work of faith," especially amongst students and academics in continental Europe. The same principle surely applies elsewhere.

The Swiss industrial gentleman who had invited us to settle down in Switzerland after our wedding understood this position perfectly and therefore offered us one of his chalets at a normal rent. My job would be to direct his research laboratory for a set number of weeks in the year, and he then would undertake to give me an agreed number of weeks free annually to hold evangelistic meetings all over Europe, but especially in the universities, just as I pleased. I suggested he reduce my salary to compensate for this added freedom to do the work of an unpaid evangelist which lay nearest my heart.

Although Beate would have less money to lay claim to than if I had taken a normal full-time scientific job and salary and given up the idea of university evangelization as my aim in life, she willingly accepted the idea of less money against more freedom to do God's direct evangelistic work. Here again she has always been willing to deny herself personally, and thus to show herself a true disciple of the Lord Jesus Christ.

The Swiss industrial gentleman mentioned was a real Christian in making these arrangements. He insisted, too, that I should have the additional claim to a certain percentage of any invention of mine which his company could use commercially over and above the small regular salary.

So, we said good-bye to our "garden of Eden" in San Nazzaro and set out for Central Switzerland where the gentleman's laboratory was situated. We found that our industrial friends had prepared an apartment for us in one of their chalets there and had, in addition, made all arrangements necessary to lend us the money to buy the furniture we needed to set up house.

However, we now had a very difficult job indeed before us—namely that of telling the dear old gentleman that neither Beate, nor I, had ever borrowed any money to buy anything we could not pay cash for. With many thanks we therefore turned the kind offer of a loan down. Their kindness knew no end, however, and he was not in the least miffed that we had turned down his offer of a loan, for every Sunday in the following months the old gentleman would telephone us to ask us to come up to lunch with him and his family.

He never told us what he may have privately thought about a young couple that had queer ideas about ways and means of financing a household when he himself had to take up large industrial loans on a regular routine basis to run his own huge business! It was enough for him that we had sensitive consciences about financial matters and that fact alone appeared sufficient guarantee for providing a safe working basis for the plans he had for a collaboration with us, even though we had impossible old fashioned ideas about debts, loans and finances. What we did we at least based on the Book—and that was sufficient for him.

But we did buy a single couch and the bed linen for it with some spare pocket money left over from our honeymoon. The two of us slept on that single couch for the first months of our marriage. We never managed in later years to part with that single couch, but have kept it as a memento of those early days of our wedded life. It is still in the spare room that my father-in-law used to use when visiting us in later years in Einigen and is now sometimes used during the day as a sofa.

I have often wondered in how far the happiness of those days was coupled with our early resolve to contract no debts at all and to buy nothing we could not pay cash for. For we took the Word of Scripture seriously: "Owe no man *anything* except to love him" (Romans 13:8).

Much of the misery which accompanies many a family life today would certainly seem to be coupled with the ease with which debts can be contracted for both the major and minor amenities of life, and which the family cannot really afford.

Of course, if one is wishing to live according to principles such as we had very consciously laid down together, it goes without saying that one has to find the bride willing to say "no" to herself in this way—for no one can be a disciple of the Lord Jesus without being willing to say "no" to himself or herself (Matthew 16:24). I have experienced the outstanding blessing of God in finding just that young lady—and I know it too! Then and to this day, she has shown that she is capable of saying "no" to herself, that is, she is capable of denying herself. Just to take a look at her figure (and weight!) is sufficient to convince the discerning person of this fact!

After meals (mostly on Sundays) at the Christian gentleman's home, which was always first class, the daughters would gather with the parents at the table for a little Bible reading. It went without saying that it would be my privilege to take on this little pleasure. Both the parents delighted in these after-lunch impromptu Bible readings in honoring the Holy Scriptures at their Sunday table.

CHAPTER IV

OUR WORK
AMONGST STUDENTS

During my first good-will visits to German universities from England directly after World War II, I became acquainted with a number of academics who invited me to give lectures on my scientific research. In the course of these, I also pointed out the philosophical implications of this research. Increasingly I was asked to hold lecture series at universities, often on issues of science and religion.

One of my greatest hindrances to becoming a Christian had been Darwinism as it was and still is being taught in schools, universities, places of higher learning and the media. If we really arose by chance—and not by plan—and if we were only the accidental product of evolution by means of mutation and natural selection from non-living matter to the first living cell up the whole evolutionary ladder, the Genesis Report of the Bible could not be true. In that case, we are not specifically designed and created in God's image (Genesis 1:27). And if the Bible can not be trusted in its first pages, why should it be trustworthy and reliable in the following pages? If it can not be trusted regarding our *origins*, can it be relied upon regarding our *destiny*? Was Man not created by a Creator with a special purpose and aim, and presented with certain absolute values as the basis of mankind's functioning and well-being? Was Man only a chance product without any meaning or goal in life, and consequently without any fixed moral standards of good and bad? These are the capital questions of life on which our whole existence and way of life is based. As I had struggled for so many years to answer these questions and to convince myself of the complete trustworthiness of the Bible, it was my strong desire to focus much of my research on the science of origins in order to be able to help other intellectuals in their problems in this area.

After the second world war there was for a number of years no other (Christian) scientist on the European Continent, lecturing in universities on the subject of origins from a creationist point of view. Only years later did younger scientists join me in the same effort.

Most of our first lectures took place at the university of Marburg in central Germany. In Marburg, I sometimes lectured from the same pulpit as the famous liberal theologian, Professor Bultman. Ironically, Professor Bultman's elaborations had tried to negate the historicity of the biblical accounts by mythologizing them, while I, from my scientific background, tried to show the accuracy of biblical accounts and their trustworthiness.

In that post-war time, young people were quite lost and really did not know what to believe. All the old pre-war and wartime ideologies and utopias of the "Third Reich" had been smashed and young people felt totally disillusioned and deceived. Thus, many were very open and receptive for eternal truths, and auditoriums were often crowded. Many turned to God and became Christians, not wanting to rely on erring men anymore, but on the eternal God.

Sometimes we were invited to speak in seminars or retreats by the Intervarsity Fellowship (IVF), or by the Students Mission (SMD) in Germany and Austria. On other occasions we were directly invited by university departments to give lectures on relevant topics. The most wanted topics were always "Man's Origin, Man's Destiny" and "Why Does God allow Suffering and Pain?" In later years, "Causes and Cure of the Drug Epidemic" became very popular.

I will only mention a few of our experiences while lecturing to students at various times and places.

THE RETREAT

During the semester holidays, we often carried out retreats centered around a specific theme organized by the SMD or the IVF for students in country resorts. Thus students and speakers had ample time together for an exchange of thoughts, for fellowship and for Bible study. It was a time of growth and of decision. We usually had a great time together.

Everybody knows that the Germans are philosophers full of intricate questions and profound problems, and not to be satisfied with easy answers. Years ago when I had just learned the German language, I visited Germany for the first time. I gained the impression that every second sentence started with "aber" (but)—they were always questioning or contradicting everything. This is, of course, not a bad habit, but very time consuming all the same.

It was and still is the habit of German students to stay up late into the night to dispute and endlessly discuss problems on one's mind. Of course, next morning they had difficulties getting up at the right time and were late. This happened regularly in students' seminars and retreats, and I did not approve of this. This was at the beginning of my work with students and I was not yet experienced enough to handle this situation. Every evening they came to my room with hundreds of problems and questions and stayed until after midnight. Warnings and jokes to make them realize the inadequacy of their behavior were in vain. "Only one more question," was their excuse.

I locked the door of my bedroom. However, I always slept with an open window. Hardly had I fallen asleep when I was awakened by an unusual noise. Through the window crawled several dark figures and sat down in front of my bed. One of them began: "Just one question..." and then they started disputing, arguing and unrolling their theological problems.

Very displeased and sleepy I dismissed them at once, remarking that so late at night the Holy Ghost did not work anymore.

Next morning for the first lecture, I only quoted Bible verses:

"Abraham rose up *early in the morning*....to a place where he stood before the Lord"(Genesis 19:27; Genesis 21:14; 22:3).

"Jacob rose up *early in the morning*"(Genesis 28:18).

"And the Lord said unto Moses: Rise up *early in the morning*" (Exodus 8:20; 9:13).

"Moses rose up *early in the morning*" (Exodus 24:4; 34:4).

"Joshua rose up *early in the morning*" (Joshua 3:1; 6:12).

"Job rose up *early in the morning* and offered burnt-offerings" (Job 1:5).

Ezekiel: "*Early in the morning* the Word of the Lord came to him."

David: "I will wake *early* and praise thee" (Psalm 57:8; 108:2).

The apostles were *early* in the temple (Acts 5:21).

"*Jesus rose up early in the morning a great while before day...and prayed*" (Mark 1:35).

I did not add much to those self-evident verses and left the students to reflect on them.

The positive effect became visible the following evenings and mornings. They had learned their lesson.

A VISIT TO PROFESSOR HEIM

On one of our lecture tours to the university city of Tübingen, during the first time of our marriage. I made the acquaintance of the well known German theology professor, Dr. Karl Heim. He was a firm pillar of biblical theology in the midst of so many liberal theologians on the European continent.

When I was in Tübingen, Professor Heim invited me to his home on his eightieth birthday. There were quite a number of people present at the celebration. I asked him if he would kindly answer me two questions, as he was an authority for the evangelical world on the European continent. He said, he would love to answer the questions.

My first question was: "Professor Heim, what is your position towards Genesis?"

My second question: "What is the best way to witness Christ to our modern generation?"

Karl Heim was a very kind gentleman. He thought for a while and then gave his answers.

"The first question is difficult for me to answer. You are a natural scientist. I am not a scientist myself. I rely in these questions on my friend Professor Freiherr von Huehne."

We knew Professor von Huehne quite well. He was a Christian, too, but a theistic evolutionist, as many of the older generation on the European continent were.

"The second question," he said, "is easier to answer for me. The best way to witness Christ to the modern generation is the *living Christ in us.*"

I never forgot this answer as it was so to the point.

COLOGNE

In January 1983, Professor Ellinger, who held the Chair of Business Studies at the University of Cologne, invited me in January 1983, to give a three day lecture series at the university, which he had organized together with his assistants and students. He was an outstanding Christian, competent in his field and a good friend of ours for many years. He later held the presidency of "Wort und Wissen," an academic organization which was also involved in the preparation of this lecture series.

The evening lectures in the university auditorium on "Origins" were so crowded that the students sat everywhere. When the seats were all taken, they sat on the floor. And when the floor became crowded, they even climbed on to the window sills, which were quite high, so that the students had to climb up like monkeys.

The students were very attentive and asked many questions. Many of them heard for the first time a scientist's witness for a Creator and wanted to get more involved in their search for God and the Truth. Several decided to commit themselves to the Christian way of life.

One evening, on January 21, Professor Ellinger and his hospitable wife invited a number of professors at the University of Cologne to a meal into their home with their wives. I was asked to give a short introductory address on "The Roll of Genetics and the Environment in the Shaping of our Character." The professors then engaged in an extensive discussion on the talk. This topic was always a hot iron politically; left wing representatives maintained that the sort of environment a person is living in wholly determines his character, and by altering the environment you can change his character for the better or the worse.

On the other hand, the right wing advocates will hold to the view that the genetical make-up of a person will determine his character and there is little that can change it.

Of course, both the genetics and the environment of a person are important; the interplay of the two factors really shape a character. The external environment influences the development of the genetic potential. The better the environment (home, school, etc.), the better the inherent genetics can be expressed and developed. However, if the genetical make-up is poor, even the best environment cannot bring to development or expression something that is not inherent.

Several of the respectable gentlemen came subsequently to my university lectures, and some even supported us.

BONN

At the University of Bonn, there were about 900 listeners in the auditorium. We were in the middle of a lecture series; the topic that afternoon was on origins. The students organizing the meeting had installed several microphones in the aisles so that the questions in the subsequent question and answer time would be audible to everyone.

Hardly had I finished my elaborations when a young man jumped from his seat, ran along the aisle and grabbed a microphone. His faced was distorted and full of hatred he shouted: "Comrades, I strongly protest against Professor Wilder-Smith's lecture. His science might be alright, but his goal is to lead us back into the captivity of Christianity. He is a religious fanatic. Marx and Hegel and their followers, as well as the Frankfurter Schule, have freed us from the slavery of the Christian God. Man is free to follow his own desires and not be responsible towards a transcendent Being, invented only to enslave us, as Marx so rightly warned.... I ask you to leave this room with me in protest." While he was screaming and we were pondering how to react wisely, the students from the audience started shouting: "Shut up, we know you with your communistic propaganda! We do not want to listen to you. Shut up! Get out! Leave!" There was a chorus of indignant student voices trying to stop the agitator.

When the Marxist propagandist saw that not a soul supported him, he took to his heels and left the room.

We did not have to undertake anything—we did not have to say a word. The students themselves had reacted spontaneously and solved the problem. Was it really the students? I wonder.

SIEGEN

Another time, I was speaking in the big "Siegerland-Halle" in Siegen. Approximately 3000 people had turned up for the evening. Usually many people stayed on after the lecture for questions—often until midnight. Many of the young students were full of crucial questions—the students always appreciated when somebody was willing and capable to take the time and the effort to seriously go into the many questions and problems which troubled them.

That evening in Siegen, during question time, a number of people explained how they had been helped intellectually and spiritually. Suddenly a student rose up and walked to the microphone at the front exclaiming: "This is all nonsense. I do not want to listen to it. It sounds like the Middle-Ages that we are guilty before God and need to own up to it, asking God's forgiveness. This is ridiculous...." He went on communicating his indignance. One could not talk sensibly to him, he was too excited.

Next evening after the lecture, the same student turned up for the question time. Would he try the same game as the night before? He soon jumped up to the microphone up front, but the expression of his face looked different this time. "Friends," he said, "what I spouted out to you yesterday was wrong of me. I am sorry. I knew in my innermost heart that what the Professor said was right and that his advice was the only way out of my frustration. But I rebelled against it. During the night my conscience spoke to me. I want to become a Christian. Please help me."

BREMEN

For a number of years, I lectured annually at the University of Bremen, which had a reputation for left-wing views. The lectures usually took place in the afternoons, while in the evenings I would speak in the big Matthäus-Church of Pastor Jochen Müller in Bremen-Huchting, often on characters of the Old Testament like Joseph, Samson, Queen Esther, etc.

Groups of Marxists often came to the university lectures, sometimes with the intention to disturb. Another lecturer told us that during his speech, which had somehow elicited the displeasure of the Marxists, they had rung little bells continuously, so that he could not continue lecturing, but had to break off. Through God's protection we did not experience such disturbances.

The Marxist students generally stayed until question time and then sharply attacked the lectures. This was, of course, an excellent way of communicating with them. A number of them, when they noticed they were being taken seriously and not just browbeaten—as unfortunately sometimes happened—became reasonable. I often had the impression that they provoked us in order to get some answers to their many unsolved social and personal problems.

I loved the students and the young people with their many questions and their open minds. And I think they felt this love. It is wonderful that so many of them eagerly search for the meaning of life, for betterment in an unjust and suffering world. It is our desire to lovingly help them in giving answers and a direction for their life.

Throughout the forty and more years of lecturing to them I found that it is usually the same problems and questions that occupy their minds all over the world.

Beate always accompanied me to my lectures. She firmly supported me in every way, especially in prayer. In Bremen, a lady student with a little daughter at her side once approached her after a lecture. "Are you not tired of always being in the background while your famous husband is admired and always in the center of attention? How can you endure that role? I just got a divorce, because I could not longer bear to be *only* a wife and mother. I am now going to realize myself." She looked really miserable and bitter.

"My dear lady," Beate replied, "I am so sorry to hear about your frustration. May I give you an honest answer?" "Of course, that's why I asked you. Besides you do not even look miserable. Don't you have the need and desire to realize yourself? Is it not high time that we women play the same role as men?"

"You are right," she said, "we women need also fulfillment and realization of ourselves. Yet, I experience the attainment of that goal in a different way.

1) "I believe that the role of a woman is not the same as a man's, especially in a family. There is diversity of talents and of tasks. I am happy that my husband does the lecturing and stands in the center of attention in public life. I see it as my role to support him so that he can best exercise his task. This I do by trying to create a little paradise at home from where he (and our children) can draw their strength. I am of the opinion that a woman is much more talented to create a home paradise than a man. She has a finer instinct to sense what every member of the family needs and how to realize it. I also

see my role in supporting my husband and my children with my prayers."

2) "In my experience, happiness and fulfillment originate in serving others with my will and with my gifts. Happiness is never an end in itself, but a wonderful by-product of making other people happy. What is more fulfilling, and realizes our character better, than making our fellow men happy through using our talents and imagination to this end? By chasing after happiness and self-fulfillment as an end in itself you will always want more and more—and never be ultimately satisfied."

In this age of demanding your rights and of realizing yourself she had never heard anybody speak like this to her.

We will tell more about our students lectures later on.

CHAPTER V

An Invitation to a Penitentiary

BUTZBACH

Through our lectures, we got to know and corresponded with a fine gentleman who was a social worker at a high security penitentiary in Butzbach, north of Frankfurt. A number of the convicts in this prison had been high-ranking Nazi officers, scientists and medical doctors who had been involved in killing and torturing people in concentration camps, as well as carrying out painful and inhumane experiments on them. For example, they wanted to find out the lowest temperature sailors could endure when a ship was sunk in the war and how to revive quickly. So, they cooled inmates of the concentration camp down to very low temperatures and then tried to resuscitate them. Of course, some died during the experiments, for the others it was a cruel torture they had to endure.

It was not an easy job for the young, well-trained social worker to take care of those hard-bitten men, but he tried his best. When he heard that we were passing by Butzbach on one of our travels, he asked us to come and visit the penitentiary and speak.

As far as I remember, about fifty or more convicts were locked in with us and the social worker. My young wife was the only female and everyone stared at her. I talked to them for about forty-five minutes, leaving time for questions. One of the medical doctors expressed that he did not believe in God at all. I asked him why? His answer was: "If God existed he would not have allowed our experiments on the prisoners of the concentration camp, he would have stopped or punished us." His perverse reasoning shocked me. I told him that maybe God gave them a last chance to repent for the cruel things they had committed. If they did not repent, there surely was eternal punishment awaiting them.

Of course, these men were facing life-long prison sentences or even the death penalty. Only a few seemed to feel sorry for the wrong they had inflicted on other human beings.

CANARY ISLANDS

Years later, in March 1985, we were invited to a prison in Las Palmas on the Island of Gran Canaria. An active English missionary had started some Christian prison work there. He asked me to speak on drug abuse as a number of inmates had been convicted of drug dealing. "And," he declared "drug abuse and dealing continues even inside the prison."

So we went into the prison—quite a different building from the Butzbach one. It was the old fortress, Salto Negro, very old-fashioned with thick walls and very dark. It was, I would say, a very unhealthy abode for four hundred men and twelve women. I spoke to a roomful of about one hundred prisoners, convicted of theft, drug abuse, tax evasion, etc. Men of different nationalities were present, as some of them had tried to escape to the Canary Islands, but had been caught via Interpol.

One young Englishman—not the criminal type—explained to me that he had been sailing with his boat from England to the Canary Islands. While stopping in Southern Europe, he had taken aboard two other young men at their request, together with their luggage. While waiting to get through customs in Las Palmas, the two disappeared from the boat and he was left alone. The customs officers found heroin and LSD in the luggage and he was sentenced to several years in prison. Of course, nobody believed his story.

We had a very profitable time with some of the prisoners, some of whom had become Christians through Mr. Murphy, the British missionary, who took such good care of them.

SWITZERLAND

Another time I spoke in a prison was in Switzerland. As a known specialist and advisor in drug abuse, I was invited twice to talk in a closed rehabilitation institution for drug addicts near Zürich. It was a modern establishment with a farm attached to it so that the mostly young people could work physically and regenerate outside in the fresh air.

I brought my animal menagerie and a young scientific assistant with me for the demonstration to show them the harmful effects of drug abuse. Very soon we built a friendly relationship with the inmates, especially when I offered to let them help me with the animals. Many of them were very fond of animals and loved to hold or feed the rabbits and mice. At first they were afraid I would hurt the little creatures. But when they saw that I treated them gently, I quickly won their confidence and they were ready to listen to what I had to say to help them in their deplorable situation.

CHAPTER VI

MY FIRST TWO BOOKS ON ORIGINS

I believe it was John Wesley who said that to initiate and sustain any really effective work of God it was necessary to provide suitable specialized literature. This would educate the people who come to be Christians in their problems, so that they could make a useful contribution to the Christian culture of the society in which they live.

The attacks of so called science directly or indirectly against the Christian Gospel are no less vicious today than they were at the time of the Wesleys. At the time of the Wesleys alcohol (particularly gin) was considered to be the best medical treatment for a host of minor illnesses. This view was most dangerous, for addiction to gin was the major medical problem of the land in those days. So, Wesley started to produce literature to correct this almost universal evil in England.

Today in Europe and the USA, a great problem is the teaching of Evolution in the schools and universities there. For in Europe it is taken today as an incontrovertible fact of science that Darwin has made the postulate of a divine Creator superfluous for the educated person. If God is scientifically superfluous to creation, then Christ who called Himself One with the Creator God, automatically becomes superfluous too. Thus, since Darwin, the preaching of Christ particularly in academic circles has become increasingly lacking in urgency. Chance and time are assumed to suffice to effectively replace Him by evolutionary processes.

We needed to show that a) there is really no clinching scientific evidence for Darwinism, and b) Darwinian theory cannot be falsified (Popper). If these two points are proven, Darwinism becomes utterly unscientific in its very nature, and therefore, c) the Gospel which had been for so long rendered "superfluous" by Darwinian theory, needs to be looked at again by scientists. Indeed this is urgently necessary, because science today is effectively without any scientifically sound theory of biogenesis.

So, we decided we would produce some literature specifically for use in the European academic world and prepare books on the relationship of science to the biblical account of the origin of life on Planet Earth. Obviously, the preaching of the Christian message in academic circles must deal with the "Origins" aspect of biology. For pretty well all science courses in universities take the view that biology *in toto* arose by purely naturalistic chemical processes over the passage of millions—if not billions—years in the past. This discredits the biblical account from the first book onwards.

Such naturalistic processes are universally presented in these science courses sufficing as to exclude the need for the assumption of any and all supernaturally controlled events to explain the origin of life. This aspect of creation must, for the scientist whom one wishes to help, be treated fairly and squarely both scientifically and theologically. *That is, it must be shown that scientifically speaking naturalistic, materialistic Darwinian science is inadequate to explain biology and its origin.*

Christian apologists working in academic circles, especially in European Christian circles, have largely neglected this aspect of Christian outreach. For example, they have often treated the problem of the origin of information and genetic language as exemplified in the structure and contents of the genetic code in an inadequate manner. Sooner or later the thinking and unbelieving academically trained person, listening to the preaching of the Gospel, will ask himself how the biblical story of Adam and Eve and the Garden (which the Lord Jesus believed to be historically true) lines up with the official Darwinian account of the origin of things biological.

For it is clear that not only did the Lord Jesus believe in the historicity of the Garden of Eden and Adam and Eve, but that the Apostles Paul and Jude did too.[1] Thus, if Darwinian science has proved that Adam and Eve and the Garden are non-historical myths, then the substance of what Paul and the Lord Jesus believed and taught on origins is a non-historical myth too. Thus, the *historical truth* of the Christian faith falls or stands with the *historical truth of Darwin's theories*. This should be made perfectly clear when preaching the Gospel in academic circles.

Thus in 1966, we wrote the first book for the European universities entitled *Herkunft und Zukunft des Menschen* (*Man's Origin, Man's Destiny*, 1968). I offered the manuscript to a well known evangelical publishing house in Germany who took it enthusiastically and signed a licensing agreement with me to publish and distribute it immediately.

I had just accepted a visiting professorial chair at one of the big ten universities in the USA.

When we returned to Europe after a year's tenure in the United States I inquired about *Herkunft und Zukunft des Menschen* and found out that the publishing house had indeed printed the book (as they were legally obliged to do), but had sent a copy of the book to a well known Christian German professor of mathematics to vet before distribution to the public. The good professor was and still is a convinced theistic evolutionist of the Teilhard de Chardin genre and recommended that the book not be published since it would in his view upset some Roman Catholics and most biologists too. He said not a word about the truth or otherwise of its

---

1. See Luke 3:38; Romans 5:14; 1 Corinthians 15:45; 1 Timothy 2:13–14; Jude v. 14.

contents, but based his opinion on what he considered to be expediency. This is indeed a bad policy for any Christian interested in the truth of Jesus Christ's teachings, who after all called Himself "the Truth."

The professor's fears were, of course, entirely illusory, for many Catholics reject the scientifically poorly founded views of Father Teilhard de Chardin and stand four square on a supernatural creation according to the Old and New Testament revelation.

So I went to another Christian publishing house, which had seen that the days of the old Darwinian theories, which collide frontally with the Scriptures and much of fundamental science too, were numbered. This second publishing house was interested in supporting scientists who were Christians taking the lead in scientific thought in this area. It signed on and paid for the book *Herkunft und Zukunft des Menschen* immediately.

The whole first edition of the book was sold out in a matter of a few weeks; whereupon the first publishing house, which had been afraid to publish the book, was seriously put out. It asked if it could have the whole edition back again from the second publisher, who had bought it from them in the first place. Such a course of action was, of course, not possible since the book had already been distributed publicly and was therefore beyond recall.

The book *Herkunft und Zukunft des Menschen (Man's Origin, Man's Destiny)* has since become a Christian classic in many languages of the world. It has seen multiple editions. The 1994 edition in English has come out in the USA with some new and original pictures of dinosaur footprints in Texas showing clear human footprints firmly planted in their centers. (The human who made the footprints in the dinosaur prints probably figured that if the marsh would support a huge Brontosaurus the same footprints in the marsh would support his own much smaller weight too!) The newest German edition appeared 1995.

In the 1994 English edition of *Man's Origin, Man's Destiny*, photographs of a human milk tooth found on the edge of a dinosaur footprint in Texas are shown, too. I regard this twofold evidence as clinching today that dinosaurs of some species certainly existed at the same time in history as human beings did—which certainly does not leave adequate time for Darwinian evolution to have occurred over millions of years. Instead, it totally supports the biblical revelation concerning origins and history.

More and more scientists today, even those who are antagonists of the Christian position,[1] are coming to the conclusion that the whole spectrum of biology came into being *suddenly* and not slowly over millions or billions of years.

This agrees with the Christian biblical position too. *But if the purely historical position of the Bible turns out to be reliable, what if the account it gives of the eternal future destiny of man turns out to be absolutely true too? What if the eternal consequences of Christ's death and resurrection are true for me personally in the future?*

The second book I wrote with the same aim in view was complementary to *Man's Origin, Man's Destiny* and was entitled *Die Erschaffung des Lebens (The Creation of Life)*. It, too, has become a Christian classic in several languages.

---

1. See for example S. J. Gould.

CHAPTER VII

AN EXAMPLE ON THE ORIGIN OF CODES AND LANGUAGE

Darwinians, and others too, often forget that no languages or codes have ever been known to arise exclusively by stochastic, materialistic processes.

If one were to find, say, poetry written in English on sheets of plant tissue lying around under trees in the garden. One could scarcely expect to win much credibility in scientific—or any other circles for that matter—by maintaining that both the language in which the poetry was expressed, as well as its grammar and structure, all arose by solely chemical materialistic processes. This would amount to saying that nothing in the nature of what we all term personality had any involvement in the arising of either the language of the poetry or of its intrinsic beauty and symmetry. Who would believe you if you maintained that pure chemistry wrote the poetry in English? and that no personality guided the chemistry in writing the poetry in English? One would not expect such far-out theories to find much of a receptive scientific audience.

And yet modern biologists believe without a whimper of protest that the genetic code which bears the beauty of so many forms of biology (think of some butterflies or tropical fish as well as the fantastic coral reefs on the Great Barrier Reef in Australian coastal waters) all arose solely by stochastic chemical means without any personal guidance by a personal Creator at all. The whole concept can only be termed hair-brained because it would, if true, be without precedent in all our experiences as scientists. If the whole concept were not clothed in Darwinian jargon, most people would disregard it out of hand. For, who in his right mind would ever believe that a language and code storing such beauty as we have mentioned arose without the personality of supreme intelligence behind it.

Of course, the real reason why far-out ideas, such as beauty and language, arising without an author ever caught on is because years ago scientists did not know what the origin of a language meant in scientific terms. They believed (and still do to some extent) that the adjunction of mere letters of an alphabet to produce syllables *produces meaning*, that is, that if one produces by chance alignment of letters the word "cat," the meaning and properties we associate with "cat" would be produced at the same time too. Some of my later literature on origins has gone in detail into this common error propagated by certain modern biologists.

By analogy we say that language and poetry in our experience always arise in *personality* riding on aggregates of matter, which we habitually designate as persons. Therefore, we assume that the language and poetry we found on a piece of biological tissue in the garden might have arisen in an analogous manner too, namely by some kind of personality guiding the chemistry behind the language. The materialist does not appear to use this type of logic at all, saying instead that he knows only about purely chemical reactions and that therefore chemical reactions alone must be the originators of all genetic language, codes and information. He does not know how to describe the aggregate of matter we call personality and how it goes about originating information, language or code, and therefore maintains that no such thing as person or personality really exists. Thus, for him, only impersonal chemical reactions can be behind the origin of the information, language and code we see all around us in nature and biology.

But he has not the slightest clinching evidence behind his naturalistic, materialistic assumption of *"no personality allowed in theories of origin."*

CHAPTER VIII

LITERATURE PRODUCED TREATING A VARIETY OF SUBJECTS

Our literary work was spreading rapidly on the European continent and then in the Anglo-Saxon world. At first most of our lectures took place in Switzerland, Germany and Scandinavia. But later, we were spending more and more time in the United States lecturing and publishing new literature in English this time.

The following list gives an idea of the type of literature we produced at first for European students, but soon also for American readers as well. Most books written between 1965 and 1993 originated from the many problems and questions put to us by thinking young people in the course of our lectures. By writing the books we thought we could help and reach more academics in their needs.

As already mentioned, our first two books—now become classics—were *Man's Origin, Man's Destiny* (1968) and *Creation of Life* (1970), first published in the United States at Harold Shaw Publishers. Some years before the two books had been published in German at Hänssler Publishing House, Neuhausen-Stuttgart.

The third book, which also appeared in Harold Shaw Publishers in 1969, was *The Drug Users*. In my Pharmacology courses, at the University of Illinois, I had met several students who were engaged in drug abuse and had come to me confidentially for advice. The drug culture was in full bloom. As a pharmacologist and chemist this was my field of expertise and I put a great deal of research into it. Soon I gained wide ranging knowledge through constant confrontation with the abuse of drugs that was going on around us. I felt I had to write something about this to instruct young people and help them to understand themselves and their situation. Out of these considerations grew my book *The Drug Users*.

Years later, in 1974, as drug advisor to the NATO troops in Europe and Asia in the rank of a three-star general, I authored another book on the prevailing drug problem: *The Causes and Cure of the Drug Epidemic*. At that time not only the U.S. troops and the USA, but also many European countries and their armed forces, were infested by drug abuse. Besides my work as NATO drug advisor, I was invited to lecture in universities, high schools, to the secret police, teacher training colleges, parents meetings, churches and hospitals on the topic of drug abuse. I knew that threats by the police and other authorities were useless. Young people like to experiment, even more so if prohibited. My method was to educate the people so that they understood what they were doing to themselves. To inform them about the nature and effect of drugs; their proper use and their abuse, about the danger to your body and mind if misused.

On October 26, 1983, I was invited by the national Swiss Television for a program on the drug problem in which Eva Metzger interviewed me. In that program also some sections of a film of my drug demonstrations in a Zürich teachers' college were shown to the public so that they could realize the awful consequences of drug addiction, what kind of prevention could be taken and what sort of curative measures were available.

The TV program was such a success that it had to be repeated six times, mostly at prime time, in the Swiss Television. The telephones of the TV Studio were blocked for hours, the book *Causes and Cure of the Drug Epidemic* was sold out, many people wanted help.

I had clearly stated in my program that the only alternative open to the disillusioned generation taking refuge in drug experiences was to experience the satisfying presence of God in their hearts every day.

One of the most read of my books is the little book called *Why Does God Allow It?* which appeared at first in 1978 in German and later on also in English. The question: "How can a good God of love create such a bad world? Why can He permit the suffering, the injustices, the cruelties and the miseries in our world? Should He not stop it and intervene if He indeed were a loving God?" This question plagues most thinking people who cannot find a valid answer. It keeps them away from being able to believe in a loving personal God. In trying to answer that age-old problem I wrote the booklet, and later—as I realized the tremendous need—the more detailed book *Is This a God of Love?* which was based on two older manuscripts written in 1955 and in 1960.

Other works out of my pen were: *He Who Thinks, Has To Believe* (1979), a challenging little book mixed with science and fiction. Or *Terrorismus: Das Kriminelle Gehirn* (*Terrorism: The Criminal Mind*, 1979), a booklet on the tragic consequences of today's permissiveness. One book treats the miraculously engineered functioning of our brain: *Der Mensch, Ein Sprechender Komputer* (*Man, A Speaking Computer*, 1982).

To give some help for the stress and frustration of our modern life I wrote *Der Mensch Im Stress* (*Man Under Stress*) in 1973.

In 1981, after some new fundamental discoveries in the field of information theory had been made, a new work of mine: *The Natural Sciences Know Nothing of Evolution* appeared first in German in the Swiss Schwabe Publishing House, and then in English through The Word for Today Publishing House. This together with *The Scientific Alternative to Neo-Darwinian Evolutionary Theory* (1982) is a very helpful book for academics and scientists, providing them with a firm scientific foundation why I consider Darwinian evolutionary theory to be completely unscientific. In the second book, I try to present my alternative theory.

A useful book for students and people who want to be scientifically and biblically informed is the German *Evolution Under Cross Examination*, published in 1983. It quotes the most common questions asked about evolution and tries to give scientific and biblical answers.

The students who came for counseling often told me that marriage for life according to the Bible did not meet the needs of couples today. Why not marry on the principle of commercial leasing? They had apparently never seen a really happy old couple. So in 1978, we set about writing a book on Christian marriage aimed especially at me to be called *Kunst Und Wissenschaft Der Ehe* (*The Art and Science of Marriage*). My better half wrote the art side of marriage and I treated the scientific side of the marital relationship. It found an enormous market among students and other candidates for marriage, but was widely read by older couples too, who often had difficulties in their marriages as they grew older and needed counseling.

In view of the widespread misconception in Europe concerning baptism—due to the State Churches' practice of infant baptism—we even ventured into the area of theology and baptism. In Europe, this is a source of endless confusion and strife. The little book called *Baptism, Its Influence on Christian Devotion* was the result of this venture.

When the problem of vanishing finances began to trouble many citizens, I tried to treat the causes of inflation, which is in effect state controlled devaluation of the currency in which earned wages and students' scholarships are paid. The severe inflation produced by the state impoverishes not only students, but everybody who earns a salary. The book designed to combat this state managed robbery was entitled: *Inflation, Der Dieb Im Haus* (*Inflation: The Thief in the House*, 1983).

Other books I produced about this time, included: *God, To Be or Not To Be, The Abdication of Scientific Materialism* (1979), and a little book on Philippians 3 in German entitled, *Divine Principles in the Shaping of a Personality* (1978).

Aids, Fact Without Fiction was produced in 1989 when the HIV crisis started to become epidemic inside and outside the homosexual culture and inside the academic scene. There was so much false information produced by the media all over the world that many people became victims because of this deception. I felt I had to speak out for the truth—even if it was terrifying—to help save lives from this devastating illness. I was glad that The Word For Today had the courage to publish the book in spite of enmity from various quarters.

Most of the books appeared first in German and have since been translated into English and other languages. They were then published in the United States of America and other countries as well. A number of these titles have appeared in Scandinavian languages too and some (for example: *Why Does God Allow It?*) in Russian, Romanian, Croat, Italian, Hebrew, Finnish, Norwegian and Danish.

CHAPTER IX

THE USE OF THE FILM AS A MEDIUM FOR THE PROPAGATION OF THE GOSPEL

In October 1978, I was invited to speak at the International Media Conference in Amsterdam, Holland. We returned in October 1980, when I spoke at the World Conference for Evangelical Communicators in Amsterdam on "The Relevancy of the Christian Message to a Materialistic World." Acclaimed Christian authors and media people from all over the world met and gave their lectures. Bishop Festo Kivengere from Uganda, Dr. Everett Koop—the later Surgeon General of the United States—Dr. Francis Schaeffer and myself were interviewed by Dr. Ouweneel, the Dutch scientist, for a special TV program on apologetics.

During the first conference, the EO (Evangeliske Omroep) team of the Dutch National Television, who knew my books, approached me about producing a film series in English aimed at students and other people struggling with Evolution.

They intended to produce a film series from the creationist point of view as an alternative to the many evolutionist films presented in television. They were of the opinion that I was the scientist and the personality to prove and explain the case for creation and to point out the weaknesses and errors of the evolutionary theory. My wife and I thought and prayed about the project and accepted the challenge.

In the course of six months, the EO (Evangeliske Omroep) part of the Dutch Broadcasting Company, which had at its disposal fabulous amounts of facilities and man power, sent a crack team up into the mountains of the Bernese Oberland near Einigen to work with us on a series of films entitled *The Origins Series*. This series won awards for contents and for technique. Originally the series consisted of seven films, each film self-contained and treating a specific area of origins. Topics included: The Origin of the Earth, The Origin of Man, The Origin of the Genetic Code, Dating, Fossils and Missing Links, etc. The Films for Christ Association of Phoenix, Arizona, U.S.A., took on the license and distribution of the Series and shortened them to five self-contained parts.

As many Dutch are heavy tea drinkers and smokers, my wife prepared endless pots of smoked tea for the TV team during these weeks of filming in Switzerland. It was an excellent team of young Christian men who knew their job well: technically, artistically and some even scientifically. We spent a profitable time together.

Many parts of the series were filmed in the mountains of Switzerland near our home.

Later on, we all traveled together to England where I was filmed in Darwin's study in Down presenting Darwin's theories, and then by analyzing them, explained why according to today's scientific knowledge these theories were no more tenable.

We drove to Piltdown filming the memorial place put up in remembrance of the finding of the Piltdown Man and pointed out the big well known Piltdown hoax.

In the British Museum in London several codicil and proof material for the series were documented.

The films were first shown several times in the Dutch television with great success. When I and my wife traveled in Holland to speak in universities or elsewhere people used to recognize me and talk to us in the streets, or even offer to carry our suitcase.

These *Origin* films and videos were translated into several languages including Russian, Norwegian, Chinese (Cantonese and Mandarin), Mongolian, Polish and German. For political reasons within the European evangelical groups the *Origins* film series was not produced in German for pretty well fifteen years although I needed it urgently for Pro Universitate and the lectures I was holding all over German speaking Europe.

So we used regularly the English edition of *Origins* which most German speaking European academics understood perfectly well.

CHAPTER X

SPEAKING AT DUTCH UNIVERSITIES

As a result of our *Origins* film work with The Dutch EO TV team a series of lectures at Dutch universities was organized for me in November 1980. I started with a lecture at Utrecht to approximately 250 students.

On the next day after a talk to the Christian College at Amersfoort, we proceeded to Amsterdam. There I had been invited by Dr. Wind to speak to about twenty professors of the Free University on "To what extent is the Evolutionary Theory scientifically feasible?" Although there were advocates of various origin theories present among the professors, we had a very good time together and I was asked to come back another time.

We had several lectures at Utrecht University. At the second lecture on "Materialism and the Genetic Code," the students expressed their appreciation by presenting us with a beautiful bouquet of flowers and the book *The Eighth Day of Creation* by H. F. Judson. It was encouraging to see how many students were open to new scientific truths, to weigh them, to accept them and to alter their conviction accordingly.

In Eindhoven, I spoke first at the university and then in the evening to the general public. Many people were very grateful and talked to me till late. I had to fly back to Switzerland the next day.

Another time the people from EO had arranged lectures at Delft and also at Leiden.

CHAPTER XI

REACHING FAR AWAY PARTS OF THE EARTH

During our Australian tour in 1987, my wife and I traveled out into the Australian outback with Professor John Rendle-Short. We came across a sort of barn out on its own. Professor Rendle-Short volunteered the information that his group had recently used that same barn to show my *Origins* films to the locals (engineers and other high officials) who lived in the "Outback" there.

We have experienced similar surprises in the far North—in the area of the "three countries corner" where Norway, Sweden and Finland meet and where the Lapplanders graze their reindeer. They too have seen the Norwegian version of *Origins* during the winter months when they were at home from their summer's nomadic life with the reindeer herds.

In February 1989, I was invited to Poland to speak to a Christian Medical Society on the "Implications of Darwinian Evolution for the Christian Today." A number of Polish doctors and scientists—even one or two from Czechoslovakia (at that time) had taken the risk of attending. On entering the platform, the president of the Society, Dr. Abraszowski—a worthy white-haired old medical professor—came up to me and cordially shook my hands, nearly embracing me before about 300 colleagues.

Now Englishmen are sometimes rather more conservative than other nationalities about showing their emotions. So I was somewhat taken aback at this sign of apparent affection from a perfect stranger, until I found out the complete story. Which was somewhat as follows:

The president of the society (who had so warmly greeted me) had been brought up under the communists and had been a convinced atheist—as he thought, on scientific grounds. Remember that Ockham taught scientists many years ago always to use the simplest explanatory postulate there is to deal with any phenomenon. That is, never suppose a complex explanation—like that of a God to explain the origin of everything—if something simpler will do. To invoke a God or a Creator is like taking a musket to kill a mosquito. If chance will do to explain the universe and biology rather than resorting to the explanation of a Creator, then the principle of Ockham's Razor[1] should be invoked to cut down the complexity involved, by avoiding additional "Creator" postulates.

It is much more simple (i.e., in harmony with Ockham) to postulate that chance and time made the universe, biology and all that is in it, rather than postulate that a good but invisible God up in the sky made such a bad creation. The "God Postulate" introduces, for example, the whole problem of evil. This would not arise if no God had been brought into the scheme of explanations.

Therefore, in common with most academically trained atheists, our erstwhile atheist and communist believed that one must not postulate "unnecessary" theistic theories to explain the universe and biology.

Our president was thus a convinced "scientific" atheist. But one fine day the communists sent him to Jordan on a medical aid mission. There he met and got into conversation with an American medical man who was a Christian. The American was informed by the Communist that all Christians were

---

1.   Ockham's theory was: If there were two solutions to a problem you should always accept the less complicated one.

Christians only because they were ignorant of real science. Whereupon the Christian informed the Atheist, that he could only be an Atheist because he knew far too little real science!

The American invited his Polish colleague to a film series which was just at that time being shown in Jordan. It was the *Origin* film series in English. The many various scientific facts given clearly and convincingly impressed the Polish medic deeply. He had never thought about these aspects of science, was convinced and became a Christian.

His wish from that time forth was to meet me in the flesh as it were. Hence the cordial outbreak on the platform in Poland! After which there was a session in which we dealt with the thousand and one questions of all the medic and scientists present which needed answering, especially in an atheistic country.

People such as the former atheist of Poland and others have now taken good care that the *Origins* films have been shown on public television in Poland and other former Communist countries.

One wonders why this has never been possible in the West.

Is it possibly to protect the effective Darwinian monopoly of thought in the Western media? Because if so, it *should be born in mind that atheistic and socialistic thought and practice brought Communistic states to their knees only a short while ago— and might do the same here, now that Socialistic atheistic thought seems to be taking over western thought here too.* Perhaps the West, too, is on the verge of going the same way as Soviet Russia for the same reason. The loss of absolute values by the take-over, which Communistic thought effected in Russia. These facts of recent history should be pondered by western statesmen before they too are overtaken by them.

Is it not highly significant that Germany, after wreaking Naziism on the world, was forced to undergo

"Entnazifikation" after the war and that thereby anyone who had carried out Nazi war crimes was punished for it? Where are the decommunistic trials going on in former Soviet Russia? Germany and the Germans were rightly "denazified." Why were Russia and Russians never "desocialized" or "decommunized? Was it because the victors were only victors by dint of superior military strength and not by difference in politics or ideology?

Have our present leaders in Western Europe allowed the ideology which animated Soviet Russia to migrate to the West and animate them, so that they are now in no position to judge the communists and socialists they vanquished in "decommunization" legal trials. The rank socialism in the West is proof of the fact that they are rapidly bringing the Western States to their knees just as the same spirit and ideology brought the Eastern Communists to their knees. The total atheism which inspires most of our official biology tells the same story. And yet we, in the West are supposed to practice real science. In reality, we practice just as "unscientific" a science as the communist scientists, which brought them not only to total scientific bankruptcy, but also to spiritual and financial bankruptcy.

In Russia, it was recently estimated that some 70 million people had seen the *Origins* films by means of the public television service. Having been stuffed full of "scientific" atheism for seventy years by the Communists, the public is now showing the "nausea reaction" by wanting to hear the other side too. The films bring just that.

In general, it does not seem to be clear to the average Western mortal that information theory today gives the absolute lie to all materialistic origin theories, for the simple reason that no known language, grammar or code has ever originated in chance processes.

CHAPTER XII

THE CLINCHING PROOF THAT THE "FOX AND MILLER PROOF" IS UNTENABLE

Fox and Miller showed that some racemic amino acids which occur in biology can be obtained by passing electric currents through mixtures of methane, carbon dioxide and ammonia. What he omitted to say was that these amino acids were all racemic mixtures which cannot under any circumstances be used directly for biosynthesis. For biosynthesis requires optically pure amino acids and cannot use mixtures of left handed and right handed amino acids.

From a purely chemical point of view, *all biological tissue contains what are known as optically pure molecules. Every chemist worth his salt knows that such cannot be produced by any purely Darwinian chance processes.* The science known as thermodynamics forbids it. Yet, most universities calmly continue teaching *Darwinism as the scientific explanation of biogenesis* claiming that chance produced all the codes, grammar, chemistry and language of the genetic code as well as the optically pure substances which make up the biological tissue of all species.

In order to lay a really sound basis for an atheistic origin of biology, biogenesis must be shown to have occurred purely chemically and thermodynamically. However, chance processes such as Darwinian ones do not provide such a mechanism. Christians have never really seriously addressed themselves to this ideal manner of settling the question of whether the origin of biology is materialistic or metaphysical in a scientifically clinching manner once and for all.

CHAPTER XIII

OUR FIRST PLACE OF RESIDENCE

As mentioned earlier on, we took up residence in Central Switzerland in the village of Wolhusen and lived on the top story of the Chalet known as Friedeck for the first year or so of our married life. Later we moved, at the request of the owner, into the roomier middle story of Friedeck.

During those first years the rigor of the war years began to make itself manifest in us both, for my good better half was often so weak that she had not the strength to take the short walk into the village to do the shopping. She had to make the trip by stages from one bench to the next, waiting at each stage until she had recovered enough to negotiate the next stage. Every evening after I returned from work in the laboratory and library we set about writing the literature and preparing the lectures we needed for the next lecture trip. But carrying out two professions was strenuous to say the least. After a time the fresh mountain air and the good food strengthened us both considerably.

During the four or five years we lived in our chalet in Wolhusen, my parents-in-law used to come to spend their summer vacations with us in the chalet. Particularly my mother-in-law loved the mountains. She became rejuvenated every time she came to stay with us. After all she had been brought up in the "Eulen-Gebirge," a mountain range in Eastern Germany, and could never reconcile herself to life in the great city of Frankfurt/Main.

So when we carried out our mountain tours in Switzerland, she was usually at the front of the column next to her son-in-law. On such tours we had the most delightful fellowship in discussing our plans for the future. She was absolutely at one with us in her concern for the academics of Europe who were for practical purposes unreached by the state church or—for that matter—any other Christian organizations. This despite the fact that the state churches absorb millions of dollars annually to serve their church organizations, money which is extracted from taxpayers under the rigors of the law, payable at the same time and under the same conditions as other taxes. Of course, if one resigns from the church, no church tax is due, but many people, although not expressly Christian, did not like doing that. After all, who will bury them when the time comes? The New Testament Gospel is largely unknown in organizations maintained by such means.

As the years flitted by we had success in finding pharmaceutical products for the treatment of leprosy and tuberculosis. The firm was able to exploit these inventions commercially, so that we became financially less dependent on a salary and could live more on the licenses from patents which I had won. But the elderly gentleman who invited us to get married and settle down in Wolhusen in the first place began to ail, and after four or five years of living there, we saw that we would have to be ready to change workplaces because it was uncertain into whose hands the laboratories would fall after his death. The member of the same family who took over the laboratories after his death was very kind to us, but asked me to work full-time there—we had produced a sizable income from patents even working only part-time. He reasoned that the firm's income from part-time work could now be increased considerably if we worked full time. But I was not ready for this reasonable, but for me, unacceptable logic, so I began to look around for another job.

Just at that time I was asked to do some pharmacological work for a professor in Geneva whose father (a famous

professor of theology) we knew about. So I talked with the son
(a man of about sixty years then) about theological matters as
well as about scientific ones. Although he himself confessed to
be an atheist he found that my theological views agreed pretty
much with those of his deceased father, whom he very much
respected.

CHAPTER XIV

PRIVAT DOCENT
AT GENEVA

The upshot was that this professor asked me to become his collaborator as P.D. (Privatdozent) in Geneva.

So I turned down the full time job in Wolhusen and took on the offer of "Privatdozent" (privat docent) in Geneva University at the Medical School, the job the professor had offered me. There was at the time no real salary attached to a P.D.

In some countries of continental Europe a Ph.D. does not suffice for a professorial chair at a university, one has to become "habilitated" before one can become a professor, that is one must become a "Privatdozent" before becoming professor. This is not the case of course in England, or the United States. But the title of P.D. carried an enormous reputation in continental Europe, even though at the time it carried practically no salary.

As P.D. in the University of Geneva, I earned for two lectures and two laboratories a week the princely sum of thirty-two Sfrs. *annually* (thirty U.S. dollars). But I took it on because it gave me the key to lecture in most universities in Europe on account of the academic worth of the title alone—and in the USA too—wherever they knew about the European university hierarchical professorial system.

I had enough publications where I was the first author, to be admitted for my P.D. examination. So, there was only one more hurdle to take and that was that of the public lecture, which had to be given before the whole assembled university (in French, of course).

Now, the French speaking city of Geneva and its university are exceedingly keen on the French language. One is not considered educated if one cannot speak (perfect) French. So the public examination for P.D. is held in French before the students and professors, who are chiefly interested in finding a reason why one should not be a P.D. in their worthy city.

After we had moved to Geneva and been there for some weeks, I was cited to speak at the P.D. examination. I mastered only school French, which I had never really spoken. Being perfectly fluent in German is no help in the eyes of French speaking Swiss. It is indeed rather a hindrance, since there is a good deal of antagonism between the French speaking and the German speaking Swiss because their mentalities are so very different.

So, I walked into the crowded main lecture hall at the appointed hour, put my hand into the ballot box and took out one of the tickets on which was printed the title of the subject on which I was to lecture. I had given them three subject titles on which I could lecture and these three titles were randomized in the ballot box. So one had to be ready to treat any one of the three subjects; I did not know what precisely I was going to lecture on as I entered the lecture hall.

The subject I had taken out at random was: "The Oral Treatment of Diabetes" (in French, of course). There was one other condition to be strictly observed. One had to speak for exactly sixty minutes plus or minus one minute. If one spoke for fifty-five minutes, the likelihood was that one would fail the examination. If one went on for sixty-five minutes the same result was likely—failure too.

Over and above this, the professors or the students present could ask any questions they wished on the subject of the lecture. Such questions and my replies too had to fall within the time limit, which fact could bring one's calculations on the time limit seriously into disarray. And all this had to be carried out in good French. The great difficulty was that the questions could and were often asked in various, sometimes outlandish, French dialects.

The upshot was that, after the lecture and after a few minutes of consultation, the committee of professors pronounced me P.D. of the Medical School of the University of Geneva.

The Medical School of the University of Geneva was at that time particularly glad of my help, because that university had a large contingent of American students studying medicine there because they could find no room in the United States medical schools. These young Americans used to rely on me and my lectures for information on most of the newer developments in medical science as they came up. This was particularly so in the tutorials I gave.

In spite of the difficulty of the P.D. examination, there is one thing it did not seem to do: It did not seem to improve, as far as I could see, the ability of the professors to lecture in a manner acceptable to or understandable by the students—or any other mortals for that manner. Many European professors are little interested in giving good lectures. This is mainly because one is rarely promoted on the basis of good lecturing ability, but mostly on one's ability to attract good research grant money, of which the university usually takes some forty percent as overhead "on-costs."

That is why the application form for academic posts applications in the USA and in Europe figure a column entitled "grant record" so prominently. In other words, can the university looking for a new professor expect the candidate to pay his own salary from his own grants? If not—judged by his grant record—his chances of landing the job are reduced. Thus, the new professor should in reality pay his own salary, or at least a substantial part of it!

So, I started lecturing at the University of Geneva Medical School, living meanwhile on my patent licenses. The research I did was in the field of tranquilizers and local anesthesia.

However, hardly had we settled in our little flat in Chêne-Bourg in Geneva when we had a great surprise. Pay-day for the other assistants came round and the professor sent them all round to me—for me to pay them! They were, of course, all his own personal assistants doing his own work. We had agreed that our finances would be regulated by my receiving only my P.D. "salary" and the professor would have his proportion of any discoveries I might make and which could be commercially exploited. But never was it agreed that I pay his assistants as well.

I asked for his written assurance that such irregularities would not occur again. I had been warned by the other assistants that we could expect trouble of this kind and that action would have to be taken in no uncertain manner... immediately.

So I did not turn up for work for a time, so that he would know that there would be no further nonsense of this type.

One day when I was out shopping with my wife in the city he drove past us in his large and beautiful Bentley, espied us, stopped, was conciliatory and asked me to come back. So I did. But he later tried a similar trick once more.

CHAPTER XV

THE GROWING FAMILY

Just before we left Wolhusen in 1956 my better half told me she was pregnant, and that she would prefer to have the confinement at home with her mother in Frankfurt. In any case she did not wish to enter hospital for the confinement. Under the Nazis, as a girl she had seen far too much of state medicine.

We looked around in Geneva and found a new apartment for us to move into after the confinement in Frankfurt. Of course, the new apartment was not complete on the day we had to move in.

This was another reason why we decided we would take advantage of a midwife working at the Nordost Gemeinde in Frankfurt who knew Beate well and was very experienced. If complications arose there were plenty of good hospitals in Frankfurt in the immediate neighborhood of the Nordost Gemeinde.

The nickname of the Nord-Ost midwife amongst the members of our family was "Gustl." She was very "matter-of-fact" in her attitude and not afraid of taking on responsibility. My mother-in-law was kindness itself to Beate and me and understood why Beate wanted to be at home with her for the birth of her first baby.

The labor pains came on slowly, but the actual birth of our eldest son Oliver was a process of more than twenty-four hours. He was born on January 23, 1956. Oliver was a healthy, fine child with an enormous appetite! My dear wife managed to nurse him for several months. She did it the same way with all our four children. To the unprejudiced, the result has been most encouraging.

Not only are the children healthy and strong, they all stick together with the other children and with us. I praise God for them every day of our life—and for their valiant mother.

In Geneva, we attended the Assembly of the Open Brethren in Cologny near Geneva where we found a family of wine farmers who were the leading brethren in the Assembly there. Old Alexis Corthay, the "father" of the Assembly took a liking to us. He was a thinking man and ministered frequently in the meetings. He had a kindly, mild and intelligent face and was never tired of questioning me about the scientific aspects of biblical creationism.

We now return to the story of the three other children we had been entrusted with in the meantime.

When I accepted the one year visiting professorship in Chicago in 1957, we knew that my wife was pregnant for the second time. So, the delivery would have to take place in the United States. We thought that it would probably be difficult to find a obstetrician willing to carry out a confinement at home. But my wife, on account of her experience as a girl under the Nazis, still wished to have the confinement at home.

When the university asked me if we needed help with housing, we answered yes and signed on for a "staff apartment" in the building where other members of the teaching staff also lived. For the price the university asked we thought it would be habitable. But in reality, it could hardly be described as that—for a young family at least.

We decided to take the transatlantic flight with Panam from Frankfurt to O'Hare Airport in Chicago. The Head of the Department of Pharmacology met us there, telling us not to put our luggage on the ground for even a minute, because sharpsters had luggage containers with false bottoms which they placed over the luggage they wanted to steal and which was then immediately out of view. Later on, they walked off with the stolen luggage when the owners had left in confusion.

The professor then kindly went with us to buy some groceries and saucepans, etc. He then took us to the staff apartment which had been reserved for us. It consisted of one rather dingy room, a pull-out bed, a small sized kitchen table, a couple of plates and practically no cutlery. It was dirty, and there was no bed-linen.

So I asked the professor if that was the way they received their visiting professors? He cheerfully replied: "Sure, if we can get away with it." This one remark taught me volumes on the type of treatment I was to expect in the real American world, for the professor himself was a fine man with whom we later became very friendly.

CHAPTER XVI

PETRA'S BIRTH

The date for the confinement was rapidly approaching and we could not think of carrying it out in the staff apartment of the university. So I began to look around for something more suitable and found it in the house of an Irish policeman. The policeman and his wife lived upstairs in a house on Iowa street, and we were to have the downstairs flat at a reasonable rent.

The next thing was to find an obstetrician willing to take charge of the confinement at home. We searched among our colleagues until three weeks before the great event was due. A young woman physician—a recent immigrant from Europe—said she would do it, but then backed down a few days before the due date. So, we had no one to help and my good better half began to be really anxious.

The church we attended was frequented mostly by German immigrants. There we found an old missionary doctor, who had worked for years in China. He said he had often delivered women in the backs of bullock carts. Iowa street was better than that, he thought, so he would help us. This he did with humor and skill.

Before the birth, I personally scrubbed down the whole house with Lysol solution to reduce the risk of infection as much as possible.

The confinement on May 16, 1958, went off well and our second child, a daughter, was safely delivered by Dr. Seiler. She was—and still is—a beautiful little girl (now big) with blond curls. But after a week or so, she contracted thrush. So I sent for Dr. Seiler. Before he had taken off his overcoat he asked me what formula we were feeding Petra on. So I said it was "Mother Nature's formula" thinking he would understand British humor. He looked at me, genuinely puzzled, and said he had never experienced that particular formula.

So I told him plainly that my better half was feeding the baby herself. Without a word he proceeded to put his coat on again. I insisted: "What do you recommend me to do, I cannot let the baby go on like that, she cries too much." Rather impatiently he said that as long as my wife was nursing the baby with human milk our little daughter would soon be well again, but that in the meantime I should paint her tongue with gentian violet—the standard treatment. So I did, and she soon got well again. From that time on, after she had overcome the thrush, she was a very happy child.

So we spent a happy year in Chicago. On weekends we did quite a lot of preaching at the Damen Street church where some of the German immigrants met. We also spoke often at the Fellowship Deaconry at Elburn west of Chicago. One of the fathers of the catholic church, Monsignore Schuhmacher, who had devoted his life to working among the down and outs in the slums of Chicago and was now eighty-two years of age, took a liking to us and asked us to help him several times, which we did happily for he was a godly man with whom one could pray.

Meanwhile I was, of course, in touch with the University of Geneva in Switzerland. They had apparently missed my tutorial and lecture work there and made me an offer of a chargé de cours position if I would return. As we wanted the children to have a British schooling, we prepared to return after the year in Chicago was over.

CHAPTER XVII

Back to Switzerland Again

We booked a passage on the night sleeper train from Chicago to Montreal and boarded a minute freighter, the *Catherina Sartori*, on the St. Lawrence River for Europe. The worthy captain of the 500-tonner steamer asked if I wished to entrust my family and myself to such a small boat; the Atlantic storms could be unpleasant!

Leaving the USA involved all sorts of bureaucratic work I had not bargained for. I had thought I had just to take my wife, Petra, and Oliver, buy a ticket for the transatlantic trip and go. But no, things were far less simple than that. First of all, I had to get an exit visa to certify that I had not swindled the IRS out of any taxes. This in spite of the fact that all my taxes were deducted at source, before I could even lay my hands on any of my own money, which I personally had earned by lecturing. The state had to have its portion!

The big question was our daughter. She was born in the United States, and therefore an American citizen. To just take her in her mother's arms without American papers would have amounted to a criminal offense—smuggling a citizen out of the States, in fact. So, I had to apply for an American passport for her. I therefore applied for the forms and received a sheaf of papers full of some 400 questions (in those days). Petra was about two-months-old at the time and I had under oath to guarantee she had never been an atheist or a communist, was not suffering from any communicable sexual disease or committed a criminal act, etc., etc.

But how to sign the formula? The official said I was to take her little two months old hand and make a scribble on the paper with it and then sign as her father. So I did.

But then a photo was required, too. So, I put Petra in her little baby chair and photographed her at two months old. I pointed out that the whole procedure seemed senseless, for no one would recognize her from the photo in a month's time. That is what happens when one builds up a state infrastructure which allows no personal discretion to its officials, but treats them all as dumb machines tied rigidly to paragraphs with no effective intelligent discretion of their own.

Both the official handling the case and I spent about a week sorting it out—and wasting our own time and everybody else's too—when a word from the official ought to have sufficed. The authority of the state was reduced to nonsense by the whole procedure.

So we returned to our apartment in Chêne-Bourg in Geneva which we had sub-let for a year to an American professor doing a sabbatical leave at CERN (The European Center of Nuclear Research), Geneva. We both worried that the department in Geneva would invite me back for a specific job, pay nothing towards the journey, and then back down on the agreement with no means of redress for us.

Hardly had we got back to Geneva when the Head of Department informed me that he was sorry the chargé de cours had been given by the authorities to a junior colleague of mine. There was no apology, just a statement of fact and no redress.

Professorial chairs do not appear on the market every day. I saw that we would have to go on living from our licenses, which were still good, but thought that I had better improve my qualifications in the meantime so that I could apply for a better job when it showed up.

CHAPTER XVIII

TWO MORE DOCTORAL DEGREES

I set about working for a D.Sc. degree of the University of Geneva while at the same time doing the research necessary for a doctor's degree of the Eidgenössische Technische Hochschule in Zürich (The E.T.H. in Zürich corresponds in stature roughly to the MIT in the USA.). I spent three days every week in Zürich, while my better half looked after the family in Geneva.

She was most valiant to do this. Meanwhile, I did my work as P.D. at the Medical School at Geneva as well. After three years of hard work, lecturing and doing research and carrying out the work of a P.D., I had won two further doctoral degrees, one at Zürich and one at Geneva. With three doctorates, one British and two Swiss together, with a Swiss P.D. and a Fellowship of the Royal Society of Chemistry in Great Britain, I had some good qualifications with which I hoped to land a suitable job somewhere.

Coming back to Geneva from America had been a fiasco. My professor had no money for the job of chargé de cours, but had given it to a colleague—a job which he had promised me in writing as head of department. The officials of the administration of the University of Geneva did not seem to care in the least that their professors behaved in this rather unethical manner. At that time, the European professor often had such an elevated social standing in the eyes of the public that he could frequently do pretty much as he liked.

After I had been back some years in my old job as P.D. at Geneva, a friend of mine told me that a dean of a medical faculty in Norway was looking for someone just like me. He suggested that I contact him. He thought it would be best if I were to go and see him, as this is always so much better than writing or telephoning.

When we saw that there was no relying on the position as chargé de cours in Geneva, we concluded it would be a good thing to go and see the dean mentioned. We found out that the Norwegians were wanting to change over from German textbooks to English ones in pharmacology. They needed a professor who was familiar with both languages and textbooks to help in this process.

CHAPTER XIX

A FREIGHTER JOURNEY NORTH

A little later the Dean of the Faculty in Bergen, Norway who was a Christian, asked us to come up and get to know him. We decided to go up to Norway for our holidays and to use the occasion to get to know the faculty and administration of the university at the same time.

So, in the autumn of that year, we took a freighter up the Norwegian coast from Bergen right up to Kirkenes on the Russian frontier and then back again.

The freighter we took was a small ship, the *Diana*, plying the Western coastal ports of Norway on a regular basis. Such ships had cabins for some passengers in those days. We knew the captain. He and his crew liked taking families on board, because they were so often away from their families themselves.

While going North on the *Diana* the captain took us past a guillemot rock in the Northern Atlantic. This was a lonely rock in the icy ocean where the pelagic birds[1] live.

Guillemots have very small wings with which they both fly in the air and swim under the water. Because their wings are so small, they have to beat them very fast to support themselves in the air. The result is that when they are nesting

---

1.   Birds which come to land only once a year to nest. Otherwise they live in the open ocean all their lives.

and flying to and fro from their nests they produce a sound like a gigantic organ.

The captain turned off the motors of the *Diana* as we sailed around the guillemot island, which was in the full nesting season, so that we could hear the impressive majestic organ-like sound produced by these birds. They fly straight out of the water into the air, the beat of the wings increasing as they leave the water to maintain their airborne flight.

Once when we were out in the Arctic ocean, the captain turned off the motors and we drifted for a time in silence. Then we saw a small rowboat approaching us. On board was a boy and what were obviously his parents with lots of packages and suitcases. The captain of the *Diana* put down a rope ladder which the parents in the small row boat held firmly for the boy who then proceeded to board the *Diana*. He was going further south on the *Diana* to school. They had determined by radio telephone just where to meet the *Diana* out in the ocean and had rowed out to rendezvous with the ship. All of life revolved around these little freighters up in the far north at that time.

The captain showed us a small island with just enough room on it to build one little wooden church. There was no room for other houses on this speck of land in the Arctic ocean. The captain told us that the church was placed so centrally that the maximum number of people from the surrounding islands could make the journey to church in their own boats on a Sunday.

In the far north, with its coastal areas so divided up by fjords small and great, there are no railways and few roads. Thus, communications there are the responsibility of ships. Arctic culture is quite different from that to which we were used. Up North, after having visited Hammerfest, the northern-most settlement of the European Continent, and the North Cape, we left the *Diana* and drove inland. Our intention was to go and see the Laplanders who had their settlements area where Norway, Sweden and Finland meet (called the "Three-Country-Corner").

In contrast to the tall, blue-eyed Norwegians, the Lapps are short in stature, dark-eyed and dark-haired with high cheek bones. They are believed to have immigrated 10,000 years ago from Central Asia. Their language is distantly related to the Finnish and the Estonian languages.

Most of the Lapps are nomads during the summer-time, tending their reindeer herds and living in tents. They wear beautiful colorful costumes and sell reindeer skins and handicraft made from reindeer antlers, bones or fur as well as embroidered articles to tourists. During the winter, they return to their settlements, where the families and the old stay all year. In the settlements, they have their churches and their schools. Here they also get married.

Most Lapps are Lutherans and Evangelical Congregationalists. Little more than one hundred years ago Laestadius evangelized among the Lapps. Many Lapps became Christians. The Lapps had the habit of drinking heavily and spending much money on drinking. As a result, their families were often ruined and used to live in great misery. For that reason Laestadius taught the Lapps personal asceticism. He forbade them to touch alcohol as soon as they had become Christians and encouraged open confession of sins. He set these strict rules to save their family life.

As we looked for the Lapps, we drove through meager grasslands with dwarf birches. It was very foggy that morning and the visibility was very poor. But we could hear the Lapps laughing and talking and the barking of their dogs. As it was damp and chilly, they had lighted an open fire and were warming themselves. When they noticed us they surrounded us and offered their handicraft which was exhibited on a small table. After admiring their handmade objects, we bought a beautiful reindeer skin. At our request they kindly showed us the inside of their tent with all their everyday utensils.

CHAPTER XX

FROM NORWAY TO SPITSBERGEN (SVALBARD)

Prior to leaving, we had booked with our Hamburg Travel Agency for that summer of 1959 a passage on a small mail boat, the *Lyngen*, departing from Tromsö via Bear Island (Björn Öya) to Svalbard (Spitsbergen) high up in the North. During the summer, this boat brought the mail to various stations in Svalbard. During the colder months, there was too much pack-ice and there were no boats running up to Spitsbergen. The people up North were very isolated. At that time there existed no airports in Svalbard. The mail was sometimes dropped by aircraft in winter.

Although we had fair weather, the heavy swell of the Arctic Ocean was considerable. So most of the few passengers the ship could accommodate were seasick. At that time, such small boats had no stabilizers and rolled with every wave. Our family quite enjoyed the experience as we were already used to sea travel with all its accompaniments. Especially little Oliver was thrilled with the waves splashing on the deck and onto him. He thought it was an easy and good way to get washed. A pair of porpoises rode the ship's bow wave and dolphins played daily around the boat.

Bear Island (Björn Öya)—about halfway between Norway and Spitsbergen—was very rugged. Only one or two persons—meteorologists—disembarked from our boat to relieve some of the crew of the meteorological station located there.

The next day, on August 13, we sighted Svalbard and anchored on the southern tip of the island. Here, at Isbjörnhamna in the Hornsund, camped a group of Polish geologists—isolated from the rest of the world (there are no roads, nor transport, nor even people)—to carry through their investigations on permafrost in connection with the International Geophysical Year. They needed food and supplies. Only six persons from our ship were allowed to accompany some of the ship's officers ashore. Because of much pack-ice, the *Lyngen* had to stay out at sea and we drove to shore with a little motor lifeboat. As I was the only scientist on board, I was chosen to go along and talk to the Polish scientists in their scanty shacks. The Polish leader of the expedition, Dr. Siedledzsky, discussed his project with me and showed me some of their work on the permafrost. This was important, as an airport was envisaged for Svalbard.

They told me about the visits of nosy polar bears searching for food around their barracks, ransacking their garbage pails.

We journeyed on, enjoying the beautiful view of Svalbard and encountering one or two floating icebergs, which shimmered white and light blue. Finally, we reached Longyearbyen, the largest Norwegian settlement of Spitsbergen. We noticed massive smoke clouds over some land areas. The ship's officers explained that these were burning coal fields. They had been burning for years as a result of shelling by German warships during the last World war, when the German military had occupied the country.

Usually, young Norwegians came to Svalbard and worked there for a few years in the coal mines or as administrators, because the wages were good and the taxes lower than in Norway. Longyearbyen is the capital of Svalbard. The governor, the so-called sysselman, who represents the political, administrative, juridical and police authority, lives here. In 1925, Svalbard was declared part of Norway although other nations had also established settlements there for mining and trapping. Some of them stayed in their settlements, for example, the Russians who were still mining there. They had 2,500 miners in Svalbard, while the number of the Norwegian miners was only 500.

A young German dental technician, an acquaintance of ours, lived and worked there for a couple of years. She enjoyed her time in Longyearbyen although she was quite cut off from the rest of the world. She found the Northern Lights (borea aurealis) in the winter, the husky sledge rides, as well as the close fellowship of this small community, to be unique experiences.

S.A. Andrée, the Swedish scientist, worked here near Longyearbyen, to produce hydrogen for his balloon with which he made the fatal voyage over the North Pole in 1897. We could still see the little pieces of iron littering the countryside.

A few days later the ship sailed further north along the coast of Spitsbergen to Ny-Alesund. Outside Ny-Alesund we came across a memorial tablet indicating that in 1926 Nobile with Amundsen and Ellsworth had started their trip over the North Pole to Alaska from here in their dirigible "Norge."

It is here that our little daughter Petra took her first steps and learned to walk.

As the summer was warmer and longer than usual that year, the pack-ice had receded further north and our ship could venture further north. The captain navigated the *Lyngen* up to the Magdalenen Bucht (Magdalenen Bay). Here he and his first officer took us ashore in the small life-boat of the *Lyngen*. The *Lyngen* had to anchor further out to sea as there was no harbor or place to dock.

At the beginning of the seventeenth century, Dutch and English whalers came to Norway. For three centuries they caught whales for their whaling industries, until in 1920 there were practically no more whales left. The same fate overtook the seals. The Dutch whalers came up to Svalbard while most of the others fished further south. These whalers produced the first maps of Svalbard.

Here in Magdalenen Bay the captain showed us where the whalers, who had died on their long journey of scurvy due to heavy vitamin C deficiency, lay buried. The dead could not be buried in the ground for it consisted of solid rock. Therefore, they had buried the mortal remains above ground in caskets which had been worn down by the ravages of time. The first officer showed us human skulls and skeletons which were often quite well preserved due to the cold climate. As we were very interested in the history of the old whalers and their way of life, he wanted to present me with the loose tooth of a whaler's skull as a souvenir from Spitsbergen. But I politely refused!

For us it was most interesting to see the calving of the big glacier in Magdalenen Bay. The air over the Arctic water was crystal-clear, everything looked very near, even when it was a few miles away. From time to time, big chunks of the glacier broke off, noisily crashing into the sea accompanied by a sound like thunder. Fortunately, we were far enough away, as the huge ice-blocks would have crushed anything nearby. The glacier moved forward about several centimeters per day.

After turning to sail back south we stopped again at Longyearbyen and then headed back to Tromsö. We passed Barentsburg, the Russian coal settlement on Spitsbergen. Our captain had tried to get a permit for us to visit Barentsburg, but to no avail.

But before leaving Spitsbergen behind us, one further experience must be recounted. The captain of the *Lyngen* had set a fixed departure time from Longyearbyen. So that nobody would miss the time, he had it written down on the blackboard beside the gangway. At the set time—if I remember correctly it was 5:00 p.m.—one of the small group of passengers was missing. Nobody knew where he was. The captain waited for half an hour or so. When nobody turned up he gave the command to weigh anchor.

Half an hour out to sea we saw a small motor boat in the far distance racing in our direction with somebody waving a white flag. Everybody watched this small boat trying to catch up with us with or without binoculars. The captain reduced the speed. I think he anticipated what was to follow. The missing passenger had climbed a small mountain near Longyearbyen. On his late return, he had found his ship gone, and then had tried to hire a seaman with a motorboat to follow the *Lyngen*. At first he could not find anybody willing to help. In the end—when he offered a high remuneration— somebody agreed to take him to the departed *Lyngen*.

Of course, everybody knew that the next opportunity for our man to return to Norway or any other European country would have been in one or six months. There were no hotels at that time in Longyearbyen or anywhere in Spitsbergen. During our stay and journey in Spitsbergen, we had always had our board and lodging on the *Lyngen*. And mail boats arrived at the most once a month during the summer. There were no cruise ships as nowadays.

There was quite a heavy swell and the motor launch had a rough time making its way towards us. When the boat was beside the *Lyngen*, the officers let down the rope ladder onto which the passenger was supposed to jump and hold on to. As the waves were violent, throwing the little boat against the bigger *Lyngen* it needed great skill on all sides to succeed in this venture. But every time the launch was in the right position for the passenger to jump—a time of only one or two seconds—he missed the rope ladder and the whole procedure had to be repeated. The captain and the seaman on the launch both started to shout at the passenger who by now looked green and white and not at all healthy. In the end, the seaman gave him a big shove out of the boat towards the rope ladder at the right moment. With the help of a sailor from the crew and much pushing and dragging the man was hauled up the ladder into the ship. The captain gave him a nice little welcome speech, after which the exhausted and sea-sick passenger retired into his cabin. I am convinced that never in his life on any other occasion was he late again!

During the term vacations at the University of Bergen we took freighters along the coast right up to Kirkenes a number of times. In Kirkenes, which is on the Norwegian side of the Russian frontier, there were places marked by miles and miles of barbed wire, designating the frontier through the Arctic wilderness. At set places, there were footsteps concreted into the ground into which one was allowed to put one's feet and look with field glasses. But one was required to stand so that the glasses could not look into Russia proper, but only into Norwegian territory! What the Soviets had to hide up there in that Arctic tundra in those days is anyone's guess. Maybe it was only a bad conscience which the Soviets wished to hide!

CHAPTER XXI

A Grave Misunderstanding With Political Consequences

On completing their courses at high school, on becoming eligible to apply for a place to study at the university, it is customary for high schoolers in Norway to celebrate this great occasion. In Norway they acquire a little special peaked cap at this celebration which distinguishes them as "academics" from other mere mortals.

One year the high schoolers in Kirkenes celebrated this great occasion of becoming "academics" by going to this place on the barbed wire separating Norway from Soviet Russia and singing student songs with their peaked hats on. And thereby hangs a story. The next day the Soviets protested in Oslo to the Norwegians that there had been a "military demonstration" on the frontier. The Norwegians were terrified of offending the Communists in any way—and apologized and warned the youngsters of Kirkenes that this must not occur again.

The Communists had mistaken the academic peaked hats for a military uniform! They had not the slightest idea of the customs of their next door neighbors, the Norwegians.

We sailed down the Norwegian west coast visiting hundreds of small ports and loading and unloading freight of all kinds. Thus, we got to know many small villages otherwise cut off from the outside world. When we got as far as Bergen, we disembarked with Petra and Oliver, and went to make the acquaintance of the Dean and his family. The Dean's wife was a dental surgeon, a lovely Christian, and a wonderful character. As a young girl, she had been an officer in the Salvation Army.

We found both the Dean and his family to be delightful people. He engaged me for one year to lecture and do pharmacological research on the therapy of leprosy (leprosy had been endemic in Bergen in past centuries and Hansen had discovered Mycobacterium leprae[1] there). So, we decided to accept the visiting chair of pharmacology in Bergen and to effect the desired transfer from German to English pharmacological textbooks.

---

1.   The microorganism causing leprosy.

CHAPTER XXII

THE PASSING OF MY MOTHER-IN-LAW

When we were up in Northern Norway, we received an urgent telegram from Frankfurt to tell us that our good mother-in-law was dying, and ask us to return home immediately. But we reached Frankfurt a day too late to see her before she set out on the long journey we all must take. My father-in-law was exemplary in his great loss, for the relationship of the pastor to his wife was one of the phenomena which sustained the Nordost Gemeinde in Frankfurt. Their home was a source of encouragement to all. Just before my mother-in-law had passed on my father-in-law had applied for a small country church in an effort to give her the courage to fight the cancer of the spine from which she was suffering. But she died before this plan could be effected.

My father-in-law was due to retire from the Nordost Gemeinde a year or two later. After my mother-in-law's death, he took on a position as lecturer at the Bible school of the Liebenzeller Mission in the Black Forest. He worked there for about seventeen years in his "retirement." He was a universal favorite among the students and others in the Bible school. We sometimes held courses with him there on Bible and Science and so were able to work together. We never had any difficulties, for we understood one another perfectly. We both had one aim—that of bringing young and old to a deeper knowledge of Jesus Christ.

He had very strong views on theology, particularly on the reliability of the Holy Scriptures and published a number of books on the subject. Those are still read in the German language in which they were written. But throughout these years of being a widower, he sorely missed the warmth and love of my mother-in-law, although I never heard him complain so much as once.

CHAPTER XXIII

THE JOURNEY TO BERGEN

After this first trip to Norway, we returned to our tiny apartment in Geneva and wound up our work at the medical school. The Head of Department was surprised I had found another professorial chair and was not afraid of traveling. I believe he thought that I would continue to do the P.D. work under any conditions they cared to impose, because of my family responsibilities, and because the necessity of travel to obtain a chair elsewhere would prevent my taking on another chair. He was wrong!

Again, we took to the car (our old Mercedes 180) again with Oliver and Petra and my good wife (always willing for strenuous adventures) in January 1960, little knowing what a winter's journey to the Arctic north with two small children on board might bring.

In Gothenburg, in Sweden, we went to what looked like a decent hotel, but when we opened the door with the children on our arms, a couple—both totally drunk—literally fell into our arms down the hotel steps. With two children on our arms, the consequences, on those high concrete steps, might have been serious.

The next morning, we drove on over the Norwegian frontier to Oslo. In winter one could not drive from Oslo over the mountains to Bergen. The mountain roads were all blocked by snow and we had to take the train. So we went to the station in Oslo where the kindly station master was obviously taken by Beate's courage to travel in winter with two small children and opened up a specially heated room for us. Later, we boarded the night train to Bergen, the station master having secured us a suitable sleeping car and put the Mercedes on the same train, too.

When we got up the next morning in Bergen, we looked for our car. During the night the train had been through the numerous tunnels through which the railway line runs while traversing the high mountains separating Oslo from the West coast of Norway. The car had apparently changed color from green to dark grey in the night. In those days the line was not electrified and they used old steam locomotives which I suppose used brown coal. As a result, we were all black by the morning for the same reason.

So we put up at a hotel just to wash and spruce up before I reported to the university offices.

The old familiar problem as to where to live turned up once more. It was January. Some friends put us into touch with a contractor who had built himself a new house and wanted to sell or let his beautiful old wooden house right on the cliffs overlooking the Bergen Fjord. It was in a superb situation with a big property although not exactly the last word in comfort or modern amenities. As Helgaheim, our house, with the huge property reaching right down to the fjord, was situated on a hill, we had a splendid view over the fjord, the neighboring villages around the various bays and the island of Askoy.

From this vantage point, we later watched hundreds of busy boats sailing or steaming to and from Bergen harbor. We learned to recognize the beat of the *Diana*'s (the boat on which we had traveled north during our holidays) two stroke diesel engines whenever she cruised by us on the way north or south. At Christmas time, the *Diana* carried a huge brightly illuminated Christmas tree before its bridge which fascinated our children.

So we gladly rented Helgaheim. However, the house was situated in the village of Tertnes, in the Aasane district, some fifteen miles outside Bergen over a mountainous road. The floors were of untreated wood but from our experience with Swiss Chalets, we did not mind that. It was heated with wood by iron stoves. But the climate round about Bergen was maritime and it was situated right over the Bergen fjord. So we benefited from the warmth of the Gulf Stream. In Tertnes there was usually little snow in winter.

CHAPTER XXIV

THE BEDEHUS

In the village itself there was a little "Bedehus."[1] The Christians of the village had built the little Bedehus, because the village itself was too small to support a permanent pastor and a church. So the believers met there from time to time to pray, have Bible readings, and to celebrate the Lord's Supper.

One night a prayer meeting in the Bedehus to be taken by the pastor of the Lutheran state church in a neighboring village was advertised. So we thought we would attend to get to know the people. We did not yet speak Norwegian, so we sat at the back in an inconspicuous place. The pastor celebrated the Lord's Supper. The wine and the bread on the table were all duly covered over by a white cloth. As a Lutheran, he wore a large white ruff where an ordinary English pastor would have worn a "dog collar."

Some Lutherans are more conservative than others and we did not know to what category this one belonged. My wife came from Lutheran background, but caution was indicated where the participation in the Lord's Supper is concerned. Sure enough, although we understood no local dialect, he started the service in "Nynorsk." (In Tertnes they speak "Nynorsk" and not "Riksmål"). Both languages are official but not yet interchangeable. We had not yet learned either. The Pastor called those who wished to partake of the Lord's Supper to come forward to the railing at the front.

---

1. A "House of prayer" (when we were back in Bergen in 1993 it had been burned down by vandals).

We remained seated out of pure caution, in case he was a "churchy" Lutheran who did not recognize what he might consider to be mere Anglicans. But he had espied us and held a quite impassioned invitation for us to come forward and partake. We were not quite sure what it was all about on account of the language difficulty and remained seated until the dear man came personally to the back and took us by the hand to the front railing where we were given the elements. Needless to say the pastor was one of the "open sort" who had studied theology at the Hallesby Menighets Fakultetet in Oslo—a Norwegian conservative theological academy which for years supplied most of the Norwegian West Coast and other parts of Norway with conservative pastors.

CHAPTER XXV

SETTLING IN

My wife and I then set about taking Norwegian classes and found it relatively easy to learn. Its vocabulary is fairly closely related to German and English vocabularies whereas its grammar is typically Germanic. Both of us found that we could get by in Norwegian at the seminars and when out shopping after about six months. Most educated Norwegians speak English, so that it is sometimes difficult to find someone on whom to practice one's Norwegian. But they are delighted when they find out that one has taken the trouble to learn their own language...because so few foreigners do. Beate and I still read the Norwegian Bible every day, so we have not forgotten the language.

We soon made good friends with the Dean of Medicine's daughter and her husband who also lived in Tertnes with their family. We spent delightful times together getting to know Norwegian hospitality and customs. We loved the Norwegian smörgasbord, offering all kinds of fish, various cheeses, including the delicious gjetost (goats' cheese), the refreshing kefir and their many different choices of bread.

On May 17, the Norwegian national holiday, we watched the annual parade of the beautiful national costumes worn in honor of the day. Our friends gave Petra a beautifully embroidered Hardanger costume, which their daughter had outgrown and which she wore with great pride. Our families used to come together for Bible studies which helped us not only spiritually, but also linguistically.

Bergen is a charming old town. It used to be the most important town of the country, because of its excellent position on the coast. The harbor of Bergen was always ice-free because of the gulf stream passing it. Have you ever walked along the "Torget" and admired the colorful old Hanseatic buildings? The harbor where the dignified *Statsraad Lehmkuhl,* the old training sail ship, anchors? In the middle lies the big fish market, the landmark of Bergen where we frequently bought our fresh fish, brought in by the fishermen every day and sold: They had so many varieties that you could eat a different kind of fish every day of the week. We took advantage of it and never got tired of Norwegian fish. Meat in Norway is dear and the quality at that time was mediocre. So we preferred fish or whale meat by far.

When one takes the "Fløbanen," the little cogwheel train up to the mountain top of the Fløen above Bergen, the view from there is breath-taking looking down on the fjords and islands, the harbor with the many ships and the town. We greatly enjoyed our stay in Norway.

CHAPTER XXVI

CLIVE'S BIRTH

Meanwhile, the time of my wife's third confinement was approaching. Medicine is state-run in Norway, but my wife still wished to have the baby at home—although the hospital confinement would have cost nothing, she wished it that way. The Norwegian state encourages women to have their babies at home. They have excellent mid-wives and there is less danger of infection after the birth.

So I looked around for a mid-wife and found Fru Drønning, who lived quite near us in Ternes. Yes, she would willingly come and officiate at the confinement. Had there been any complications at Oliver's or Petra's births? No.

When the labor pains started, I telephoned Fru Drønning and she arrived shortly afterwards in our house. I had taken a little stroll with Beate in our beautiful little garden on the fjord. Clive, our third child and second son, was born so quickly that Fru Drønning arrived only just in time. We could only thank God for this.

Out of deference to the land of his birth, we called him Clive Haakon after the brave King Haakon who spent the Second World War in exile in England. For some reason Clive was Daddy's boy from the start.

As soon as he heard the sound of my old Mercedes coming over the mountainous road, he would start reaching out for me from his mother's arms as I came into the house, regardless of the laws of gravity, until he was in my arms. Then he would calm down with little grunts of sheer satisfaction.

Shortly after Clive's arrival I was preparing for a lecture at the university when an official from the Town Hall turned up and asked to see me urgently. I sent the message that I could not come at the moment as I was lecturing. But he insisted and said I would be sorry if I did not manage to come. What did he want?—You would never guess! He said that we had carried out the confinement at home and thus saved the state a certain sum of money which he wanted to hand over to me personally, which he did on the spot.

Beate was glad of the money for buying baby clothes and baby shoes. Every month after that we received a certain sum of money from the state (child benefit) for each child, which Beate used for new clothing as the children grew.

I have seldom known a state like the Norwegian State, which was so honest with its tax money that it paid back in cash, and of its own free will, money for services which are its responsibility but which the citizen had carried out himself. Try to imagine the Swiss State, for example, paying back the money we have paid in excess for garbage collection for the last ten years. We have been charged for eleven persons for all these years and yet are only two of us, Beate and me. This is, of course, because the garbage charge in Switzerland is not on the number of persons living in the house—which would be logical—but on the number of rooms in the house—which is illogical. Just consider any one of the numerous other social services one pays for and does not use. I have not had much contact to date with local tax offices wishing to refund me for anything much of their own free will. But the Norwegian State was the grand exception.

CHAPTER XXVII

THE VISIT OF THE KING

After our third child, Clive, was born in Tertnes, in May 1960, my wife and I, together with all the professors of the university, were invited to a concert evening with the Norwegian King Olaf. At that time, my brother with his wife and four daughters were staying with us for a visit from England. My wife and I were looking forward to that festive evening. Before we left the house we talked with our capable young German nurse who helped us with the children, asking her to keep a watchful eye on our little baby son. The youngest little niece was only three-years-old and very interested in the baby. "Please leave the washing-up of the dishes, we can do it later," we told Fräulein Erika, "just watch little Clive!"

We drove towards Bergen through the dark woods down the narrow, winding road leading to the fjord. Suddenly my wife grasped my hand and exclaimed: "Stop!" Her face was pale and she looked frightened. "What is the matter, dear?" I asked. "It's the baby, we have to go home. Something happened to the baby," she stammered. With great difficulty I turned the Mercedes round on the narrow winding road, ready to drive home. I had just turned round when she relaxed and whispered: "It's O.K. now, we can drive on to see the King!" You can imagine that my reaction at that moment was not the most favorable one. But as my wife's behavior at that moment was so atypical and new for her, I turned the car back again and drove on to Bergen. I quickly glanced at my watch and noted the time: 18:50. We spent an enjoyable evening with good music, speeches from and to the King, etc. together.

When we arrived home at Tertnes after the function, we asked Fräulein Erika, who was an intelligent, conscientious girl: "What happened tonight at ten minutes to seven?" She blushed and answered: "I did not want to leave the washing-up for you afterwards, so I did it. Suddenly, I heard little steps upstairs in your bedroom. I rushed up the stairs and there stood the little three-year-old girl. She had grasped the baby by his legs and had pulled him out of bed. His head bumped on the coarse wooden floor-boards as she dragged him along to the top of the stairs, down which she was planning to haul him and show him to us. I caught them at the top of the stairs and saved the baby. The baby is all right, he only has a few little scratches on the back of his head from the wooden floor. The time I saved the baby was 18:50." We thanked God for his protection. But how had my wife received the baby's "emergency call"?

Initially, I had been engaged by the Dean for one year. After the year was over, the head of department asked me if I would consider staying for a further year on the same basis as before. I accepted as we were very happy in Norway and had learned the language successfully—to the delight of the Norwegians. Most Norwegians loved the British, who had, after all, shed their blood to save Norway in the Second World War. Our research had gone well in Bergen and we had published quite a lot of work on leprostatics and local anesthesia.

We had increasing contact with the local Norwegian Christians and started publishing smaller Christian books in Norwegian. Beate also liked the maritime climate of the West coast.

But today every country has its peculiar difficulties, and Norway is no exception. The welfare state in particular is no exception. In the meantime, other Norwegians had become qualified for the position of chair of pharmacology. The question was: Why did the State University of Bergen employ a foreigner to do a job which a Norwegian could do just as well? Now that the transfer to English text books had been effected there were Norwegians just waiting for my position to become empty once again.

So we cast around for the next step to take. We now had three small children and Clive was just starting to walk when we set out for Geneva once again. We still had the same small apartment in Chêne-Bourg, which was now too small for the five of us. It was difficult to have to return to Geneva with three small children to a position which I knew could not be permanent, because it was not paid.

The faculty in Geneva asked me to lecture twice a week instead of once a week and to do more tutorials. So I put pride in my pocket and did. But I often felt like giving the administration a piece of my mind. But what was the use? They could always say: "Go somewhere else if you don't like it with us." Lots of academics in Europe and elsewhere are in the same position today. Many young medical doctors with young families start work in the operating theaters at 7:00 a.m. and do not get back home before 8:00 p.m., because the university will not employ other young doctors, even those who are jobless because they say their budgets do not balance. The real reason they have not the money is that they squander it on the administration and their huge and modern buildings. But the young doctors have to work twelve hours daily and risk breaking up their families, not to speak of the increased risk to their patients.

The tendency today everywhere is to save and reduce on the specialists who do the real work and increase on the administration, which costs a lot of money and is of little profit financially, nor academically, nor for the patients. Resources are squandered on facilitating and modernizing the administrators' lives—and their number—while complaining about lack of resources and the inability to employ a few more doctors to relieve their overwork. This overwork is associated with the risk of qualitatively mediocre work because of long hours and fatigue. Statistics show that the recent colossal increases in medical costs are mainly the result of increased administrative expense rather than any increases in the cost of purely medical activities such as the salaries of doctors and nurses, medicines or medical equipment. In addition, the interference of the under-worked administrative staff in matters previously purely the province of clinical and medical staff—who undergo years of specialized training to learn how to take such life and death decisions—seriously impairs the quality of the medical services provided.

CHAPTER XXVIII

A FULL CHAIR AT THE UNIVERSITY OF ILLINOIS

After two or three years, a job as full Professor of Pharmacology turned up at Illinois where I had already spent a year. The Senate there initially offered me an Associate Chair of Pharmacology. This I turned down on the grounds that with three European doctoral degrees, and a P.D. on top of that, I was no longer interested taking an associate chair.

Their reply was that they would reconsider the full chair proposition *after* I had been back at Chicago in an associate chair for some years. Remembering the words of the professor who met me the first time we were in Chicago "that the University would try anything it could get away with," I turned that offer down too out of hand and said I would not invest in another Atlantic journey at my own expense with four little children unless the full chair were assured me by the Senate *before* I set out.

We had to consider too that during these years I had worked for the two Swiss doctorates, and we had been entrusted with another son, Einar. This meant that the responsibilities we had to take on in our travels were even greater than before. We now had four little ones to think of instead of three. Evidently, I was very interested indeed to hear the response which the Senate in Chicago gave to my most recent missive.

This time, however, they got the message and by return mail I had the official invitation for the full chair of pharmacology in the College of Pharmacy together with the post of Head of Pharmacological Research at the Medical Center. This was a good post since the University of Illinois is one of the "Big Ten" Universities in the United States.

But they still offered to pay nothing for my traveling expenses. So we set out by freighter from Antwerp for the USA at our own expense.

On the Atlantic Ocean, after we had left Antwerp, we received a radio message to say that my good father had died, so I could not even go to his funeral. This made us both sad.

We had crossed the Atlantic on an empty corn and wheat freighter owned by a Swiss Christian who earned his living by supplying the Swiss government with American cereals. Because it was totally empty, the boat stood so high out of the water that it caught the wind in a most uncomfortable manner. Off the U.S. coast we ran into a hurricane and had to heave to for several days and put out the sea anchors. The children used the heaving of the ship, when the floor of our cabin behaved as though it were a wall, to slide up and down on cushions.

Eventually we arrived at Philadelphia only to find that the longshoremen were all on strike and would allow no one to land. The captain allowed us to stay on board: he had no other option.

We had brought with us a brand new Mercedes 190 which was transported on deck and had been exposed for many days to the Atlantic storms. The captain came privately to me one day and said he did not know how long these longshoremen would delay us, and that they were a tough lot to deal with. But he was ready for them. He planned to invite their leader into his office and talk with him over a bottle of whiskey. While he was doing that, he would instruct his crew to take the ship's electric crane and unload us and our car while nobody was looking. But I must get everything ready to be up and away before you could say "Jack Robinson." So I paid the captain for the extra week's enforced board and lodging on the ship and prepared to leave.

We got our four children ready and put all our luggage into the car. The captain disappeared into his cabin with a large whiskey bottle, our car was hitched to the ship's crane and away we were. On the quay-side I pressed the starter button, but the motor showed no signs of life. Obviously the salt water had done its work by shorting out the spark plugs.

We were afraid the longshoremen would see us struggling with the motor. But I had the spark plugs out in a very short time, cleaned them, and then tried again. Away she went this time on two cylinders, picking up on all four as we drove out of the dock area.

CHAPTER XXIX

THE JOURNEY TO CHICAGO BY CAR

We drove out gingerly onto the turnpike in the direction of Ohio and Detroit. The traffic was very heavy compared to the European scene to which we were accustomed. After driving some hours we noticed that the turnpike had suddenly become empty of traffic and on the Western horizon before us was a huge dark bank of clouds. It was obviously a weather front which was the reason everyone had disappeared and sought hotels.

Suddenly a howling blizzard broke upon us, and it became so cold that the carburetor of the new Mercedes froze up completely. One could only keep going by putting one's foot hard on the accelerator and pulling on the hand brake so that one did not go too fast, so keeping the motor hot enough to overcome the icy blast of the blizzard. In the end we stopped at a garage to take on gasoline and asked where we could put up with our four children. Everything was full up to the last room. A kindly policeman saw our plight and went to a private house for us. He asked the good lady of the house to put us up for the night, which she graciously did. The next morning we went outside to inspect our car—and could find it nowhere. It was totally buried under several feet of snow. So we dug it out, thanked the good lady, paid what we owed her and set out again for Chicago.

This time we did not wish to live in Chicago itself. I thought of how much my mother-in-law had suffered by life in

Frankfurt. So we sought a house in Wheaton, a suburb about thirty miles from the center of Chicago. There were plenty of houses for sale in Wheaton, but we did not have the money for the deposit to buy one and therefore looked for one to rent. We still did not wish to bind ourselves by debt. So we sought and sought and sought again until we found a businessman who wished to go abroad to work for a number of years. He offered to rent us his furnished house and we moved in immediately with the four children. We were most grateful for this solution.

Chapter XXX

The Brain Wave

I used to leave home every morning about 7:00 a.m. for the one hour train journey to the Chicago and North Western Station in Chicago. From there it was not far by foot to Polk Street and the Medical Center where I worked.

In winter, the severest part of the journey was that in Chicago itself. It was here that I found out truth of the name "windy city" for Chicago. The icy blast from the prairie in January was something that even a person who had survived the climate of Stockton-on-Tees could scarcely put up with. But even the icy prairie blast had its uses. One day in January, I left the overheated train from Wheaton to proceed to the Medical Center, and as I left the Chicago and North Western Station an icy blast hit me on the pedestrian crossing outside the station. I suppose the blast must have given me quite a shock, for as the wind struck me I had a sudden brain wave which solved a problem of evolutionary theory I had been thinking about for some ten years. It suddenly flashed into my mind that time allowances alone will never bring any reversible reaction to completion, but merely to equilibrium. Biological reactions are mostly reversible ones, so that no matter how many billions of years the Darwinian scientists propose, they will do nothing to bring any biological processes to completion: They will just perfect their equilibrium. Thermodynamics controls just that vital point.

All I needed to do next was go to my office and write up what I had "seen" in that "flash." It took me the best part of a day to do so. It was a revelation to me to experience how much thought the brain can handle in a "flash." How evolutionists and others can ever imagine that such a rapid functioning organ, as the brain undoubtedly is, arose by chance chemical reactions is a mystery to me. But that is not the only mystery, there are even bigger ones around.

The brain and all the organs of the body are built on the basis of a blueprint—the genetic code. To my mind, to seriously believe that any blueprint could have had its origin in chance betrays a total lack of knowledge concerning the origin of any code, grammar or information.

One says that in the seconds before a car collision (or other accident) one's whole life often passes before one's consciousness as if on a screen. I assume that forms of stress release some mechanism in the brain which bring up slumbering experiences in a matter of split seconds. If an icy blast from the North American prairie releases such solutions to thermodynamic problems which have been slumbering for years, I suppose even such icy blasts have their uses!

The administration of the University of Illinois had promised me the full chair of pharmacology at the School of Pharmacy together with the position of Head of Pharmacological Research for the entire Medical Center to make the full chair more attractive for me. The second position was never implemented, since the professor of pharmacology at the School of Medicine objected, believing it was his sole right to exercise. So about once a year I showed the Dean of the administration of the College to which I was attached their official letter of invitation to that position. He said that the position had not changed and I must therefore wait a bit longer. So I waited for a full five years for them to honor the position for which they had invited me to come at my own expense..... which I finally thought was long enough.

Meanwhile my classes and lectures prospered and I had some 180 students in my classes. I had good students with whom I had an excellent relationship. The classes I gave on the causes and cure of the drug epidemic found a particularly wide echo, as did the adult education evening classes, which became quite popular.

Once, during the last session before the holidays, my Chicago students asked me if I would grant them a special favor. I asked them: "What favor?" The answer was: "Please, Professor, would you continue lecturing for another half an hour?" That was an astonishing request as usually students wish to rush out of the classroom for their holidays. So I asked them: "Why do you want me to go on? What do you want me to lecture on?" They looked at me spell-bound replying: "Anything! You can lecture on anything. We just love listening to your Oxford English accent!"

I had a good relationship with my colleagues and with the Dean. With some of them I am still in contact after many years.

The following amusing little story happened many years later when we were back in Switzerland. One summer evening when our artist friend, Frank Wagner, and his wife visited us for a long weekend, we decided to take the romantic boat round-trip on Lake Thun.

It was a beautiful mild summer evening and we boarded the nostalgic veteran paddle steamer *Blümlisalp*. The *Blümlisalp* had lain on dry dock for several years and just been restored to its original antique form. We were admiring the exceptionally golden sunset when we espied an elderly couple walking on the deck. "Don't they look English?" Beate remarked to me. I agreed. And, in fact, they were English. I greeted them and the gentleman began talking to us: "We have come several times to the Bernese Oberland for our holidays," he said, "and we love this area."

"I used to have a good friend with whom I worked together as Professor of Chemistry in Chicago. When I returned to

England at about the same time as he returned to Switzerland, my friend advised me to spend my holidays near Thun in the Bernese Oberland. He loved this area and thought it to be the most beautiful place on earth. Actually he owned his home there although he was English. I followed his advice, and every time I came here I tried to find him. I looked through the telephone books for his name but was never successful."

"What was his name?" I asked, "Maybe, I can help you?"

"His name was Dr. Wilder-Smith." "Wilder-Smith? Well, that's me!" He stared into my face, and then with a glimpse of recognition he exclaimed: "Of course, it is you!!"

At the same time in scrutinizing our opposite, we identified him as my colleague and friend at the University of Illinois, Dr. Lloyd. What a coincidence: on the same boat, at the same time! Dr. Lloyd had actually bought a ticket for a different boat in Thun that evening. The nostalgic *Blümlisalp* had caught their eye when passing by so that they had spontaneously changed plans and boarded the *Blümlisalp*.

Of course, we all were very happy about this unexpected reunion. We met one another several times, renewing our friendship from olden times.

During my time at the University of Illinois, I was awarded three Golden Apple Awards for the best courses of lectures by the students and four Senior Lecturer Awards for the best series of senior lectures. The last Golden Apple Award was inscribed: "He not only made us better scientists but also better men." This remark made me very happy.

CHAPTER XXXI

HAPPENINGS IN THE FAMILY

At home in Wheaton, Beate did not have much help from me in the family, because I was often away from 7:00 a.m. to 10:00 p.m. (when I was doing the adult education evening classes). At the end of the winter season, I was often yellow from not having seen the sun or daylight for so long.

One day, Oliver, our oldest son, who then was twelve years old came to my wife and told her that he had given his heart to the Lord Jesus Christ and that he had decided to follow him. She was more than happy. "Please, tell Daddy too," he added. My wife replied: "Daddy would be so pleased if you told him yourself." In the evening after I had told the children's Bible story, and the light was switched off and it was dark in the room, Oliver told me about his decision.

This was a very happy day for us parents. We learned over and over again how good and important it is that the oldest child first take the decision to become a follower of Christ. It made it much easier for the younger children to follow in the same footsteps. The younger ones respected Oliver and they had an example and forerunner in the Christian way of life instead of a tempter in wrong corrupted ways. There was an interval of only two years between each of our children. They were therefore always very close to each other and did most things together.

The church we attended in Wheaton was Bethany Chapel (a church of the Open Brethren) where I sometimes helped with the ministry on Sundays. We were very happy there and the children loved their "Bethany Builder" Classes. We gained many, many friends and found it much easier to make friends in the United States than in Europe. While attending Bethany Chapel on Sunday in Wheaton, Einar, our youngest son, sometimes sat with us in the church service while the three older children took part in their Sunday School classes.

One Sunday the Lord's Supper was administered. It was made clear that those who loved the Lord were kindly invited to partake of the bread and the wine. There were no other children present. Suddenly, Einar pulled at my sleeve to attract my attention. I looked at him and he whispered: "Daddy, am I also allowed to take part? You know, I love the Lord Jesus." I did not know how to answer. I knew I could do great harm to the little boy by saying "no," which he might misunderstand as if I was doubting his genuine faith. On the other hand I had no idea what the practice of Bethany Chapel was with regard to children. Many churches do not admit children to the Lord's Supper under a certain age. Then an idea struck me. When the bread and wine was passed around I shared my little piece of bread and then my individual little cup of wine with Einar. His face lit up and looked happy as he knew he was accepted and taken seriously.

CHAPTER XXXII

A New Offer

At this time, I was approached by the American Agency for International Development (A.I.D.) in Washington regarding a professorial chair for pharmacology in Ankara, Turkey. They asked me especially to introduce a program for post-graduates there.

I consulted with my Dean about the matter, who was very nice. I asked him to give me a firm date for the implementation of the second position, which they had promised me, but which was effectively blocked by a colleague of mine in one of the other colleges. The Dean said he could not influence the second professor towards changing his attitude. So I set a deadline of a month for the resolution of this problem. When nothing happened, I accepted the A.I.D. offer and took on the position of full professor of pharmacology at Ankara, Haceteppe University, Turkey.

CHAPTER XXXIII

FETA
THE STH IN BASEL

In the sixties, I was invited several times to Basel by Dr. Samuel Külling to speak to his students' class at the Bible School in Chrischona on the first pages of Genesis.

A few years later, in 1970, Dr. Samuel Külling founded in Basel, Switzerland, the first academic theological institute of higher learning in a German speaking country which held to the inerrancy of the Bible as its fundament. Here, finally, theologians could be educated with a sound biblical basis for their job as pastors compared with the liberal theology taught at practically all our universities. It was a big step of faith and much resistance had to be overcome until the FETA (Free Evangelical Theological Academy) in Basel could be established. Dr. Külling is the rector of the Academy.

Today, the FETA, renamed STH (Staatsunabhängige Theologische Hochschule) in 1994, is well established and enjoys a high academic standard. When we visit evangelical churches in Germany or Switzerland, we usually can recognize if the pastor was trained in the STH in Basel, because students there have learned to present a structured, intellectually and spiritually well-constructed sermon not found in many other places. We are grateful that Dr. Külling and his colleagues had the vision and the courage to start the STH. It is a great blessing to our generation and fills an important need in the sector of evangelical academic thinking and education.

Until 1970, no theological institute of higher learning on the German speaking continent taught the subject "Bible and Natural Sciences." As a scientist with considerable research in the field of origins, I was asked by Professor Külling to teach that subject. From 1972 onward, I showed and taught the students of the STH that the biblical teaching of creation was true and in agreement with the facts of science. I disproved with scientific arguments, the hypothesis of evolution. Practically all Christian institutions of higher learning in German speaking countries taught theistic evolution at that time.

Gradually, younger scientists became involved in research on origins in their own field of expertise. They became convinced of a creation of the world and life by an intelligent transcendent logos in contrast to an accidental origin and evolution of life. Today, there are a number of good natural scientists who hold to the anti-evolutionary and creationist point of view.

Arthur in his laboratory at the University in London

Beate as a music student at Frankfurt, Germany

After the engagement

The newly
married couple

Dr. W.S. teaching students at the lab at the University of Illinois

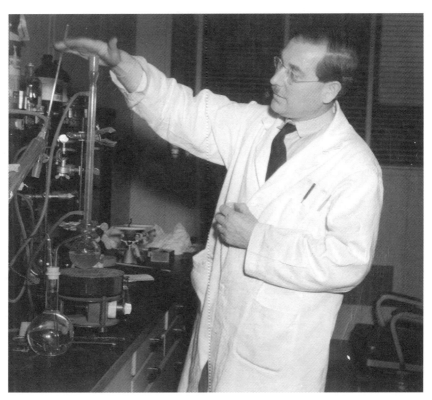

Research at the University of Illinois

Continuing education classes for pharmacists
at the University of Illinois

Dr. W.S. speaking at a natatorium in Wuppertal, Germany

Oliver and Petra
in our Norwegian home

Young family in Norway

Clive and Einar, our two youngest sons

"Helgaheim," our Norwegian home near Bergen in Tertnes

Our ship *Lyngen* in Spitzbergen

Lyngen in Magdalena Bay in Spitzbergen

PART IV

THE LATER YEARS

THE JOURNEY TO
TURKEY IN 1969

In the summer of 1969, we once again went through all the bureaucratic exercises of obtaining exit visas from the United States. We bought a new car, a station wagon, built to our own specifications from American Motors for the four children and all the luggage.

On June 18, we set out for Canada and Montreal. In Montreal we boarded the Norwegian freighter *Ørnefjell*. The freighter had cabins for twenty to thirty passengers. Near the coast of Newfoundland, the ship's crew sighted large schools of cod in the water which awakened in the captain and his seamen the desire to do some fishing—although it was illegal. So they sent huge clouds of black smoke into the air making the coast guard believe the *Ørnefjell* had engine trouble and therefore stopped for two hours out at sea. Now everybody— the crew and the few passengers—began fishing. Even our children were allowed to take part. As the fish were plentiful, we caught a good number of them. The captain caught an enormous fish, so heavy that it could not be lifted with the line. So the seamen put down the ship's rope ladder, the captain climbed down into the water, took the huge cod into his arms and carried his prey up the ladder onto the ship.

The result of our successful catch was that we had to eat cod most of the following days until finally we met another steamer which relieved us of a load of cod and of our daily monotonous menus.

After an otherwise uneventful Atlantic crossing, the *Ørnefjell* landed at Le Havre. From there we took a boat to England to visit our relatives and then headed home to Switzerland via France. On the way, we stopped at Bayeux to admire the beautifully wrought famous wall tapestry there showing the Norman invasion of England in 1066.

After four weeks at home in Einigen, we set out in our new station wagon towards Yugoslavia and Greece for Asia Minor.

We drove over the Grand San Bernardino Pass via Milano to Venice. The beauty of the Grand San Bernardino mountain world captivated us. We visited the old hospice on the pass where the monks had lived with their St. Bernard dogs, trained to rescue the lives of people lost high up in the mountains, in ice and snow.

We stayed overnight in a suburb of Venice, because all the hotels in Venice were booked. Venice, La Serenissima (the most serene), with its narrow canals, romantic gondolas, bridges and old palaces marked by its art and history cast a special enchantment on us. Together with the famous Piazza San Marco, our imagination was set back into long by-gone years when Titian, Tintoretto, and Veronese created their great artistic works here.

From Venice we drove to Triest and then into Yugoslavia. Here the roads began to deteriorate. The traffic was heavy and the driving discipline bad, there were multiple accidents. A big crane lay toppled across the road and damaged cars blocked the traffic. First we drove through today's Slovenia to Rijeka (Fiume) where we found lodging in a private bed and breakfast. The people were very hospitable and loved children. They made us very comfortable. We all enjoyed the bathing in the Adriatic Sea.

The next day we traveled South along the coast through the beautiful spa of Split and turned inland at Opuze towards Metkovic. Between Mostar and Jablanca—in the mountains of

Hercegovina—we had some hair-raising experiences. The mountainous roads were relatively new and had obviously been built by engineers with little experience of the consequences of the traffic and weather conditions there. Recent heavy rains and storms had washed the roads out in places and we saw cars deep down in the mountain ravines that had gone down with landslides hundreds of meters to the bottom of the valleys. It was still raining.

After one of these landslides, traffic was blocked for half a day, while we waited for emergency repairs to be made to the road. Hundreds of cars were blocked in the queue, which slowly disengaged itself over a makeshift bridge replacing the long washed-out section of the road. It was late evening as we drove into the next little village near Jablanca with hundreds of other motorists to look for lodgings for the night in the wildest of mountains. We were grateful that God had protected us so far in the midst of all the surrounding dangers.

But there was nothing to be had—except at one lady's of very doubtful reputation. For an enormous sum of money she took us all in for the night. She wanted to know if we wished anything to drink before we turned in. We were all worn out after the hair raising driving on the mountain roads, so we accepted her kind offer. It turned out that she had nothing but a kind of "gin" or "rakı" which went down one's throat like fire and which the children just could not stomach. The house had neither washing facilities nor a toilet.

The next morning Einar and later Oliver became sick. We had some Ovomaltine and milk powder with us which we gave them to drink. Would we be able to make it over the continually deteriorating mountain roads with so many risky diversions?

Our journey continued from Jablanca to Serajevo, the town so well known for the assassination of Duke Ferdinand which had caused the First World War in 1914.

Further North we passed Tuzla. As soon as we left the mountains, the roads became better. In Bosnjaci, a farming village with large herds of geese running around, we tried to find lodgings for the night as the children were still sick. But there was no accommodation to be had. So we drove on to Belgrade where we found a motel in the southern suburb of Avala. After a good night's rest Oliver and Einar felt better.

From Belgrade we took the road southward to Nis. At the bakery shop in Nis, I had to communicate in Russian to buy some milk and bread. Nobody understood any English, German, French or Italian. My Russian, which I had not used for years, had become a little rusty, but it was good enough to make the shop-keeper understand what we wanted.

With the improving road conditions we could advance much quicker in today's Serbia, from Belgrade to Nis, to Leskovac and Vranje.

In Macedonia, after Skopje and Titov Veles, the landscape became bare with thousands of sheep grazing on the hills. We also saw numerous storks everywhere; a fascinating sight for our children who had heard fairy tales about storks but had hardly seen any.

Towards evening we reached Gevgelija at the Greek border. Here we stayed in Motel Varda, a big beautiful place. This place was so different from all the accommodations on previous nights that we enjoyed it immensely. The large grounds were marvelously landscaped; a very romantic park full of flowers and running fountains. Under full silver moonlight accompanied by classical flute and piano music, we took our evening meal outside on the gracefully built terrace of the hotel.

The following morning we crossed the border to Greece (August 28). Via Thessaloniki we journeyed to Kavalla, Xanthi and Alexandrupolis. En route we enjoyed several times swimming in the warm Aegaen Sea. Around Alexandrupolis, the Greek military were engaged in large-scale maneuvers when we arrived there in the dark. We spent the night in a motel near the sea. Between Ferrae and Kesan, we crossed into Turkey and drove on through Malkara, Tekirdag and Silivri towards Istanbul. Things had slowly begun to change as we approached Asia-Minor. The general public there had entirely different habits and customs.

In Istanbul, the traffic seemed to us like a madhouse. Almost every car showed signs of damage—which was not surprising! Cars drove on both sides of the road at the maximum speed with the drivers honking and shouting at one another. Our only desire was to get out of this chaos.

At that time there was no bridge over the Bosphoros, so we took the ferry across and put up on the Asian side of Turkey in a small common lodging house at Kartal. The owners were intrigued to see us on the road with four small children, all of a much lighter skin and hair color than themselves. Already the customs officials at the frontier had shown their delight in our fair-haired, blue-eyed children by wanting to kiss and touch them. But the children thought rather differently about such matters, shrinking back from such foreign figures.

The roads in Turkey proper were not too bad, but the standards of driving were unbelievably bad. If, for example, one was on an upward incline and approaching its summit, traffic coming from the opposite direction would think nothing of overtaking—entirely blind. During our stay in Turkey we saw countless cases of head-on collisions caused by maneuvers of this type. The driver who overtook without visibility would usually defend himself by maintaining that the other driver with whom he collided head-on "disturbed him during overtaking." It would seldom occur to them that overtaking without adequate visibility was at the root of the evil.

Eventually, on August 30, we arrived safely in Ankara. I drew up at the steps of the modern building of Hacettepe University. When I had found the Dean's office, I stepped in to tell the General Secretary we had arrived. There was, however, not the slightest trace of warmth in his welcome. He did come out to our car rather, I thought, because his duty required such a gesture. But at that time we had not yet learned just what his code of conduct and etiquette requires of him with respect to foreigners.

However, the General Secretary stood back in unconcealed amazement on seeing the new six cylinder green station wagon and burst out in English: "Allah must love you all very much." The doctrine taught by the Koran is perfectly clear on this point: Allah blesses all those whom he loves with worldly goods...just the same doctrine that some Christian extreme Pentecostals wrongly teach today, too. However, the Muslim also teach the converse of this doctrine, namely that poor people, not blessed with worldly goods, are in fact cursed by Allah. They are therefore often treated accordingly—poor beggars are not to be pitied—as they are the accursed of Allah himself. Hence the mercilessness often seen in Muslim life.

To stave off Allah's unfriendly eye, the poor beggar will repeat sacred texts from the Koran invoking Allah's blessing on all passers by. During the month of Ramadan each text repeated by the Muslim has a special value both for the one who recites the text and for the one who hears it.

Once we went with the whole family down to Tarsus where the Apostle Paul originated. We saw all the antiquities which tourists are shown. But what touched us most was, however, not Paul's fountain or Cleopatra's baths and how they were heated. What touched us most was a poor half-demented girl of about fourteen years old being chased and stoned through the city by a horde of ragamuffin boys. She was shrieking in terror—the boys were aiming their stones effectively, and they obviously hurt the poor half-witted child.

Now our boys had been taught to respect and protect weaker and sick persons and just could not abide a scene like this. So they picked up sticks and stones in defense of the girl before you could say "Jack Robinson." If we had not taken counter-action immediately, there would have been a pitched battle with these ragamuffins and our children.

It took us a long time to understand the teachings of the Koran, which are the basis of the Turkish mentality. Their mentality is very much dependent on these teachings. They live in them far more than many so-called Christians live in the teachings of the Bible.

CHAPTER II

AN APARTMENT IN ANKARA

At sunrise, we were awakened by the call of the muezzin from the minaret of the mosque. Our first concern was to find an apartment for our stay in Ankara. But how to proceed? We knew there existed a German Embassy School in Ankara. Maybe they could give us some advice? The teaching staff must have gone through similar housing difficulties? Or the various embassies? But neither the people at the German School, nor at the various embassies, could help us with our housing problem.

After some searching, my wife met an English lady in the street who could speak some Turkish and who had heard by the grape-vine that in the A block of Atatürk Bulvarı an apartment had just been vacated by a lawyer and his family. As we did not yet speak a word of Turkish, the English lady was kind enough to accompany my wife to the "Kapıcı" (caretaker) of the A block. He confirmed the vacancy of the apartment—which was even furnished. The Kapıcı had an apartment key, but no address of the moved owner. He showed us the place and suggested—as did the friendly couple from the neighboring apartment—that we move in at once. They all would try and find out the address of the owner in the meantime.

The apartment was really too small for our family. But it was extremely difficult to find something suitable. The apartment at least had hot and cold water and a bathroom.

The apartment was on the sixth floor and had an elevator which other houses did not possess. Most houses in Ankara were not well equipped. This house was in a relatively modern block in Kavaklidere near the Polish and the Czech Embassy. (By the way, at that time, Dubcek was Czech Ambassador in Ankara after falling in disgrace with the communists. There he was kept under strict surveillance by the Russian Embassy, later he was sent back to Czechoslovakia.)

So we moved into the apartment, although the curtains were in a very dilapidated state and the refrigerator was broken. Our kind neighbor lady, Mrs. Taylan, came with us to the electricity, water and gas administration to get this official part settled. Of course, the water was not safe for drinking, it had to be bought from the "Suçu" (Water seller). And nobody was safe from cockroaches, no matter where one lived.

The greatest difficulty arose from the fact that the water was often turned off without any warning for hours at a time, at any time of the day or night. Since the water and sewer lines ran in the same tunnels, this meant that the sewage contents leaked easily into the neighborhood of the drinking water lines which often showed a negative pressure due to the shutting off of the water pressure. There had already been outbreaks of cholera due to this practice. So we took the precaution of always boiling the water before using it to wash vegetables or dishes. Even with such precautions most Europeans and Americans suffered from hepatitis and other disabilities.

The American Commander of the NATO forces kindly offered to let us fetch water in containers from Balgat—the U.S. compound—for our personal use.

We soon found out that the owner of our apartment was a relative of the rector of the Hacettepe University, a lawyer living in Izmir. He fully agreed to rent us his flat in Atatürk Bulvarı. He was a kind gentleman and even had the apartment renovated—which it badly needed.

Soon after our arrival in Ankara my wife and myself started Turkish lessons with Abdullah Bey, Professor for English. We learned enough to get by with shopping or asking the most fundamental questions in daily life. I often went up to the huge compound on which the British Embassy was situated and helped the staff out with lectures and talks in their chapel. It was surprising to find that the nice little chapel they had built for the Anglican services there, had the standard type of chapel bell, but that the bell could not be rung. For, said the Turks, the sound of it might penetrate beyond the confines of the British compound and that would be counted as making Christian propaganda on sovereign Turkish, i.e., Muslim property—which was strictly forbidden. On the same line of thought the Anglican Pastor was not permitted to wear his dog collar outside the British compound, to say nothing of his ceremonial robes, of course. That would again be tantamount to making Christian propaganda on Muslim soil.

My colleagues at the university made no bones about it, for them I was an utter heathen. I was curious to know just why they thought so. The person I asked told me readily, in a matter of fact sort of way: "You so-called Christians are all the same; in practice you are really the purest of heathens. You do not fast. You do not pray." For the Muslim, to pray is to touch the ground with the forehead, and to prostrate oneself before Allah a set number of times daily, to demonstrate submission to the will of Allah.

So I answered: "But I do pray; in secret, and I do fast; but not to be seen by men." So when the Muezzin gave his call to prayer from the minaret that evening and they all got out their prayer mats, I was careful to shut my office door. Similarly, I did not eat anything while they were all fasting during Ramadan. As soon as I took care to do this, I was accepted and invited to their little feasts when the Muezzin allowed them to eat again at sunset.

Another point should be observed if one is to find the way to their hearts. They consider the title "Son of God" for Jesus, the Christ, to be blasphemous—and they have their reasons. For if Mary was the Mother of God as the Catholics call her, then God, they think, had sexual intercourse with a female human being and Jesus was the outcome of this sexual intercourse. This they consider to be blasphemous and a very serious matter indeed, confirming them in their fixed view that Christians are in reality heathens.

So when witnessing to a Muslim, one should avoid unnecessary upsetting titles of the Christ, thus taking into account their prejudices and background.

CHAPTER III

THE TURKISH MILITARY

One Sunday afternoon we took the children out for a drive on the hills behind Çankaya, to get some fresh air. While we were walking on the dry hills, a column of ancient Turkish army trucks came rumbling by—full of Turkish infantry soldiers—having been on maneuvers. The trucks were all very ancient and had obviously not been serviced for a long time. One of the trucks broke down, and in spite of the fact that the driver got out and fiddled with the carburetor, no sign of life appeared despite extensive use of the electrical self starter. I saw that if he went on pressing that starter button like this, he would have no battery left to feed his ignition system.

So, although I was not in my old clothes, I went over to help him. He was an ordinary Turkish soldier who obviously knew nothing of internal combustion engines. There was, I guessed, water in the carburetor. So I showed him how to take the float chamber off, clean it out and restart the motor. It was pathetic to see his relief when the motor burst into life, for at that time Turkish soldiers got beaten with the lash if they returned to barracks even a minute too late, and they fear that lash. That is one reason why Turkish academics were so keen on getting commissions as officers when they have to do their military service. Officers do not get beaten, of course.

There was another point connected with military service in Turkey which ought to be mentioned. If an academic was married to a foreign national, that is, to a non-Turkish wife, and then got called up to do his military service, he could not obtain a commission as an officer as long as he is married to the foreign wife. In order to escape the risk of undesired treatment, he must become an officer. *But he could become an officer only if he divorced his foreign wife first.*

The Turks make little of this fact by pointing out that he can always marry her again after his military service is over, so that the hardship is not too great. The fact is, however, that the officer on being demobilized often does not remarry his first wife but takes another, maybe younger one, while he has the chance to do so legally and without expense.

The Muslim religion has always been shaky on the point of women's rights and still allows polygamy, although Atatürk forbade it. But what Atatürk and other politicians do and promulgate in Ankara does not find much respect in the more distant parts of the country. The remarkable fact is that in spite of this weakness with respect to women's rights and the growing strength of women's rights in the West, the Muslim faith is spreading in the West at a fast rate even while women's rights are so much emphasized. One wonders how much the Western female converts to Islam really know of the real nature of the Muslim faith where women's rights are concerned—or, for that matter, how much they know of the attitude to women of the Christian faith, which they are forsaking. One wonders also how much our politicians know in depth of the Muslim faith and nations in general, with whom they are making their political contracts.

In Turkey, we had a good deal of social contact with the American, British and German Embassies. As a result, we saw first hand some of the problems that have to be dealt with by the diplomats. One example will suffice for our purposes here: A German girl had met and married a Turkish academic while he was working in Germany. When they went back to live in Turkey things rapidly went wrong with the marriage—as they almost always do if the couple starts to live in Turkey. Young Western-minded German girls do not like being under the absolute rule of the Turkish mothers-in-law as Turkish girls often had to be—and accepted as perfectly normal. On top of that she sometimes had to put up with other wives as well! She has none of the freedom a Western girl considers to be her inalienable right today.

When the husband joined the army they were divorced. So she went home to Germany, taking the little baby boy with her. Her husband did not take the baby boy, because he did not know how to look after babies, and Turkish men do not do what they consider to be women's work. She brought up her little son as a normal German boy, he went to school in Germany and never learned Turkish.

Then one day, out of the goodness of her heart, she thought she would like to show her ex-husband his child, now a little German boy of some six or seven years old. So without consulting anyone she took off for Turkey and visited her ex-husband with her little son.

One morning the son was missing and no one could find him. Her husband professed ignorance of his whereabouts. The poor mother was distraught; the boy did not speak Turkish. The boy never turned up again and the mother had to return to Germany without her son.

He had disappeared completely without a trace.

I asked a friend of ours at the German Embassy what one does in such cases. The answer is, that according to Muslim law, valid in Turkey, the son belongs to Allah and to the father. The Muslim will not respect the laws which we respect. To them we are "heathen," and so they do not regard our laws as valid over theirs. In this case, the fact that the mother had born the child and brought him up would have little weight. In short, the German Embassy could do nothing, nor could anyone else. So the mother lost her child who was stolen in the night.

As our newspapers and schools do not deal with these matters, young Western girls do not know when they are playing with "fire." They just do not know the facts of other cultures and religions. They think that having sexual relationships with members of the opposite sex of other cultures and religions is innocuous, or no different to having social intercourse with such members of other cultures.

CHAPTER IV

THE CRADLE OF FORMER CIVILIZATION

Our stay in Turkey was rendered all the more valuable by our experience of living in the very cradle of a former civilization. We explored the ancient ruins of Ephesus and Tarsus, where Paul grew up. All along the southern coast of Turkey one finds the ruins of the ancient Greek culture that existed here 2000 years or so ago—the beautiful mosaic pavements, the sites of ancient temples showing what a superior culture the ancients who lived there developed. It was fascinating to visit the old places mentioned in the Bible. One example is the seven churches mentioned in the Revelation of John. We stayed one night in a motel near Pamukkale—the Biblical Laodicaea—and swam together with numerous tortoises in the warm waters gushing out of the earth into a pool. In Ephesus, we came to understand why in the New Testament it says that Paul in the amphitheater of Ephesus talked up to the people, amphitheaters being built that way. We tried the acoustics in the theater ourselves. It was superb, with whispering audible right to the back of the amphitheater.

The present day Turks have built their lean-to shacks against the walls of beautiful ancient temples. The stark difference between the building cultures then and now could not be displayed more effectively than by such juxtapositions in modern Turkey. But even more so, the spiritual culture then could not stand more starkly in contrast to today. There is not a trace today of the strong Christian culture that once thrived in this area of the earth. It is today, spiritually speaking, totally burned out.

HATTUSAS

North East of Ankara, we found the ruins of Hattusas, the former capital of the Hittites. The Hittites are spoken of a great deal in the Holy Scriptures. They were the military experts of the Middle East in Old Testament times and David employed them as mercenaries to form the mainstay of his army. Uriah, the husband of Bathsheba, was a Hittite (2 Samuel 2).

Bathsheba was a very beautiful woman with whom David fell in love. To cover up the fruit of his adultery with her, he sent her husband to fight in the most dangerous part of the front-line where he was, as planned by David, killed.

When I was a boy, liberal theologians and archeologists used to teach that the Hittites were an Old Testament myth. They maintained that such a people as the Hittites had never really existed. This, they thought, proved that much of the Old Testament was historically mythical, including the story of Adam and Eve and the Garden of Eden.

In Turkey, one may see today the ruins of the capital city of the Hittites, Hattusas, at Boghazköy with the huge, massive stone pillars which served as gate-posts for the gates of the city. In these stone walls one can still see the holes in which the gate hinges hung. Next to the main gates there are small low passageways through which one can still crawl, as the ancients used to do when the main gates were closed. There are also the remains of their large libraries showing a very considerable culture.

A dictionary was found in this library. It was edited in several languages, proving not only that the Hittites existed and were the bearers of a very well developed culture, but that they hired out their people as mercenaries to King David. Besides maintaining imposing military organizations throughout the Middle East, they also built and inhabited the imposing city of Hattusas with its spacious library facilities.

The theologians of Bible-critical schools were not a little wrong in thinking that the Bible was historically incorrect, they were massively wrong, for the Hittites' capital city, the dictionaries to their and other nations' languages as well as their massive architecture have now all been found by modern archeologists. I personally believe that not only has the biblical history proved correct, but that the history of the future—the prophecies too—recorded in the Bible will turn out to be at least as correct.

KAYMAKLI

Not very far from Ankara we also discovered the two underground cities mentioned by the Apostle of the letter to the Hebrews (Hebrews 11:38). The Apostle speaks of the martyrs who were forced to live in the caves and holes of the earth for the sake of their faith on account of the Roman persecution. The cities under discussion, e.g., Kaymaklı, are entirely underground and invisible from the surface. A ventilation shaft leads from the surface downwards to a layer dug out in the soft sandstone. Here there are many, many small rooms and what amounts to real apartments deep in the earth.

There are chapels with Greek New Testament texts still painted on the walls. Everywhere in the passageways there are niches in the walls, still black with the smoke from the oil lamps placed to light up the dark passages. The entrances to these underground cities were closed by huge blocks of sandstone, carved out of the same sandstone into which they were quarried. They are like large wheels, let into sockets over the entrances to these underground cities.

The Roman legions were always on the look-out for the inhabitants of the underground cities. In these hidden cities there were even underground graveyards, cut into the rock, where the dead were buried. There were also underground wine presses for pressing out the grapes with channels cut in the sandstone for draining the juice. Grapes were harvested there above ground, of course, and then brought down into the underground cities to be made into wine. The inhabitants of these cities must have been a good deal smaller in stature than we are: the passageways are about five feet high and we had to crouch to enter some of the rooms. There are some seven levels of "apartments," one above the other in Kaymaklı, with some of the lower levels being under water today so that one can visit only the upper levels. In the area there are two such cities connected by underground passageways.

The Turkish caretakers looking after these ancient monuments took a liking to us and our children. When discussing the meaning of all these works one of these men told our eldest son that "the ancient inhabitants of these cities were Christians, but not like the present generation of Christians, for rather than compromise in matters of faith they lived underground for years. The ancients knew how to deny themselves, which most of the modern ones have forgotten how to do."

GÖREME

In the neighborhood of Kaymaklı lies Göreme, which consists of dwelling places hewn out of the sandstone pinnacles which have thus been made hollow. It looks like a moonscape today. The story goes that when the Roman persecution stopped with Constantine's conversion, the inhabitants of Kaymaklı came out of the underground city. But they did not know how to build surface buildings, only how to hollow out the sandstone rock pinnacles. So they took the pinnacles of sandstone around Göreme and hollowed them out. Then they made windows in them and so made their first surface dwellings, using the same building techniques as they had used in building the underground cities. "Göreme" means in Turkish "You cannot see me" because, of course, being hollowed out of natural rock pinnacles all you can see are the windows the people cut through the sandstone to let light and air into the dwellings.

In this district (Göreme), the Turks today continue to do what the ancients did, hollowing out the sandstone rocks and using the resultant caverns to keep their wines cool during the warm summers.

CHAPTER V

FOSSIL BEDS AT KIZILÇAHAMAN

Another time, we went on an expedition from Ankara with the American Chaplain, with whom we did quite a bit of ministry, to see the fossil beds at Kizilçahaman. There we saw literally thousands and thousands of fossil fish, and plants of all imaginable sorts and kinds. Some of the fish were most interesting, having been overtaken by death right in the middle of eating one another. One fish was in the process of swallowing his neighbor, and had been fossilized right in the middle of the very act. So, the fossilizing process must have been very quick and sudden and certainly not a slow process over millions of years.

CHAPTER VI

STUDENT, UNIVERSITY, AND NATO RELATIONSHIPS

If we restrict ourselves to the kinds of experiences in Turkey, which I have reported up to present, that would give an entirely false picture of the real situation when we lived and worked there. Quite a few expatriates in Turkey fell ill with what was commonly known amongst us as "frustration hepatitis" after a few months of residence there. We had deemed ourselves to have escaped this disease, but as we were leaving Turkey after two years there, I also fell victim to it and it took me a long time until I was wholly recovered from it.

The disease was undoubtedly a true hepatitis—one's eyes and skin became yellow and one felt really awful. One had one great desire, namely to get out of Turkey to a country where one could drink milk and water, eat cheese products in safety and be in a country where everything worked as it ought to.

What I am reporting on in the next section is strictly factual, but highly unpleasant—if not unbelievable to the average European. However, in order that the reader may know what is really going on regarding his tax money and its funneling to developing countries (which Western politicians often seem to know little or nothing about) I propose to recount here some of our daily experiences at the University at Ankara. This university, by the way, practically lived on U.S. aid programs, which amounted to millions of U.S. dollars per annum.

CHAPTER VII

THE PEACE CORPS

There was, and still is, a dire need in Turkey for instruction in the English language, as well as in technical and agricultural matters. In teaching English at the Universities in Ankara, the Peace Corps did excellent work. I got to know the Peace Corps Director personally and admired him for his perseverance in spite of the insurmountable difficulties which confronted him.

There were about seventy Peace Corps members who taught English at SSU (one of the three universities in Ankara). The whole concept was an exemplary exercise in personal and national sacrifice, and voluntary poverty to help a developing country. The Peace Corps had a contract with the SSU until June 1970.

In January 1970, students in Ankara went on strike against "American Imperialism" in connection with the presence of the Peace Corps in Ankara, members of which were teaching English there for the merest pittance of pay. The students boycotted and picketed the three universities in Ankara, and there was some shooting and killing amongst the left- and right-wing students.

One day, during a General Forum of students at SSU, one of the firebrand leaders said that he personally would crack the skulls of any of the Peace Corps dogs ("Köpekler") who turned up again at SSU to teach English.

The Rector was informed of the speech and to save his own skin—he was classified by the students as an "American dog" himself for the simple reason that he had accepted so much money and help from Uncle Sam—he immediately conceded to the students and fired the whole of the Peace Corps from SSU *in absentia* with no notice at all. This was in direct contravention of his contract with the Peace Corps and with the U.S. Embassy.

The other foreign professors at Ankara were furious at this betrayal of their fellow countrymen, who had done such an excellent job without even being paid for it. They said "No Peace Corps, no ex-patriot professors either." But a lot of violence occurred: a Turkish Professor was shot dead in front of the university, leaving a young wife and three small children. The Peace Corps evaporated overnight. Soon everybody forgot what had happened.

The other foreign professors had problems of their own: The Turks had already unilaterally withheld parts of the foreigners' own personal salaries. This despite the fact that Uncle Sam had already paid the salary in advance in full for the Turks to administer.

The Turks considered any attempt by the United States or other donor countries to retain administrative control over the funds "an affront to Turkish sovereignty." They stuck to this position so unbendingly that Washington caved in and paid the whole money out to the Turks to "administer" by themselves, with no strings attached except to pay the expatriate professors' salaries. As a result the Turks withheld part of the salaries with impunity, including my own salary. Thus the expatriate professors, some of whom had given up well-paid, tenured jobs to help the government aid program were delivered into the hands of the Turks without any chance of redress. The politicians who did this were warned time and time again by the Americans living in Turkey of what the consequences for Americans who had signed on for Turkey would be.

CHAPTER VIII

CAR-BURNING

Just before the above events something else occurred. The United States Ambassador, who had helped the Turkish universities to acquire large sums of American dollar aid, went to inspect the university at which I was stationed. He was duly received by the rector and taken into the administrative building for the official reception.

When the Ambassador and the Rector glanced out of the window a bit later they saw a truly shocking sight. The students had overturned the Ambassador's car parked in front of the building and had set fire to the gasoline which ran out of its gasoline tank. The car was totally destroyed. This is how the students thanked the representation of the United States who had built the university and was still supporting it for them.

In another incident, the commander of one of the larger NATO units, with whom I was personally on very friendly terms, sent his brand new American Motors Ambassador car on a mercy mission to SSU. An elderly Turkish lady was desperately ill and needed immediate hospital treatment, and the good commander sent this elderly lady to our hospital in his new car. When she had been duly delivered into the treatment ward, the students surrounded the commander's car, drove off the Turkish chauffeur, overturned the vehicle and set it on fire with its own gasoline.

This happened almost in front of my office window. As far as I could ascertain no one was ever punished, and the damage done to NATO property was not paid for. A number of students were arrested, but then released at the request of an expatriate British professor who certified that the students concerned had been in his lecture at the time of the incident.

Car burnings of this type continued sporadically until the Military Government of Professor Erim replaced that of Demeril in the Spring of 1971.

CHAPTER IX

SUPPLIES OF DRUGS AND CHEMICALS

One of the great difficulties one encounters in carrying out scientific research in developing countries concerns the supply of chemicals and apparatus. At the universities and research institutes in Ankara one could find desolate technical apparatus everywhere. Much of the modern equipment had been a gift of the USA, Germany or other Western countries. But as soon as the equipment needed any repairs, the expensive technical apparatus was not used any more and lay around desolate, because there were no spare parts or know-how to be had in Turkey. It was too complicated and troublesome to import the spare parts. In Turkey this was particularly difficult, because of the unbending attitude of the customs officials in questions of customs and duties on apparatus and research chemicals. Even gifts from developed countries were taxed at such impossible rates that it was often not possible even to receive a gift of chemicals or a piece of apparatus.

CHAPTER X

New Experiences in Dealing with People

One day a Turkish colleague of mine in the institute returned from a stay of some months in the United States and found he could not get hold of certain chemicals he needed for research purposes. So he turned to me for help, as the items he needed were not available in Turkey.

I advised him to try his American friends, as Uncle Sam was often a good deal more helpful in such matters and often made gifts for work in developing countries. He had, of course, already asked and received nothing, so I was his last hope.

As it happened, I was going to Switzerland in a few days. Would I try there? I said I would try, but that the chemicals would have to be paid for as the Swiss were not used to giving gifts of chemicals worth hundreds of dollars. If he would guarantee me the money, I would buy what I could and he could reimburse me afterwards. Thus we agreed as we parted.

In Switzerland, I spent three full days at laboratory furnishers looking for the chemicals he wanted. I paid nearly three hundred U.S. dollars out of my own pocket for the chemicals. On returning to Ankara (in Turkey one was allowed to take into the country customs free anything one has on one's own person), I took in my three hundred dollars worth of chemicals duty free having stored them in my own pocket— perfectly legal in that country.

In Ankara, I triumphantly produced the chemicals—or at least the bills for them. However, when I showed the bills to my Turkish colleague who had ordered them specifically from me, he sulkily told me he did not want the bills, but only the substances! This was warning enough to me after my many experiences with the habits of the country. But then he added that I had been under a misapprehension for he had been expecting me to do as they do in America, that is to scrounge or to beg the drugs from wealthy companies. This was, of course, a direct untruth, for I had gone to great lengths to point out that I could not do in Europe as our friends the Americans do in the goodness of their hearts.

However, my colleague maintained that he had no money and was not going to pay for the materials I had already advanced money for. I had now only one method of proceeding: I had the chemicals I had bought in my personal possession and that is where they were going to remain. After a few days, a physician in the hospital heard through the grape vine that I had brought some glucagon with me which he was needing urgently for his work on diabetes. So, I sold him half the glucagon I had brought with me on a cash and carry basis. Gradually other Turks heard that I had a little store of things not obtainable in Turkey. I gradually sold everything I had on a strict cash and carry basis and recouped myself partially for my trouble.

Here we find the root of one of the great difficulties in dealing with the generality of Muslim people. In the Koran they have no specific remedy for sin or wrong doing. Their great subject of prayer to Allah is to get him to overlook sin, that is, become unconscious of it. Apology and repentance for sin in the Christian sense is not their way of dealing with wrong. Allah does not deal with it that way. He overlooks its existence. He who apologizes (repents) is in fact in a weaker position than the one of whom one asks forgiveness. So the Muslim tends to do what even many Christian lawyers recommend: "do not admit anything."

The Muslim also says that Allah made man of good material and that therefore man is good. He can say this because Allah resolves not to see the evil—for which he reveals no remedy except that of refusing to see it—because he is supposed to have made us good.

The idea that god (i.e., Allah) settled the sin question by paying the price for it himself, is foreign to Muslim theology. For Allah does not deal with sin and wrong doing, he only makes himself "unconscious" of it by overlooking it.

When my Turkish colleague who had asked me to fetch the chemicals found that they were diminishing rapidly he suddenly found that he had some money after all, and I sold him the small residue I still had of the substances he had needed so urgently. But he never would admit to me he had lied outright to me on two counts. In the first place, I had told him I could not scrounge in Europe the things he wanted, and in the second place, he said he had no money: But on no account would his Muslim principles allow him to repent, or even acknowledge the wrongness of his way of going on. It would never enter his mind to "make a clean breast of things." The principle is to deny that wrong doing, alias sin, exists at all. Do not see it; that is, deny its existence.

There is one cardinal sin which no Muslim cares commit, it is that of being found out or caught red-handed, that is, never let sin come to light and never lose face, always cover it up. Unless we understand these simple principles we will never understand the perfectly transparent mentality of our Muslim friends. *Nor will our politicians ever be able to make successful treaties with them. Because their ways of thought are quite different to those of our Christian culture.*

For my research work at the university I had a good and intelligent laboratory assistant working for me. One day I gave him the task of verifying the melting point of a certain chemical which I needed in my research for a new drug. It was very important that the substance we used for the new drug was pure. After a time F. Bey approached me with the chemical, declaring that the melting point was 230°C. As I had my doubts by looking at the substance, I asked him if he was sure that it was 230°C. Yes, he was quite sure, he said. "Did you really examine the melting point?" "Yes, of course. I have just done it." I just could not believe it, the chemical looked impure to me. "Let's determine the melting point together," I said. When I repeated the experiment together with him the substance already started to melt at 215°C. The substance was impure and the melting point therefore much lower than he had stated. Apparently he had never done the experiment. "Now, F. Bey," I asked, "what do you have to say to that?" "Well," he said, "on the bottle it says the melting point should be 230°C." "Why did you not tell me the truth? The consequences could be severe. Don't you owe me an apology?" He angrily looked me straight into the eyes and answered: "You do not understand. Why should I owe you an apology? You would even expect an apology of Allah, would you not?" "Certainly," I said, "if he had lied to me."

CHAPTER XI

DISASTER RELIEF

Turkey, being an earthquake zone, is always in danger of such natural catastrophes. While we were there during the two years 1969–71, two major earthquakes occurred. Both caused widespread damage and misery. In Ankara the shocks were hardly felt, but to the southwest and east of Ankara the shocks were very severe indeed, with much loss of life and damage to property.

Some professorial colleagues of mine went to the disaster area shortly after the major shocks had occurred and helped in the relief work there. They had nothing but praise for the international organizations which helped directly to relieve the suffering especially amongst the poor populations of those earthquake areas. Some of the families were so poor that they had never seen a five lire bill (at that time about the equivalent of thirty cents, U.S.).

In order to give the shortest possible account of relief work in Turkey, I will cite here without much comment one or two incidents which were widely discussed in Ankara at the time. After the second earthquake, Western Germany sent a planeload of West German woolen blankets to Ankara for the victims. But there were immediate difficulties at the airport because of the scandalously high customs demanded by the Turkish Customs for the gift blankets. The German authorities were unable or unwilling to pay such customs duties for gift rugs for poor Turkish victims.

There was hurried telephoning all round Turkey and in the end some senior military authority reportedly instructed the customs authority to let the consignment through, without further difficulties. This was duly done. A few days later, however, the markets in Ankara and Istanbul were flooded with the best German woolen blankets at considerably higher prices than normal for such goods.

On trying to get to the bottom of this I was informed on good authority that "someone else had taken the Baksheesh," whatever that meant. I did find out though that only a small percentage of those woolen blankets got through to the catastrophe area in Bingöl.

One day my good wife asked me to bring back some butter and cheese on my way home. Now butter and cheese of the Turkish kind were not relished much by the expatriate families, as there was much TB among the cows there, so I bought some of the imported variety.

On my arrival home my wife, as is her frugal wont (for which I am truly grateful), gasped at the bill. It was twice the regular price. On opening the butter wrap we had another surprise, for there on the inside was stamped very clearly that the butter was a gift from the American people to the Turkish people, not to be sold or exchanged. Cheeses of all kinds, similarly marked in English as being gifts from the West German, Danish and other nations, were sold regularly and generally at fabulous prices all over Ankara and Istanbul. If one raised an eyebrow or was so silly as to show such wraps to the Embassies of the nations concerned, one was merely laughed at. I tried, so I know.

CHAPTER XII

THE INTERNATIONAL USE OF A.I.D. FUNDS

One afternoon I was sitting in my office overlooking Ankara. There was a serious student boycott of the university in progress when some of the other members of the department came suddenly into my office and politely asked me to leave. On asking why I should leave, they said they were doing me a favor because they did not wish for me to be kidnapped with the other foreigners. This may have been true, for I had a quite good rapport with some of them, but I think reality lay somewhere else, for the truth was that they really did not want me to see what I now in fact was in the process of seeing.

For suddenly there was the deafening noise of powerful helicopters flying low, directly overhead. They were American machines with Turkish markings on them. They flew straight towards the Middle East Technical University. There had been a lot of trouble. The underground passages of the huge new American built campus, through which the electrical mains, the sewage and the water lines ran, were full of arms and weapons of all sorts. The students had blockaded themselves in these areas and held the military at bay in a state of siege for several days, with no professors allowed in or out.

Things had now come to an impasse; this was the meaning of the helicopters, which had come to break it. I watched them fly, heavily armed, over METU (Middle East Technical University) and circle round the brand new campus. Then the real trouble started—the students began to fire at the gun ships and the helicopters returned fire. The students had retired into the dormitories, apparently thinking that the gunships would spare these new American built buildings. In this point they were mistaken, for the gunships literally let rip at everything, regardless of cost.

As soon as the military had put down the revolt and arrested hundreds of students, the whole place was searched for arms. The underground passages mentioned were crammed with equipment of all types. It took the Turkish Army some six months to sort out the arms in those passages, for there was enough to equip a small army in the underground passages of METU. Think, however, of the millions of American dollars wasted on "education" of this type under the A.I.D. (The Agency for International Development) programs and paid for by the American taxpayer.

What modern educational leaders seem not yet to have grasped is that both in Turkey and in America all education needs to be squarely based upon a modern moral basis. Without the chaotic results like those reported above are to be expected.

CHAPTER XIII

THE RULE OF LAW IN TURKEY

As Turkey is a member of the NATO, freedom of conscience and religion are guaranteed—at least on paper. In practice it is quite different; there is no religious freedom whatsoever. Islamic law strongly limits religious freedom for non-Muslims. It is even unlawful to ring the bells of the little chapel on embassy grounds on Sundays.

A Turkish gentleman, an acquaintance of ours, traveled by bus from Istanbul to Ankara. On the way, the police carried out a raid. They found a Bible and some Christian literature in his brief-case. The policeman took the Christian literature with him and told our friend to pass by the police office in Ankara where they would return his booklets to him. When he turned up at the police station in Ankara they took Mr. B. straight into custody. The police kept him there, in jail, without a trial, for weeks. While "waiting for some information," he was imprisoned together in a cell with about sixty other people: criminals, drug offenders, a number of people from Eastern parts of Turkey involved in blood feuds, etc. They all lived together in this one room, with a bucket in the corner and few other amenities. Once a day they received a thin kind of soup. As the food was bad and scarce, relatives and friends—if there were any nearby—were sometimes allowed to bring food for the prisoners. But they had to stand in line for a pass to visit and bring food.

When our friend's wife in Istanbul learned that her husband had been imprisoned, she traveled with her baby daughter to

Ankara to be near him. Most of her friends and relatives refused to take her into their home—they were afraid of getting involved with the police. So we offered to put her up. We prepared some Turkish "Pide" (pastry with ground meat, onions, tomatoes on top baked on a metal sheet) for her husband. She stood in line for an admission pass. When she was admitted the guards poked into the "Pide" with long knives to make sure there were no weapons or drugs concealed in it. When she finally entered the cell with the deformed food a crowd of hungry inmates surrounded her. Those without someone to bring them some food—especially from Eastern Turkey—were very hungry. By now they all knew that Mr. B. had been taken into custody for being a Christian. "As a Christian, your Master Jesus Christ expects you to share your food with the hungry," they exclaimed. They knew that much of the Bible. So, our dear friend willingly and kindly shared his food with the hungry crowd although very little was left for him.

Our Turkish friend sat in detention for weeks without having committed any illegal act. The police knew that in Turkey, as a member of NATO, according to the law they had signed, there should be freedom of conscience and religion. The only means of punishing Christians was to put them into detention for an indeterminate time, and then finally release them.

When nothing happened, I visited my colleague, the son of a President of Turkey, a medical doctor at the American hospital in Ankara. He was a friendly gentleman who had spent some years in the United States. When I explained the sad case of Mr. B. being retained in detention without a cause, he promised me to talk to his father about it. Next day he told me disconcertedly that his father was not able to do anything, as the military had taken over this case. So that even the president could not interfere. Finally, weeks later, our friend was released without trial and without any explanation.

CHAPTER XIV

OUR CAR NUMBER PLATES

In Turkey, foreign professors and many of those helping with various aid programs were required to have Turkish customs number plates on their automobiles. These were blue in color, and for Ankara bore the local code, O6 ZZ, followed by a number. For my plates I had to pay an exorbitant fee, because the Embassy had not taken care of the exemption required for us professors. Other foreign teachers in schools, etc., were automatically exempted from these enormous fees.

One arrived in Ankara using one's national number plates and then got them exchanged for the ZZ plates. This process was in practice highly athletic, for it meant commuting from one Turkish office to the next on a more or less full time basis for more than three weeks. Some minor form or paper would allegedly be missing at each office. The missing paper would have to be *personally fetched immediately otherwise the processing of the papers would be interrupted* which in practice meant stopped. To restart the process was accompanied by so much office running that one would do almost anything to avoid the process getting stopped. Only those who have dealt with Eastern offices know what this means. After nearly four weeks office running, I got to the stage where I was within an ace of getting my plates, when the police officer handling the case found that I had committed the most heinous of all crimes: I had bought a foreign casko car insurance policy for a quarter of a million U.S. dollars with the Winterthur office in Zürich. The Winterthur was a Swiss insurance company doing an enormous amount of business in both Asiatic and European Turkey.

The good police officer showed the utmost ingenuity in devising reasons why I should *not get the plates and therefore not get the use of my car.* First, he said that it was a Swiss policy and therefore not valid in Turkey. So I had to write to Switzerland to obtain written confirmation that the policy was valid in Turkey. The second attack was based on the assumption that the Winterthur company had no office in Turkey. I showed him the address of the Turkish office of the Winterthur. It was in Istanbul. The third attack was that the policy from Istanbul was valid only in European Turkey on the other side of the Bosporus.

I then had to get a letter from the company to say that the policy was valid everywhere in Turkey, i.e., both in European and Asiatic Turkey. Then came the fourth line of attack to prevent my using my car: an attack which the officer considered to be impregnable: It was that no one in Turkey ever used a Swiss insurance for their car. I proved to the dear fellow that the Winterthur was doing a roaring trade in Turkey. But he would not relent, although this whole process took weeks to work through. One almost needed a separate office to do all the writing of letters they demanded, as well as a servant to do the office visiting needed. The fifth line of attack was very serious indeed, because the green insurance card everyone had to have was not in the Turkish language. This "final" attack he positively threw at me. Therefore, said he, an ordinary police officer on the street could not check me or my green card. So I pulled out my green card and showed to him that it was written in French, which was an official language in diplomatic circles in Turkey.

But he was not finished even yet, for to have given way after I had demolished his five objections would have caused him loss of face—a devastating thing to happen to anyone in the East. So, he said he wanted a green card of mine for himself so as to be able to refer to it at all times in case of doubt. Of course, he thought that if I had no green card on my person when checked on the street, then I could not use my car at all and he would have won the battle with the foreigner: prestige and the maintenance of prestige being the most important cornerstone in Eastern society. I smiled my very best smile at him, made a little bow to show that I acknowledged his superiority over myself and that he had won. I handed over to him as *a personal gift my green card*, to keep in his own office. Then I telegraphed to Switzerland to the Winterthur office in Zürich for a *reserve spare green card*. They knew me well in Zürich and I knew that they would send me one free of charge by express mail from their offices in Istanbul. Which they, of course, willingly did—the next day I received my spare green card.

The police officer concerned was a giant of a man with a huge handle-bar mustache. We parted the very best of friends. In fact, he ordered tea and biscuits for us both and we celebrated the end of the war without him even guessing who had really won. He obviously thought he had won the battle for "seniority" over me and had successfully stopped me from using my car, not realizing I could replace the green card without any difficulty any time I chose.

CHAPTER XV

CURRENCY STABILITY AND A.I.D. IN DEVELOPING COUNTRIES

When we went to Turkey in 1969 the rate of exchange of the Turkish Lira (TL) to U.S. Dollars was roughly ten to one respectively. On the black market it was easy to get fifteen or sixteen TL to one dollar. But the risk of being caught by the police was considerable. Most people could see that a devaluation of the Lira was on the way, the only problem was "when?"

When we left for Switzerland to take our vacation there in the Summer of 1970, the university owed a number of professors—including myself—salaries that had not been paid. While we were away on vacation, the Turkish Lira was drastically devalued—some 35%. That is, of the considerable sum owed us by the Turkish universities some 35% was lost in devaluation while we were on vacation. With the devaluation, prices in Turkey just soared out of control. The price of gasoline, because it was imported, rose well over the amount of the devaluation.

We professors protested against this development. The result was interesting. To compensate for our loss of income our *U.S. dollar salaries but not our Turkish Lira salaries* were increased by a small percentage, but not by nearly the amount we had lost by the non-payment of salaries and by the devaluation of the currency. That is, in the last analysis the

Turkish catastrophe was farmed out immediately onto the unsuspecting American taxpayer.

By careful management of the news in the United States, the American taxpayer has little idea of what is being done with his tax dollar. Up to present, when difficulties arise abroad in education or aid programs, and are accompanied by e.g., large scale riots causing heavy financial expenditure, this extra, unbudgeted expense is quietly farmed out on to the American taxpayer.

CHAPTER XVI

HOW I BECAME A
DRUG ADVISOR

A great number of U.S. troops were stationed in Turkey, as it was a NATO member and a near neighbor to the then hostile Soviet Union. The Turkish population, for a great part, were not very friendly towards the American military. Kidnapping of GIs and bombs by left wing activists were frequent. Thus, many U.S. servicemen were frustrated—besides the boredom that an army endures during peacetime. So an increasing number of soldiers turned to drugs, mostly to hashish and LSD.

One day in Ankara the U.S. Commander's son was caught experimenting with drugs and put into a Turkish prison. In Turkey, the punishment for being involved in drugs is severe. Very few Turks took drugs, although they had huge plantations of poppies and handled the seed daily on their kitchen tables. But they did sell drugs to U.S. soldiers and other foreigners, earning a lot of money by doing so. Finally, the Commander's son was "kidnapped" out of the prison and immediately flown back to the States. The Commander had to retire.

The higher officers, intimidated, approached me through the U.S. chaplain in Ankara, whom we knew well, asking me to help combat the enormous drug problem they had with their servicemen. Nixon, then President of the United States, ordered his generals to do something, quickly, to diminish drug abuse by the troops. They looked around for a drug expert to instruct the troops in a way the servicemen would approve of.

As there was no American available and I had taught pharmacology for several years at the University of Illinois, they asked me, despite my being British. I accepted the challenge and started to lecture all over Turkey to American soldiers and their dependents. I explained to them what the different kinds of abused drugs did to their body and to their psyche, demonstrating the physical effects using animals, such as rabbits and mice. I was also invited to lecture in schools as a preventive action. I thoroughly enjoyed this activity with the young U.S. soldiers and pupils, and was glad I could help a number of them.

CHAPTER XVII

MILITARY AND DIPLOMATIC PRIVILEGES

Before leaving for Turkey, we AID-professors were told by the U.S. AID authorities that there would be no PX[1] or other privileges for us such as the majority of the foreign "colonies" enjoyed in Turkey.

The Peace Corps worked on exactly the same basis, too. They too had no PX or other military privileges either. On the other hand some of the AP (AIDs Program) higher officials lived in pomp which made the diplomats of some smaller nations green with envy.

The Muslim regards riches as a sign of approval by God (Allah) himself. If you are poor, it is because God has not blessed you and is *displeased with you.* Therefore, the Turks were not in the least grateful to the fine young men of the Peace Corps (or other organizations) for coming to help them in poverty. On the contrary, they were sure that Allah was the enemy of the Peace Corps, because its young men had taken on voluntary poverty to help them, the Turks. The basically different ways of thought between the two cultures, Christian and Muslim, is such that misunderstandings quickly arise unless one understands the other on a very mature plane of thought.

---

1. Base exchange, shopping facilities for the U.S. forces, where products could be bought which were often not available to the general public. The PX was also accessible to diplomats and other U.S. groups.

With respect to the Peace Corps, therefore, the Turkish reaction was as follows:

a) The Peace Corps people are only pretending to love us and to want to help us. In reality they are the servants of the CIA interested only in spying on us.

b) No one voluntarily becomes poor to help his neighbors; there must be an ulterior motive.

The reason I mention these things is this: Why burden the already overburdened U.S. taxpayer with non-productive expenses amounting to millions of dollars per annum. There are practically no checks or balances in the system as administered at present. And such checks and balances cannot be built into the system by people who are entirely ignorant of the basic philosophy of the people who need the checks and the balances. The founding fathers of the United States knew their system and built in the checks and balances accordingly. The modern diplomat who administers the AID programs does not seem to understand the basics from which he should proceed in order to administer tax payer's money correctly.

I have now set out the reasons why the Peace Corps and other valuable AP relief work being carried out in developing countries is not only despised, it is often considered to be a spying operation even by many of the most religious Turks. Any well educated diplomat or AP worker ought to have known that one cannot apply programs which *presuppose Christian ways of thought (i.e., voluntary poverty) to non-Christian systems without trouble arising.*

CHAPTER XVIII

ALLAH'S GUESTS

In spite of all that has been said above, which applies more to the consequences of *religious* and *official rules*, we met and appreciated many Turkish people with wonderful character traits. One excellent characteristic was their gracious hospitality, from which many Christians could learn.

Our family was eager to visit the places of the New Testament, among them Ephesus. After some very interesting hours visiting Ephesus in the burning summer sun, we all felt tired and dehydrated. Clive, having a very light skin, was really wilted and exhausted. So, we sat down at the side of our car under a tree. Suddenly the door of a house nearby opened. A lovely Turkish girl walked straight towards us. In her hands she carried a plate with an exquisitely arranged, cut, juicy watermelon. She bowed in front of us and handed us the plate. We did not quite know how to react. But she graciously smiled at us and said: "You are Allah's guests! Please accept it!"

Her mother was watching her all the time from the window.

So with many thanks we took the delicious fruit. It was just the best thing to quench our thirst, much better than Turkish water, which you cannot drink until it has been boiled for a long time. Our children, indeed we all, eagerly ate the melon, being refreshed and revived by it. The girl and the mother watched us with delight. But this was not all. Hardly had the young lady disappeared into the house, when she came back with another plate—again artistically arranged—with a different kind of melon. "You are Allah's guests!" She repeated. She would be greatly hurt if we had refused their kind gift. And indeed we were most grateful for this refreshment and the most generous hospitality towards strangers like us.

We once were invited to a party with leading military and academic leaders in Ankara. The hospitality was—as always—excellent. My wife's table partner was a very courteous colonel of the Turkish army. During the conversation, while the coffee was being served, he told her the following. "When you are offered coffee and you do not want another cup, don't say: 'No, thank you.' Nobody will take notice of your answer, and your cup will be filled again. You have to learn and know the sign, for example how to place your spoon, until they react and believe you. Otherwise they will only think you are being polite but that you do not mean it." But the difficulty is that the sign is not always the same in different parts of Turkey! He told her, that once, when he was stationed out in the wilds in Eastern Turkey he had not succeeded in finding out the "sign." He constantly said: "No, thank you, I have had enough." But nobody believed him and only thought it was a polite gesture. So they kept on filling his cup, which he could not just leave and asking directly did not do anything.

So that afternoon he drank, if I remember correctly, about forty cups of coffee!

CHAPTER XIX

FATMA

Our neighbors in Ankara were educated delightful people, and exceedingly helpful in every respect. Our children were good friends with their children.

All foreign families and Turkish families who could afford it had household help. Firstly, many Turkish women needed the money for their families. They had very little. And secondly, help in the house was very inexpensive. Turkish women liked to work, especially for foreign families, because they earned more for shorter working hours.

Fatma, one of our faithful Turkish helpers, was between forty and fifty years old and a real treasure in the house. After a short time, she knew exactly how our house ran and what needed to be done. She seemed to read our wishes in our eyes. She was faithful, excellent with children, very clean and good in every household skill. And yet she could not read or write; she had never learned it. She—like so many Turkish women, especially in the country—had never gone to school, because from early childhood on girls had to work. It was often different with boys, especially the oldest sons; they went to school and were very important in the family.

But Fatma was not uneducated. When we talked with her about politics, health treatment in the family, every day life and news she was perfectly informed and up to date. She learned everything from the radio or from other people she asked and talked to. She eagerly used her eyes and ears. She was a devoted Muslim. Several times during the day at the call of the muezzin she disappeared into one of our bedrooms, unrolled her prayer mat, bowed towards Mecca and prayed. She ate with us at the table and observed us praying and reading the Word of God. Once a Turkish man knocked at our door to sell his butter. When he noticed that we were foreigners, he immediately withdrew to leave. But Fatma told him: "Come in. Don't be afraid of these people, they pray." We would have loved to take her with us back to Switzerland. But she was married and had a family.

CHAPTER XX

THE KAPICI

Our shopping was done by our "kapıcı," a kind of janitor which every house possessed. In former days, Turkish ladies were not allowed out on the streets, they were supposed to stay at home. For this reason the kapıcı not only carried out the duties of a janitor but also had to execute all types work outside the house such as shopping.

In the morning, the kapıcı would come to the door to collect our shopping list and some money. Some hours later he would bring us the groceries. He usually knew the price of the goods. But as his arithmetic was poor we added up the prices ourselves, left the appropriate sum with him and took back the remaining change.

Once my wife cleaned our car herself during the siesta. This nearly caused a riot amongst the kapıcıs along our road. A lady cleaning her car? Unheard of! Where was the kapıcı? Didn't he know his duties? They summoned our kapıcı and went for him. Had my wife not quickly intervened and clearly explained that it was not the kapıcı's fault they would have given him a beating. Beate had wanted to clean our relatively new car herself because the kapıcıs often used dirty cloths which scratched and damaged the finish of our station wagon.

Once a group of kapıcıs gathered around our Rebel while our kapıcı proudly explained his colleagues that the tailgate of the station wagon could be opened two ways: sideways and downward. He wanted to demonstrate this, but operated both mechanisms at the same time with the result that the entire tailgate came off and stuck in his hands with a few loose cables hanging around between the back of the car and the tailgate. It was good that I knew how the mechanisms functioned and with some effort was able to repair the damage.

CHAPTER XXI

THE EDUCATION OF OUR CHILDREN IN TURKEY

The immediate question for us on arriving in Turkey, in August 1969, was: What are we going to do with the children's schooling? The Turkish schools were out of the question from all points of view. Although the children picked up the Turkish language more quickly than we did, the type of instruction they would have received in a Turkish school would never have prepared them for university examinations in Europe.

We did not dream of ruining the children's chances of a career in Europe just for the sake of our own careers in Turkey by sending them to Turkish schools. The Turks would not have permitted it anyway. They encouraged the expatriates to have their own schooling systems, knowing that European higher education was not compatible with the Turkish school system, which was in many ways linked to the Koran.

Before we got to Turkey, Beate had found out that there was a very good private school of the German Embassy in Ankara. The director of the German school, Mr. Kahmann, was a typical German schoolmaster of the old type and personally a delightful man. He received us both heartily and was not afraid to take on our children although they had changed schools so often. The difficulty with our children was that they spoke German at home, but had been to British and American schools. The result was predictable. They wrote English according to the English orthography—but they wrote German according to English spelling too. Over and above that, the German language still has a strict difference between the "Du" form of address for close friends and in the family, and the "Sie" form for polite address in society. English and many other languages (such as Norwegian and other Scandinavian languages) have long since given the difference up and address every one with the same form.

So when our children addressed the director of the school in the familiar form of "Du," everyone, including the director, was most intrigued. But Mr. Kahmann, the Director, unraveled the cause and never batted an eyelid at being addressed in the "Du" form by our children. It was like addressing the King or the Ambassador as "Bill" or "Chuck" or "Harry"! We quickly remedied this little faux pas at home.

Mr. Kahmann asked my better half to come and teach Music, Orchestra and the Recorder at the school. This she did, and had a delightful relationship with the children at the German Embassy school the full two years we were in Ankara. Mr. Kahmann asked me to sit on the School Council, which I did. All of this brought us into close contact with the German Embassy staff, the German expatriates in Ankara and with the German Ambassador himself.

Germany, from the time of the Sultans, always had a close relationship to Turkey—closer perhaps than that of most other Western nations.

The fact that our children spent two years at the German school in Ankara gave them an excellent basis in grammar, mathematics and orthography both in English and in German, for German grammar and spelling rules are strict, and taken a good deal more seriously than in British or American schools.

When our children attended British public schools[1] later on, they found they were well in advance of the British system in everything but the natural sciences, where the UK system was

---

1. Public schools in Britain are paradoxically private boarding schools.

well in advance of what they had learned in the German system. But their languages, grammar, mathematics and spelling were very much in advance of that of their British confrères.

During our time in Ankara, Clive, our third child, was asked by the Turkish radio in Ankara to help with the English language program given to the public once a week. As he possessed a very clear and melodious voice, he was chosen to pronounce and read the words for the Turkish students learning English.

CHAPTER XXII

THE SUMMER VACATION IN TURKEY

After the cold winter in Ankara, we often motored down to the Mediterranean south coast where it is much warmer and where the orange trees grow. There we bathed in the Mediterranean Sea with the children, and got away from the fog and smog of Ankara.

One spring we all motored down to Silifke and put up at one of the new hotels right on the sandy beach. It was delightful to get up in the morning and go straight for a morning dip in the clear warm sea. I had just taken a good morning dip when I heard an unearthly wail coming from the direction of our hotel. One does not hear such a wail in western countries. I also saw my wife running over the sandy beach and signaling me to come urgently. She said something dreadful had happened in the hotel room next door to us, would I come and help immediately.

So I ran with her to the hotel and found the lady who had occupied with her husband the room next to ours setting up the unearthly wail. Her daughter of about seventeen who had occupied the next room was lying on the bed and looked as though she was in high fever. She was as pink as a cherry. I took her pulse and could find none. She was dead. The poor mother begged me between the wails to bring her daughter back. People in such countries often have a belief that Westerners can do anything—that is, if they want to. And if they don't bring back the dead it is really because they don't really want to.

Between the dreadful wails, I found out that the daughter had taken a shower in her room the evening before. She had sat under the stream of hot water and apparently fallen asleep there. The water was heated as it ran through the system—there was no storage boiler. As far as I could see the gas burner had "struck back," as they sometimes do. When this happens large amounts of carbon monoxide are produced. The carbon monoxide escaped into the bathroom, and the girl under the shower fell asleep breathing carbon monoxide, and never woke up. The parents found her under the shower the next morning.

On investigating the gas heater we found that a bird had built its nest in the chimney, which accounted for the carbon monoxide escaping into the bathroom. I told the Turkish doctor who came to certify death the cause of the accident. He had the room sealed so as to prevent further trouble.

But after two or three days, I saw that guests were being put into the same room again, using the same bathroom. No effort had been made to prevent birds from building their nests in the chimney of the gas heater. Life is cheap in such countries.

When the Turkish parents realized that their daughter's death was final, and that I, as well as a quickly fetched Turkish medical doctor, could not revive her, they started to wail and shriek in their sorrow. The wild lamentations of the professional Turkish mourners could be heard for hours from afar off. It was such a wretched hopeless wailing noise that it frightened and haunted us for many days afterward.

CHAPTER XXIII

Our Children and the Music Conservatory in Ankara

Our three boys and our daughter are all like my wife—they are all musical. So we wanted them all to learn an instrument. Petra chose the violin, Oliver chose his mother's instrument, the violoncello, and the piano, Clive and Einar each chose the silver flute. So the immediate problem for us was to obtain a violoncello for Oliver and a violin for Petra.

Now the Turks are excellent craftsmen. Regularly a number of their best craftsmen were sent to Mittenwald in Germany where they learned to build violins and other instruments. We went round to the conservatory, where these craftsmen worked to order the two instruments. We were told that it is important to fix the price in advance, otherwise the instrument could cost anything up to the value of the national debt. So with the help of a German lady, a violinist, married to a Turk who taught at the German school, we fixed the price and the date of delivery.

At the agreed time, we went round to the conservatory and found that the two instruments were ready. Both looked beautiful. So, in my ignorance of Turkish customs, I prepared to pay the agreed price, but met immediate resistance from the craftsman. No, I could not do that, the cello had turned out so excellently, it was a quality instrument beyond all expectations. He would have to demand a much higher price, he had fixed with me. He was sorry, but he could not have foreseen that it would turn out to be so extremely good.

Just at this time the Turkish university had started withholding my salary, so that I had no cash to spare. So I told him I could not pay the extra amount. The violoncello builder would have argued the hind leg off a donkey, so I told him I did not want to deprive him of the money for a good instrument. If he could find someone to pay the extra money I would congratulate him, he should take it at once. When he saw that I was not prepared to argue any more he took the money I offered him, but I nearly lost my instruments.

In between their customary bargaining, the Turkish tradesmen offer you çay (tea) and sweets and ask a hundred questions to find out your whole life story. In the end they will usually say to you: "As you are a German (as my wife was) and have blue (or any other color) eyes, I am willing to give you my valuable instrument for the very low price of x Lire (the price you had agreed upon before hand). But only because I like your eyes (or whatever), and like the Germans. I worked in Germany for a year. But this is a special price for a friend. Of course, I will not profit anything."

You will thank him very profoundly for his kindness. On leaving he will happily shake hands with you. Usually, the whole affair of bargaining, tea drinking and personal conversation, until you finally receive your instrument, takes a good portion of your day! But if you do not play the game with them they will be hurt and disappointed.

The fact is that the Turks just love arguing about prices—for them it is the spice of life, and if you pay what they demand they despise you. If you go to the market to buy some strawberries—there are wonderful strawberries to be had in Turkey—and if the normal price is twenty lire a Kg—they will ask of you at least 100 lire for a Kg. If you turn your back knowing the real price, they will shout after you first of all eighty lire a Kg., then sixty lire a Kg., then forty lire. But they will call you a foreign dog if you pay the originally demanded 100 lire per Kg. They love to argue, bargain and chisel about prices, and love people who will play at that delightful game with them. To pay the exorbitant prices they ask for, because they are poor people, is an absolutely wrong philosophy, for they just love to bargain—it is for them the very spice of life.

CHAPTER XXIV

FRIENDS IN NEED

One day, as we were sitting with the children on the Mediterranean beach, a despatch rider arrived in front of the hotel and asked for me. He had an Ankara number plate on his little motorcycle, so I guessed his mission had something to do with the university there. And I was right. The envelope he handed me was marked "urgent." Inside I found a little note in the handwriting of an American colleague we knew who worked at another university.

He said that his wife, who had four little children about the same age as our four, had discovered a lump in her breast and needed advice as soon as possible. They did not trust the local doctors there, would I come and advise them as soon as possible? In London, I had worked for four years on breast and prostate cancer, so the dear people thought I was the man to turn to. In Turkey, if one needs a message delivered quickly and surely, the best way is always a personal despatch rider. The telephone often did not work—except on the off-chance.

So we packed our bags and told the despatch rider to ride back to Ankara with a letter to the same person (Professor K.) who had sent the original message to us. It said: "We are all on our way to Ankara and plan to be there this evening."

I told the distraught couple that there was only one piece of advice I could give them, and that was to go to the American military hospital in Wiesbaden, Germany. Although we professors did not have the right to ask the military to lend us the use of their facilities, we did ask them to make an exception in this case. So one of the American chaplains with whom I worked closely fixed up an appointment for the good Mrs. K. in Wiesbaden. They examined her thoroughly there and referred her urgently to the Mayo Clinic in the USA. I advised the K.'s to telephone the Mayo and to fix this up—which they did.

But what was to happen to the four children, all going to school in Ankara—and to the father at work in the university? The children had to be fetched every day from school on account of the kidnapping campaign, and they also had to be looked after. What to do? For such a serious operation Mrs. K. could not and should not undertake the journey and surgery alone. A woman needs the support and presence of her husband if she has to undergo an operation of this gravity.

It was therefore decided that Dr. and Mrs. K. travel together to the USA and leave the children with us.

We had four children ourselves of about the same age as the K.'s children. If their children did not mind sleeping on mattresses on the floor of our small apartment, my wife would take them and see they were fetched from and taken to school every day and properly fed.

Now this was something the children just jumped at. Of course, they did not realize the seriousness of their mother's condition except maybe the oldest daughter. For them it was four new children to play with. Now, family K. was American, of course, and spoke English. At home we spoke German. Over and above this, the K.'s perhaps did not take their Bible quite so seriously at that time, but they were by no means anti-Christian. Thus, Bible reading and prayer in the family were matters a little new to the children. From youngest childhood on it was the custom in our family that every night we told our children a Bible story out of the Old Testament.

The call went through the house at bed time—promptly at 8:00 p.m. "The Story." All activities in the house stopped and everyone hurried to the bedroom where the story was to be told. We never had trouble getting our children to bed at night because they were all looking forward to the thrilling story—a new one every evening. The K.'s children got used to the story telling routine too and looked forward to it just as our children did. I used to withdraw for half an hour before 8:00 p.m. to thoroughly prepare the story, reading it through again carefully so that the children got an accurate and fresh account of the contents of the biblical history. This takes time and discipline on the part of the father who does it, but may I say after nearly forty years of practicing this habit, that the profits of such a discipline are well over one hundred fold. By doing this job accurately and with common sense, the children learn to love the wisdom of the Holy Scriptures and to read the Bible for themselves.

So we changed the story language to English and fixed up eight mattresses on the little bedroom floor we called our own. We told the eight children the stories of Joseph and his brothers, of David and Goliath, of King Saul trying to spear David his faithful servant to the wall and David dodging him at the very last moment, and others. They were all entranced and could not hear enough.

It was a delightful time for all of us—enormously heavy on my good wife, but rewarding. These four K. children are now scattered all over the world and are active Christians and a blessing everywhere. The most important thing they learned was, I think, that to live or try to live out the biblical message is the most satisfying method of living that exists on earth.

From time to time we received telegrams from the anxious parents at the Mayo Clinic. They kept on reading of the kidnappings in Ankara in the American press, and so feared for the safety of their little ones. So we assured them, with the very poor communications we had at our disposal, that we brought the children to and fro from school every day, that all were very happy and looking forward to their parents' return.

Mrs. K.'s operation at the Mayo was successful and after many weeks the parents returned with a new experience of the goodness of God to them personally. After more than twenty-two years Mrs. K. is still alive and active, and the children still remember this traumatic experience in Ankara with a tinge of joy. The mother was thus cured of her breast cancer and is now teaching English in foreign countries—I believe she is teaching at the moment in China.

But one thing happened to us which I must not forget to report. The parents were, for a small child, away from the children a long time. When they did eventually return, the smallest child had become so attached to our family that the parents had become strange to him. It took some time for him to get used to his own mother and father again after having got so used to us and to our four children. But in spite of that "getting strange to one another," I believe that the overall effect of such a traumatic experience for the family remains permanently positive and that the character is shaped by experienced truth: "All things work together for good to those who love God" (Romans 8:28).

CHAPTER XXV

OUR TENURE OF TWO YEARS IN TURKEY EXPIRES

Towards the summer of 1971, we began to think of returning to Switzerland. In 1969, we had lived in the house we had built near Bern in Einigen on the Lake of Thun for a short period of time. When we went to Turkey, we had rented the house out to a Christian artist friend of ours, Frank Wagner and his family. Frank Wagner wished to paint in the neighborhood. He spent two years in Einigen painting the delightful little churches which are dotted all around the Bernese Oberland and the Lake of Thun. When we came back to Switzerland from Turkey we found him a small house a few yards from our house, which he could rent at a reasonable price. So we had delightful fellowship with him and his wife for the first few months after our return.

CHAPTER XXVI

ILLNESS OVERTAKES ME

Hardly had we returned to Switzerland when I fell ill. After just one month, I began to be totally off my food and to have no strength at all for the daily work. This worsened for well over a month. My good wife then called in the local doctor—a nice old man with considerable clinical experience—who examined me thoroughly but could lay his hands on nothing specific. But he did say however he had never seen anyone so utterly exhausted as I was.

Just at this time, while I was laid up the local authorities began to question me about a residence permit. Of course, I had no job in Switzerland, so that they had a perfect right to ask me. All I could say was that they had permitted me to build a house in Switzerland and I wished to carry on my lecturing work at European universities. They replied that this did not warrant my living in the Bernese Oberland—which at that time was in a militarily restricted area. If Switzerland were attacked, the Swiss planned to yield the lowlands which are militarily difficult to defend and retire to the mountains (the "Reduit") which they could defend against all comers.

The doctor treating me had, like most academics in Switzerland, a military rank too—for Switzerland has only a very small professional army. He understood this rather precarious situation. He thought, however, that the acuteness of the cold war which was then being waged would wear off with time. So he kindly wrote to the local authorities, saying that he had seldom seen a person more in need of recuperation in Switzerland than me. He told them I was a friend of the country who had a Swiss P.D.[1], as well as two Swiss doctorates at two leading Swiss universities. Would they kindly give me an extended year's residence permit? And the dear good people did!

During one of these days—the doctor still had not been able to find a diagnosis for my illness—my wife looked at me quizzically for a long time. Then she said: "I think you have brought your troubles with you from Ankara. I would say that you are suffering acutely from hepatitis A. The whites of your eyes are a dirty yellow." And on close inspection they were. So we told the doctor about it—and he agreed. It took me several months of nursing by my good wife until I got over "Turkish frustration hepatitis."

By working in the garden and taking long mountain trips with the children and my wife I slowly regained my strength, but it took months of patient nursing by my wife before I was fit enough again to take on lecturing at Swiss, British and German universities. When I was fit enough I started to lecture again at European universities and the Swiss were kind enough to give me a residence permit as a roving professor for this purpose. This permit I still have. But it took me a good six months of rehabilitation to get back into some sort of form again after the two years at Hacettepe University in Ankara.

---

1. Privat-docent.

CHAPTER XXVII

THE ROVING COMMISSION: THE EDUCATION OF OUR CHILDREN

After we had got back from Ankara to our house in Switzerland in July 1971, the whole weight of the Turkish experience came over me like a flood and I fell ill as recounted above. My good wife nursed me for months besides running the house and looking after the schooling of the children. Oliver, the eldest boy, had to prepare for his university exams, which in Europe is a major undertaking. We knew that for the development of the children's personalities, both academically and morally, good schools were essential.

After much consideration and many prayers, we fixed Oliver up at St. David's College, a boys' boarding school in Wales, North England. He was soon doing well academically. He also started a Christian Union at the school where the principal, Mr. Mayor, a fine Christian gentleman, did his best to further every pupil according to his gifts. Oliver became a Prefect and later on Head Boy of the school as did his two younger brothers Clive and Einar later on when they attended the same school.

We chose English schools for two reasons:

1) As far as we know English boarding schools are at their best teaching sciences. Our sons wished to read

medicine and needed a good scientific education. As we had traveled and moved in many foreign countries, our children already knew several languages and were not so much in need of good foreign language teaching, the weak side of the British school system.

2) To our knowledge, children were much less ideologically indoctrinated and psychologically manipulated in British boarding schools than in the European continental schools, the latter having resulted in the destruction of many families.

In 1975, Oliver started his medical studies at Liverpool University. At first, we tried to get him into the University of Heidelberg, so that he would be nearer home. But the European Union had not proceeded far enough to allow this. The Germans would not recognize British exams and vice versa. Petra and the two younger boys we sent to the Swiss secondary schools. So we had our eldest boy in England in school preparing for the British university and three younger children in Swiss schools.

It soon transpired that the Swiss curriculum did not fit in with the Anglo-Saxon curriculum. Petra was interested in the sciences, like the boys were, so we had to take care that each child should have an equal chance of a career in Europe.

After one rather unhappy year for Petra in the Swiss secondary school in Thun, we transferred her to Westonbirt School for Young Ladies, a good girls' public school, where she passed her O-Levels, and later on to Dean Close where she took her A-Levels. Thus, the children all followed a curriculum which would fit them for European universities.

All our children were active Christians when they entered school. We parents prayed that God might keep them in their faith and protect them from the many temptations. The first year my wife used to write to the children nearly every day—

later on two or three times a week. We thought it necessary to tell them all the little events at home so they would not lose contact. They also knew that we had to live very frugally to be able to pay the high school bills for four children and they honored this fact by also spending very little, although some of their friends came from wealthy homes and lived accordingly.

At boarding school, our children met many children from broken homes who did not know a happy home life. Our children saw the need and tried to help. Over Christmas and during the summer holidays they brought various friends home to Switzerland for skiing and hiking.

One of the young boys—he was already sixteen years old— wrote us a letter after his holidays with us in the Swiss mountains which ran approximately as follows: "Dear Prof. and Mrs. Wilder-Smith, Thank you for a wonderful Christmas in your home. I enjoyed the good food. I enjoyed the skiing in the mountains. What I most enjoyed was sitting around the blazing fire-place reading together from the Word of God and being permitted to ask as many questions as we wanted to... Would you mind my calling you Mom and Dad?"

Some of these young friends have become active Christians and later started Christian homes.

When Clive, our second son, entered the English Boarding School, he—like all new pupils—had to pass an entrance examination. When it came to the subject of Scripture, the chaplain asked him many questions about the Old and the New Testament: "Who was David's father?" What was the name of Abigail's husband?" or "Tell me the names of Joseph's brothers."

At the end of the examination Clive received 100%. The chaplain asked Clive: "When and how did you learn all your Bible knowledge?" Clive paused to reflect for a moment. Then he replied: "I think I always knew it." He could not remember a time when he did not know these biblical stories. From his earliest childhood he had listened to the Old and the New Testament accounts told by Daddy every evening. And he so lived in it that he was sure he had always been familiar with these stories.

Before their time at the British Public School, Clive and Einar, the two younger boys, stayed with us at home and visited the Swiss secondary school in Spiez. For boarding school, they had to take the long journey to North Wales. The separation was very hard for the children and for us parents.

They took the night train from Thun at 10:00 p.m. to travel on a sleeper to the English Channel coast in Northern France, and then on by cross channel steamer to England. The channel crossing was often very rough notoriously so. Many people would rather cross the Atlantic than the English Channel!

How we used to wait for the telephone call from North Wales that the children had arrived safely at school and were in the capable hands of the headmaster there, who was a personal friend of ours!

These long journeys alone at such a tender age made our children mature before their time, it also made them mature in their trust of the Lord Jesus Christ to help them in the difficult situations which life brings with it. In the positive sense of the word they became self-reliant from an early age But it was hard for their parents—especially their mother—to entrust such young ones to the hurly-burly of life.

The three boys all decided to read medicine. Cliver did so in Liverpool, but the younger boys started some years later in Heidelberg, Germany. By their time the European Union had proceeded far enough for the Germans to recognize the British school exams, and university, and medical degrees and vice versa.

After our daughter Petra had successfully passed her entrance examination for the university, she enrolled as a student for dentistry at Guys Hospital Medical School in London.

During their student time, our children had to work hard and exercise a lot of self-discipline. First of all, this meant acquiring the best grades in order to be admitted to medical school. Germany and many other European countries had a numerous clauses restriction for reading medicine. Thus, only a few of the very best student candidates were admitted to the medical courses every year. All four of our children made the race: Oliver in Liverpool University, England; Petra in Guys Hospital Medical School, London; and Clive and Einar in Heidelberg, Germany. The children and the parents had to live very frugally to be able to afford the education. But I think it did not harm any of us in the least. We all had to deny ourselves a number of things. Many things which could not just be "bought" we prayed for. So, we experienced answers of prayers which made us not only dependent on our Heavenly Father, but showed us his loving care even in the smallest things.

CHAPTER XXVIII

THE LORD MAYOR'S DINNER

Just one story to confirm the above.

Petra was for some time the student speaker for her class together with a male student. Once a year the Lord Mayor of London gives his well-known Lord Mayor's Dinner, a sumptuous public dinner to the aristocracy, celebrities and the leading brains of the country. As student speakers, Petra and her fellow student speaker were invited to this honorable event. They felt very honored. There was only one dilemma. All the other wealthy guests would be immaculately and expensively dressed.

Petra—as a poor student—could not afford expensive clothes. So we prayed about it. Then she adventurously started out with a rather meager purse for Knightbridge (the expensive shopping area in London) to purchase a dress for the festive occasion.

She ventured into one of the exclusive boutiques and looked around for a suitable robe. The dresses were beautiful, but the prices exorbitant, not really cut for her purse. Suddenly her eyes fell on a very pretty dress. Its style was elegant, but not overloaded. She tried it on; it fitted her perfectly. However, a seam was torn open. She pointed it out to the shop assistant who replied: "Because of this defect we have lowered the price very considerably as you can see." And truly, as she looked at the adjusted price tag she could hardly believe her eyes.

413

Can you imagine how our Petra felt? She took the exquisite dress, fixed the seam herself and wore it together with her gold necklace, which we had given her for her eighteenth birthday.

In the evening she went with her escort—the fellow student speaker—to the Lord Mayor's Dinner. When she was introduced to the long row of highbrow nobility in their gold, pearls and richly adorned attire she attracted many an admiring glance and compliment. How graciously God had answered her prayer and provided her with the necessary outfit even for the famous Lord Mayor's Dinner.

CHAPTER XXIX

THE INTERNATIONAL CHRISTIAN BUSINESSMEN'S ASSOCIATION

I have worked for well over twenty years with the IVCG[1] and they were the first to ask me to come and lecture to them on our return from Asia. This fellowship works on the same principles as the CBMA[2] in the United States and was started in Switzerland more than thirty years ago. It has carried on a fruitful ministry in Switzerland, Germany and Austria for many years. The initiator and president of the IVCG was Dr. iur. Guggenbuehl in Zürich, an outstanding lawyer and businessman and a fine Christian, with whom I worked together for many years.

The IVCG functions as follows: Many businessmen who would never enter a church or a religious meeting were invited by Christian friends to a festive dinner in a first-class hotel or restaurant. After the meal, there followed a speech by some renowned speaker treating a relevant topic or problem of economy, politics, science or other. While trying to give thorough solutions to the treated topic, the speech always ended by pointing out the main problem of mankind: A disturbed relationship to its Creator and the resulting malfunctioning of the world and mankind. The first remedial step is to restore an intact personal relationship to our Creator

1. The abbreviation stands for the German name: Internationale Vereinigung Christlicher Geschaftsleute.
2. Christian Businessmen's Association.

by the removal and forgiveness of our sin through the Lord Jesus Christ so that man can again begin to function the way he is supposed to.

In many towns in Switzerland, Germany and Austria the IVCG has monthly dinners. Once a year an international conference takes place in each of these countries with many participants from all over, where people meet or make friends. I was often a main speaker at these conferences and dinners, together with other professors and leading business experts.

Many businessmen, young and old, of all kinds and walks of life started a new fulfilled Christian life at these meetings and also helped others to achieve it. We gained excellent friends through this work, which is still going strong.

Our main organizer for businessmen's dinners and lectures in Austria was our personal friend Friedrich Aberham in Vienna. He was a good businessman himself, full of joy and Viennese humor. He and his wife were people of prayer and we were often guests in their hospitable home in Vienna.

From 1974 on he organized regularly lecture series at universities for students and academics, as well as in various lecture halls for the general public. Usually, the auditoriums were crowded and numerous people—especially students— would stay behind to ask their questions of academic and personal concern. There were so few men who were able to communicate with them logically in today's language about their intellectual and personal problems.

AUSTRIA

An Austrian businessman had taken part in some of the IVCG banquets in Vienna where I had spoken and become a fulfilled Christian. Some time later we met his son as a student in Vienna, who told us: "My father had been so blessed by the talks at the IVCG banquets in Vienna that he sent me there to study. He knew that Wilder-Smith was lecturing in Vienna every year, so he wanted me to experience the same blessing."

The greatest part of the Austrian population is Catholic, which accounts for their piety and reverence towards things religious, but also for much superstition. Many of them longed for a close relationship with God, into which they gladly entered as soon as their intellectual and personal difficulties were removed.

Fritz Aberham used to drive us to our lectures in Salzburg, Linz, Innsbruck and even down to Graz. Once he drove us to Graz in his car—I think it was a big Chevrolet—on the highway which was practically empty. It was late in the evening after a lecture series in Vienna. As we were rather tired, he told us one Austrian joke after the other, with his typical Viennese charm, to keep us awake. We laughed a lot. While driving he seemed to have forgotten about speed limits. I happened to look at the speedometer and could not believe my eyes: the speedometer needle had disappeared into the dashboard—he was driving so fast that it was no longer registering!

From our lectures on "Science and Faith" in and around Vienna a number of home Bible studies originated, which Herr Aberham regularly took care of. Students and businessmen who had become believers grew into fine mature Christians who were active in or started various Christian outreaches.

One of our last times in Vienna we parked the car near the university, and my wife and myself walked to the auditorium. A young couple ran after us. Out of breath, the young man addressed me: "Professor Wilder-Smith, I only wanted to let you know that a year ago I attended your lectures. You started your lecture with a short prayer which is very unusual in an academic setting. I sensed: This man has a living relationship with his Father in Heaven. The whole evening lecture God spoke to me so vividly that I wanted to have this personal contact to God, too. I committed myself to God through Jesus Christ and became a Christian, and now also enjoy a personal relationship to the Heavenly Father. I wanted to thank you and I thought it might make you glad to know this."

After the Iron Curtain had fallen Fritz Aberham also took us to Bratislavia in (then) Czechoslovakia to speak there. People were very eager to listen as they were tired of the all pervasive materialistic propaganda. They were open to new scientific findings and ideas which opened up horizons for eternal truths. The room was full to the last seat and the presidium was held by a few academics amongst whom was the Vice-President of the Czech Academy of Sciences.

Fritz Aberham's sudden death in August 1991, from a brain hemorrhage while rowing with his grandchildren on the Danube was a hard blow to us and many others.

GERMANY

Another good friend of ours amongst the leading businessmen in the IVCG with whom we worked together for over thirty years was Willi Bolender from Hannover, Germany. He started and then for many years excellently organized businessmen's dinners and conferences all over Northern Germany. He also arranged very popular Bible seminars for the public in Hannover, usually based on the wealth of Old Testament stories, like "The Wisdom of King Solomon" (Proverbs), "Today's Meaning of the Book of Esther," "The Development of a Character" (Daniel), "The Life of Samson," etc.

It would lead too far to recount all our pleasant memories with good friends in this work all over the German speaking countries. In Swiss cities like Zürich, Bern, Basel, Schaffhausen, St. Gallen, and Geneva, I was invited regularly to speak to the businessmen. A very faithful prayer partner and quiet friend through all our ups and downs in life was Herr Henoch Altherr from St. Gallen; never pushing himself into the front, but always ready when needed.

I spoke regularly at IVCG dinners, breakfasts and conferences over many, many years. We often combined these ministries with lectures at universities and high schools.

In high schools the most relevant subjects were always "Causes and Cure of the Drug Epidemic," because of the growing drug problems in schools, and "The Origin of Life." Young people wanted to know where they came from and what was the meaning of life. Those two questions are closely related: If man was a product of chance, obviously there was no real meaning in life. Most schools and universities teach that men arose accidentally and therefore there was no meaning or purpose in life. However, if life and man was created and planned, there must be a purpose behind it. I spoke in hundreds of schools and always enjoyed the open and honest questions of the youngsters.

BASEL

In November 1976, I was holding a three day lecture series at the auditorium maximum of the university in Basel. The first evening's program was on drugs with animal demonstrations. After noon on the first lecture day, one of the organizers told us that a lady politician did not approve of using animals to show the audience the effect of drugs, and therefore would cause the "Grossrat" in Basel to call off the evening lecture. I kindly asked for an immediate appointment with the lady politician, which she granted me. When I explained to her the procedure of the demonstration, that no animal—as far as man can say—would die or suffer pain, she permitted us to go ahead. To confirm what I had assured her, I invited her for the lecture and reserved for her a place up front in the first row. Afterwards, she was quite content and even thought it a good idea to warn people of the effect of drugs in this way. It might save many a life from destruction by drugs.

In Austria it was in Vienna, Linz, Graz, Salzburg and Innsbruck where I lectured over and over again through many years. We will never forget the good fellowship we had at the yearly IVCG autumn conferences in Fuschl and later in St. Wolfgang while exploring the Word of God and enjoying the beautiful scenery.

Germany was certainly the country where I lectured most except in the last years, when I traveled and lectured extensively in the United States, New Zealand and other overseas countries. I repeatedly spoke in Hannover, Bremen, Frankfurt, Karlsruhe, Pforzheim, Giessen, Marburg, Hamburg, Siegen, Cologne, Kaiserslautern, Nurnberg and Erlangen to mention only the larger cities. In the areas around Stuttgart, the Black Forest, the Siegerland, I spoke in many lecture halls and churches. It would just be too much to mention them all.

The IVCG had an annual conference located each year in a different place within the German speaking countries. In Switzerland the big Whitsun Conference of the IVCG usually took place in Zürich.

In October 1971, the annual conference took place at Bad Teinach in Southern Germany in the Black Forest. European business men were just beginning to notice the problem of drug abuse of various kinds and were looking for help with counseling in this area. Thus, I was invited to speak on "The Causes and Cure of the Drug Epidemic."

After the lectures I had a delightful surprise: I saw a face in the audience which I thought I ought to know. It turned out that the owner of the face had met me for the first time in Harpenden in England, where he had been a prisoner of war. I had visited his camp and ministered the Word of God to him there and he had never forgotten that. I had come to the camp with my friend Mr. O.C. Hartridge, who regularly did Chaplains' work in the Harpenden camp, and whose well known radiant face had for a long time been a solace to those ex-soldiers in captivity. Mr. Hartridge who brought Georg Brinke over from Switzerland to help with the German P.O.W.s, and it was Georg Brinke who had asked me to go to Switzerland after seeing the POW work. So, all this came back to my mind when I saw Heinrich Notz, the former German POW, sitting there in front of me in Bad Teinach. Heinrich Notz remembered the old days of hunger in the camp and brought apples and potatoes for me with him to Bad Teinach—just in case I was hungry there, and to make up for the food I had often brought him into the POW camp. After many years, it was a little attempt to say "thank you" for the service we had rendered them while they were in captivity after the war.

Heinrich Notz and his story were duly introduced to the two or three hundred businessmen attending the conference. They cheered this good man who still lives near Bad Teinach, and thanked God for the Christian impulses he had received in the most unlikely situation.

CHAPTER XXX

THE FOUNDING OF PRO UNIVERSITATE

Through my scientific work on origins, as well as through my books, we won many faithful friends in the academic world, but also a number of bitter enemies.

At first it seemed to me that I was the sole scientist on the European Continent defending the theory that life could only have arisen in connection with a source of information, an intelligent creator, because life was so full of information and design. We soon found out that other scientists and thinkers were also interested in that line of thoughts.

During the twenty years or so in which we had been active in producing literature suitable for European academics—brought up from the cradle to the grave on "scientific materialism"—my wife and I founded an e.V. (registered society)—under Swiss law for holding seminars aimed at the education of students and others in re-introducing into science, Christian thought and values.

For the first year, we rented a Swiss school—empty over the summer vacation—and invited professors and other capable lecturers to hold, during two to four weeks, lectures offering scientific alternatives to the materialistical basis of the dominant Darwinian evolutionary theory. We critically examined the consequences of the forms of materialism behind the evolutionary theory. The name of the e.V. (registered organization) which we registered for legal purposes was "Pro Universitate."

We were determined from the outset not to form just another Christian organization with its sub-groups and paid traveling secretaries in every university city, because in the end such organizations always seem to degenerate into little Christian ghettos. They then sooner or later lose contact with the real academic world round about them. We wanted to remain totally decentralized and decoupled from all power politics—especially from Christian denominational power politics—and have achieved at least this end.

In October 1975, Professor Dr. Alma von Stockhausen, a German lady professor of philosophy and theology at the University of Freiburg wrote us a letter, asking to meet us. She was interested in my rejection of the Darwinian theory of evolution on scientific reasons and had read my book *Man's Origin, Man's Destiny*.

Professor von Stockhausen was convinced on philosophical and theological grounds that man and biology could not have originated by Darwin's evolutionary theory, namely as a result of millions of deaths and the suffering necessary for this evolution. This idea does not correspondent with the nature of a loving God, a Creator, whose nature is self-sacrificing love abundant and who gave Himself that we may live. Death and suffering are the philosophical consequences of sin, of the fall of man, rather than the method of creation.

Professor von Stockhausen had sought for a natural scientist who confirmed her philosophical standpoint of origins from scientific reasons. Her mother, Dr. Phil. Elisabeth von Stockhausen, born Countess of Bernsdorff, knew of her daughter's concern. When she read in the church newsletter of the Osnabruck diocese that the American scientist Dr. Burdick was lecturing at Munich on a topic such as "Fossil Remains (Pollenanalysen in Fusspuren): Do they confirm Evolution or

Creation?" she told her daughter about it. Professor von Stockhausen, highly interested, telephoned to Munich and learned that Dr. Burdick would also lecture on the same topic at Basel which was much nearer her home.

After the lecture in Basel, Prof. von Stockhausen invited Dr. Burdick to lecture at her academy at Bierbronnen in the Black Forest. Dr. Burdick accepted. But as he spoke only English, communication was not easy, Prof. von Stockhausen understood some English, but was not used to conversing in this language. She sent one of her German students to fetch Dr. Burdick by car from Basel. In his lectures, Dr. Burdick showed that much of the current evolutionist fossil dating needed reconsidering. By analyzing pollen found in fossils, which by evolutionists were supposed to be millions of years old, it was discovered that they must be much younger and therefore more in agreement with the creationists' theories. Dr. Burdick presented a strong case against the theory of evolution and for the theory of creation. After the lecture, he handed Prof. von Stockhausen some of my literature.

The same student chauffeur was to drive Dr. Burdick back to Basel to his hotel. As the student had become antagonistic towards Dr. Burdick on behalf of his lecture, Prof. von Stockhausen thought it wise to accompany them in the car to Basel.

They left Bierbronnen at 10:30 p.m. The student driver suddenly started to drive faster and faster. When they reached Basel he raced through all the red lights in the city. The two in the back of the car, Dr. Burdick and Prof. von Stockhausen, became extremely frightened. Actually, the student experienced a schizophrenic fit and was out of control. In the end, the car came to an abrupt stand-still across the road, in front of a tree. The driver dashed out of the car shouting: "I believe in Jesus Christ" and disappeared into the dark. By now it was past midnight. The two shocked passengers, pale as the death, emerged from their backseats.

Seeking a telephone box Frau von Stockhausen telephoned the police to rescue the car and drive Dr. Burdick to his hotel. The police also tried in vain to find the sick student driver. A few days later he took his life.

Professor von Stockhausen then tried to order my book *Man's Origin, Man's Destiny* at the Herder Publishing House. They told her that this book did not exist. After telling them that she would go to another book shop, they finally procured the book for her.

Full of joy at having found the scientific confirmation of her philosophical conviction—having by now read *Man's Origin, Man's Destiny*—Prof. von Stockhausen asked for a meeting.

She afterward told us that the shocking experience in the car, which could easily have ended in death seemed to her like an attack of Satan to prevent her from meeting us—which later led to a very fruitful collaboration and complementation in our Christian students' work. But God had intervened and protected.

Of course, we were delighted to make Professor von Stockhausen's acquaintance when she visited us a few days later. She was accompanied by the well known embryologist Professor Dr. Blechschmidt, who had meanwhile also read *Man's Origin*, and his son Meinulf, a devout priest.

Professor Blechschmidt's name is well known for his *refutation* of Haeckel's Biogenetic Law[1] by his long careful research on human embryos. He thereby confirmed that man is a special creation—human right from the beginning—and not a descendant of animals. His collection of human embryos is world famous.

We had a delightful afternoon together.

---

1. The human embryo in developing from the ovum passes through the same changes as did the species in developing from the lower to the higher forms of animal life.

Professor von Stockhausen's point of view confirmed what I had shown at length in my books, that chemical biogenesis could not have occurred spontaneously, because it needed an intelligent Mastermind behind it. And the same applied to the origin of species; each species needed extra specific information added to it, which was not intrinsic in raw matter.

This first meeting of the minds between Frau Professor von Stockhausen, Herr and Frau Professor Blechschmidt and ourselves was the beginning of a life-long cooperation and friendship. They often helped us as lecturers in our Pro Universitate seminars. These we had started in 1981 in order to re-introduce Christian thought into academic thinking, which had been totally taken over by materialism.

Frau von Stockhausen, with a similar goal in mind, had founded an academy at Bierbronnen in the Black Forest, where I lectured many times from 1976 onward. We were always received with cordial and excellent hospitality.

At the academy in Bierbronnen Professor Carsten Bresch, a biologist and evolutionist from the University of Freiburg, and myself led a lively dispute on evolution versus creation, which was later continued by correspondence and published in the two magazines *Factum* and *Agemus*.

On January 20, 1976, I was invited by Frau von Stockhausen to lecture to her philosophy class at the Pädagogische Hochschule (College of Education) in Freiburg and critically analyze Jacque Monod's book *Chance and Necessity*, one of the communists' favorite sources. The lecture hall was crowded. The ASTA, a group of Marxist students, had been organized to disturb and disrupt my lecture. They kept on changing the volume of the loudspeaker constantly. In the end they gave in when noticing that neither the audience, nor the speaker, showed any signs of terminating the lecture. In the course of the lecture, the Marxists even became convinced by my arguments showing the untenability of Monod's hypotheses and surprisingly their initial aggression turned into genuine enthusiasm.

Professor Blechschmidt and his wife lectured in an unforgettable manner on the uniqueness of man. Using slides, they showed the development of a fertilized human egg—a distinguishable *human* embryo from the first day onwards until the ninth month. He compared the human embryo with animal embryos, which were at all stages different from human ones and clearly showed the untenability of Haeckel's biogenetic law.

A great help and very popular in our students' seminars was Professor Kitchen from Liverpool University, an Archaeologist and one of the greatest Egyptologists today. By means of his excavations and his great knowledge of Egyptian history, archaeology and hieroglyphic characters, he had shown that the Old Testament records are reliable in every respect.

For example: Joseph was sold by his brothers as a slave for twenty shekels of silver. Through excavations several records on stone tablets were found referring to the sales price of slaves. The price of slaves varied according to the times. By the amount of the price it could be ascertained that a slave cost twenty shekels of silver at exactly the time the Bible gives for the period of Joseph's life.

He also pointed out on the basis of his historical research that men and civilizations had not risen by evolution from the very primitive upwards to today's highest(!) development, but rather that civilizations had undergone undulation. That means that the rise and fall of cultures and civilizations follows one another, very often determined by the moral standards of those generations.

Pro Universitate has become a small but very active family of students and professors who have attended or lectured at Pro Universitate seminars in many European countries. Our habit was to lecture in a university or a large church hall. After the lectures, students often asked for more information. Then we would invite them to a coming Pro Universitate Seminar—say in Switzerland, Germany or Denmark. In Ringköbing, Denmark, for example, we rented a whole Christian boarding school with its facilities for up to eighty students for two or three weeks.

Another friend and supporter of the Creationist view of origins was Professor John Rendle-Short, a pediatrician in Brisbane, Australia. As a student, I had known and respected his father, a prominent surgeon. Both were well-known in the medical world. I met Professor Rendle-Short junior for the first time at an international medical conference in Toronto in July 1972. In the morning, we both rode the same bus to the conference center. As the bus was crowded, we had to stand while we were discussing the origin of man. Professor Rendle-Short was inclined to believe in theistic evolution. I explained why I regarded any kind of macro-evolutionary process to be impossible both scientifically and from the Christian point of view. At that moment, the bus stopped unexpectedly and Professor Rendle-Short fell. He later told me that at the same moment he also was struck by the realization that, indeed, evolutionary theory was scientifically and biblically untenable. Laughingly he explained that both shocks occurred at the same time. Later on Professor Rendle-Short founded the Creationist association in Australia and contributed much to the movement. We stayed with him and his gracious wife on our Australian lecture tour.

But in our work we did not only receive flowers and honors, but also brickbats; we did not only win friends, but also vehement opponents. One of our fiercest opponents was Professor H.v.D. who opposed us wherever he could. He even went so far as to write to the universities where I had earned my doctorates to undermine me. He intended to expose me publicly, as he considered I could not have acquired three earned doctorates besides my FRSC. Of course, the rather surprised British and Swiss universities concerned confirmed all my doctorates as genuine, although the University of Zürich at first could not identify my name amongst its doctorates throughout the years. The reason was that H.v.D. had not supplied my correct full English name Arthur E. Wilder-Smith to the university. H.v.D. triumphantly wrote us in a letter that he had found out the "deception" that I had not earned a doctorate at the ETH Zürich. He said that he would keep quiet and not publish the swindle if in future I would refrain from trying to publish our dispute. Thereupon I telephoned the ETH in Zürich who immediately recognized me under my correct name. They put the situation right to H.v.D. by letter. They could, of course, not have been expected to find me under the wrong name.

H.v.D. also contacted the Royal Society of Chemistry inquiring about the authenticity of my title of FRSC ("Fellow of the Royal Society of Chemistry") and at the same time asked them what the letters FRSC stood for. The Royal Society of Chemistry was not impressed by this rude ignoramus, who called himself an academic, and had not the slightest notion of their world renowned higher institute of learning in England. The Institute did not even care to answer H.v.D., instead passed his letter on to me, spiced with some comments.

CHAPTER XXXI

The Position in Scandinavia and Elsewhere

NORWAY

As a result of my books being read by academics in many other countries I received letters and invitations from all over the world.

We had met Steinar Thorvaldsen as a mathematics student in Trondheim during our two years' stay at the University of Bergen, Norway where he was involved in Christian students' work. From that time on we regularly corresponded with one another. Later, he became lecturer in the high North at Tromsö where we visited him and his family in September 1985, on our return from the North Cape. We worked together on several occasions.

In February 1979, Dr. Thorvaldsen and some other professors and students organized lectures at the universities of Trondheim, Bergen and Oslo. In Trondheim, a seminar series took place under the aegis of Rektor Inge Johansen on the topic "The Limits of Science: Materialism in Science and its Consequences. On the Way to Building Sound Science." The speakers were Dr. Udo Middelmann, the son-in-law of Francis Schaeffer, and myself. Udo Middelmann treated the philosophical aspects while I addressed the scientific side of the topic. The seminar lasted four days and was well organized. Not only students but also a number of older academics actively participated in it.

After the seminar in Trondheim, I was invited to give a four-day lecture series to students in Bergen, which was very well organized by Greta Larsen and her colleagues of the Christian Studentlag. There was a great interest in the chemical and informational aspects of the origin of life. I also had to speak at the Teachers Training College in Bergen.

In Oslo, as well as in Bergen and Trondheim, we were interviewed by the media.

As briefly mentioned above, I was invited to the North of Norway in September 1985, in Tromsö. I spoke at the university, in the Teachers Training College, in the high school and also in a church, all organized by Steinar Thorvaldsen.

We were shown the beautiful modern "ice-church" with its colorful church windows and the fine organ, which fits in so well with that Northern landscape. In the evenings the strong intensive Northern lights radiated all over the dark sky.

For the weekend, we took a car trip over the border to Finland with a group of Christians. Here, in a small log cabin, we enjoyed the wild unspoiled nature on walks along the fjord. We found a rusty steel helmet of the German Wehrmacht—forty years after the end of the war.

Two of my books, *He Who Thinks Has to Believe* and *The Natural Sciences Know Nothing of Evolution*, were translated into Norwegian.

FINLAND

In April 1981, Dr. Matti Leisola in Helsinki, who is also Privatdocent in Zürich, invited us to come to Finland for a lecture tour in several Finnish universities (Helsinki, Turku, Tampere, Lahti, Joensuu, Jyväskylä).

Our visit to Finland started with a TV program in Helsinki on the Origin of Life, followed by a lecture tour to the universities. Thousands of interested students, teachers and professors attended the lectures and most of the big newspapers and magazines published articles on my lectures.

Dr. Leisola superbly translated my lectures from English into Finnish. Everywhere the question of man's origin and his destiny was of vital interest. The auditoriums were usually crowded and the discussions vigorous. I still remember, e.g., our lecture at the University of Helsinki where the Rector was rather a materialist. He had organized a conference with a number of lectures on origins running simultaneously. When we were introduced to him, he assigned us to a small lecture hall, and gave the "big auditorium" to a strong Darwinist, because he thought he would draw more listeners. A long time before the lectures began a huge mass of people streamed into our small lecture room and it rapidly became clear that not everybody would fit into it. In the end, the Rector had to give us a bigger lecture hall. When he saw the endless stream of people moving into the hall, he very reluctantly let us have the biggest auditorium which was filled to the last seat.

People were tired of always listening to the same propaganda of the Darwinian explanations of origins and were eager to learn of viable scientific alternatives. Over and over again, we experienced the eagerness of students and open-minded academics to study and examine new scientific data on biogenesis and the origin of species.

Dr. Leisola wrote the following comments about Dr. Wilder-Smith's time in Finland for his seventieth birthday: "In 1974, a friend of mine presented me with the book *The Creation of Life* by Professor Dr. Wilder-Smith. The contents of the book profoundly affected me and changed my biological convictions totally. For the first time in my life it became clear to me that the facts of biology directly revealed the existence of God to those who were willing to observe and listen.

"Another rendezvous with Professor Wilder-Smith which changed my life took place in 1980 when I had the privilege of meeting him personally: first in his home in Switzerland and later during his tour of several weeks' duration in Finland.

"The central role of the Word of God in his personal life and that of his family was an example and an encouragement for my whole family. In August 1980, Prof. Wilder-Smith and I met some Finnish professors to organize a lecture series at the University of Helsinki for the following year.

"In late Spring 1981, the peaceful scientific life of Finland was thoroughly shaken up, when Professor Wilder-Smith arrived in Finland after a long U.S. tour. At Easter the Finnish television showed a program on Professor Wilder-Smith's views on life and its origins. This program was followed by a lecture tour to five Finnish universities. Thousands of interested students, teachers and professors attended his lectures. All major newspapers and magazines published articles on Professor Wilder-Smith. After his lecture tour the editor received several hundred letters for and against his creationist position.

"Two of Wilder-Smith's books, *He Who Thinks Has to Believe* and *The Natural Sciences Know Nothing of Evolution*, appeared that same year in Finnish.

"The personality of Professor Wilder-Smith and his courageous confrontation with the materialistic thought system of this world undoubtedly encouraged Finnish Christians. Many of them had never before heard such scientific arguments for the truth of the Bible.

"As everywhere in the world the young generation in Finland is beginning to see how totally unscientific and purely religious the evolutionary stand point is.

"In this new revival of critical thought persons like Professor Wilder-Smith have played a pioneering role.

"I want to congratulate him on his seventieth birthday and wish him many more years of blessed and fruitful activity. This dying world is badly in need of people like Wilder-Smith." P.D. Dr. Matti Leisola, University of Helskinki and later on at the ETH (technical university) in Zürich, December 22, 1974.

DENMARK

Dr. Peter Öhrström is Reader in Logic and Physics at the University of Aalborg in Northern Denmark. He is also the founder of *Origo*, a magazine for students and academics, and is very active in Christian work amongst teachers and students.

In the autumn of 1985, Dr. Öhrström invited us for the first time to Denmark. He had organized several speaking engagements for me at various places in Denmark. On October 1, we started out with three days of lecturing at Vejle Fjord Höyskolen, a boarding school. The next day, Dr. Öhrström drove us to the University of Aarhus for lectures to science and medical students on the "Origin of the Genetic Code." An interview with a lady reporter followed.

We flew on to Stockholm for a three-day conference on origins. Back in Copenhagen, Dr. Öhrström had organized a TV debate for me on "Evolution versus Creation" with Professor Nils Bonde, Lecturer in Paleontology. Although our views were different, we got on well personally, which helped a lot with the communication. Professor Bonde kindly accompanied us to the station so that we could spend a little more time together, which we appreciated.

On October 11, Beate and I took the train to Ringköbing. I had been asked to teach a three-day course for Christian teachers on "Evolution/Creation" and related topics. The course was held in the Christian high school. The Headmaster, Mr. Mogens Kappelgaard with his wife and staff extended excellent hospitality to us. He showed us round his ideally planned school. As the school is not used and empty during summer holidays, we inquired about the possibility of holding a Pro Universitate seminar there. Mr. Kappelgaard very kindly offered us the school for this purpose.

Together with some Christian teachers, Dr. Öhrström helped us to carry out Pro Universitate student seminars in Denmark at a very low cost. This was important so that finances should be absolutely no bar to any student who was sincerely interested in the answers to modern materialistic science, but whose financial means were perhaps slender. The Danish State supports all educational efforts to instruct its citizens, and thus they also supported our students' seminars.

We used the venue in Ringköbing for Pro Universitate for two successive years, 1986 and 1987. Danes, Germans, one or two Norwegians, Swiss and Austrians took part in the Pro Universitate seminar. Everybody loved it; the hospitality in the school was warmhearted and first-class. In the following years we then switched back to facilities in Central Europe and Switzerland to avoid long and expensive travel for most of the students to and from the seminars.

The director of the school in Ringköbing told me that evangelical Christianity was at a low ebb in Denmark, but that many parents, dissatisfied with the materialistic teaching and bad discipline in the state schools, send their children to the Christian boarding school. In the three to four years they spend there, many see and experience—often for the first time—what New Testament Christianity is; something quite different from "Churchianity." And a good percentage of these children become Christians. The love and harmony of New Testament Christianity possesses a very strong attraction for such children indeed. By this unexpected route, God is slowly but surely evangelizing Denmark far more than by mass meetings or church organizations.

From 1988 onwards, Dr. Öhrström organized further seminars and lectures for students and academics in Copenhagen and Aalborg where we were then invited to speak.

SWITZERLAND

Most of our Pro Universitate seminars took place in the mountains of Switzerland. Year after year we treated subjects like:

- Evolutionary Theory: A Critical Analysis

- The Supernatural: Reality: Time and the Transcendental

- Society Without Absolute Values: The Post-Christian Alternative?

- Self-Realization of Man: Personal and Social Aspects

- The Physiological and the Psychological Meaning of the Easter-Event

- Today's Crisis: A Consequence of Wrong Thinking. A Possible Solution: a) Manipulation, b) Genetic Manipulation, c) Metanoia

- Society in the Breaking: Is There a Way Out?

- The Secret of Creativity: Information the Third Pillar of the Universe

- The Concept of Man: Basis of Society

We tried to give scientific alternative answers to the atheistic views which are generally held today in institutes of learning and in the media.

After the lectures, which required a lot of concentration, the young participants often used their free time to hike in the mountains and to enjoy the beauty of nature. Sometimes we organized an evening tour on Lake Thun onboard of one of the steam boats, to admire the sunset and then the subsequent moonlight over lake and mountains, while discussing problems or striking up valuable, lasting friendships.

The last of the many seminars we held in September 1993, in Kandersteg in the Bernese Oberland. This seminar was to celebrate fifteen or more years of Pro Universitate work, and was thus to be a thanksgiving seminar. This special seminar was not a public, but rather a festive occasion for invited long standing Pro Universitate teachers and participants. It was an opportunity for those residing not too far from the Bernese Oberland to reflect together on the topic "In the Beginning was the Word (the Logos)." It took place at the old historic Ruedihus in Kandersteg.

In the first presentation our good friend, Dr. Peter Öhrström from Aalborg University, Reader in Logics and Physics, pointed out that the meaningful word (logos, information) was the fundament to all communication which had to be based on absolute values. In the beginning must have been the Logos (information) to make logical communication possible.

Professor Dr. Alma von Stockhausen, in her specialty of philosophy, explained likewise that a philosophy not based on absolute values leads to total nihilism: existentially, morally, intellectually.

As a natural scientist, I showed by means of the genetic code that the whole realm of biology is based upon specific information. This genetic information could not have arisen stochastically, but needed a first intelligent Designer, a Logos.

On Sunday morning, Reverend Dr. Armin Mauerhofer expounded the existence of the "Logos" before the origin of everything else, based on the first verses of the Gospel of John.

Mr. Brümmer and Mr. Napierski delighted everybody with their exquisite performance of ancient music on the harpsichord and the classical guitar, which harmonized so well with the antique Ruedihus in which the seminar was held.

The owners of the Ruedihus, Mr. and Mrs. Maeder, with their first-class cuisine, did their best to honor us as guests in the beautifully elegant old-fashioned wood-paneled rooms.

The lectures, the fellowship, the talks, the excursions in the beautiful alpine world were delightful and refreshed us in body, soul and spirit. We were so grateful for all the blessings God had bestowed upon us during the years of the Pro Universitate Seminars and for the close collaboration with all the outstanding lecturers and friends.

CHAPTER XXXII

OUR FIRST EXTENSIVE LECTURE TOUR IN THE UNITED STATES IN 1981

Dr. George Hillestad, who initially published our books in the United States, organized a speaking tour for us all over the United States in 1981. The tour was to last six weeks.

We started out from Zürich on February 19, 1981. In New York, Kennedy Airport, we had to pass through the U.S. customs. The airport was dirty and looked neglected. The customs officers treated every person suspiciously and like a criminal. We promised ourselves never, never again to enter the United States via New York—a promise we have kept until the present!

From New York we continued our flight to Puerto Rico where we visited the university in Ponce for a few days.

In Boston, Dr. Hillestad joined us for the start of the lecture tour. We arrived in a turbulent blizzard and only after circling around for a long time and two or three unsuccessful landing attempts did the pilot safely bring down the plane on the runway.

After a radio program in Boston, we had several extensive TV programs in Norfolk, and then traveled back to Boston for a talk to businessmen and a lecture at Park Street Church, as well as an article in the Cape Cod Times. Our kind hosts were our life-long friends Frank and Elizabeth Wagner. Frank is a first-class painter who exhibited his maritime paintings regularly at the Royal Academy of Arts Exhibition in London.

On Sunday, March 1, I spoke twice at church services. We then took the U.S. airplane to Toronto. At the People's Church I discussed the topic "The Great Debate, God or Chance?" before an audience of 1,700. Oswald Smith, then ninety-two years old, was present, also at the lively question time afterwards.

Our tour continued to Guelph University and then in a small sixteen-seater airplane to Purdue University, Lafayette, where the auditorium was crowded and people very enthusiastic. In between, there were always interviews from newspaper and radios. These were often conducted in the taxi between the airports and the lecture halls. Each day I had to speak two to four times in addition to the press, radio or TV interviews. On top of this schedule, we traveled nearly every day to a new destination. In the end, we hardly knew which town we were in and what calendar day it was. We realized that our tour program looked very good and interesting on paper but strength-wise was very hard to realize.

From Lafayette we flew in a Piper eight-seater through the clouds to Athens/Ohio and the next day to Columbus. We were so grateful that God blessed the lectures. We knew we were only his instruments whom He was so gracious to bless. In Ohio on Sunday, March 8, 1981, I spoke three times in the Grace Brethren Church of Pastor John Willett, followed by a TV Press Interview. Each service was attended by about 950 people when I spoke on "The Six Days of Creation." The audience were very open and receptive.

CHAPTER XXXIII

THE CHICAGO DEBATE

Right afterwards, on March 9, 1981, we flew on to Chicago and to the Urbana Campus of the University of Illinois in Champaign. There we watched students standing in line to get into the big auditorium for the evening's debate. Two professors, Dr. Woese and Dr. Weber debated me on the topic "Life's Origin, the Creation Alternative." Some 1,935 students and professors were crowded into the auditorium. The TV team was ready to televise the whole debate. Before it began, I approached my two colleagues, Dr. Woese and Dr. Weber to shake hands and exchange a few friendly words with them. But they turned their back on me pretending not to see me. Thereupon, I approached them from the other side; I thought it important to conduct the debate in a gentlemanly way. But demonstratively they again turned away from me. I felt sorry for this attitude. But I noticed that the TV team had filmed this introductory scene for the public. The debate went well and many of the students understood that life just could not have originated without intelligence, without a Creator.

After several weeks into our tour, Dr. Hillestad also realized that our speaking program was extremely tight. It was the first tour he had organized and on the later tours he allowed for more breathing time in between. He was a very good and reliable friend who could also take a good joke, when one day—I was exhausted and suffering from a migraine—my wife teasingly remarked: "Dr. Hillestad, if you kill my husband, you will have to reckon with me." He then really tried to relieve us of extra work and allowed relaxation by showing us places and objects of touristic interest. The traveling, praying and working together united us to a harmonious team and we enjoyed the company of each other.

On March 10, our tour led us from Urbana to Minneapolis. At the university, I treated the subject of "Causes and Cure of the Drug Epidemic" in the afternoon and in the evening "Is Man Genetically or Environmentally Controlled?" and on the next day more topics on biogenesis and evolution. Dr. Owen and his colleagues had organized and prepared the lectures well in Minneapolis, which made a great difference.

In Kansas City, two more lectures followed on the next day. On Friday I spoke at my old College, at the University of Illinois in Chicago where I had been professor years ago. It was a pleasure to meet some of my old colleagues again and even Dean Webster, now quite advanced in years, took part in the lecture I gave on drugs, their use and their abuse.

In Wheaton, our hometown twelve to fifteen years ago, we visited some of our old friends with whom we had kept in touch throughout the years. Our special friends, the Dr. Acuñas—our children had gone to the Christian Grammar School together with their children and had been friends with them—invited us for a meal and took us around all the nostalgic places from years gone by.

On Sunday morning, I preached at Woodside Chapel in Maywood, Illinois, and stayed with our faithful prayer friend, Miss Findlay, who in the evening took us to Moody Church. I preached there to a good crowd on "The Great Debate." Moody Bible Institute and the Church are situated in an unsafe area of Chicago. After the service and the many questions we were fetched by car to the Marriott Hotel. We were to leave early the next morning from O'Hare airport. Dr. Hillestad, the driver, the two of us and a young man tried to get into the small car, but in vain; there was not enough space for five persons. While trying to solve the space problem in the car I finally asked the driver: "Is the young man joining us in the car your son?" "No," he answered, "I was of the opinion that it was your son." "No, it is not our son." "Is it Dr. Hillestad's son?" "No, it is not his son." We were perplexed. The young man did not say a word, but had already conquered himself a seat inside the car. Now the perturbed driver addressed the young man: "Who are you, why did you try to get into the car although there is not enough room for all of us?" We were starting to feel a little unsafe. "Well," he said, "maybe you would have driven me home." We hoped he was telling us the truth and had no other intentions. Dr. Hillestad gave him some money and pointed out to him the bus station right opposite the street. Now, we were all able to board the car and reached the hotel after midnight.

We took an early plane to Des Moines. I had been invited to speak the next day at the Senate House at Des Moines at a Hearing on the "Seven Postulates of Darwinism." We rushed directly from the airport to the TV station for an interview on Channel 8 and right afterwards to the Senate House for the Hearing, which was a preparation for the future vote for a bill on teaching Creation besides Evolution in schools. A public luncheon followed.

In the evening, I gave a lecture at Iowa State University in Ames, showing that the model of creation is more scientific than the model of evolution based on the analysis of the origin of the genetic code.

Then followed a number of interviews and lectures at the University of Columbia, St. Louis, at the University Houston, Texas, at the Azusa Pacific College, and the Christian Heritage College in San Diego.

In San Diego Professor Dean Kenyon, the author (together with Gary Steinman) of *Biochemical Predestination* from San Francisco State University came to visit us for two days. We had corresponded with one another but never met. It was a real pleasure to talk shop with one another on scientific problems in which we both were involved, especially on biogenesis. I had to think of Proverbs 27:17: "Iron sharpeneth iron; so a man sharpeneth the countenance of his friend."

Over the weekend, I spoke in several churches in San Diego, and the next week at USC, Los Angeles, and at the University of the Pacific in Stockton.

On March 25, 1981—I felt very exhausted and tired after the endless lecturing, interviewing and preaching—I was invited to speak in the evening in Calvary Chapel, Costa Mesa. When I and my wife entered the building Pastor Chuck Smith welcomed me so cordially—like a long lost brother—that I felt refreshed and at home right away. His face shone with God's love and kindness. This church later became our spiritual home in the United States.

In the evening I spoke on "The Seven Postulates of the Evolutionary Theory" and used the work of Sol Spiegelman of putting together a living virus, to stressing my point. The audience was between 3000 and 4000—most of them young people. Pastor Chuck Smith asked me to come back the following year when on my next U.S. speaking tour.

From that time on we returned many, many times to Calvary Chapel, Costa Mesa, and became close friends with Pastor Chuck, who always was to us an example of faithfulness towards the Bible and of God's love.

In a later chapter, we will tell more about the work of the Calvary Chapels.

Our next stop on our tour with Dr. Hillestad was Boston. Interviews with the *Boston Globe* and several TV and radio stations took place, as well as lectures in Park Street Church and other churches and societies. We also visited Stoney Brook School on Long Island, a good solid Christian school, and spoke three times to the entire school and once to the faculty.

CHAPTER XXXIV

THE MYSTERY DEBATER: A DEBATE AT THE MIT

A big surprise awaited us when back in Boston. A debate "Evolution versus Creation" had been fixed for me at the distinguished MIT (Massachusetts Institute of Technology).

Until the great day of the event, nobody had yet disclosed to me the name of my opponent, nor did I know what his field of scientific specialty was.

But a few hours before the debate, when I insisted on some specific details for the evening, our MIT liaison showed us a poster fixed to the walls everywhere in and outside the MIT campus.

The advertising poster read:

Dr. A. ERNEST
WILDER-SMITH
Ph.D.,Dr.ès.Sc.,D.Sc.,F.R.I.C.

v.s.

THE MYSTERY DEBATER
Ph.D.,Dr.ès.Sc.,D.Sc.,D.D.S.

"Evolution and Creation:
a Controversy Revisited"

Wednesday, April 1
8:00 p.m.   Free

We had to laugh. The organizers had fully profited of the fact that a joke was allowed on April Fools' Day.

Fortunately, our responsible MIT host could let on to us some more information about the "mystery debater." He was Dr. J.L., a doctor of dentistry. The academic titles printed behind his name were fake titles—just imitations of my own titles—except the last one D.D.S. for his dental degree. This little "academic alteration" was "justified" on account of its being April Fools' Day.

The subject of the debate and the ingenious poster attracted a huge crowd of people. One must not underestimate that students—and not only students—love to watch a cock fight—which they expected to take place on account of the hot subject.

Our moderator was Dr. Philip Morrison who was in no way unbiased. When he was afraid that the scales of the balance in the auditorium might go down in favor of my creationist explanations of the origin of life, Dr. Morrison, the "neutral" moderator, took sides by supporting the evolutionist mystery debater.

The students reacted spontaneously. Sometimes, when they thought an answer hit a bull's eye, they became hilarious and threw their hands into the air.

Debates are always difficult for me: Not the scientific material or the debating itself. And not the answering of questions and explaining of facts and problems.

What is of real concern to me in debates is to win your point and not lose the colleague you are debating. Because by hitting very hard or treating your opposite as an enemy you can embitter your opponent and harm his soul. We always ask God to give us wisdom and a heart full of compassion and respect so that we can convince our colleague of the truth as I see it, but at the same time show him our respect for his person and his efforts. I am of the opinion that it is sometimes more important to win your brother than to win your point. And yet, it is our task to defend the truth so that others can be helped. But to practice it in the right manner needs extreme wisdom in discerning the clear factual truth from the loving respect to the person one is debating. It is easy to fail in this area.

CHAPTER XXXV

AN INVITATION TO A CONFERENCE ON HEALTH FOODS

I was invited to speak at all sorts of conferences—sometimes only distantly connected with the Christian ministry. But if I was permitted to speak freely and without any restrictions I accepted.

An instance of this sort of ministry took place on October 29, 1989, at a Health Food Conference in Bad Lahnstein on the Rhein. I was asked to give a scientific talk on "Conception, the beginning of man's biological time frame" and on "The interaction of the genetic make-up of man and his environment." The organizers wanted to profit from my general scientific know-how while the going was good! As there were quite a few scientifically interested people present who believed that no scientifically trained person could trust the Biblical report on the Creation, they questioned me about the origin of life and man from a scientific point of view.

In Europe, most academics have been taught to believe that life probably arose spontaneously from dead matter by chance and purely chemical means over long time periods. They ignore in fact that all life functions on the basis of receptors and acceptor sites fitting very precisely into one another just like a hand fits into a glove. This close fit permits chemical reactions to take place at the comparatively low temperatures of life. Glove and hand systems like this necessitate mirror image structures like left handed and right handed gloves. No life, as we know it today, is possible without such receptor and acceptor fits required for the metabolism of all life. But we must not forget that the entropy status of the left handed molecule necessary for all life is exactly equal to the entropy status of the right handed molecule. That is, it is exactly as difficult to create a right handed molecule as it is to create a left handed one. This all adds up to one result: Chemistry left to itself with *no informational guidance from outside will always produce an equal quantity of left handed and right handed molecules.*

This is an empirically provable fact. A long molecule consisting of higgledepiggeldy left handed and right handed radicals, will never fit into another long molecule consisting of higgledepiggeldly sequenced left handed and right handed radicals. Put technically, therefore, because specific configurations involving either exclusively left handed molecules and the right handed molecules are needed for acceptor and receptor systems, and because the left handed form has exactly the same entropy status (equal degree of complexity) as the right handed form does, it is *theoretically impossible for life to have arisen by chance without outside input of specific information to ensure that the right handed—or the left handed form—is being exclusively formed.* A simple scientific fact of this type throws out all purely materialistic theories on the origin of life.

Thus, when the organizers at Bad Lahnstein asked me to speak on the significance of science in the question of the origin of life, I willingly complied. Even a question such as that of the significance of entropy status to the origin of life can be made comprehensible to non scientists if one takes the time to do the job properly.

Chemistry alone is not capable of distinguishing between optical isomers, the material basis of life, because the left handed isomer has exactly the same entropy status as its right handed isomer. For this reason, the chemical processes behind biological synthesis always, without exception, deliver a racemic mixture of 50% left-handed and 50% right-handed form—unless creative information is supplied to select the isomers necessary for the correct "fit" for the metabolism of life. Without the correct "fit"—as based upon the correct optical isomer—no acceptor-receptor systems can be produced to liberate the metabolic energy needed to support life's processes. In practice this means that information has to be supplied to the chemical syntheses to guide them into the correct paths to produce left or right isomers to construct the machinery of life's processes for releasing energy. Interestingly, the information required to distinguish between optical isomers of identical entropy status has only been demonstrated in connection with biology—or more specifically with the brain—for the information necessary for it is not merely potential information, but actual information of the creative kind.

Such information of the creative kind does not arise stochastically, but—as far as we know today—always arises in a brain of some kind. Put differently, one can usually trace back the origin of information of this type to a brain or a person, for a functional brain is usually coupled to a person of some kind with all the accompanying mysterious properties.

If persons are relevant to questions of the origin of life, then, obviously, moral questions enter the picture too. So for the last lecture of the conference at Lahnstein, I agreed to speak on the moral side of the question of the Origin of Man. That is the side where will and purpose play their role in guiding chemical reactions into paths, which chemistry alone cannot determine. The philosophers amongst us seemed to be entranced at this development, because it opened up vistas which were apparently new.

Most of the health oriented audience—they were almost 1000 people—had never listened to thoughts of this kind. They received the spiritual message at the end of the lecture with great openness.

CHAPTER XXXVI

OUR SECOND UNITED STATES TOUR IN 1982

Our second great U.S. lecture tour took place in April 1982. The tour was again well organized by Dr. Hillestad. We flew out to Boston where we stayed one night with our friends, the Wagners, and continued next day via Atlanta to Augusta in Georgia. Dr. Carl Fliermans, a first-class microbiologist, whose specialty was legionaris morbus (legionnaires disease), and a group of excellent academics had invited me to speak at various venues. The same evening, on April 14, I spoke at the First Presbyterian Church at Augusta. Next day I had an interview with a newspaper and lectured to 250 students at the Medical School of Georgia.

In Birmingham, I addressed the staff of the Medical School in the morning and spoke to the church on "Brainwashing and Manipulation." I spoke at a breakfast for scientists followed by a long and lively discussion with some geologists on geological dating.

On Sunday, April 18, I preached twice at Briarwood North Church, each time to about 1,200 people and once to Briarwood South on "The Great Debate." The topic of the evening lecture, again to a large audience, was "Why Does God Allow it?" After the lecture the College Group met and put scientific, as well as theological, questions to me.

On Monday, April 19, we drove to the Montevalla University where I taught a biology class on Scientific

Creationism. In the following chemistry class when teaching chemical evolution, I noticed very little knowledge of chemistry. This complicated the lecture considerably when trying to explain the difference between intellectual and chemical information.

But we had a pleasant conversation with one of the professors there who was a Christian and a theistic evolutionist. When I explained why life could not have started spontaneously from non-living matter, he told me after the lecture with about the following words: "Being a Christian I always had the vague impression that Darwinian evolution could not be the solution to the origin of life. But I had no other explanation. Now you have shown us the scientific background, the creationist alternative seems to make more sense to me."

An interview on TV Channel 6 and the videotaping of three interviews on drugs, on the problem of suffering and on "He who thinks, has to believe" took up a great part of Tuesday, April 20. In the evening, I addressed the Christian Medical and Legal Society at their banquet on the topic "Causes and Cure of the Drug Epidemic." I enjoyed talking to colleagues with a good appreciation of the subject.

The next five days we spent in Washington D.C., lecturing two evenings at the University of Maryland on "The Great Debate" and "The Origin of the Genetic Code." The students were full of questions and searched for valid answers. I also had the opportunity to talk shop on these important subjects with some professors. Some were at first quite antagonistic, but changed their attitude during our conversation.

We lodged with a young academic couple. They put us up in their cellar, a note-worthy place which caused us many a smile. There was no water because the plumbing was in a bad state of repair. The dark damp room looked to say the least as if it needed a good cleaning. When the people above us used the bathroom during the night (or during the day) we had the pleasure of listening to a very special kind of concert. Because the plumbing and the masonry of the bathroom above us were also defective, our hosts had placed vases and chamber-pots into the cellar to catch in it the running water dripping through the ceiling. It sounded not directly like a bell choir, but with increasing defects from above and more pots and vases down underneath it might evolve into a musical choir in the course of many more years of chaos.

We enjoyed Washington with all its impressive buildings: the White House, the Senate, the different presidents' monuments. The beautiful city was in its Sunday's best as it was the time when the dogwood trees blossom. The delicate blossoms looked like porcelain. One morning Dr. Hillestad took us on a sightseeing tour through Washington and Georgetown. What struck us deeply in Washington was the great contrast of beautiful magnificent buildings and suburbs and the shockingly dilapidated slum areas full of misery.

I spoke in various churches, big and small, breakfast meetings and seminars in and around Washington. On our last day in Washington, April 26, we met Dr. Everett Koop in his office at the Hubert Humphrey Building to exchange our experiences and our concern in the field of drug abuse.

On the next day, a radio program at the 700 Club awaited us, and then we traveled on via Indianapolis to Lafayette. After an interview with a journalist, Ray Moore, the same gentleman who had arranged the big lecture at Purdue University last time, had organized a meeting at Purdue University: "A.E. Wilder-Smith Answers His Critics" as a kind of continuation to the lecture given here a year ago on our first speaking tour.

Our next place was Champaign. First a radio program with phone-in questions. In the evening, a lecture in the big auditorium of the university on Evolution and Creation with 600 students and professors present.

On April 29, in Los Alamos, New Mexico, where I lectured to a number of scientists of the secret city and others in the civic center. From there we flew to Denver and gave a week's series of evening lectures at the big Calvary Temple with Pastor Blair, and also spoke twice at the University.

On our way to California, we stopped over for a few hours at Las Vegas. What we saw there greatly disturbed us. We were glad to move on. The same evening I spoke to the students of the Saddleback College on Creation, elaborating on the experiments of Fox & Miller, optic activity and Fred Hoyle's calculations.

After one talk at Pastor Burnett's church in Dana Point I was invited to speak four evenings at Calvary Chapel Costa Mesa (May 9–12, 1982). The people at Calvary Chapel and especially the many young people there are always enthusiastic and it is a pleasure to talk to them. They are keen to learn to defend their Christian belief. Here I spoke on "The Criminal Mind," "The Effect of Environment and Genetics in a Person," "The Great Debate: Evolution or Creation" and "The Drug Epidemic."

As I had had some correspondence with the scientists of Loma Linda University in the past, I enjoyed meeting their science professors during one of the following days and talking with them on various origins topics of mutual interest. I also addressed their students.

Our last speaking engagement on this second U.S. Tour was in San Diego. Dr. Hillestad had looked after us very well on the whole tour and during the last days in San Diego he showed us the points of beauty and interest in his home town. In the evening, he took us to the Coronado Hotel, a really special occasion for us. On May 19, we boarded the airplane back to Zürich.

CHAPTER XXXVII

THE APPRENTICES IN SCHAFFHAUSEN

In Europe, the effective outreach of the established churches to young people is often weak. So, certain free church groups in the city of Schaffhausen decided they would start a series of lunch time meetings for the apprentices in their area and Dolf Meyer, the initiator, asked me if I would be the first speaker.

Of course, since the time available was that of their lunch break, one had to take care not to get the apprentices late for work after the meeting. Since the scientific knowledge of these young people was not very profound, the subjects had to be carefully chosen. It was decided therefore to make a start with the subject: "My Genes and My Environment." In the course of the lecture I showed the relationship of the genetic make-up to the character of a human being.

I managed to keep well within the time allotted me in the lunch break of these apprentices. Encouragingly, at the end of the talk they seemed to understand the relationship between genetics and character, and what can be done towards breeding out detrimental genes from the gene pools of human beings without the process descending to a sort of operation in cattle breeding.

CHAPTER XXXVIII

SWISS SOLDIERS
ARE OUR GUESTS

My good wife was at home when in the evening of November 7, 1971, a knock came on the front door. It was the time of the annual maneuvers of the Swiss Army. A drenched officer was standing out in the appalling rain. The mountain side on which our house is built was simply pouring with water. So he asked very polity if his men, who were in the middle of their maneuvers, could take refuge for the night in our garage. He had asked the neighbors, but they said their cars were in their garages and there was no room. We had two cars in our garage, but my good wife said, that people were more important than cars and she would drive out the cars to make room for the soldiers. So she did.

The officer and his men were most grateful. The Swiss do not have a large professional army. Everyone in Switzerland has to do military service, starting when they are in their teen years until they are fifty or so years old. Every year the service time required of a soldier gets shorter. My wife gave the soldiers shelter in our garage and on the floor of our library downstairs—they are not allowed to sleep in beds while on military service.

We could not have had better guests in our home. During the time they were on military service it rained cats and dogs all the time and they always came in soaked from head to foot. My wife gave them a hot water heater so they could shave and wash when they came in from their duties outside.

After about a week, they moved on to another site for maneuvers. When the men got home after some weeks, there followed a large arrangement of flowers with a thank-you card for my wife, signed by all of them for having looked after them with hot water for washing and making tea when they came in out of the cold.

CHAPTER XXXIX

MORE DRUG LECTURES

I considered teaching the European students at their universities as my main activity. However, when the NATO authorities approached me in February 1972, asking if I would be prepared to help them further in their drug control programs, I thought that I could easily arrange the lectures in the European universities so that I could manage both jobs.

The U.S. Generals of the army and of the airforce invited me to give drug lectures and demonstrations on their European bases.

In Chiemsee, Southern Germany, a number of generals and myself met to discuss the practicalities and to set up the contract. Late at night—I was already in bed—General Pearson knocked at my door and asked me to sign the contract. I explained to him that I would give my signature under one condition. "What condition?" he asked. "Under the condition that I have the freedom to offer an alternative to drug abuse." "Which alternative?" "People take drugs because they cannot cope with the grey drudgery of army life; they cannot alter the situation they are in, so they try to get out of it by altering their state of mind through drugs. Older people take alcohol to anaesthetize their consciousness, reality being too unpleasant. Younger people—like your soldiers—try psychedelic drugs to expand their consciousness to experience more excitement because reality is too drab. The alternative to drugs is to experience the joy and fulfillment that God offers us in a living relationship with him. It is the Christian message." "I agree," answered the general, "but you must promise me not to upset the atheists and people of non-Christian beliefs." This I promised.

I was given the rank of GS15 (equal to Brigadier General), which in the course of the next few months was increased to GS17 after I had served at countless military bases. I had at my disposal helicopters and staff to fly with the animals to the various NATO bases, where I would lecture to thousands of soldiers and officers.

So on February 14, 1972, I set out from Einigen to Wiesbaden, where the NATO authorities put me up in the NATO hotel General von Steuben. I was asked to inspect the laboratories they had set up to control the urine drug content of all NATO staff. At any time, any soldier or officer could be asked to produce a urine sample with no warning. This would then be tested for drug content so that if any soldier or officer had taken any morphine or cannabis that fact would show up in the urine and punishment be administered.

The NATO people had set up a perfectly furnished laboratory for this purpose. And it certainly made the NATO staff careful about taking drugs, because the central administration could find out quickly and with good certainty just what the drug status of their staff was. Even generals could be asked for a urine sample without warning. Of course, if the personal physician had put a patient on, say morphine as a pain killer, that would show up in the urine too. That a doctor might give a patient codeine had to be taken care of in the administration too. For codeine being methyl morphine would show up as a morphine derivative in the urine too. In these laboratories they could test for morphine, amphetamine and barbiturates and so keep their fingers on the pulse on the drug status of the NATO staff. All this cost enormous amounts of money.

I spent a week looking over these facilities before fixing up appointments in various bases. I then started lecturing to the soldiers and officers on just what drugs like hashish do to the body and why the military cannot risk their soldiers taking these drugs, because their reflexes become unreliable. One can beautifully show this effect in animals so that a soldier can convince himself that it is very unwise to have powerful machinery at one's disposal if under the influence of, say, tranquilizing drugs; one may endanger one's own life and that of others, too.

In the following few years I was invited to lecture and give demonstrations on drug abuse using animals in countless military bases belonging to NATO in Germany, Spain, Italy, as well as in Turkey. The British would never allow a demonstration using animals on their soil, because of the anti-vivisection leagues so active in Great Britain. NATO had the difficult job of working under the different and sometimes contradictory laws of the various countries in which it worked.

Once I had to give a drug demonstration in Bitburg, Germany. About 1000 GIs were assembled to watch and take part. In the front rows sat the brass: all the high officers. The drug lectures were compulsory for all the military troops.

My assistants in white coats were ready, with the mice and rabbits lined up in their boxes. When I tried to put on my white coat for the animal experiments, I realized the sergeant had given me a coat that was about three sizes too small. I asked the assisting sergeant to lend me his coat, but he refused. So I rolled up my shirt sleeves and performed the demonstration in my shirt.

I explained the effect of the different drugs on the human body:

- how amphetamines are apt to kill, especially when taken in a group,

- how tranquilizers suppress learned skills so that one becomes accident-prone,

- why morphine, alcohol and other drugs develop dependency,

- that psychedelic drugs are a stepping stone to harder drugs and make one lazy.

My intention was to show the audience not only the benefits of drugs administered *medically*, but also to make them understand how very dangerous drugs could be when *misused*. I explained how each drug reacted differently according to: a) the setting, b) the set, c) the given dose, d) the individual involved.

Using a rabbit which had been medicated with tranquilizers, I showed them how learning capability was suppressed. The rabbit was unable to learn anything even if the same trick was repeated over and over again. While demonstrating this effect suddenly a tall broad-shouldered GI stood up. He started to walk like a robot towards me at the front of the lecture hall, his eyes rigidly staring on me. "I must have help, I must have help immediately!" he shouted. I handed my demonstration rabbit to one of my white-coated sergeants to repeat the experiment while I took the GI by the hand and disappeared with him in the restroom—there being no other room at hand.

"What is the matter?" I asked and tried to talk him down, because I realized that he was having a drug trip. He answered: "While concentrating on your experiment I experienced a drug trip. Every time I have to concentrate hard on something I experience a trip. It's driving me mad. I cannot stand it any longer!"

"What drug have you been taking?" I inquired. "I have not taken anything for several months." "What did you take before that time?" I found out he had been taking LSD and amphetamines on top. Now I understood. He was suffering from flash-backs: drug trips which one can experience a long time after having consumed the drug, especially when mixed with amphetamines.

"I work in the accounting office of the army. We have to prepare the accounts for the auditor. Every time I concentrate on my papers they start to burn from all four corners with a blue flame, eating their way towards the center of the page. When the four flames meet in the center a horrible grimace appears staring at me. I cannot bear it any longer, I need help!"

I tried to quiet him down and handed him to an assistant so that I could finish my lecture and talk to him afterwards.

Later, I spoke confidentially to his superiors. He got a release from his office work. Plenty of hard manual work in fresh air, vitamin C and a healthy life may eventually free one from the unpleasant experience of flash-backs.

I have met pastors who had stopped taking drugs years ago and were living a normal life. Yet, often when they concentrated on preparing a sermon for Sunday they experienced a flash-back—they went on a drug trip. Only much fresh air, hard work in the garden and regularly taking vitamin C over a long time period finally freed them from the unpleasant experience of flash-backs.

I very much enjoyed my work amongst the NATO troops. Although it was not an easy task, I found it a great opportunity helping young people.

A few months later the sergeant who had refused to lend me his white laboratory coat came with his family to visit us in our home in Switzerland. He had in the meantime become a Christian. "Do you know, Professor, why I refused to give you my white coat that day? I myself had been a drug addict. I had volunteered to assist you at drug demonstrations to acquire the needles I needed for my injections. My arms were full of needle scars from drug injections. Of course, I did not want anybody to see the scars. But it gave me a shock. I became a Christian and was freed from drugs. I wanted to tell you this."

The day the sergeant and his family came to call on us we experienced an amusing little incident.

Only a few hours earlier we had returned from a lecture journey to Germany. It was a Sunday. All shops, as usual, were closed over the weekend and our cupboards were empty. We had just finished our lunch with the last provisions and intended to take a little nap after the long journey and the long nights of the previous strenuous week, when the bell rang. Curiously, I opened the door. There was the sergeant, his wife and three kids. They asked, if they could pay us a little visit as they were just passing through our area on their way to the mountains. "Come in, make yourself comfortable. Have you had your lunch yet?" The children yelled: "No, we are so hungry!" I had committed a faux pas, as I realized at once, because there was no food in our kitchen which to offer them. I consulted with my wife. Finally, we found a tin of mushrooms, a package of pastry shells and some tinned vegetables. My wife did her best to make a nice meal of it. When she entered the dining room where our guests by now were seated the boys shouted: "Uuh, we don't like mushrooms!" Perplexed I remarked: "My boys, you will either eat the mushrooms or go hungry, because there is no other food in our house." Then I offered the mushrooms to our children, and they loved them. As soon as our little guests observed with how much gusto our children devoured the pastry shells filled with mushrooms and vegetables, they asked if they could not try a little of it after all. It did not take much time for all the food to disappear. "They tasted really good, we imagined something quite different," they confessed.

I thought this little incident was a good analogy to Christian life. Non-Christians often imagine that life with Christ is dull and not enjoyable, because so many Christians look so uninviting and boring. But if they see us believers delighting and flourishing in our relationship with Christ they are attracted to try a taste of that desirable life too—and experience the goodness and fulfillment of it—just like the little boys with the mushrooms.

During my years as a three-star general in the NATO forces as Drug Advisor, hundreds of thousands of servicemen went through my hands. I think that with my helicopters and the assisting staff I visited about every NATO base in Europe.

CHAPTER XL

Public Lectures and Speaking in Churches

We now move back a number of years in time to learn some more about my various speaking engagement in churches, public halls and Christian circles all over Europe. As soon as I had become a Christian, I was often invited to speak in churches or halls to the public. This started first in England and soon spread to the European Continent.

As my only condition for speaking was that we were not restricted in what we were going to say, we were invited by many different Christian and non-Christian organizations, groups and churches.

FRANKFURT

After our wedding and on settling down on the European continent, I was quite often invited into German and Swiss churches to speak. From time to time I was even asked to preach the sermon on Sunday mornings, although I am not an ordained pastor. In the beginning, as a young Englishman I was still unfamiliar with the rites and rules of the different European continental churches. That once caused me to commit a serious faux pas. An elderly Lutheran pastor in Frankfurt invited me to take over his pulpit on Sunday to preach to his congregation. This was a great honor as he usually shielded his pulpit from other speakers.

I arrived by train that morning wearing a light brown suit. Pastor V. looked at me, aghast. I asked him what was the matter. "Your suit, your brown suit. You cannot preach in it. It would desecrate my pulpit." I felt very sorry to cause him this distress. What could be done to remedy my great fault?

Suddenly with a sigh of relief he said: "I know, I have the solution." "I'll give you my ecclesiastical gown to wear on top, that will cover up your brown suit." And that is what we did. As he was a very short man his robe covered me like a miniskirt and my brown long legs and arms must have been very obvious. I must have looked like a scare-crow. But Pastor V. was content and that was most important.

It would lead too far to tell about all my lectures in Frankfurt—which were quite many; one series taking place outside our lecture building in the center of Frankfurt while the riots against the "Startbahn West" (the extension of the United States military runways on Rhein-Main Airport in the eighties) were raging nearby. The police brought in buses with "heavies" to counter-act the aggressive left and green attacks and sometimes even caught and punished the wrong people— innocent onlookers.

HANNOVER

A place where I spoke frequently at IVCG (International Christian Businessmen Association) banquets and conferences, or in lecture halls and churches was Hannover. Our able organizer there was usually Willi Bolender. His family and ours were friends over many years. In later years, Ingo Butschkau and Karl-Heinz Benatzky, all businessmen and active Christians, helped in the organization.

The first times I spoke to the general public in Hannover was in August 1964. The town was still badly bombed after the war with many destroyed buildings. A huge tent was rented to welcome people to my lecture series. Many families had lost fathers, husbands and sons, and were deeply hurt in their hearts. My desire was to reach their hearts by pointing to the terrible consequences of sin manifested in the wars, enmity and destruction which had struck us so cruelly. This was not what God had meant the world to be. The painful suffering in the world was the consequence of first Adam's sin. From then onward mankind's and our sin had resulted in enmity towards God and our fellow men.

God created us with a free will so that we can chose between right or wrong each time such a decision is put before us. Unfortunately, we often prefer wrong to good. If we only realized how the consequences of each single sin ruins not only the one who commits it, but also his whole environment and his fellow men. For this reason, God cannot consider our sin lightly, but takes it so seriously. Fortunately, God provided a remedy. Separation from God due to sin can be remedied by repenting and confessing our wrong-doing to him. To pay for our sin Jesus Christ, the Son of God, took sin on Him. He died for it on the Cross so that we need not bear the punishment any more. By believing in His salvation and committing our life to Him we can have fellowship with God and communicate with Him. We are His children and He is our Father who cares for us.

After one of my speeches in the tent in Hannover, one young man approached me. He told me he had accidentally passed the tent and curiously peeped into it. What he heard interested him, so he stayed. "But who," he asked, "who is this Jesus you talked about? I have never heard his name before this evening. Can you tell me more about this person?" Of course, I did. I told him about God's love to us, of his sacrifice in sending his son Jesus into our world to save each one of us from our sin so that we could live in fellowship and peace with him and our fellow men. I also gave him some literature so he could learn more about the Lord Jesus Christ.

When in the following years the city of Hannover was more and more completely rebuilt, we were able to use better auditoriums like the academy of music, the town hall or hotel conference rooms for specific seminars.

During my life, I spoke in many countries and continents in churches and public halls. Hardly anything in life is more fulfilling than when hopeless, frightened, burdened and desperate people accept God's salvation in Christ and become joyful, hopeful children of God.

On June 10, 1983, I spoke at the "Kirchentag" of the Protestant State Church (bi-annual meeting of Protestant church groups lasting several days and treating a large variety of topics) in Hannover on the subject "Evolution—the Creed of our Modern Time." Some 3000 people were attending the lecture and the discussion afterwards was very lively. The "Kirchentag" messages of the Protestant Church in Germany are mostly liberal and pluralistic. But under the aegis of Pastor Kemner and his evangelical center in Krelingen a few Bible believing theologians, businessmen and scientists got together and had decided it to be important to offer a spectrum of Bible based relevant lectures at the same time to the ten thousands of visitors.

BIEDENKOPF

On our travels we sometimes experienced God's special protection. I remember the lecture series in 1973 in Biedenkopf, Germany, which started on April 28. Every evening a group of Communist youngsters attended and afterwards bombarded me with questions and their usual slogans and phrases. Some of them were hostile, others changed their attitude on noticing that there were answers to their questions and that we were not fighting them.

After one such evening a shrill telephone bell woke us up at night. It was 2:30 a.m. "I hope nothing is wrong with the children?" my wife remarked. And then we realized it was not the telephone in our hotel room that was ringing Was it the one on the corridor? We slipped on our dressing gown and rushed into the corridor. There we noticed that it was not a telephone bell sounding, but the alarm of the elevator. Accompanied by impatient knocking on the elevator walls, voices shouted: "Open the door, open the door, we are stuck! Help us quickly!" We tried our best to help, but in vain. Next, we attempted to find a member of the hotel staff or other responsible person, but the hotel was totally empty. Not a soul to be found. What should we do? There were not even other hotel guests in the house. We wandered through the whole hotel, but could not find a single person. And, of course, we were total strangers in this area.

Meanwhile the knocking increased in desperation. My wife had the idea to enter the hotel office and notify the police by telephone. This was easier said than done with the complicated telephone system. We pressed one, two, three...ten buttons which all started to blink and buzz but were not able to get into contact with the outside world—or with the police. Meanwhile, we had discovered the telephone book and the number of the police station.

In the middle of our despair, the hotel door opened and a man entered. He was apparently the only other guest, returning late to his bedroom. We asked him for help and the three of us together finally managed to call the police in. All the time the inmates of the elevator—in claustrophobia— hammered, scolded and shouted at us to hurry up and free them. By now they had already been stuck in the little cabin for two hours.

When the two policemen appeared we had to explain the whole situation. At first they were suspicious of us, but soon they understood the situation. They helped us switch off the blinking and buzzing buttons in the office. One of the policemen found the room underneath the roof with a manual winch to bring the elevator to the next door. The second policeman waited in front of the elevator when the door opened. Two young, not very trustworthy looking men in workmen's overalls with deep pockets full of various tools emerged. One of them—quick as lightning—slipped through the policeman's legs and disappeared through the door into the darkness. The policeman took hold of the second young man and asked him what their intentions had been in entering the hotel in the middle of the night, as they obviously were not guests. He stammered, that they had come to get something to drink. "At 2:30 a.m.? You know the restaurant closes at midnight. Besides the restaurant is on the ground level and you got stuck between the second and third floor. You had better come with me!" With a firm grip the policeman took the man to the police station. It seemed to me that the worse of the two had escaped.

With grateful hearts we returned to our beds. We had been the only people in the hotel that night, and God had protected us from the burglars. They had gotten stuck—and we had to rescue them. No wonder they did not like our idea of notifying the police. They had insisted that we should liberate them ourselves, only agreeing after nearly two hours when there was no alternative.

The next morning we found out that the owners of our hotel possessed a second hotel nearby where they also lived. For that reason our small hotel had been so deserted during the night.

BERLIN

Maybe I should add a few words about our repeated lecture series in Berlin. Our first invitation to Berlin was in 1973. I had been invited by the NATO Commander, U.S. General Win. W. Cobb, to give drug demonstrations to the troops in Berlin. At that time, only certain airlines were allowed into Berlin, because the airspace of the Russian occupation zone had to be crossed by planes. The Russian command was that the foreign airplanes had to fly at a very low set altitude, otherwise they would be shot at. We experienced bad weather several times when flying to Berlin, which could be really unpleasant at such low altitudes.

After a talk on January 23, with General Cobb, a very intelligent and pleasant personality, and later with other high officers, I spoke at the Outpost Theater to some 500–600 troops with animal demonstrations. The front rows were occupied by the brass. It was interesting to watch the soldiers. Because they were ordered to take part in the drug instruction, the GIs usually entered the room showing their aversion openly. They lounged in their seats, pulling their caps over their faces and closed their eyes ostentatiously. They did not want to listen to another sermon on drugs ending with all the threats and punishments for taking them.

When the soldiers suddenly heard a lecture on how certain drugs negatively affect your body and your soul and that it was their *own* responsibility to look after their health they listened. They sensed that here was a person caring for them individually and in their health. The caps over the GIs faces disappeared one after the other. Gradually they sat upright and took a personal interest in the demonstration. The questions afterwards showed how well they had listened.

There followed other big drug demonstrations in the afternoon and on the next days with new troops in the Outpost Theater. I also spoke to several American high school audiences and was interviewed by the TV and other media.

One morning General Cobb sent his chauffeur, Herr Schultze, to show us round West Berlin. We visited the sad Berlin Wall with the memorial crosses for the victims who had been killed on their flight from the East.

One eighty-year-old lady who had tried to jump out of the window to flee to the West was shot in the air while jumping.

Herr Schultze took us also to Checkpoint Charlie where we saw the different devices which East Germans had invented to flee over the border to the West: cars specially adapted to hide persons, diving devices to traverse the Elbe or other rivers, tools with which tunnels were dug underground for escaping into the West. On each device a little story was attached about the moving efforts people had taken to flee into liberty. During my stay in Berlin, I also spoke at various American schools.

A special experience was our little visit behind the Iron Curtain. General Cobb had kindly arranged it for us. He sent Herr Schultze to drive us to Checkpoint Charlie and to wait there under the installed TV camera for our return from East Germany. The border control was very severe and rude and lasted a long time. We had to change into an East German bus. The seats were taken apart and not an inch in the bus was left without strict control. We were not allowed to leave the bus during the whole tour, only under supervision at the Russian war memorial and at the Hotel Berolina where no East Germans were admitted. At Hotel Berolina where we were locked in, we were advised to buy some snacks. At the counter I asked for some oranges. No oranges. "What about a banana?" "No Sir, no bananas." "And pineapple?" None either. I gave up, because their apples did not look very appetizing. Of course, I had asked for these southern fruit for an obvious reason.

A Spanish lady in our group suddenly panicked when realizing we were locked in. She rattled at the doors in vain. They were pressure locked doors. I squeezed my finger through the middle enclosure. "Sssssssst," and it opened. To make sure, nobody would hinder us leaving the hotel, I remarked in rather a loud voice to the nervous Spanish lady: "I think they may not have locked us in. The door just did not work. But now it is working. Come along." They obviously did not dare to oppose us. So the whole group swarmed out of the hotel to try some contact with the outside world. But immediately we were asked to board the return bus to West Berlin. They, the Eastern officials, were sorry, but our time was up!

In the autumn of the same year, 1973, we were back in Berlin. This time, for three public lectures in German in the Urania Hall. The first evening on "Drugs, Addiction and the Subconsciousness" was very well attended. Drug abuse was rapidly increasing and many young people and parents were becoming frightened about the extent to which it was spreading.

As affluence was increasing, indifference towards spiritual things was growing. So the second evening's topic was: "The Nation's Problem: Affluence, Stress, Decay and Self-defeat."

The last lecture of the series was on "Materialism: Scientific, Philosophic and Life-style, All Equally Destructive"

From this time on, we repeatedly returned to Berlin for lectures to academics, to businessmen and to the general public.

The biggest outreach took place in May 1983. Herr Lattka and some other academics had organized a lecture series in Berlin. The series had been well prepared long before by an efficient team. It started with a lecture in the School of Theology on the Problem of Evil. For five consecutive evenings, I spoke in the crowded Baptist Church on "Faith and Science." Many young people were present and wanted answers to their various questions.

In the mornings, I usually lectured in universities and high schools. The first morning the director of the Robert Koch high school had asked me to address the pupils on "Evolution: Philosophy or Science?" We had an animated question time which left teachers and pupils thinking about the evidence against evolution.

The next morning a lecture was arranged at the Free University on "The Natural Sciences Know Nothing of Evolution." The numerous students were very open and cooperative. Berlin was supposed to be a difficult auditorium, because East and West met here and clashed. Many people were pro-West, because they feared the Communism from the East. On the other hand a great number of Eastern Marxist ideologists had been secretly channeled into West Berlin by Eastern Communists to undermine Western politics. But we appreciated the exchange of thoughts with them and experienced little aggressiveness. Not until three hours later did we leave the place because of the many honest questions put to me. Of course, after such a lecture I was usually worn out. Students shot at me from all sides with their manifold complicated questions from all areas of science and non-science. One had to react quickly and wisely. How good, we had the promise from One who is Wisdom Himself to give us the right answers at the right time and that I could rely on Him. I love students and I love thinking people, they are a challenging vis-à-vis to me. And I think they react to it positively which creates a good relationship and basis for solving problems together.

I lectured in the Technical University the next afternoon. Again the attendance was good. The students here had chosen the same topic as in the Free University. A mentally deranged student disturbed the lecture and had to be removed. Afterwards the attention was good and the response positive.

Both university lectures were video-taped for further use.

At the end of the week a dinner for persons in responsible public positions was arranged. Politicians, academic people, businessmen and other high-ranking guests were invited for this evening on "Stress," a rather relevant subject for such an audience.

The following year, 1984, we chose Berlin for a Pro Universitate Seminar on "Everything possible, everything allowed?" involving the power of manipulation in the media, the challenge of technological medicine (genetic manipulation, which our son, Dr. med. Oliver Wilder-Smith lectured), and today's crisis, a consequence of a disturbed relationship between man and science.

The final lecture, open for the public, took place on Sunday, November 25, in the big Apostel-Paulus-Church on "Time and Eternity." Twelve hundred people attended. The event was framed by classical music.

Chapter XLI

Some Hobbies

Because of my schedule densely filled with teaching, the consulting, the writing and the speaking engagements—all of which I greatly enjoyed—there was little time left for any extra hobbies. One of the activities which our family enjoyed together was hiking in the Swiss mountains. In God's beautiful nature, with the colorfully blossoming mountain meadows in front of you and the gigantic snow-capped ten thousand footers behind them, the murmuring brooks beside you and the ringing of the cow-bells around you, hearts automatically begin to admire God's creation and wisdom and cannot but praise the intelligence behind such manifold beauty. We often observed in our guests, what a peaceful, but exulting influence mountain scenery exerts on people of all kinds.

Another hobby greatly enjoyed by our whole family is classical music. My wife, our children and myself love classical music, either playing ourselves, listening to it or singing together at the piano. What a wonderful gift *good* music is, ennobling and enriching the soul! After a day of concentrated and busy work, what a refreshment it meant to us to listen to a concert by Mozart or a fugue by Bach. Music was an inspiration and help to me in all my work. How beautifully, for example, Haydn translated the first verses of Genesis into music, doubtless by God's inspiration. Haydn knew masterfully to describe the different works of creation and to glorify God, the Creator, in musical form.

As a balance to my intellectual and spiritual work, I love gardening while thinking and working out new scientific or

476

spiritual ideas. Here too it gives me great pleasure to observe God's nature and discover the great Logos down to the smallest detail in biology. It shows me the Creator's love towards men, that He not only created the world purely functionally, but that He also made it to be beautiful and enjoyable.

Another relaxing activity is fishing, which I enjoy especially on our holidays, in Norway in the sea, in Finland and in Scotland in lakes. Switzerland is not the best place for fishing, it is very expensive to buy a license. Our children share this love for fishing with me.

CHAPTER XLII

PROFESSOR WILDER-SMITH'S SEVENTIETH BIRTHDAY

On December 22, 1985, we celebrated my seventieth birthday. God had so graciously kept me in good health and I was able to continue my lecturing, my writing and traveling as before. We wanted to thank Him for His goodness and celebrate this joyful day together with friends and colleagues from many parts of the world.

Our good friend Willi Bolender and his wife in Hannover had arranged a great feast at the Queen's Hotel near the Deer Park in Hannover, the place were I had often spoken to Businessmen. Here we also had held seminars for students and intellectuals. About sixty people—relatives, friends, and colleagues—were invited to this occasion, celebrating and praising God for His blessings and help throughout all the seventy years of my life.

The Factum Publishers in Berneck, East Switzerland, dedicated a whole issue of the *Factum Journal* (a Christian periodical for intellectuals) to honor my work as a surprise for me.

There were scientific contributions and congratulations from colleagues of various corners of the world: Dr. Duane Gish for the Institute for Creation Research; Professor Dr. Ellinger, Professor Dr. Blechschmidt and Professor Dr. Kuhn from Germany; Dr. Osterman from Austria; Dr. Kitchen and Dr.

Burkitt from England; Dr. Leisola from Finland. Professor Dr. Thürkauf and Frau Professor Dr. von Stockhausen also from Germany, as well as Willi Heider for the work done amongst the German Prisoners of War. General Willard Pearson from the USA who was Commanding General of the V.-Corps in Germany when I was NATO Drug Advisor in Europe also expressed his appreciation.

I was deeply touched by all the literary contributions and kind wishes.

CHAPTER XLIII

THE HUXLEY MEMORIAL LECTURE IN 1986

In 1985, I received an invitation from the president of the Oxford Union in England, Ms. Wilson, to take part in a debate. As most of my respected readers will know, the Oxford Union is considered the foremost debating club in England. Most of the great politicians like Churchill or Margaret Thatcher learned and practiced their debating skills here in younger years. It is the exclusive club which Oxford students and other ambitious members—if admitted—join to attain excellency in political rhetoric and debate.

The debate was to take place on February 14, 1986, and the motion before the House was formulated: The Doctrine of Creation Is More Valid Than the Theory of Evolution. Professor Wilder-Smith, University of Illinois Medical Center, Chicago, and Professor Andrews of London University, were invited to give their scientific reasons as to why the doctrine of creation is a valid scientific explanation of the origin of life and the various species of life.

Our opponents—defending evolution—were to be Professor Maynard Smith (author of *The Theory of Evolution* and *Game Theory* and *The Evolution of Fighting*) and Professor Richard Dawkins (the author of *The Selfish Gene* and *The Blind Watchmaker*).

The debate took place in remembrance of the famous public debate under the auspices of the BAAS (British Association for the Advancement of Science) in the latter half of the nineteenth century. This debate was carried out by T.H. Huxley and Bishop Samuel Wilberforce who was also Professor of Mathematics (son of the great Wilberforce who was instrumental in freeing the slaves and abolishing slavery). That debate had became a milestone in history. On account of this debate, Christian teaching of creation was considered to have become obsolete. Bishop Wilberforce's argument was the following: Behind every watch exists a watchmaker, likewise behind every creature stands a creator. He was convinced that life was created by a creator just as every watch was made by a watchmaker.

Huxley denied Wilberforce's statement. He cited the famous example of the six eternal apes fastened to six typewriters with endless supplies of paper. If these six apes were to hammer for an endless period of time at random on the typewriters one would in the end also find the 23rd Psalm of David amongst all the other texts they had written. Huxley said that the probability formula demanded such a result. Bishop Wilberforce was shocked by Huxley's statement but could not contradict—as a mathematician—when Huxley cited the probability formula:

> *Where Time is Infinite, the Probability is 1. Given endless time, the probability is that everything will happen by chance. Given long enough time, the 23rd Psalm by David will be produced by chance without David. And likewise life can be created by chance without a Creator, if given enough time.*

The audience accepted Huxley's logic and Wilberforce lost the debate.

Since that debate, the hypothesis of a Creator God is considered to be superfluous in scientific circles. As a consequence of the Huxley/Wilberforce Debate the name of a Creator is taboo in most leading scientific journals.

The debate on February 14, 1986, at the Oxford Union where I was invited to present the creationist side, was in memory of the above mentioned debate over 100 years ago and was called the Huxley Memorial Lecture. Before the debate commenced it was agreed between both sides that no religious or non-scientific material should be introduced into the debate.

Two students of the University of Oxford first gave their scientific reasons for accepting the concept of creation as the valid scientific explanation of life as we see it on earth now. An American colored student was especially intelligent and witty in his exposé. Two others spoke out for evolution and presented the usual old arguments for evolution.

My reasoning for the creation model, briefly summarized, included three main arguments.

1) I showed that the probability formula which Huxley used to prove his point of chance producing life was not valid for the origin of life. The typing of the apes on the typewriter produced *irreversible* results, whereas the organic-chemical reactions which produce the basis of life are always *reversible*. Huxley's formula cannot be applied in *reversible* reactions as I have shown in my various books on biogenesis.

2) Only information theory can explain the genesis of self replicating information storage and retrieval systems (i.e., the DNA molecule) in biology. Such systems cannot arise solely as the result of the random forces of natural law but *can only arise as the result of information* (surprise effects), which *cannot be derived from natural law.*

Darwin's formula of life is:

a) matter + time + energy = primeval life

b) primeval life + time + natural selection = evolution (evolutive speciation)

The creationist's formula of life is:

a) matter + time + energy + I (information) = primeval life

b) primeval life + time + energy + I (information) = speciation

It is not our business as scientists to specify just where the factor I (information) came from (although we may hint at some possibilities).

3) For my third point I presented the scientific research of Professor Vollmert from the University Polymer Institute in Karlsruhe, Germany. He showed the impossibility of chance arising of any vital or macromolecular proteins under the experimentally simulated Darwinian conditions used by Fox and Miller (see Bruno Vollmert's book *Das Molekül Und Das Leben*, Rowohlt, 1985).

I also mentioned my own research on optical activity in biological chemistry, which proved Fox and Miller's experiments wrong. (See my books *The Natural Sciences Know Nothing of Evolution* and *The Scientific Alternative to Darwinian Evolutionary Theory*, TWFT, Costa Mesa, CA.)

After the debate was over, Richard Dawkins attacked me not on my scientific discourse, but on the basis of my beliefs. Professor Andrews brought up the point of order that no religious considerations should play any role. The president demanded that Dawkins sit down.

Professor Maynard Smith appreciated my scientific approach but said that I believed in a small tribal God, which was not acceptable today. He believed that the whole, big universe was God which was a superior belief. Again, I was attacked on purely religious grounds, which was entirely out of order.

In the end the creationists won some 114 of the votes from the voting public of about 300—which was quite surprising, as the Oxford Union represented the materialistic naturalistic evolutionary viewpoint of biogenesis.

The debate was never published. As most Oxford Union debates are given nationwide publicity in the press, in radio and in television. There may well be some cogent reason for the total cover-up which the whole debate subsequently experienced.

In December 1986, I received an inquiry from the Radcliffe Science Library, Oxford, asking if I had ever really held a Huxley Memorial Lecture on February 14, 1986. No records of my having held the lecture as part of the Oxford Union Debate could be found in any library. No part of the official media breathed a word about it. So total is the current censorship on any effective criticism of Neo-Darwinian science and on any genuine alternative.

CHAPTER XLIV

OUR JOURNEY BEHIND THE IRON CURTAIN IN 1980

In 1980, our good friend Siegfried Lattka in Berlin had the idea of organizing a tour behind the Iron Curtain for my wife and myself. This was to include Eastern Germany and Poland, as he had relatives and many friends in Görlitz at the East German-Polish border. He saw the great spiritual need of these people and felt a spiritual burden to help them. In those days such a trip was not easily arranged. The communistic state was atheistic and anti-Christian. My books against Darwinian science and Marxist materialism were well known in the Eastern countries; they were on the black list and prohibited. How could I expect to receive an entry permit from the East German authorities? And would it be safe once we had gone behind the Iron Curtain? A leading lady in the East German "Kirchenleitung" (church leadership) had already formally and publicly expressed her disapproval of my philosophy. So, the Western authorities strongly discouraged my journey to the East. The British Embassy in Bern said that they would not take any responsibility for us if we traveled behind the Iron Curtain.

Quite by accident, Mr. Lattka who took care of all entry permits and traveling formalities, met the British Consul in Eastern Germany who was very helpful. He advised Mr. Lattka to risk the trip, but asked him for every detail of the intended journey, so that he could cover us and keep an eye on us during all stages of the trip for safety's sake. We thought this a great idea. Of course, we were not allowed to speak publicly, but to say a few words of greeting was not prohibited.

In Spring 1980, we started out from Berlin in Mr. Lattka's Mercedes. Mrs. Lattka very kindly prepared sandwiches and fruit, as well as hot and cold drinks in thermos bottles for provisions on our journey, because the Iron Curtain countries were very short of food and rationed. She had also bought and put into the trunk of the car packages of coffee, chocolate, men's shirts and other articles which were unobtainable in the East.

After a thorough and strict control of persons, papers and the car, we entered the DDR (German Democratic Republic) at Check Point Charlie where the tank canons at the border gate were pointed directly at us and everyone crossing the border.

Leaving East Berlin and driving through the country side, two things struck our eyes:

1) The woods were fenced in by barbed wire and it was strictly forbidden to enter; they were full of military.

2) The fields were badly tilled and sowed; over and over again rows were left empty—as if the sowing machine had run out of seeds without anybody noticing it. It seemed that nobody really cared. Evidently there were no incentives for the farmers, as they did not work for themselves but for the colkhozes (collective farms).

THE VISIT AT THE SORBES' VILLAGE

Our first stop was at a village called Schleife. The village was one of seven villages inhabited by the Sorbes of Slavic origin. The Sorbes emigrated to Germany in the fifth and sixth century from Russia—from the area behind the Don River. These people are deeply rooted in the Christian faith. Through the many centuries they have kept their own language and culture alive in midst of Germany. When we visited them they still spoke Sorbic.

Until the Iron Curtain fell they had their own school and church. Mr. Lattka introduced us to their pastor, Pastor Maiwald, who gave us a tour around the village. He took us to a Sorbic farm—alas empty, as under the Communist government it had been joined to the kolkhozy (the village collective farm). The Sorbic ladies—their husbands were at work on the kolkhozy—showed us the stables and barns.

Then they invited us into the old farm house where they had festively laid the table and lovingly prepared a typical Sorbic meal for us. Grown-ups and children wore their Sorbic costumes. They were Christians and after the meal, to honor us, they sang their old beautiful hymns and read a Psalm to us, all in their Sorbic tongue, although they spoke German with equal facility.

They took us to a small house where they kept and sold their handicraft; beautiful hand crocheted laces, daintily and colorfully painted eggs and other art-work. The ladies presented us with three beautifully decorated empty eggs delicately worked in wax-technic after the Russian style. We still have them in our home

GÖRLITZ

In the evening, we arrived in Görlitz and were made welcome in the home of the reformed pastor, Pfarrer Naumann, and his hospitable wife. Dietrich Heise, the excellent youth evangelist, had helped to arrange our meeting with various active Christians in the East.

Görlitz is a beautiful town with historic, ornamented patrician houses which have become sadly dilapidated under Communist rule. (Since the fall of the Iron Curtain, East and especially West Germany have invested a lot of money, beginning to restore the beauty of the old buildings which may still take some time till its completion.)

Here in Görlitz, Beate's father was born and spent part of his boyhood. Of course, we visited the Landeskrone, the mountain he climbed as a child, and other places he had told us about, although the magnificent old buildings and the market square in their dilapidation saddened us.

Next day, we met Bishop Wollstadt, a fine evangelical Christian man who tried his best to further the biblical message inside the church under Communist rule. That was a hard task. He had won the respect of the State authorities on account of the outstanding social work he accomplished.

Bishop Wollstadt—besides his duties as a Bishop in the Lutheran Church—headed a big home for physically and mentally handicapped, the "Martinshof." He had built up the "Martinshof" on a Christian basis. It was exemplarily run so that he gained the respect of everybody. All the handicapped people loved him. We observed his loving relationship to the sick when he talked with several of them as he showed us around. Of course, the State was very happy about this well organized institution which relieved them of work and financial obligations which otherwise would have fallen on them.

In the evening, a crowd of Christians gathered in the church room. As I was not officially allowed to speak but only to express some words of greetings; my guests encouraged me to rather extensive greetings. Everybody present was obviously very suspicious of every new person that turned up and was unknown to them. Perhaps he was a Communist spying on them?

The people asked me a lot of questions. Many of them had read my books, which several had brought with them. They must have been smuggled by some brave persons into Eastern

Germany and I was asked to sign them. Some people handed me albums. At first I did not know why. When I opened them they were full of copied pages of my books, hidden there so that Communist spies could not find them.

POLAND, 1980

One or two days later we started on our way towards Poland together with five East German friends. At the Polish border we met with some difficulties. One of the multitude of papers necessary to cross the border was missing. To apply for, receive and pay for that paper cost us three or four hours of waiting around and answering unending lists of questions. A long line of innumerable cars was waiting to cross the border and many of them were stripped and thoroughly searched.

As we were expected that afternoon in Dziegielow for a meeting we had to hurry to arrive there in time. Therefore Herr Lattka sometimes drove his Mercedes up to 160 km/h if the road permitted it. The speed limit was 90 km/h. We were doing quite well until a police car sighted and stopped us demanding from us "Westerners in a Mercedes" a high fine. We now tried to stay within the speed limit, but it seemed that they were after "West Marks" and soon stopped us again. Our East German friends, who knew and showed us the way always drove in front of us. In their little Wartburg they drove exactly at the same speed as we did. We pointed out that fact together with our East German friends. Luckily one of the East German youngsters spoke some Russian—apparently Poles and Russians understand one another's language. In the end the Polish police let us go without a new fine—but also without an apology.

It was late when we arrived in Dziegielow. The crowded audience had patiently waited several hours for us. We had a profitable time together with old and young, all of them showing the marks of suffering on their faces. A group of students was eager to learn answers to the atheistic teaching in schools and universities which they could not harmonize with their Christian faith.

Dziegielow is a center of evangelical Christianity. There is also a deaconry and the deaconesses work as nurses to sick people and also teach Bible studies. In this area repeatedly revivals took place. Gospel campaigns are regularly held in this place and many people turn to Christ and experience His renewing power.

We stayed overnight in Ustron with our good friends Mr. and Mrs. Lisztwan and their two daughters. They made us very welcome in their home and prepared a nice meal from their meager rations—a real sacrifice as they had very little food themselves. While chatting together we found out that Mr. and Mrs. Lisztwan had known my wife's grand uncle (and grandparents), who had been instrumental in a spiritual awakening in that area.

VISITING GOLLNOW, 1980

The young East Germans together with Mr. Lattka had planned a special surprise for my wife. They intended to drive us for the Whitsun weekend northward to Gollnow in Pomerania, the place where my wife had spent a great deal of her youth. Next morning we started out. In the afternoon we arrived in Gollnow where Beate with her family had spent so many happy years of childhood. But her old paternal house with all the familiar neighboring buildings had disappeared. In their place blocks of shoddy mass slums had been erected. During the fighting of the last days of the war, the town had been badly destroyed. Among the few buildings in the town center which had survived the war was her father's church, although the steeple had been partly shot away and only repaired in a shortened form.

The city wall in all its old beauty was still standing, but the slums made a ridiculous contrast against it.

The greatest shock of all to my wife was not only that not a single face in her home town was recognizable, but that the whole culture and language of her youth was gone, too. No one spoke a word of German, even the name of the town had been transliterated into Polish. The streets had all been renamed and the empty shops had Polish inscriptions on them. This was an entirely strange city and had nothing to do with her old childhood world.

Unsuccessfully we tried to find a bed for the night, but there was no room and certainly no food. After a long consultation between the five East Germans and us three West Germans, we decided to try to find a transport camp. After we had nearly given up we at last found a camp with one or two buses parked in front of it. On entering, the proprietress greeted us kindly—and even in German. She bustled around and produced an excellent meal for all eight of us from secret cubbies. It consisted of vegetable soup, fish, bread, and some Polish delicacies. Afterward some of the East German fellow-travelers got out their guitars and we all sang spirituals. The proprietress liked this, but said the communists didn't, so would we please wait until all the other guests had gone and the doors were closed. We did. Afterward Herr Lattka went into the back office with the good lady and presented her with some new shirts for her husband and chocolate candy. She was absolutely delighted and put us up in neat little timbered huts—part of the camp—for the night.

The next morning, after having washed in an open general bathroom, with very little water and primitive sanitary arrangements, the good lady treated us to a breakfast which was sumptuous for the Poles, but for us Westerners just sufficed to keep body and soul together. It was Whit Sunday and our dear friend, Herr Lattka, packed the rest of his presents (brought from West Germany) and presented them as a Whitsuntide gift to our East German friends and travel companions. These gifts were all those things they could never buy in their shops: coffee, chocolate, candy bars, special foods like ketchup, etc. We all stood under the trees in the woods and sang Whitsuntide hymns. I gave a little address followed by a prayer. It was a most unusual Whitsun service, standing in the woods with no church.

But the greatest surprise came last. We went to pay the bill, which meant a solemn conclave between the proprietress and our West German host. Nobody saw the deliberations—not even us. But two beaming faces emerged after a period of tense waiting—we did not know whether or not we had enough money for such luxuries as we had enjoyed. Now came the supreme moment: the bill was twenty-five DM (West Mark, which was so more valuable than their East currency) which equals twenty U.S. dollars for all eight of us, including a sumptuous evening meal, eight beds in three block huts and breakfast! Everybody was delighted and we proceeded on our way to the rigors of another inspection on crossing the Polish—East German border.

In Poland and in East Germany we met active groups of Christians who had stood firm and suffered bitterly for it. But the hunger for God's word and for Christian fellowship was very great. The position of the few evangelicals in Poland is aggravated by their being a small minority in the Catholic state church.

THE MEDICAL CONFERENCE IN CIESZYN, 1989

In 1989, I received an invitation from Poland to speak at a conference for medical doctors in Cieszyn. I accepted and in the second half of February my wife and myself departed by Swissair to Poland.

Our first flight stop was Cracau. Good friends, the Marcols, met us at the airport and they drove us by car to Ustron where we stayed with their parents, Mr. and Mrs. Lisztwan, and their sister's family for a few days. In Cieszyn medical doctors from different parts of Poland and one or two Czechs, who had secretly crossed the border, took part in the conference over the weekend. It was here that Dr. Abraszewski, one of the leading doctors of the Polish Christian Medical Association, presided over one of the lectures and told us the story of his remarkable conversion in Jordan on account of our *Origin* Films shown there.

I also spoke to the doctors at the hospital where Dr. Wartak, the organizer of the conference, a fine Christian gentleman, worked. They asked me to speak on the drug problem which was also starting to bother them behind the Iron Curtain.

SPEAKING IN A COMMUNIST HIGH SCHOOL

One morning, on February 23, 1989, some Christian high-school students had succeeded in arranging a lecture for the upper grades on "New Discoveries and Research on the Origin of Life." We were first led to the office of the directress of the high school, a convinced and hard communist, who cross-examined us quite intensely. But she was interested in the topic.

So when the lecture started, the directress with a great number of her teaching staff participated in the lecture to the upper grades.

I lectured, as I was used to lecturing all over the world, on the untenability of evolution and materialism. From my scientific research and the newest discoveries of information theory and genetics I showed them that a metaphysical source of information, a Creator, is unavoidable for an honest intellectual and that materialism cannot explain the origin of life and should therefore be abandoned. I am a naive Englishman who is used to speaking his mind freely without hiding the truth for political or other reasons. My wife afterwards confided to me that she had felt uncomfortable and prayed a lot for God's protection as I was saying things which surely must have irritated communists. Her neighbor in the lecture room, a catholic science teacher, told her he was a Christian and agreed with my thoughts, but would not dare to express them so openly. During the lecture, each time when he thought that I said something dangerous, he kept on commenting to her: "He should not say that!... This will have bad consequences for him! Oh no, they will not swallow that! ...He will not get away with that remark! I wish, he would not say so much!"

In the end my wife whispered to her teacher neighbor: "Leave my husband alone and let him say what he has to say."

The lecture was over. A very good discussion with the pupils followed. The directress of the school rose and said: "Professor and Mrs. Wilder-Smith, thank you for your visit to our school and the interesting lecture on the topic. One thing particularly impressed me during your lecture. I have hardly ever seen anybody speak with so much love to my students. Thank you very much."

She presented my wife with a lovely bouquet of flowers, and to me she gave a hand-carved wooden picture.

AUSCHWITZ

On February 28, 1989, Anna and Jurek Marcol drove us in Lisztwan's little Polski Seat to Cracau. En route they showed us the concentration camp Auschwitz, which was still in the same state as in 1945 when the Russians liberated the inmates. We were deeply disturbed looking at this place of utmost suffering and misery; the gas chambers, the incinerators where thousands of men, women and children had been put to death under extreme agony and anguish. The sacks full of human hair, shorn before death and sold for money, the crutches, glasses, shoes and clothing reminded us of the individual needs of each person and moved our hearts deeply. Even the suitcases with the personal addresses—home town, street, title—on it were exhibited.

How could any human ever been capable of such ferocious cruelty and bestiality? And yet many of those henchmen and inhumane torturers had started out as normal people like ourselves. Is it that each of us bears the possibility of committing these satanic bestialities if we choose a certain life-style? I often pondered on this serious problem. May the answer be contained in the following thoughts? If a person knowing right and wrong is placed before a decision and deliberately chooses wrong, it will leave a mark on his character and harden his conscience, the fine instrument that God has given each person as a compass through life. If he continues to deliberately choose wrong instead of right, his conscience will gradually harden more and more and his character will deteriorate. In the end he will have destroyed his God-given conscience. He will feel no regret doing wrong and will even enjoy it. Of course, it is a struggle each person has to fight between two transcendent powers, between God and the Devil, between good and bad. Man has a free will. To whatever side he turns and to which spirit he gives himself, by that spirit he will be possessed. But if we continue to constantly decide for bad against better knowledge, there might be a point of no return. This might be the state where man enjoys wrong-doing, and exercises cruelty and bestiality.

It is a serious warning to all of us to use the fine, God-given compass of our conscience wisely during our journey through life, so that we can be a blessing and not a curse to our fellow-humans and ourselves by, choosing God and His will.

In Cracau, I spoke to a crowded free church, mainly attended by young people and students.

After our time in Cracau, we flew on to Warschau where we spent a few days at the Theological Academy lecturing to the students from different Christian denominations: Lutheran,

Orthodox, Free Churches, etc. One of the elderly lecturers translated my lectures very ably from German into Polish.

In Warschau, we went sight-seeing on our own, as the market place and some of the historic buildings were worth seeing. When we wanted to find the place where the Jewish ghetto had been, which Hitler and the Nazis had so cruelly destroyed, nobody could give us any information. Although a number of people understood some English when we asked them it seemed to us that the younger generation there had somehow forgotten their past. It took us a very long time to find an old gentleman who finally could show us the way where the old ghetto had been. On arriving at the location we found the impressive monument with inscriptions remembering the sad and cruel happenings of the past. We still could sense the immense suffering in the atmosphere there, which lay heavily on us.

In the evening of March 3, we took the airplane from Warschau back to Zürich.

CHAPTER XLV

Simon Greenleaf University

The Simon Greenleaf University, formerly School of Law in Anaheim, California, was named after Simon Greenleaf, a Christian Lawyer. The school's concern is to train Christian lawyers who would not only become first-class solicitors, attorneys and barristers, but also excellent advocates for the Christian faith.

With the deterioration in the structure of the American legal system, the School of Law seeks to reverse this trend by educating lawyers committed to the biblical foundation of law, rights and institutions established by God.

The University also offers courses in Christian Apologetics and Human Rights.

In 1986 Dr. John W. Montgomery, The Founder and then Dean of the school, invited me to lecture on October 25 to the whole student body on "The Origin of the Genetic Code." Dr. Montgomery and Harold Lindsell received us cordially. The students were very involved and eager to be well instructed in scientific matters to be able to defend also the statements of the Word of God concerning origins.

From this time I regularly taught in Simon Greenleaf on the area of science and apologetics. In 1990, I gave a three-month course on "The Origin of the Universe" in the position of Distinguished Visiting Professor. At the 1990 graduation ceremony Simon Greenleaf University awarded me with an honorary LLD degree.

The same year, on November 6, 1986, I was asked by Dr. Margaret Helder of the Christian Science Association in Canada to speak at the Jubilee Auditorium in Edmonton, where 3000 people attended the lecture. The following day at the Jubilee Auditorium in Calgary I spoke on the same topic in front of 1,200 listeners.

CHAPTER XLVI

OUR AUSTRALIAN AND NEW ZEALAND LECTURE TOUR

AUSTRALIA

The Australian Creation Science Association asked me in 1987 to speak at their annual summer conference in Brisbane. As I had been in contact with Professor Rendle-Short, their president and founder, for several years and had followed their good work I accepted gladly. In January 1987, we flew via Bangkok to Brisbane. People came from all over Australia to take part in the conference. There was much interest in the controversial subject of "Evolution versus Creation" as the state educational system only taught evolution as the explanation of biogenesis without presenting any alternative theories. Quite a number of parents home schooled their children because of the one-sided, purely materialistic instruction in most schools—not only in Australia! They wanted to teach their children the creationist view as well. I think it is only fair to teach children the whole spectrum of information available, to give them all the facts so that they later are able to form their own balanced opinion.

Unfortunately, it is very common today for children—and grown-ups—to be manipulated into preconceived opinions by people who are only interested in fostering their own ideologies on others. Children should instead be taught the whole spectrum of information and fact available in each area so that they can form their own independent opinion based on the knowledge available.

During the conference, January 5—January 10, I was supposed to speak at least once a day on special topics relating to origins with a discussion time following the lecture. The main subject of the conference was: "The Evolution/Creation Controversy." Other scientists from Australia and the United States contributed their research findings and lectured on their scientific specialties. The presidency of the conference was held by Professor Rendle-Short.

One afternoon my wife gave a report of her life under the Hitler regime. She pointed out how Hitler's aggressive Darwinism had led him to his hatred of Jews and to the establishment of extermination camps.

After the conference, we spent some delightful days with the Rendle-Shorts in their home in Buderim at the Sunshine Coast. I spoke at several churches and also at a radio station in Brisbane.

Prof. and Mrs. Rendle-Short took us into the woods near Kenilworth where a Bellbird Colony nested. Except in the bird park in Walsrode, North Germany, we had never seen or heard a bellbird. But its clear bell-like voice so enraptured us that we had always cherished the wish to meet a bellbird in its natural habitat. Here our wish was granted to our delight.

The Rendle-Shorts also took us to the rain forest and showed us the typical plants and animals. Most thrilling were the songs and sounds of the rain forest birds. Many of them sound so different to the birds we are accustomed to. At our departure Mr. MacKay, an Australian scientist, presented us with a cassette of the rain forest birds' calls, which we often play back for our enjoyment. The cat-bird with its cat-like mew-sound astonishes us anew each time.

The many Australian marsupials which we met frequently on our outings were most exciting and interesting as well. We also saw a duckbill platypus, a most interesting animal which up till now we had only seen in zoology books.

On January 22, the Rendle-Shorts drove us to Toowoomba, towards the outback where their son practices as a medical doctor. As we passed a building in a remote area, Prof. Rendle-Short pointed to it saying: "Your *Origin Films* were shown in many places in Australia, even in this hall." In Toowoomba at the TV station, Dr. Tony Wheeler and myself debated on "Evolution versus Creation." Dr. Wheeler did not answer or enter into any of my questions regarding and critique of the hypothesis of evolution. He just stated the central points of the theory of Darwinian evolution as taught in schools—and that was it. When confronted with a significant scientific point of evidence for creation in the following discussion with the public—the small room of the TV station was crowded with 200 people who listened in and wanted to take part—his answer was very unspecific. One of his arguments was: "Creationists always address laymen and do not move in scientific circles."

My reasoning was to show, by means of information theory, that the origin of life and the origin of species was only possible by introducing an immaterial source of information or intelligence. To show the difference between Darwin's evolutionary theory and the creationists' theory I set up two equations:

1. a) Darwinian formula:

m (matter) + e (energy) + t (time) = Life

b) Creationist formula:

m (matter) + e (energy) + t (time) + i

(information) = Life

2. a) Darwinian formula:

cell + e (energy) + t (time) = Species

b) Creationist formula:

cell + e (energy) + t (time) + i (information) = Species

NEW ZEALAND

We then continued our journey to New Zealand where a rather busy schedule awaited us. In the United States, Dr. Martin, director of the CRI in Orange County had previously jokingly warned us: "When you go to New Zealand, you have to take a survival kit with you!"

On May 20, 1987, we arrived in Wellington, the administrative capital of the country. We always felt—even on our second visit to the city, that it was not easy to speak here. At the university, a debate with Professor Gordon Hewitt, a classical evolutionist, was arranged on May 26. He brought along the usual ideas on Darwinian evolution which were easily defeated—but nevertheless he held firmly to them. We learned afterwards that in younger years he had been a Christian Crusader, but now belonged to the Skeptics Society. Other lectures and an interview by the Evening Post followed.

We moved on to the South Island of New Zealand and spoke in Nelson and in Christchurch to students at the university, in churches as well as on the radio. In Christchurch we met many active Christian academics of different professions who impressed us greatly by their devoted Christian lifestyle.

In Dunedin, we were again invited to speak to the students and in churches. On May 28, we flew on to Invercargill, the southern-most town on the South Island. Our good friends, the Melhops, graciously exercised hospitality towards us in their home on several visits—not only toward my wife and myself, but later on also towards our children. I spoke on Sunday in their church and gave a lecture series of three evenings. My wife addressed specially invited ladies in Mrs. Melhop's sitting room telling about her experiences and God's protection during World War II.

The Melhops showed us around the area. It was a rare feeling to stand at the southern-most tip of this continent with nothing but thousands of miles of water in front of you. We felt like the passengers of the *Dawn Treader* in C.S. Lewis' eponymous book when they reached the end of the world.

THE TUATARA, THE LAST SPECIMEN OF AN EXTINCT GROUP OF REPTILES

Mr. Melhop and his friend Mr. Gay took us into the Tuatarium in Invercargill one afternoon. This was a separate part of the natural museum there, especially built for the tuatara. A scientist, specialist on tuataras, had the task of looking after the tuataras and studying them. The Maoris named this reptile "tuatara" which means "peaks on the back," a reference to the spines. In spite of their lizard-like appearance they are so different in their skeletal features that they clearly belong to a separate order. The tuatara are a kind of small dinosaur, miraculously the sole survivor of that old kind of reptile, which the evolutionists say faded out 50 million years ago. They have their home on Stephens Island in Cook Strait and on a group of islands in the Bay of Plenty. Because Stephen Island has been invaded by kiore, or native rats, the tuatara there are decreasing rapidly. Now biologists are trying to protect them from extinction by bringing some of them to the museum. These tuatara are still exactly the same as in the Lower Triassic age (200 million years ago according to evolutionists) only a little smaller. I wonder what that tells us about the evolutionary theory!

The tuataras have a long life span. They can grow over one hundred years old. "George," who had been brought to the tuatarium, was to be calculated over one hundred and fifty years old. With a length of 600 millimeters, he was one of the largest tuataras on record.

We met "Henry," a male at least eighty years old. He sat on my arm and he was quite friendly although he can get temperamental and even furious. His diet consists of non-stinging insects or juvenile white mice and newly hatched birds. The tuatara will seldom eat food that is not alive.

The tuatara's eggs do not have a hard shell but a parchment-like covering and are laid in clutches of eight to thirteen. The male must have a body temperature of 22°–26°C while his sperm are forming, or else the sperm will be infertile. Egg laying occurs ten months after fertilization—usually between October and December. A female may take several nights to excavate a hole which measures up to half a meter (half a yard) in diameter and twenty centimeters deep. Once laid, the eggs are covered over and abandoned. Ground incubation ranges from twelve to fourteen months. If the temperature is too cold, egg development stops. A prediction of a hatching date is therefore almost impossible.

Growth studies suggest that they are fully grown by the age of sixty years. At least twenty years are required before sexual maturity is reached. The tuatara is noted for its low metabolic rate. During hibernation, in periods of low temperature, its heart beat is irregular and can be as low as one heart beat per four minutes, while at high temperatures the pulse rate can rise to thirty to forty per minute. Few other animals have such a wide fluctuation.

For night vision—like other nocturnal animals—they have an optical system for intensifying the amount of light entering the eye under poor light conditions, comparable with the optical system of modern reflecting telescopes. We were astounded by the wonderfully designed functional concept underlying such a so-called primitive animal. Obviously an intelligent Designer stood behind such a unique creature!

Mr. and Mrs. Melhop took us inland to their holiday home in Queenstown. On that journey we appreciated the characteristic landscape of southern New Zealand: endless rolling hills with meadows full of white sheep, but hardly any people around. It is the land of 60 million sheep and three and a half million people.

On our air travels we admired the beauty of the country; the matchless extensive beaches, the green pastures and the high snow-covered mountains—all close together in comparison with other countries.

Flying back to the North Island, I spoke at most universities of the country. In New Plymouth, on July 14, our kind host took us up Mount Egmont, the highest elevation of the North Island. I lectured at Hamilton and Hastings, in Napier and in Palmerston North, where the university hall was so crowded that students sat enthusiastically on the floor and stayed on afterwards for question after question. One of our hosts took us to Rotorua on July 17, to show us the warm geysers there, which reminded us of our visit to Yellowstone Park in the United States some years ago.

Before returning back to Auckland, we had to give a talk in Tauranga, at the Bay of Plenty, where there are many fruit and kiwi plantations. Later after the talk in a college, we were shown around a big station, packing kiwis for export.

In Auckland, we were met by Pastor Aitkins who made us very welcome. He drove us to the big church of Takapuna Assembly of God where we were introduced to Pastor Wayne Hughes, the main pastor of the church. We stayed with Professor Tan, an oncologist, and his wife who extended us first class hospitality and spoiled us with their exquisite Chinese cuisine.

I spoke in the Takapuna church on subjects concerning science and the Bible. The big church hall was always crowded and Pastor Hughes, his staff and his family supported and encouraged us in every way. Here in Auckland I also spoke at the university to students, talked on two radio stations and was interviewed by the newspapers.

The next day we flew from Auckland via Hawaii to Los Angeles. In Hawaii, we took a stop-over of three days and spoke at the local Calvary Chapel under the direction of Pastor Stonebraker.

CHAPTER XLVII

THE SEVENTY-FIFTH BIRTHDAY

In the middle of 1990, my husband started occasionally complaining of pains in his legs which sometimes made walking difficult. At the university hospital, the Inselspital in Berne, he had a neurological check-up including measuring of nervous conduction in his legs. But nothing could be found.

So he continued his lecture tours in Austria, Germany and Switzerland at universities, high schools, churches and in the media. In December my husband would be seventy-five. We all had the impression that he had aged during the last months. Little did we know that three months later he would have to undergo serious surgery.

On December 22, 1990, we celebrated his seventy-fifth birthday at the Dorint Hotel in Beatenberg above Lake Thun in the Swiss mountains. The "children" and myself had planned to make his birthday a dignified and joyous festival remembering God's blessings and kindnesses in my husband's life.

We had invited friends, relatives and colleagues. Guests were present from virtually each stage of my husband's life.

As frame for the festive evening program we had chosen King Arthurs' Round Table. Our son Oliver appeared in the role and costume of Merlin who had come back from ages ago to the event of the day. Together with Einstein he had just invented a time machine which could transfer people backward or forward in time and space. At first try Merlin landed us—the honorable audience—too far back in the past. Yet the appropriate background music was very pleasant to listen to with the old music of that past age masterly played on harpsichord and classical guitar by two friends from Germany: Herr Brümmer and Herr Napierski.

At second try Merlin took us with his time-machine to the old Tudor farmhouse in Cholsey, England, in the year 1915, when my husband was born. The joy and pride of the parents showed in their faces.

In the same manner the anniversary guests were taken by Merlin to many important stages of Wilder-Smith' life. At the same time slides of appropriate old scenes and persons were projected by Clive and Einar to put us also visually in the right location.

Invited guests present who had been present in these periods of life gave short accounts of their involvement. Two former German prisoners of war reported how their life had been changed by my husband's ministry to the prisoner of war camps in England.

Professor Ellinger and Professor Scholler, who knew my husband from his work in the universities in Europe, also gave lively accounts of time spent together. Others reported about the work amongst businessmen, where people had been reached at dinners and breakfasts who would never dream of entering a church. There were also young guests who had taken part in his lectures as students.

Herr Lattka vividly recounted the risky and eventful tour behind the Iron Curtain to Eastern countries. Some very close personal friends shared what my husband's friendship had meant to them in their life. The brilliant laudation about his scientific and spiritual achievements, his research and his books was given by Frau Professor von Stockhausen. The excellent cuisine of the Dorint Hotel added to the success of the evening.

My husband concluded the program with a talk on Jeremiah 23:5–8.

Singing and a concerto by Johann Christian Bach for flute and piano, played by Einar and his fiancée Annelies, rounded off the delightful evening.

In summarizing the past years, we were amazed how the Lord in His goodness had blessed and protected our life. We had so much reason for praise and thankfulness.

CHAPTER XLVIII

THE OPERATION

After his seventy-fifth birthday, my husband was often tired and felt dizzy. Walking became increasing difficult.

On January 5, 1991, our youngest son Einar and Annelies, both medical doctors and devout Christians, were married in Thun, Switzerland.

My husband had difficulty sitting through the wedding and felt uneasy and unwell. At last our sons, all medical doctors in different specialties, suggested: "Daddy, the doctors could not find any cause for the problem with your legs. Why don't you put your head into a NMR scanner?[1] Maybe that will give us an explanation?"

Our youngest son was registrar in the neurology department of the university hospital, Bern. The NMR scan showed a huge meningioma in his head above the brain which had obviously been causing all of his unpleasant symptoms by pressing on the brain.

The operation took place on March 6, 1991, in the Inselspital of the university of Bern. Thousands of faithful friends all over the world prayed with us. Although the apprehension was great we knew ourselves to be in God's hand. Several friends telephoned me in the morning quoting the Bible verse of the day: "I shall not die, but live, and declare the works of the Lord" (Psalm 118:17). It made my heart confident, that this wonderfully appropriate verse had been

---

1.   NMR = nuclear magnetic resonance.

chosen for today of all days in our "Losungen" (daily Bible verse) read daily by most German speaking evangelicals.

After seven or eight hours of surgery—this day seemed to be one of the longest days ever to me—our son Clive telephoned me to say that the operation was over.

Our children were a great support to me. Clive, our second son, a gastro-enterologist, then engaged in medical research at the University of Berne, was in communication with the neurosurgeon during the whole time of the long surgery. As he was the only one of our sons on the spot he checked all the medical preparations and arrangements at the hospital in a very capable and loving way. He watched over every movement and was present every minute of his busy schedule.

For the surgery Oliver, our oldest son, specialist in neuro-anesthesia and intensive care, had taken leave and came from Geneva University hospital to assist us. He accompanied his Daddy to the anesthesia room before the start of the surgery. Afterwards, he kept a watchful eye on the treatment in the intensive care unit.

After the surgery both sons, Oliver and Clive, very conscientiously daily checked my husband's state of health and every therapy. It surely must not have been easy for the doctors to treat a patient with so many medically trained sons. But the whole medical staff was very kind, efficient and helpful in every way. The care in the Inselspital was good, and—best of all—we were allowed to visit there any time.

Our daughter in California telephoned nearly every day and supported us in prayer and love, as did our son Einar and his wife Annelies in Dunedin, New Zealand, where they had meanwhile moved from Switzerland.

How very grateful I was for the medical and spiritual support of our children!

Hundreds of American friends from Calvary Chapel Costa Mesa, from Simon Greenleaf School of Law, many relatives and friends from Europe and from all over the world stood by us. We experienced what a blessing good friends were. God had answered all our prayers. The surgery was successful. Our hearts were full of thanks and praise.

After two weeks my husband was already able to leave the hospital and come home, although still very weak. Oliver and myself spent a restful week with him in the Black Forest, enjoying the first spring flowers there and taking long, but restful, walks. How good it was to have our beloved husband and father home again!

To regain his bodily strength, my husband intensively worked every day in the garden. As our daughter's wedding was planned for June 29, he prepared the garden beautifully for this occasion so that flowers, trees and bushes as well as the lawn looked their Sunday best. The fresh mountain air and manual work helped him to rebuild his physical strength.

My husband was particularly talented at producing first class juices and jellies from our garden fruits. These were famous among our friends and relatives. The family usually picked and cleaned the fruit while my dear husband, using his expertise as a food chemist, concocted the most delicious juices and jellies. At Petra's wedding reception these garden products—black and red current juice, josta and gooseberry juice, grape juice, blackberry and raspberry juice—were the most desired beverages.

CHAPTER XLIX

OUR DAUGHTER'S WEDDING

A dear friend of my parents came from Frankfurt, Germany, to help us with Petra's wedding preparations. We had much fun with Frau Knörich while we baked the many cakes, cocktail pastries and cookies (no mixes, all hand-made!) after German, Swiss and English tradition.

On June 29, the wedding of our daughter Petra—a dental surgeon and laser expert at the University of California in Irvine—and Marc Allmeroth—a fine Christian Californian lawyer from Long Beach—took place in the Castle Church in Spiez, our neighboring little town on the Lake of Thun.

The reception and toast given by my husband to the newly married couple were held in our beautifully prepared garden. As a surprise for our American guests, we had invited two Alphorn players in Swiss costumes. These gentlemen thrilled everybody with their Alphorn music.

In the evening the dinner, the speeches and special entertainment took place in the Grand Regina in Grindelwald. Einar and Annelies played Schumann and Bach on the flute and piano. Irene Moser sang Israeli folk music and the young people played humorous and relevant sketches from Petra's and Marc's life, bound together in Goethe's great poem on love:

Whence are we born?—from Love...

How would we be lost?—without Love...

What can help us overcome?—Love...

Can one also find love?—through Love...

What does not let us weep for long?—Love...

What shall always unify us?—Love...

Of course, the meaning of Johann Wolfgang von Goethe's poetry finds its deepest final truth not in human love, but in God's Love, which was eagerly pointed out.

The celebration ended at midnight with my husband's talk relating to the last line of the above poem: "Unifying factors in matrimony" showing that love and forgiveness, as well as joint prayer and Bible reading, are the main unifying factors in matrimony.

Next day the couple departed for their honeymoon in Greece.

In the end it took almost six months until my husband had fully recovered from his surgery and felt strong enough to start his lecture tours anew.

CHAPTER L

OUR VISIT TO EAST GERMANY AFTER THE LIFTING OF THE IRON CURTAIN

In September 1991, we were both invited back to Eastern Germany for a lecture series in Görlitz. As the Berlin Wall had fallen, it was easier to travel and our oldest son Oliver accompanied us. Herr Lattka had arranged with some of the city fathers to invite my husband for some relevant lectures. They had the difficult task of rebuilding Görlitz, not only materially, but also socially after the communistic regime had been destroyed. The heads and thoughts of people were still full from years of Marxist indoctrination.

So we took off for Berlin, where we were supposed to join Herr Lattka in his car for Görlitz, near the Polish border in East Germany.

At the airport in Zürich, when passing through the passport control, one of the customs officers recognized my husband from a lecture he had given to about 1000 Swissair pilots and officers a year ago in Zürich on "How to Deal With Stress." This was the time when several airplanes had been hijacked by terrorists, and stress among pilots and crew was considerable. Apparently, the officer had appreciated the lecture, as he spoke to us in a very friendly fashion.

The first evening in Görlitz took place in a circle of medical doctors and scientists. It addressed the topic "Is Darwinistic Evolution still relevant?" Professor Wilder-Smith treated the seven main postulates of evolution by Kerkutt and showed that not one postulate of evolution was valid. The subsequent discussion was long and animated as the materialistic training of thought over so many years of communistic rule had been deeply imprinted in the academic's convictions. Most Christians among the doctors and scientists were theistic evolutionists "because to survive in a Marxist country, the only option for a scientist who is a Christian was to compromise and believe in theistic evolution."

The next three evenings my husband spoke on topics which the East Germans had chosen: "The Drug Problem"—a problem which had increased with the lifting of the Iron Curtain, and *Man's Origin, Man's Destiny*,—an issue to be reconsidered, as Marxist materialism had just fallen to pieces. The last evening in the church handled the eternal question "Why Does God Allow Suffering and Evil?" People in the East had suffered so much, that the problem of why all the suffering and so much evil in this world existed vexed many of them. The church was crowded and afterwards many came with personal problems, which they wanted to talk over with us afterwards.

One day Herr Lattka gave us a tour of the area. We visited Herrnhut, Count Zinzendorf's village, where year after year the so-called "Losungen" (Bible verses for each day of the year) are drawn by lottery. Count Zinzendorf, a very active Christian, was the founder of the Herrnhut Brethren. Many of his followers lived together in Herrnhut, a very clean and well cared for village.

A terrifying sight on our tour met us at the power plant in Hagenwerder. Black fumes rose into the air from a row of huge factory chimneys. The poisonous stench was unbearable. In the area a number—I believe it was over a dozen—of the nearest surrounding villages were empty ghost towns: their inhabitants had been evacuated from their homes because of the continuing extension of the open-cast mining of lignite. The sight was depressing and the air badly contaminated. Behind open windows the curtains swayed in the wind, skinny cats wandered along the deserted village streets, and in the little gardens lots, scanty grey vegetables waited in vain for hungry harvesters. To rescue the village church, it had been transplanted to the Northern part of Görlitz.

One free afternoon, Oliver and myself wandered through the old city center of Görlitz. It was very encouraging to observe the changes that were taking place. Some of the historic buildings were already renovated and others were scaffolded for restoration. Best of all, people had taken the initiative and opened little shops. The spirit of hopelessness and depression seemed to have given place to hope and enterprise. This was also the time when people were open for new ideas and spiritual truths. Would we Christians use this opportunity wisely and fully?

CHAPTER LI

SPEAKING ENGAGEMENTS

IN THE U.S.

In August 1992, we left again by Swissair for a longer lecture tour in the U.S. Pastor Chuck Smith had again kindly invited us to speak in a number of Calvary Chapels. The first weeks we stayed with our daughter Petra and her husband Marc in their beautiful little apartment in Long Beach. We had a wonderful time together, as this was our first visit in their new home in California since their marriage over a year ago. During this time my husband intensively worked on his new book *The Time Dimension: Its Relationship to the Origin of Life*. Soon his various lecture obligations started, first an interview with the Los Angeles Times which was done quite objectively by the journalist Dana Parson.

Next on the agenda was a talk to the College Group of Marc's home church in Long Beach on evolution and dating methods. My husband discussed the recent findings of extensive beds of *fresh hadrosaur bones* (Kyle L. Davies, *Journal of Paleontology*, vol. 61, No. 1, 1987) in the Colville River in Alaska, which caused some heart searching in certain geological circles. These were *fresh* bones and not fossilized and were established by experts to be hadrosaur bones, that is duck-billed vegetarian dinosaurs. (More about these findings in A.E. Wilder-Smith's book *The Time Dimension: Its Relationship to the Origin of Life*, published by TWFT, Costa Mesa, 1993).

Another interesting discovery was described in the scientific journal *Canadian Geographic* (1986–87). On Axel Heiberg Island, Northern Canada, *a forest of massive redwood stumps had been found in the polar region,* (See *The Time Dimension*) showing a vastly different vegetation from today's barren polar desert in that Northern region. Again the wood had not been fossilized, but was perfectly fresh: one could split it, cut it, carve it and burn it. It must have been preserved by floods of immense proportions, followed by a rapid change of climate.

These findings were very exciting for the college students, because they create grave questions and problems for evolutionary geology and dating. On the other hand, they encourage and confirm creationist science.

On September 2, my husband accepted an invitation by Hank Hanegraaff, the president of the Christian Research Institute. He had arranged interviews on the call-in programs on his radio station between himself and my husband on Biogenesis and on AIDS. Because of much interest and a multitude of call-in questions from the public, the program had to be extended for another hour. In former years, my husband had hosted various programs and call-ins with Dr. Walter Martin, the founder of CRI.

During the next weeks, Prof. Wilder-Smith repeatedly spoke in Calvary Chapels. We always appreciate their great love and faithfulness to God's Word. Their special identity mark is love. Calvary Chapel Costa Mesa is our spiritual home in the U.S. and the friendship of Pastor Chuck Smith and his wife mean much to us. In one way it is astonishing—and in another not at all astonishing—how fast and how many Calvary Chapels come into being, and how rapidly they grow. God obviously blesses their ministry, because they serve Him with an undivided heart.

Lectures followed in the church of Greg Laurie, in Riverside, whose evangelistic work among young people impressed us greatly. Every Monday evening his Bible Studies are frequented by several thousand young people of various walks of life, training and convictions. Every time a number of them make a decision and become active Christians.

My husband also preached in Pasadena Calvary Chapel with Pastor Xavier Ries and at his brother Raul Ries' church in West Covina, at San Juan Capistrano with Pastor Chuck Smith Junior, at Vista, at San Diego, at Downey, at Temecula, at Chino Hills, and the Moreno Valley at Redwoods and also at Pastor Neely's Warehouse Ministries in Sacramento. Very impressive to us was the church of Joe Focht in Philadelphia, which seemed to be bursting out of all seams because of its rapid growth.

OUR LAST VISIT TO NEW ZEALAND

On October 26, 1992, we were on our way to New Zealand. We had a stop-over of three days on Fiji before flying on to Auckland where my husband lectured again in the Takapuna Assembly of God. Our over-all topic this time was "Logos in Biology."

He spoke on Auckland 1ZB, a one-hour radio call-in program with Robin Harrison. The show was then prolonged for another hour. A few days later another radio program followed with Leighton Smith on the same station.

For this visit we were again guests to Professor and Mrs. Tan, who looked so well after all our needs.

At Dunedin airport, we were met by Einar and Annelies who were working for two years at the university hospital. Einar, who had already been registrar in Neurology at the University Hospital in Bern, wanted some more experience in internal medicine abroad. Annelies needed some more training in general medicine. We stayed with them in their beautiful rented home near the fjord in St. Leonard's. They used their house to invite people for Christian fellowship. When we visited there, they organized two evenings for intellectuals from the university and asked my husband to speak to them on scientific topics and give his Christian testimony.

All his free time during our Australian visit my husband worked on his manuscript "The Time Dimension."

Einar and Annelies showed us the only mainland albatross colony in the world on the Taiaroa Head of the Ontago Peninsula. On the same peninsula, the Yellow-eyed Penguins also nest. We watched them coming in from the sea like little men climbing the steep sand dunes, always at about 4 o'clock in the afternoon.

In Dunedin, we met Dr. Michael Denton who wrote the book, *A Theory in Crisis*, which helped many people to recognize the weakness of evolutionary theory.

On November 23, we both took the "Intercity" train to Christchurch. It runs along the beautiful coastline through the country to Christchurch. A special romantic touch on this train is that they offer the old English tradition of afternoon tea with scones, strawberry jam and Devonshire Cream. In Christchurch, my husband had a program on Radio Rhema, where we both had been interviewed on our first New Zealand tour 1989. The topic everybody was interested in—and also afraid of—was AIDS. This was also the topic of the radio program and of a number of lectures Wilder-Smith gave on this New Zealand tour.

We took the bus from Christchurch to Timaru to visit our faithful missionary friends, the Bruce family, who lead a students hostel with mainly young people from Asia. At the same time they teach "religion" in various schools. They use both activities to spread the Gospel and in their loving and competent way reach many a heart spiritually.

In Dunedin, several churches asked my husband to preach on Sundays. November 29 was very special for us; in the morning my husband spoke in Hannover Baptist Church on "The Nature of the New Birth" referring to the Old Testament story of the serpent on the pole. In the evening of the same day, our son Einar gave the sermon on "Magdalene and the precious nard." His discourse showing that the motivations of one's actions often count more than the action itself stayed with us. It was the first time that Einar and his father spoke on the same day at the same place. Our hearts were full of thanks.

Other lectures followed in churches, in the Evangelical Library and in the YMCA before we flew back to the U.S. During the night on the plane my husband got a cold which affected his voice. By the time we reached Hawaii, his voice was totally gone.

For the stop-over in Honolulu, Pastor Stonebraker had organized a debate between a professor from a local college and Prof. Wilder-Smith on evolution. But how could he debate without any voice at all? We asked the Stonebrakers to take us to a doctor. So they drove me to their son's General Practitioner whom my husband asked for some oral prednisolone besides some antibiotic. Next morning my husband's voice was back and he agreed to the debate in the evening, hoping the voice would stay until then. With God's help the debate went well. The opponent in the debate was not hostile and in spite of different convictions, the evening ended in a friendly atmosphere. He was a theistic evolutionist, but no atheist, which at least gave us some common ground.

After the strain of the evening, my husband's voice was again completely gone. But now he had the time to let his voice be cured by time.

Back in California, in December 1992, Pastor Chuck Smith offered us a delightful house, only a ten minutes walk away from Calvary Chapel Costa Mesa. It was beautifully situated and we fell in love with the place. The house was lovingly furnished and prepared by Pastor and Mrs. Chuck Smith personally and by friends from the church. It was filled not only with everything necessary, but also with many extra signs of love and imagination. We were overwhelmed by so much love.

We stayed in this house until the middle of January. My husband was able to work on his manuscripts, read new publications and develop his thoughts for lectures and the new book. From here he started a full speaking and lecturing program in a great number of churches, many of them Calvary Chapels which had sprung up during the last ten years and grown immensely. In some of them he spoke to audiences of several thousands, consisting mainly of young people. It is contagious to see their love of the Lord Jesus Christ, of the Word of God and towards one another and people in general. No wonder God's blessing is on them.

How much we cherished the friendship and faithful prayers of all those Calvary Chapel friends, especially later on during my husband's suffering and sickness.

From 1987 onwards, The Word For Today, the publishing house of Calvary Chapel, Costa Mesa, directed by Jeff Smith, has gradually taken over and published most of our English literature. We enjoyed a good collaboration with their team, which was very helpful in every way.

In the middle of January 1993, we flew back to Switzerland to attend to the hundreds of letters waiting for us—which took both of us several weeks to get through. Wilder-Smith also gave several lectures and radio interviews in Switzerland.

We prepared the manuscript for a little book on "Baptism and Christian Devotion." for U.S. publication with The Word For Today.

CHAPTER LII

ADELINE'S DEATH

On March 6, my husband's oldest sister, Marjorie, telephoned us from Oxford, England, to inform us that their youngest sister Adeline lay very seriously ill in the Battle Hospital in Reading and was dying. She had at the most two to three days to live, the doctor told us when we telephoned him. The next day we both took the next possible flight to London and went straight on by train to Reading. Bruce, Adeline's husband, said that she had been in a coma most of the day and not responsive. My husband demanded an appointment with the doctor who had stopped giving her any medication or food "because she was dying." They only gave her diamorphine for her pain. We asked the doctor to continue with antibiotics and liquids. After a day Adeline briefly opened her eyes and was able to speak a little, although she was confused, perhaps because of the diamorphine. She was very weak and the abscesses on both her thighs were enormous. She was a little better for maybe two days. On March 12, Adeline died in the hospital. She had been ill for a long time.

CHAPTER LIII

BACK IN THE UNITED STATES

Late in April 1993, we were back in the United States doing more lecturing and writing. We had started writing our Memoirs hoping that our life experiences might be of help to others.

In the second part of May 1993, my husband was invited to lecture for several days at the Calvary Bible College at Twin Peaks situated in the beautiful San Bernardino Mountains. As before, we were cordially received by Dr. Larry Taylor, the Principle of the School, his staff and the students. Calvary Bible College had students from all over America, as well as a few from Western and Eastern European countries. It is always a pleasure to lecture to the enthusiastic students there, so eager to learn so as to be well equipped for their later ministry. Professor Wilder-Smith taught them about the origin of life, treating chemical evolution and the laws of entropy, about current and new dating methods, about the basis of information theory, etc., so that they might be able to understand the serious problems of evolutionary theory as presently taught. He also covered dimension theory by means of black holes and the allegory of Flatland.

To better equip the students for counseling, they were instructed on AIDS, on today's drug abuse problem, on stress and how to cope with it, and on the criminal mind and its relationship to our permissive society. Many of those young Bible College students will later be pastors of big new churches and will be faced with many of the serious problems of today's society. So they will need optimum equipment to meet these urgent needs.

At the end of June, we started out on a tour to Russia for some lectures on Materialism and Modern Science. Pastor Paul Smith had inaugurated a program in St. Petersburg to help young people there to reconsider and rethink their materialistic upbringing. He had asked my husband to aid in this program. People from Calvary Chapel had by this time started churches in Moscow and other Russian places.

On our journey to Russia, the group stayed for the first night in the London Airport Hilton. During the night my husband fell acutely ill and had to be taken to the nearest hospital in Hounslow. We could not continue the journey to St. Petersburg and had to return home to Switzerland. This illness was found to be the consequence of my husband's previous cranial surgery, and was aggravated by special stress or exhaustion. After some days of rest and care, he was better.

In August, we traveled to Millstatt Castle where Pastor Chuck had invited us to help in two retreats for groups of young Yugoslavs and Hungarians.

As already described in the chapter on Pro Universitate, we celebrated the fifteenth anniversary of Pro Universitate in September 1993, in the beautiful old Ruedihus at Kandersteg under the theme "In the Beginning was the Word."

CHAPTER LIV

BEATE'S SIXTY-FIFTH BIRTHDAY

As my sixty-fifth birthday was approaching, my husband and our sons put their heads together in a "secret conference." "Mutti," they asked me, "for your great approaching day, would you prefer a celebration in style in Switzerland with friends and relatives, or would you rather go on a journey with us to a destination of your choice?"

Just before my birthday we had planned to hold the Pro Universitate seminar in Kandersteg. So I thought it would be a splendid idea to go on a journey with my husband and our children. "The destination of your choice?" After conferring with them, we all agreed on Norway where we had spent delightful times thirty years ago when my husband had worked for two years at the University of Bergen.

We had been back in Norway previously during holidays. It was one of our favorite countries. In the summer of 1985, Oliver and the two of us had traveled up the entire Norwegian coast by the so-called Hurtigrutene (fast boats). The Hurtigrutene run up the coast every day of the year, substituting for trains, especially in the North (no trains North of Trondheim). They stop at a great number of islands along the coastline, which could hardly be reached otherwise. These boats run day and night stopping about fifteen to twenty times at important ports along the coast and on islands.

In 1989, Oliver, Clive, a friend of ours and we both had again traveled the same route North in December in the dark winter season up to Harstad; there were only a few hours of twilight a day. We were sometimes the only non-Norwegian passengers on board—there were no tourists, only locals. This was not the tourist season, it was two weeks before Christmas. Up North it was minus 30°C (-22°F)—bitterly cold—with ice and snow everywhere. But, as we had been expecting the severe cold, we had brought enough warm clothes with us—four or five layers—to really enjoy ourselves. We explored every stop; the snowy landscape of the islands and the coast with the illuminated villages, the Lofoten islands: a Christmas dream come true. But most beautiful were the Northern lights (aurora borealis), moving in different colors like curtains over the dark Nordic sky in red, green and white. The Norwegians call them "God's Neon Lights."

Coming back to my sixty-fifth birthday trip, my husband, Oliver and Clive lovingly organized it all. Unfortunately, Petra and Marc in California could not get leave to join us on the trip. But Einar and Annelies had just finished their year at the hospital at Dunedin in New Zealand and would join us in Bergen.

We flew via Copenhagen to Bergen. I will never forget the magnificent golden sunset which poured a warm red light over the many small islands in the glittering North Sea below us.

In Bergen airport we climbed into the eight-seater van which our sons had rented for our ten days in Norway. We drove to the little hotel overlooking the beautiful old Hanseatic town of Bergen. It was good to practice the Norwegian language again after so many years of absence. My husband and myself still had the habit of reading the Norwegian Bible together every evening in bed.

How good it was to breathe again the fresh salty sea-air and to listen to the cry of the sea gulls and the oyster-catchers!

What fun to explore the lively fish market, where thirty years ago we always had bought the fresh, delicious fish. Every morning the fishermen would come into the pretty harbor directly adjoining the market place with their little fishing boats and sell the catch of the night to the customers. Fish is the main food of the Norwegians, but there are so many varieties and it is so fresh that one never gets tired of it. The market officials scrubbed the place every afternoon. It was so clean that there was never a fishy smell around after fish booths had been cleared away in the afternoon.

We strolled through Bergen, the Hanseatic quay with the old colorful wooden-ware houses and shops. We admired the beautiful hand-knitted Norwegian pullovers in the shop-windows.

Next evening—Einar and Annelies had meanwhile joined us—my husband invited us all together with some friends from thirty years ago (the Shorts) to a festive birthday meal in Hotel Admiral from where we enjoyed a glorious view of the harbor with the old training sail ship "Statsraad Lehmkuhl" and the mountains behind.

The next day we visited Troldhaugen, the home of Edvard Grieg, situated on idyllic grounds. He composed his music in a little wooden cabin right near the fjord. The old piano with his own music on it, his coat, hat and walking stick are still on the same place as in his life-time.

Every year the Grieg music festivals attract many music-lovers from all over the world. Before the building of the new Grieg Hall near the house intimate concerts were held inside Grieg's home at Troldhaugen. Of course, now all the concerts take place in the big Grieg Hall in front of which a statute of the great musician is erected.

One day later, we left Bergen and headed inland in our van towards the mountains along the picturesque Hardangerfjord. In Kinsarvik, we boarded the little ferry across the fjord to

Utne and then drove on through the Hardanger Vidda, a forbidding bleak mountain area. Our goal was Hovden, a small mountain resort where we had rented a large rustic log cabin. Together with Ute and Carolin, two girls from an acquainted family, we spent our time taking long, extended hiking tours in the multi-colored autumn mountain forests to lonely lakes and some times along hidden trails of elks and reindeer. We cooked and lived according to Norwegian customs; various kinds of fish, brown bread with gjetost (brown goats' cheese) and plenty of kefir (a kind of yogurt).

We much enjoyed our visit to the silversmiths in the Setesdal. In this valley, they hand-craft delicate silver jewelry for the traditional Norwegian costumes and other art works to sell. The old silversmith's art runs generations back in the same families and is passed on from father to son to grandson, etc. The old silver-smith we visited and his son, Torleiv and Hallvard Bjorgum, played the "Hardanger Fiddle," an artistically ornamented violin with four or five extra sympathetic strings. The latter are steel strings placed under the fingerboard through an opening in the bridge and serve as resonance strings. The fiddle is played to old folk music and dancing, and is not easy to master. While we visited there the young silver-smith took part in an international contest in Geneva, Switzerland, where he won the first prize.

On Sunday, we attended church in the little wooden church in Bykle with the famous, magnificent rose-painting on the inside walls.

The rope for ringing the church bell hangs down right in the middle of the aisle between the two rows of pews. A lady church warden rang the bell shortly before the service started. How glad we were when the Lutheran pastor held his sermon in Riksmål, and not in Nynorsk. We could perfectly understand what he said and he preached a very good biblical sermon on Lazarus. Most of the hymns we still remembered from thirty years ago and we gladly joined in the singing. After the service, we found out that we were no strangers to the pastor and other friends present. They knew of my husband's books and films, which had been translated into Norwegian.

In the evenings, we all sat together around the fireplace in our cozy log cabin reading and studying the Hebrew letter and exchanging thoughts about it.

Before traveling back to Switzerland, we visited Mr. Skagen, one of our old-time friends around Bergen, with whom we had stayed in touch through all the years. His dear wife had meanwhile left this earth for a better place.

We were grateful for the wonderful time together in Norway. God was so good to us.

CHAPTER LV

THE SECOND SURGERY

Petra and Marc spent the following Christmas with us in French Switzerland.

After Christmas my husband went for a check-up in the Inselspital in Bern. This revealed that the meningioma above his brain had started to grow again, and that a second surgery could not be avoided. It was a great shock for us all. We prayed about it and agreed to have the operation performed on March 14, 1994.

Again, thousands of faithful friends around the world prayed for the long surgery. Shortly after the operation complications arose; a venous sinus thrombosis occurred. A long time of very patiently borne suffering followed. All the time my husband was the perfect gentleman he had always been. For a time it seemed that his health would recover.

On February 27, 1995, our first grandson, Adrian, was born to Einar and Annelies in Bern. My husband was utterly delighted when we saw Adrian a few hours after his birth on a visit to the hospital. He had always been very fond of little children.

In the Spring of 1995 walking became so troublesome for my dear husband that he had to use a wheel-chair for moving about. He usually sat in his wheel-chair on our big terrace overlooking Lake Thun and the snow-capped mountain giants, Eiger, Mönch and Jungfrau. He so much loved that magnificent view, he loved God's beautiful creation. When our Finnish friend Mrs. Raija Bopp visited us we often sang together. One of the last hymns he sang with us was "Der Himmel steht offen, weisst Du warum? Weil Jesus gekämpft und gelitten darum..." (Heaven is open for us. Do you know why? Because Jesus had fought and suffered for that purpose...) He rejoiced in the assurance of that knowledge. One evening when Mrs. Bopp left us he said to her: "Mrs. Bopp when I am no more, please look after my little nightingale." He loved listening to my singing and playing on the piano. And he was always thinking of others and never complaining although he went through such a lot of suffering.

There were times when he became down-hearted. One night I woke up hearing him sobbing beside me. "What is the matter, my dear?" I asked. "Beate, look at me, look at the state I am in." He had been a strong healthy man all his life and now felt his handicaps strongly. Yet every time we came to the conviction that we still had so much to be grateful for. We had one another and still were together—one of the greatest treasures to be experienced in life. And we thanked God for it.

His sense of humor was always refreshing. One day after his afternoon nap when I came to his bed to help him into the wheel-chair, I jokingly asked: "May I kiss this gentleman?" His answer was: "All contributions are gratefully accepted."

During the last weeks when talking became harder for him he often looked at me for a long time without saying a word. I once remarked: "You look at me so kindly and radiantly. What is the matter?" He slowly replied: "That's only the reflection of your face and mind. What better object is there to regard?" Until the end he remained the perfect gentleman although it became more and more difficult for him to communicate verbally.

When he could hardly stand up any more I asked in Calvary Chapel, Costa Mesa, for help. Sally Mann, the wonderful competent secretary, found a strong young gentleman, Perry Huesmann, who was so kind as to come for two months to Switzerland to help me lift up my husband from and into bed. He took over part of the physiotherapy and helped us with other chores which required strength. Perry had just successfully finished his theology education and could free himself for eight weeks before his new obligations. He was a great and loving helper.

During my husband's last eighteen months of sickness, several friends were of great support to us. Without them it would have been so much harder to deal with everything. All our children stood faithfully by us in a special way throughout this time.

Clive stayed with us much of the time, although he has his apartment in French Switzerland near Lausanne. In his joyful and humorous way he helped us without getting discouraged in all of the difficult, unpleasant and hard daily jobs. He always had a word of encouragement and love for his daddy when pain or bodily impairments troubled him. With his strong arms, Clive helped him down the stairs, lifted him out of bed and supported him firmly while I washed him.

Once my husband, leaning on Clive for support, said to him: "Clive, I am sorry I need your help in this unpleasant job, I feel so embarrassed." Clive answered: "Oh Daddy, it is an honor to have the privilege of serving you. We are so glad to be around you."

Einar, a Registrar of Neurology at the Inselspital, the University Hospital at Berne, discussed the treatment and the medication of my husband with his colleagues conscientiously. When my husband was in the hospital in Bern, Einar and Annelies were so kind as to often let me stay in their home in Bern. Otherwise I had to drive daily from Einigen to Bern to be with my husband.

Our daughter Petra and Marc telephoned frequently from California. Petra flew four times to Switzerland to help Daddy and be near him. The night before his surgery she flew in from Los Angeles. As the airplane was late, the hospital was already closed for visitors when Petra finally arrived in Bern. She sneaked into the hospital through a private back door and found her Daddy's room. My husband was still awake as he knew of Petra's coming. The two had an extra special time together the night before the operation. In her loving and practical way she relieved us of many jobs.

Oliver came home from Geneva every free minute to support and help us. He also took on himself the difficult task of talking strictly to one of the doctors in the last hospital, who had a strong tendency to euthanasia and needed putting right.

I would like to emphasize that, one of the things we learned from this difficult time of my husband's illness was what an asset a good medical system is, and how dependent good medical care is on sound ethics. We often spent a lot of time and energy discussing ethical aspects of my husband's treatment. We were astounded at the prevalence of euthanasia-style attitudes, often hearing comments such as "he's had a long and fruitful life, why should we prolong his life," or "your husband has such a limited quality of life now, shouldn't we just let him slip away and stop treating or feeding him?" This is the tragic, but logical, result of generations of medical students being taught that man is only a machine which has evolved, and that no absolute values exist. Looking back at this period, I feel that I spent a large part of my time "defending" my husband against the medical system! It is so important that relatives watch over the treatment of their dear ones.

Another thing I learned was how important visiting is to an ill person. How my husband brightened up and became responsive when I or another visitor entered the room! Sometimes my husband shared a room with another patient. I experienced some elderly patients who did not have a visitor for days on end, who spent their days sitting unresponsive and apathetically, just existing in their chairs due to lack of social intercourse. Let us not forget our biblical duty in this area (Matthew 25:36), our churches need to be much more active in visiting those who are elderly or sick.

It was a real privilege that most of the time of his illness we were able to care for my dear husband at home, even when he was in a wheel-chair during the last weeks and had to be fed artificially via a gastrostomy. This was because his coordination of swallowing became progressively more impaired as a consequence of the complications following surgery. In the last few weeks of his illness, the great problem was that my husband easily aspirated after vomiting, and that this almost invariably led to pneumonia.

It was on account of another such episode of pneumonia that I had to take him to the Salem, a Christian-run hospital in Bern, in the middle of August 1995. From that time on his health deteriorated progressively. I stayed with him every day. After a week he was transferred to the palliative care station of the hospital where he received very intensive nursing. Most of the nursing staff on the unit were Christians and some knew of my husband from his lectures and books. They nursed him with great love. We had never before experienced such good nursing and care in a hospital; even my doctor sons agreed on this.

Every morning I read him the Word of God and prayed with him, even when he hardly reacted any more. I told him that I dearly loved him and that I was so grateful to have him. I sang our favorite hymns and held his hand. He sometimes opened his eyes and looked at me or slightly squeezed my hand. But he was too weak to communicate in any way. But I am sure he took much more in than was obvious to us.

He deteriorated further. When the breathing became heavier and irregular the nurses put an extra bed into the room so I could stay with him overnight when necessary. All our children were nearby. Petra had flown home from California and stayed at his bedside during the last days.

On September 14, while a nurse and I carefully washed him, my husband took his last breath. Peacefully he lay in his bed. The heavy suffering with all its pain was over.

All our children gathered with me round our beloved husband and father who was now home with his Lord and Savior. Oliver said: "Let us pray and thank God for our Daddy who had been such a loving example to all of us." Sadness and gratefulness filled everybody's heart as we together approached the throne of God committing the past, the present and the future into the hands of the Lord who had wonderfully guided our lives until now. He would also care for us in the future.

CURRICULUM VITAE OF ARTHUR ERNEST WILDER-SMITH

1915	Born on December 22 in Reading, Berkshire, England
1922—1930	Wallingford Grammar School
1930—1932	Taunton Boarding School, Somerset
1932	School Certificate with honors (Distinction in Chemistry)
1933—1935	Oxford University (Botany, Zoology, Chemistry)
1934	Oxford: First public examination in Natural Sciences
1936	Reading: B.Sc. general degree (Botany Zoology, Chemistry)
1937	Reading: B.Sc. honors degree
1941	Reading: Ph.D. (Physical Organic Chemistry) (Optically active ketones)
1943	London: C. Chem., Associate of the Royal Institute of Chemistry
1946	London: F.R.S.C., Fellow of the Royal Institute (later: Society) of Chemistry
1956	Geneva: P.D.(medical), Ecole de Médecine, Switzerland (Hypoglycemic drugs)
1964	Geneva: Dr. ès Science, Ecole de Médecine, Switzerland (Chemotherapy of Tuberculosis and Leprosy)

1964	Zürich: D.Sc.(Natural Sciences) ETH, Switzerland (Chemotherapy of Mycobacterial Diseases)
1945—1949	London, Countess Lisburne Memorial Fellow in Cancer Research, Middlesex Hospital. (Prostatic carcinoma, sex hormones)
1950 Sept. 17	Marriage to Beate née Gottwaldt (state marriage: Wallingford, England; church marriage: Frankfurt/Main, Germany)
1951—1955	Lucerne, Switzerland, Head of Research (at Geistlich Pharmaceuticals; Research: Anesthetics, leprostatics, tuberculostatics, analgesics, sex hormones)
1955—1960	Basel, Switzerland: Consultant in Chemotherapy to chemical industry
1956—1964	Geneva, Privat-Docent, Ecole de Médecine (Teaching: Chemotherapy and Pharmacology for medical students; Research: Diabetes, leprosy, tuberculosis, opioid analgesics)
1957—1958	Chicago, USA, Visiting Assistant Professor of Pharmacology, Medical Center, University of Illinois (Teaching: Pharmacology and Chemotherapy; Research: Tuberculosis, leprosy, local anesthetics)
1960—1962	Bergen, Norway, Visiting Professor of Pharmacology School of Medicine, University of Bergen (Research: Tuberculosis, leprosy, non-steroidal analgesics)
1964—1969	Chicago, USA, Professor of Pharmacology, University of Illinois, Medical Center Dept. of Pharmacology (Developing a drug abuse program)

1964—1969	Chicago, USA, Professor of Pharmacology, University of Illinois College of Nursing
1969—1971	Ankara, Turkey, Professor of Pharmacology, Hacettepe University (Teaching: Establishing a program in post-graduate pharmacology)
1970—1977	U.S. NATO Forces in Europe, Consultant and Drug Advisor in rank of 3-Star General in Drug Abuse Program to officers and servicemen all over Europe
1970—1977	Drug instruction to General Staff of Swiss Armed Forces, Police, Teacher's Seminaries
1975—1992	Extensive lecturing in Swiss, German and Austrian universities and institutes of higher learning; Speaking in students' seminars, at businessmen's seminars and meetings, churches and public halls
1979 February	Norwegian universities tour
1980	Seven films, *How the World Came To Be* with Dutch TV One film, *Drug Abuse* One film, *Dimension Theory*
1980	Dutch universities tour
1981 March 1	U.S. lecture tour (43 universities, 23 churches, 18 media)
1981 April/May	Finnish universities tour
1982 April/May	Second U.S. lecture tour
1983 October 26	Zürich: Swiss National TV interview with Eva Metzger on the drug problem (transmitted six times in prime time)
1984 April/May	Third U.S. lecture tour
1984	Scotland lecture tour

1985 October	Denmark lecture tour
1986 Oct./Nov.	Fourth U.S. lecture tour
1986 February 16	Oxford Union Debate: "The Doctrine of Creation Is More Valid Than the Theory of Evolution"
1986 November 5–8	Canada: Edmonton and Calgary
1987 January	Australian lecture tour
1987 May/June	First New Zealand lecture tour
1988 February	Denmark lecture tour
1988 June	Second New Zealand lecture tour
1988 August	Fifth U.S. lecture tour
1989 Feb./March	Poland lecture tour
1990 April/June	Sixth U.S. lecture tour
1991 March	First head operation
1991 September	East Germany lecture tour (Görlitz)
1992 Nov./Dec.	Seventh U.S. lecture tour
1992 December	Third New Zealand tour
1993 Spring	Eighth U.S. lecture tour
1994 March	Second head operation
1995 September 14	Called to be with the Lord

AFFILIATIONS

Member: British Chemical Society (since 1943)

Sigma Xi (since 1957)

Rho Chi (since 1965)

American Association for the Advancement of Science (since 1969)

New York Academy of Science (since 1992)

AWARDS

1965–1966	Chicago: "Best Teacher of the Year" University of Illinois Medical Center, College of Pharmacy
1966–1967	Chicago: "Best Teacher of the Year" University of Illinois Medical Center, College of Pharmacy
1966–1967	Chicago: "Golden Apple" Instructor Award, University of Illinois Medical Center, College of Pharmacy
1967–1968	Chicago: "Best Teacher of the Year" University of Illinois Medical Center, College of Pharmacy
1967–1968	Chicago: "Golden Apple" Instructor Award, University of Illinois Medical Center, College of Nursing
1968–1969	Chicago: "Best Teacher of the Year" University of Illinois Medical Center, College of Pharmacy
1968–1969	Chicago: "Golden Apple" Instructor Award, University of Illinois Medical Center, College of Pharmacy
1990 May 6	Simon Greenleaf University, Long Beach, CA, Doctor of Letters honoris causa, School of Law and Apologetics

CONSULTANT PRACTICE

- Consultant to BAOR on German Affairs particularly with respect to reconciliation. Rank: Lt. Colonel (1946–1947)

- Consultant to the Chemical Firm Schweizerhall, Basel, on Pharmacology and Therapeutics (1955–1962)

- Consultant to Sapos S.A., Geneva, Switzerland on leprostatics, tuberculostatics, hypnotics and anesthetics (1955–1960)

- Consultant to Bengué Pharmaceuticals, Wembley, England on leprostatics and tuberculostatics (1956–1958)

- Consultant to Armour Pharmaceuticals Corp., Kalamazoo, IN, USA on pharmacological research in Europe (1958–1960)

- Consultant on Further Adult Education, Professional Colleges, University of Illinois at the Medical Center, Chicago, USA (graduate education of pharmacists and nurses with medical practitioners in recent advances in pharmacology and related areas) (1965–1969)

- Consultant to the United States Army and Airforce in Europe and the Near East on drug abuse. Drugs involved: hashish, marijuana, cocaine, heroin, morphine, amphetamines, barbiturates, alcohol, tranquilizers and nicotine in the human. Rank: GS 17 (Lt. General) (1970–1975)

- Occasional Drug Abuse Consultancies have involved demonstrations at and lectures at: Military Headquarters of the Swiss Army in Bern and the Stadtpolizei in Zürich, Switzerland.

PUBLICATIONS

- Fifty-four original scientific publications originated from A.E. Wilder-Smith's research.

- He authored twenty-three books, written in English or German. Many of them have been translated into up to seven other languages.

- His *Origins* films, which won two awards, were translated into many other languages.

A laplander in
the far North

Our home in
Einigen,
Switzerland

Turkish
women

University buildings in Ankara, Turkey

The Warrior's Gate
in Hattuşas

Göreme, underground dwellings

Lecturing in Graz, Austria, with the IVCG (businessmen)

Our first Pro Universitate seminar in Krattigen, Switzerland

Professor Wilder-Smith
enjoyed working with students

Dr. Wilder-Smith working at home in Einigen

A.E.W.S. working in his study with Beate

Fishing in Scotland

Dr. Wilder-Smith and Karl Neuhaus climbing the Matterhorn

The Wilder-Smith family. Our log cab'n in Houden, Norway.
Starting place for many hikes.

In the Swiss moun-
tains during a ski holi-
day with Petra and
her husband Marc

"Henry," male Tuatara
(by kind permission of
the Southland Museum)

Petra and Marc's
wedding
June 29, 1991

Professor Dr. Wilder-Smith and
Beate at
Petra's wedding
1991

Dr. med. Oliver Wilder-Smith (right)
& Dr. med. Clive Wilder-Smith (left)

Dr. med. Einar Wilder-Smith
with wife Annelies (Dr. med.)

Prof. Wilder-Smith
at his 75th birthday with
Prof. Alma von Stockhausen

Prof. Wilder-Smith
at his 75th birth-
day with his
friend Prof.
Scholler

Poster announcing a debate with "The Mystery Debator"

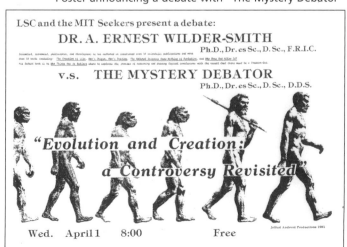